Techniques for Teaching Law

Techniques for Teaching Law

Gerald F. Hess

and

Steven Friedland

Carolina Academic Press
Durham, North Carolina

ISBN 0-89089-785-9
LCCN 99-61099

CAROLINA ACADEMIC PRESS
700 Kent Street
Durham, North Carolina 27701
Telephone (919) 489-7486
Fax (919) 493-5668
E-mail: cap@cap-press.com
www.cap-press.com

Printed in the United States of America

For
Grace and Francis Hess
and
Fran and Stan Friedland,
our parents and model teachers.

Contents

xiv   Contents

Preface

Our primary purpose for this book is to provide the reader with a teaching resource. This collaborative effort, with a great deal of help from our friends and colleagues, is intended to enhance both teaching and learning in law school. We hope that TECHNIQUES FOR TEACHING LAW will help legal educators create challenging and interesting learning experiences for their students. We believe that better teaching and learning can have a ripple effect—more effective legal education will motivate our students to become better learners and, eventually, to better serve their clients.

To achieve these ambitious goals, we have included two types of material in TECHNIQUES FOR TEACHING LAW: (1) foundational principles of higher education; and (2) specific teaching ideas from a wide range of legal educators.

The foundational principles of teaching and learning are based on the large body of research and literature on higher education. This literature is extensive, but worth pursuing. We devoted Chapter 1 exclusively to models of teaching and learning. Chapters 2 through 12 each begin with an introduction that applies basic pedagogical principles to legal education.

The heart of TECHNIQUES FOR TEACHING LAW consists of 137 teacher-tested ideas. These ideas were contributed by experienced legal educators who used them successfully with their students. We hope that the ideas are sufficiently intriguing to catch the attention of law teachers and clear enough for educators to quickly and easily implement them with their students.

We wish to thank the many people who made this book possible. First, we appreciate all those dedicated teachers who contributed their ideas to TECHNIQUES FOR TEACHING LAW. (Of course, the contributors retain copyrights in their portions of this book; it was the least we could do!) While many others contributed to putting this book into print, one person in particular deserves our appreciation. We are indebted to Paula Prather for her excellent work in all phases of this book, including discussing the basic concept, gathering teaching ideas, working with the contributors, and performing a mammoth word processing feat.

Gerry Hess and Steve Friedland
March 1999

Techniques for Teaching Law

Chapter 1

Teaching and Learning — Theory, Research, and Applications

This chapter reviews research, theories, and models that provide a foundation for much of what is known about teaching and learning in higher education. It attempts to provide legal educators with a basic understanding of teaching and learning so that they can make informed decisions about their instruction. In addition, this chapter articulates, in general terms, how the research, theories, and models apply in legal education.

Presented below are four theories of learning and three models of effective teaching. These theories and models are based on decades of research and thousands of studies, reported in hundreds of journal articles and dozens of books. Consequently, this chapter just scratches the surface of these theories and models. Many other theories and models of teaching and learning exist. (We hope that legal educators will want to pursue more directly the teaching and learning literature; the list of references at the end of this chapter provides a starting point for that worthwhile quest.)

A. Learning

A central focus of education is student learning. In law school, the core of student learning includes the substantive content, skills, and professional values critical to the education of an effective, ethical attorney. If student learning is central to the mission of legal education, then an understanding of how humans learn should help law teachers become more effective. Four types of learning theories are described below: (1) cognitive psychology, (2) intellectual development, (3) learning styles, and (4) characteristics of adult learners.

1. Cognitive Psychology

Cognitive psychology attempts to explain mental processes such as memory, thinking, problem solving, and decision-making. The goals of cognitive psychology are to illuminate meaningful, not rote, learning and

3

to develop theories that explain comprehension and knowledge utilization. In describing meaningful learning, cognitive psychology has emphasized four areas: (a) information processing, (b) knowledge structure, (c) thinking about thinking, and (d) social processes.

a. Information Processing

Cognitive research has described the basic operation of the human memory. Most humans can pay attention to only one thing at a time. Memory of new knowledge is fragile and can accommodate only a few new concepts in a short time span. Memory becomes much more stable once the new knowledge is recorded in long-term memory stores. Consequently, to acquire new knowledge, humans need to attend to the new information and maintain it until it can be encoded in long-term memory.

Isolated bits of information that students try to memorize by rote are not likely to reach long-term memory. Instead, knowledge is much more likely to be encoded and recalled later if it is meaningful—if the new concepts can be linked together in a framework. Many students are able to make sense of new concepts and encode them only after they can see the "big picture."

Another key aspect of human information processing is that it is specialized for both verbal and visual information. Thus, when students encounter information both verbally and visually, they are more likely to encode and recall it later.

b. Knowledge Structure

Cognitive theory views learning as a constructive, rather than a receptive, process. One theory structures knowledge in three stages: declarative encoding, proceduralization, and composition. Knowledge is first encoded as a set of facts. For example, "a complaint must contain a short plain statement of the claim showing that the pleader is entitled to relief" or "an environmental impact statement must be prepared on proposals for major federal actions significantly affecting the quality of the human environment." Student performance with the new knowledge (drafting a complaint, for example) is slow at best.

In the next step, proceduralization, students gain familiarity with the basic concepts and the relationships between concepts. Students integrate the new knowledge with existing knowledge. Knowledge becomes available for problem solving and students can more easily translate knowledge into action. For example, students can draft a complaint that states a claim and can analyze whether an action is likely to require an environmental impact statement.

Composition is the final step in transforming and using knowledge. Students continue to improve their ability to carry out complex cognitive skills. Composition may occur over many months or years. For example, students' ability to make sophisticated and persuasive arguments may develop throughout law school and the students' subsequent professional careers.

c. Thinking About Thinking

Cognitive psychologists name the process of thinking about thinking "metacognition," which includes two closely related learning concepts. The first concept is student awareness of how the student learns. This entails whether the student knows what strategies (reading, discussion, performance, writing) are most effective for that student to learn particular content or skills. The second concept concerns student control over learning strategies. Student control involves whether the student can plan, monitor, and alter learning strategies appropriate for the applicable subject matter and teaching style.

Student performance is enhanced when students are conscious of their learning strategies and they can modify those strategies to accommodate the subject and teaching style. Teachers can facilitate students' metacognition by drawing attention to the process of learning, modeling different ways to approach a problem, and providing feedback to students on the effectiveness of their learning strategies. For example, when beginning law students brief a case, the teacher can collect the briefs, give oral feedback to the class on the briefs, provide several samples of effective briefs, and ask students to evaluate whether their briefing is effective.

d. Social Processes

Many cognitive processes, such as strategic thinking, articulating reasons, clearly expressing ideas, writing, and speaking, are developed best through social interaction. Students learn higher-level thinking, problem solving, and sophisticated argument by observing and working with others. Group activities can provide immediate feedback on the quality of students' thinking, ideas, and expression. More highly skilled thinkers, such as teachers and advanced peers, model high-level skills. Students working in groups can collectively reach levels none of them could have reached alone. Finally, tasks that connect to the real world, such as clinical work and externships, create a potent environment for the development of thinking, speaking, and writing skills in context rather than in isolation.

2. Intellectual Development

Researchers and theorists have constructed several major models of adult mental development, including Piaget's theory of cognitive development, Erickson's model of psychosocial development, and Kolberg's stages of moral development. Perhaps the most applicable developmental theory for legal educators is Perry's schema of intellectual and ethical development.

a. Stages of Intellectual Development

Perry based his schema of intellectual and ethical development on interviews with Harvard undergraduates in the 1960s. The schema emerged from exhaustive analysis of the ways students described their experiences and transformations in college. Extensive subsequent research has confirmed the schema in adult students of various ages, in a range of colleges and universities, both in the United States and abroad.

Perry's schema creates four major categories of intellectual and ethical development: (1) dualism, (2) multiplicity, (3) contextual relativism, and (4) commitment in relativism.

(1) Dualism

Students at this stage see the world as a set of absolutes: right/wrong, true/false, good/bad. Knowledge and truth come from Authorities, such as teachers, who have Answers. The true Authorities do not disagree—facts are facts. Different perspectives and disagreements among authorities can exist because there are both Good Authorities and Bad Authorities. Students see their role as learning the truth as set forth by Good Authorities. In the law school setting, Dualists want to identify and commit to memory the Good Law.

(2) Multiplicity

The transition from Dualism to Multiplicity begins as students confront disagreements among Good Authorities. Students acknowledge that there is legitimate uncertainty in the world. Knowledge now falls into three categories: Right, Wrong, and Unknown. During the early phase of Multiplicity, students believe that the "Unknown" category is small and might better be called "Not Yet Known" because through proper procedures Answers will be discovered over time. In later phases of Multiplicity, students believe that the "Unknown" category is large and might better be called "We'll Never Know For Sure." Thus, in the later stages of Multiplicity, students conclude that it is more important to know how to think rather than what to think. On many issues students believe no opinion is any better or worse than any other opinion and there is no objective basis on which to decide what is right. In the law school setting, students in the late Multiplicity stage become adept at making arguments supported by Authorities, but have difficulty evaluating arguments, positions, and opinions.

(3) Contextual Relativism

In Contextual Relativism, students see for the first time the self as a legitimate source of knowledge. Authorities such as teachers and books are viewed as fellow seekers of understanding that have more experience than students in dealing with the knowledge and uncertainties in their field. Students recognize that there are many good arguments on most issues, that there are principles on which one can evaluate arguments in any given setting, and that they must be able to make tough choices based on those principles. In law school, Contextual Realists are able to use facts, precedent, and policy to evaluate issues, make persuasive arguments, and approach complex problems.

(4) Commitment in Relativism

Students at this stage are skilled in analytical thinking and have experience in evaluating ideas, values, and interests. Students use that skill and experience as they face personal and professional choices. As students make professional and personal commitments, they may experience self-doubt and sadness as they recognize that choices they make foreclose other choices. Students come to terms with complexity, and take responsibility for their choices. Many law students will not reach this stage of development until after law school; some will never reach it.

b. Implications for Legal Educators

When adults enter new learning situations, such as law school, they proceed through the Perry schema. Consequently, the Perry schema has significant implications for legal educators. First, the Perry schema speaks to the basic nature of education — not the transmission of knowledge, but the transformation of the learner. This view of education as transformation is consistent with the dominant conceptualization of legal education, which consistently identifies "thinking like a lawyer" as a major goal of legal education. Second, the Perry schema helps teachers understand why their students struggle with what appears to teachers to be basic concepts and skills. As applied to law school, students may write poor exams not because of their study habits but because of their stage of development as learners. Third, researchers after Perry have demonstrated that teaching/learning methods can affect students' developmental progress. For example, students can develop analytical skills, critical thinking, and independent learning through:

- An environment of mutual respect among teacher and students and enthusiasm for the course;
- Variety in methods of teaching, learning, and evaluation;

- Clear course and class objectives and clear directions for learning activities;
- Course materials with multiple levels of complexity and different perspectives;
- Examples from students' experiences;
- Active learning, such as field work, group projects, and simulations;
- Frequent and timely feedback.

3. Learning Styles

"Learning style" refers to the characteristic way a person acquires and uses knowledge. Four types of models of learning styles exist: personality models (basic characteristics of the learners), information processing models (ways of acquiring and processing information), social interaction models (ways students behave in the classroom), and instructional preferences (preferred teaching and learning methods). One of the most elaborate personality models of learning styles, the Myers-Briggs Type Indicator (MBTI), has been applied in legal education.

The MBTI is designed to assess the ways people prefer to take in information and to make decisions. The MBTI is based on extensive research and is used widely in business and education. The MBTI classifies individuals based on four preferences: Extroversion (E) or Introversion (I), Sensing (S) or Intuitive (N), Thinking (T) or Feeling (F), and Judgment (J) or Perception (P). Research indicates that significant percentages of law students have each of the preferences. Thus, law teachers should anticipate that students with each of the preferences will be in their classes and that those students will learn best through a variety of teaching/learning methods.

The tables on pages 9 and 10 set out some of the characteristics of each preference and the teaching/learning methods most appropriate for each. The Myers-Briggs scheme is quite elaborate; the tables provide a brief summary.

Table 1a. Myers-Briggs Type Indicator Summary

EXTROVERTED TYPES	INTROVERTED TYPES
Characteristics:	**Characteristics:**
* Direct energy and attention primarily toward the outside world—people and activities * Gregarious and talkative; energized by people and activity * Prefer to act first and think about it later	* Direct energy and attention primarily toward the inner world of reflection and thought * Exhausted by too many people and activities; energized by quiet and privacy * Prefer to think things through carefully before acting
Teaching/Learning Methods:	**Teaching/Learning Methods:**
* Small-group interaction * Active methods such as discussion, simulation, field work * Concrete applications of abstract concepts; problem solving	* Time to gather thoughts before participating in discussion * Working with their own thoughts—listening, reading, and writing * Opportunity to polish work before presenting it

SENSING TYPES	INTUITIVE TYPES
Characteristics:	**Characteristics:**
* Perceive the world through the five senses * Interested in facts * Realistic, practical, concrete * Accurate, steady, precise, patient * Like to keep things simple; dislike complications	* Perceive the world through intuition * Interested in possibilities * Interested in abstract concepts, implications, relationships * Creative and innovative; dislike routine and details * Work in bursts of energy when inspired
Teaching/Learning Methods:	**Teaching/Learning Methods:**
* Clearly stated goals and expectations * Step-by-step analysis, one topic at a time * Concrete hands-on experience and many examples before moving to the abstract * Opportunity to practice skills to be learned * Computer-assisted instruction, simulations, videos	* Focus on the big picture, theory, and concepts * Opportunities to be inventive, solve problems, be creative * Assignments that require individual or small-group initiative * Discussion, small-group projects

Table 1b. Myers-Briggs Type Indicator Summary

THINKING TYPES	FEELING TYPES
Characteristics: * Make decisions on the basis of thinking * Avoid emotions when making decisions * Logical, rational, analytical, critical * Need and value fairness	**Characteristics:** * Make decisions on the basis of feeling * Base decisions on personal values * Warm, empathetic * Need and value kindness and harmony
Teaching/Learning Methods: * Logical, organized presentations * Debate * Evaluation and criticism of material * Feedback of specific, objective achievements	**Teaching/Learning Methods:** * Emphasis on human values; examples with human interest * Close personal rapport with teachers * Questions concerning personal opinion * Feedback that begins with agreement and appreciation; gentle criticism

JUDGING TYPES	PERCEIVING TYPES
Characteristics: * Approach outside world by attempting to order and control it * Make decisions quickly * Well organized; make and follow plans * Work steadily on one thing at a time until finished	**Characteristics:** * Approach outside world by gathering information and adapting to it * Delay decision; keep options open * Flexible, spontaneous; not organized * Work at many things at once; may start more things than they finish
Teaching/Learning Methods: * Provide plans, schedules, organization * Assignments given well in advance * Predictability and consistency * Recognized milestones and completion points	**Teaching/Learning Methods:** * Provide options, choices, flexibility * Allow second chances and changes in plans * Student choice in assignments * Pursue problems in their own way and draw their own conclusions

4. Characteristics of Adult Learners

Legal educators can improve their teaching and their students' learning by understanding basic characteristics of adult learners and shaping their teaching methods to reflect those characteristics. Four important characteristics of adult learners are: voluntary, respectful, collaborative, and contextual.

a. Voluntary

Participation in learning is voluntary; adults engage in learning of their own volition. Adults pursue education because they want to develop new skills, sharpen existing skills, acquire new knowledge, and gain insights. Adults are usually highly motivated to learn and are willing to engage in participatory learning methods such as discussion, simulation, and small-group activities. However, adults are quick to withdraw their participation if they feel that the education is not meeting their needs, does not connect with their past experiences, or is conducted at a level they find incomprehensible. Further, most adults will retreat if they are humiliated in the classroom. Intimidation does not facilitate adult learning.

b. Respectful

Mutual respect for the self-worth of teachers and students underlies an effective teaching/learning environment. One of the central features of good teaching is that students feel that instructors value them as individuals. However, for students to grow they must develop powers of critical reflection and accept challenges from teachers and their fellow students to consider alternative ways of thinking and behaving. Therefore, a difficult but essential task for the teacher is establishing a classroom climate and culture in which students feel and show respect and are willing to challenge and be challenged.

c. Collaborative

Students and teachers are engaged in a collaborative effort. At different times during a course, and for varying purposes, the teacher and students can share leadership. Collaboration is appropriate in course and class design in which both learner and instructor have a voice in choosing course objectives, teaching/learning methods, and evaluation criteria. Collaboration is constant — it involves reordering priorities and refocusing teaching/learning activities as the course progresses.

d. Contextual

Education involves exploring ideas, skills, knowledge, and attitudes. But exploration does not take place in a vacuum. Adults learn new concepts, skills, and attitudes by assigning meaning to them in the context of their previous experience. The learning process is cyclical. The learner becomes acquainted with new ideas and skills, applies the ideas and skills in real-life settings or simulations, reflects on the experience with these new skills and concepts, redefines how they might apply in other settings, and then reapplies them in new situations.

B. Teaching

Legal educators who want to enhance their teaching skills can make use of a variety of resources and models of teaching excellence. Each year, dozens of organizations sponsor conferences on teaching in higher education and some focus on legal education. Many colleges and universities have development programs designed to help faculty with their teaching. Further, numerous periodicals address teaching in college and several target law school teaching. Moreover, most university libraries contain helpful monographs that explore teaching in great detail.

The three models of teaching excellence below have been the subject of books, articles, conferences, and faculty development seminars: (1) Components of Effective Instruction, (2) Seven Principles of Good Practice in [Higher] Education, and (3) Dimensions of Exemplary Teaching.

1. Components of Effective Instruction

One of the enduring myths of university teaching is, "Nobody knows what makes teaching effective." In fact, researchers have been exploring the components of effective instruction since the 1930s. Those researchers include educational psychologists, sociologists, and developers of teaching excellence programs for faculty. They have collected and analyzed data from faculty, from administrators, and from students in different stages of their university careers and in a variety of disciplines. Although individual research studies use different nomenclature and reach some conflicting conclusions, reviews of the overall body of that research identify common components of effective instruction. A leading author on teaching and learning, Maryellen Weimer, explores five components of effective instruction identified in a research review. These components are summarized below.

a. Enthusiasm: The Zest for Teaching

Students want to take courses from faculty who enjoy and care about their teaching. Faculty enthusiasm for teaching must be genuine. Few teachers can fool their students by faking enthusiasm for the entire course. Teachers should think about issues such as why they are pleased to be teaching that content, those skills, that course, those students, at that school, in legal education. If faculty are not enthusiastic about *any* of those issues, another line of work is in order. It is not enough for teachers to be enthused—they must also communicate that excitement to their students. Teachers can begin by telling students in the first class why they are enthused about the course. Then throughout the course, teachers can demonstrate their enthusiasm with tone of voice, gestures, facial expressions, eye contact, movement during class, and humor.

b. Preparation and Organization

Effective teachers plan and prepare entire courses and individual classes. When designing a course, faculty should address the following issues and clearly communicate these matters to students in syllabi or some other way:

- Identify course objectives (what students should be able to know and do at the end of the course);
- Choose materials (books, articles, videos, computer programs);
- Pick a variety of teaching/learning activities (lecture, discussion, small-group work, simulations, computer tutorials, field trips, writing exercises);
- Articulate classroom policies and procedures (attendance, timeliness, academic honesty); and,
- Develop grading and evaluation methods (tests, writing assignments, participation).

Each day's class should reflect the teacher's preparation and organization as well. Like most other public presentations, a class should have an introduction, body, and conclusion. Teachers can communicate organization to students during class by identifying objectives at the beginning of class, using visuals such as handouts and overhead transparencies, and reiterating key issues at the end of class.

c. Stimulating Student Thought and Interest

The ability to stimulate student thought and interest in the course is an important part of engaging students in their own learning. Two concepts, learning styles and active learning, are central to stimulating student thought and interest. Different students learn best in different ways (reading, listening, speaking, observing, performing.) Consequently, teachers can help students learn by using a variety of teaching/learning methods in the classroom. Further, many students' preferred learning style is best served by active learning. Active learning means that the students engage in something more than listening, such as discussion, small-group projects, simulation, interactive computer tutorials, field work, and writing. (Each of those active learning methods is the subject of a chapter to follow.) Research shows that active learning methods facilitate the development of higher-level thinking (analysis, synthesis, evaluation) and skills acquisition, which are critical goals for most legal educators.

d. Explaining Clearly

Clear, effective teachers are adept at ascertaining when their students are confused and at using examples to diffuse students' confusion. One way for teachers to gauge students' understanding is to look for nonverbal cues in the classroom. Indicators of students' lack of understanding include facial expressions of frustration or confusion and students conversing with one another or looking at each other's notes to try to fill in the gaps in their understanding. Another way for teachers to assess their students' confusion is to ask the students expressly, "Do you have any questions?" For this query to be effective, teachers must genuinely want to hear students' questions. Teachers demonstrate their interest in students' questions by maintaining eye contact and giving students at least five seconds to generate questions before moving on. Teachers also can assess students' understanding by asking students at the end of class to hand in (anonymously) a slip of paper with a question or by inviting students to ask questions via e-mail.

Examples are an important tool in helping students understand complex concepts. Good examples are clear, appealing, and transferable. Clear examples are concrete, brief, and include ideas known to students. Appealing examples relate to the students' experiences and aspirations and are novel, credible, and realistic. Transferable examples are those that provide a specific instance that can be generalized to the larger principle. Teachers can build a repertoire of examples by recording examples as they occur to the teacher or as the teacher reads or hears about them. Students are an excellent source of examples. By asking students to provide examples of a concept, teachers not only get the benefit of new examples, but can assess students' understanding as well.

e. Knowledge and Love of Content

Good teachers know and love their subjects. Teachers must understand the theory, structure, and key details of the subject to be effective in helping students learn. But knowing the content is not enough to be an excellent teacher. In addition, effective teachers love their subjects and communicate that love to their students.

2. Seven Principles of Good Practice in [Higher] Education

In 1986, leading teachers and scholars in the movement to improve higher education in the United States met to identify the key principles which characterize the practices at educationally successful colleges. Those teachers and scholars developed seven principles for good practice in undergraduate education. The principles were based on findings from decades of research on teaching and learning in college. The "Seven Principles for Good Practice in Undergraduate Education" became the title of the lead article in the March 1987 issue of the *American Association for Higher Education Bulletin.*

The Seven Principles have greatly influenced theory and practice in higher education. More than 150,000 reprints were requested within six months of its publication. Subsequently, educators developed a Faculty Inventory, Student Inventory, and Institutional Inventory, which are instruments designed to help teachers, students, and administrators to assess how their courses and campuses reflect the Seven Principles. Numerous conferences and journal articles have addressed the Seven Principles and two books review the research behind the principles and describe practical applications of the principles in college: APPLYING THE SEVEN PRINCIPLES FOR GOOD PRACTICE IN UNDERGRADUATE EDUCATION and THE SEVEN PRINCIPLES IN ACTION.

Although the original focus of the educators who developed the Seven Principles was undergraduate education, the principles have much to offer legal educators as well. The authors of the principles summarized them as follows:

> *Principle 1: Good Practice Encourages Student-Faculty Contact.* Frequent student-faculty contact in and out of class is the most important factor in student motivation and involvement. Faculty concern helps students get through rough times and keep on working. Knowing a few faculty members well enhances students' intellectual commitment and encourages them to think about their own values and future plans.
>
> *Principle 2: Good Practice Encourages Cooperation Among Students.* Learning is enhanced when it is more like a team effort than a solo race. Good learning, like good work, is collaborative and social, not competitive and isolated. Working with others often increases involvement in learning. Sharing one's own ideas and responding to others' reactions sharpen thinking and deepen understanding.
>
> *Principle 3: Good Practice Encourages Active Learning.* Learning is not a spectator sport. Students do not learn much just by sitting in classes and listening to teachers, memorizing pre-packaged assignments, and spitting

out answers. They must talk about what they are learning, write about it, relate it to past experiences, and apply it to their daily lives. They must make what they learn part of themselves.

Principle 4: Good Practice Gives Prompt Feedback. Knowing what you know and don't know focuses learning. Students need appropriate feedback on performance to benefit from courses. When getting started, students need help in assessing existing knowledge and competence. In classes, students need frequent opportunities to perform and receive suggestions for improvement. At various points during college, and at the end, students need chances to reflect on what they have learned, what they still need to know, and how to assess themselves.

Principle 5: Good Practice Emphasizes Time on Task. Time plus energy equals learning. There is no substitute for time on task. Learning to use one's time well is critical for students and professionals alike. Students need help in learning effective time management. Allocating realistic amounts of time means effective learning for students and effective teaching for faculty. How an institution defines time expectations for students, faculty, administrators, and other professional staff can establish the basis for high performance for all.

Principle 6: Good Practice Communicates High Expectations. Expect more and you will get it. High expectations are important for everyone—for the poorly prepared, for those unwilling to exert themselves, and for the bright and well motivated. Expecting students to perform well becomes a self-fulfilling prophecy when teachers and institutions hold high expectations of themselves and make extra efforts.

Principle 7: Good Practice Respects Diverse Talents and Ways of Learning. There are many roads to learning. People bring different talents and styles of learning to college. Brilliant students in the seminar room may be all thumbs in the lab or art studio. Students rich in hands-on experience may not do so well with theory. Students need opportunity to show their talents and learn in ways that work for them. Then they can be pushed to learn in ways that do not come so easily.

3. Dimensions of Exemplary Teaching

A leading author on teaching in higher education, Joseph Lowman, has developed a two-dimensional model of exemplary teaching. The quality of instruction results from a teacher's skill at creating both intellectual excitement and interpersonal rapport with students. Intellectual excitement and interpersonal rapport motivate students to do their best work. Excellence at either dimension can make a teacher effective with some students in some courses; excellence at both will make the teacher highly effective with most students in nearly any setting.

Lowman based his two-dimensional model of exemplary teaching on three types of research. First, he reviewed the immense body of research on student evaluation of college teachers. (Nearly 1,000 such studies were conducted from 1974 to 1993.) Second, Lowman observed twenty-five exemplary college teachers in the early 1980s. Third, he analyzed over 500 student and faculty nominations for teaching awards in 1989, 1990, and 1991.

For both dimensions of the model, Lowman characterizes teachers who rate high, medium, and low. For each rating, he describes what an outsider would observe in the classroom and the effects the teacher would have on students. In addition, Lowman reports the most common descriptive terms found in the student and faculty nominations for teaching awards. Summarized below, for the highest rated teachers on each dimension, are the most common descriptors, outsider's observations, and effects on students.

Dimension I — Intellectual Excitement

a. Most common descriptors of exemplary faculty:

Enthusiastic
Knowledgeable
Inspiring
Humorous
Interesting
Clear
Organized

b. Observer's description of teaching:

All content is extremely well organized and presented in clear language.

Relationships between specific concepts and applications to new situations are stressed.

Content is presented in an engaging way, with high energy and strong sense of dramatic tension.

Teacher appears to love presenting the material.

c. Impact on students:

Students know where the teacher is going and can distinguish important from unimportant material.

Students see connections between concepts and can apply them to new situations.

Students have little confusion about material or about what the teacher has said.

It is easy to pay attention to the teacher (almost impossible to daydream).

Class time seems to pass very quickly, and students may get so caught up in the ideas that they forget to take notes.

Students experience a sense of excitement about the ideas under study and generally hate to miss class.

Dimension II — Interpersonal Rapport

a. Most common descriptors of exemplary faculty:

Concerned
Helpful
Caring
Encouraging
Challenging
Available
Fair

b. Observer's description of teaching:

Teacher appears to have strong interest in the students as individuals and high sensitivity to subtle messages from them about their feelings concerning the material or its presentation.

Teacher acknowledges students' feelings about matters of class assignments or policy and encourages them to express their feelings; may poll their preferences on some matters.

Teacher encourages students to ask questions and seems eager for them to express personal viewpoints.

Teacher communicates both openly and subtly that each student's understanding of the material is important to the teacher.

Teacher encourages students to be creative and independent in dealing with the material and to formulate their own views.

c. Impact on Students:

Students feel that the teacher knows who they are and cares about them and their learning a great deal.

Students have positive, perhaps even affectionate, view of the teacher; some may identify strongly with the teacher.

Students believe teacher has confidence that they can learn and think independently about the subject.

References

CHARLES C. BONWELL & JAMES A. EISON, ACTIVE LEARNING: CREATING EXCITEMENT IN THE CLASSROOM (1991).

Stephen D. Brookfield, *Adult Learners: Motives for Learning and Implications for Practice*, in TEACHING AND LEARNING IN THE COLLEGE CLASSROOM 137–149 (Kenneth A. Feldman & Michael B. Paulsen eds., 1994).

Roger H. Bruning, *The College Classroom from the Perspective of Cognitive Psychology*, in HANDBOOK OF COLLEGE TEACHING: THEORY AND APPLICATIONS 3–22 (Keith W. Prichard & R. McLaren Sawyer eds., 1994).

Thomas G. Carskadon, *Student Personality Factors: Psychological Type and the Myers-Briggs Type Indicator*, in HANDBOOK OF COLLEGE TEACHING: THEORY AND APPLICATIONS 69–81 (Keith W. Prichard & R. McLaren Sawyer eds., 1994).

ZELDA F. GAMSON ET AL., APPLYING THE SEVEN PRINCIPLES FOR GOOD PRACTICE IN UNDERGRADUATE EDUCATION (Arthur W. Chickering & Zelda F. Gamson eds., 1991).

Arthur W. Chickering & Zelda F. Gamson, *Seven Principles for Good Practice in Undergraduate Education*, 39 (7) AAHE BULLETIN 3–7 (1987).

JUDITH A. STURNICK ET AL., THE SEVEN PRINCIPLES IN ACTION (Susan Rickey Hatfield ed., 1995).

Gerald F. Hess, *Listening to Our Students: Obstructing and Enhancing Learning in Law School*, 31 U.S.F. L. REV. 941 (1997).

Kurfiss, Joanne, *Intellectual, Psychosocial, and Moral Development in College: Four Major Theories*, in TEACHING AND LEARNING IN THE COLLEGE CLASSROOM, 165–189 (Kenneth A. Feldman & Michael B. Paulsen eds., 1994).

JOSEPH LOWMAN, MASTERING THE TECHNIQUES OF TEACHING (2d ed. 1995).

Paula Lustbader, *From Dreams to Reality: The Emerging Role of Academic Support Programs*, 31 U.S.F. L. REV. 839 (1997).

William S. Moore, *Student and Faculty Epistemology in the College Classroom: The Perry Schema of Intellectual and Ethical Development*, in HANDBOOK OF COLLEGE TEACHING: THEORY AND APPLICATIONS 45–67 (Keith W. Prichard & R. McLaren Sawyer eds., 1994).

Vernellia R. Randall, *The Myers-Briggs Type Indicator, First-Year Law Students and Performance*, 26 CUMB. L. REV. 63 (1995).

MARYELLEN WEIMER, IMPROVING YOUR CLASSROOM TEACHING (1993).

Chapter 2

Course and Class Planning

Most excellent instructors...plan very seriously, fully aware that alternative ways of organizing class sessions are available, which go beyond the mere presentation of materials to the promotion of active higher-order learning and motivation. —Lowman

While many people, including law professors, carry planning books and calendars to help map out their lives, it is rare that law professors possess the equivalent for their classes. Like Rodney Dangerfield, course and class planning often get no respect. Instead, there exists an unstated belief that the creation of a syllabus for a law school class, especially when guided by the compass of a casebook and its teacher's manual, constitutes more than sufficient class planning. Furthermore, the thinking goes, discrete and explicit planning is unnecessary.

Course and class planning, however, is a serious subject worthy of a law professor's time. Express attention to planning can lead to more effective teaching methods and, more importantly, better quality of learning for students. Course and class planning can help make the classroom a more productive and enjoyable place.

So why don't law professors plan and plan hard? The answer probably lies in a combination of history, culture, and difficulty. A law class generally is modeled after the law classes the teacher had as a student and designed in a manner consistent with a law school's culture. Improvement in class, even with planning, is neither easy nor guaranteed. No matter how hard one seems to try, the same obstacles often appear.

Without planning, though, the "same old way" rarely produces change, but rather leads down the same road over and over. As time goes on, it becomes all too easy to defer the responsibility for bad classes to students or to conclude that the same type of teaching experience is inevitable.

The values of planning are threefold: (1) planning allows teachers to recognize and identify strengths and weaknesses of the class, (2) planning encourages teachers to develop strategies and tactics to deal with the strengths and weaknesses, and (3) planning helps teachers and students appreciate "the bigger picture," rather than just the immediate task at hand. For example, creative strategies and tactics for overcoming teach-

21

ing roadblocks, from the types of questions asked to how to end a class on an upbeat pedagogical note, can help deal with problems so that they diminish or disappear altogether.

A. Planning Theory

Planning has descriptive and prescriptive stages. The descriptive component involves a realistic assessment of the current status of a course and how it operates. The planning process will suffer if the professor does not confront problems, such as: a lack of clear and concise goals; the parts of the course that may perplex students, bore them, or seem to provide little relevance; or obstacles like uneven class participation, students who are late for class, and students who do not attend class. Identification of strengths and weaknesses is generally a necessary predicate to effecting change.

The second stage of planning is the implementation or prescriptive phase. It is here that strategies and tactics are used to deal with the issues identified in the descriptive phase. According to Webster's Dictionary, "strategy" means "a careful plan or method; the art of devising or employing plans or stratagems towards a goal." "Tactics," on the other hand, means "a device for accomplishing an end."

Strategies and tactics can be applied to all aspects of a law course, from teaching methodology to substantive coverage. For example, a professor may plan how to better communicate to students the relevancy or interesting aspects of the Rule Against Perpetuities. Further, strategies and tactics can be used to better communicate to students the overriding goals of a first-year civil procedure course or to develop a policy to encourage widespread class participation.

The specificity of the planning strategies becomes important, much like in any business venture. While a vague and meandering business plan could succeed, it would be much better if it were designed with precision. Without that precision, it is difficult to determine whether the plan worked and, if it did, how it worked.

B. What to Plan

While course objectives comprise one obvious aspect of planning, the planning activities should not be cabined to just this one component of a law school course. Numerous other components of the planning process exist: the syllabus; the materials; the teaching/learning methods; the class environment; the opening and closing of class; and the evaluation techniques.

Within these areas, planning can reach many different subcomponents. For example, the syllabus could detail course goals, the physical environment could include how the board or multimedia technology will be used, and teaching methodology could touch on how handouts will assist with the classes. These components and subcomponents of the planning process are discussed in greater detail below.

1. Course Objectives

The most appropriate starting point in course planning is for teachers to determine what it is the students ought to be learning in the class and to expressly communicate these goals to the students. Although it is sometimes difficult to express goals with specificity, explicit objectives help teachers and students stay on track during the course. Objectives may vary from segment to segment of the course and can include doctrinal rules, specific applications of legal analysis and problem solving, and the lawyering skills used in the course area, such as complaint writing, negotiation, or interviewing.

From a seminal work on planning, PREPARING INSTRUCTIONAL OBJECTIVES, Robert F. Mager offers additional advice about planning objectives. Useful objectives communicate clearly by minimizing interpretation and have three characteristics: (1) performance—what it is a learner shall do, (2) conditions—the circumstances surrounding performance, and (3) criterion—the standards for acceptable performance.

(1) A useful objective "describes the kind of performance that will be accepted as evidence that the learner has mastered the objective." Thus, "appreciating" something or "understanding" something would not describe a performance and would fail as useful objectives. On the other hand, "writing" or "speaking" would satisfy the performance requirement.

(2) Conditions are limitations or circumstances that should be imposed to determine whether mastery of the subject is being demonstrated by the students. Examples of conditions include: reciting the rules of law without the aid of notes; analyzing the hypothetical within 30 minutes; creating an example of a rule of law.

(3) Criteria inform students about how well they should accomplish the performance task. Criteria can be used to minimize

the intangibles, those things that can not be evaluated, and to maximize the tangibles. Speed, accuracy, and quality are all acceptable criteria of performance.

2. The Syllabus

The syllabus can be viewed as instructions for a do-it-yourself building kit for learning. It describes the construction materials (e.g., casebook), the assignments for building, and its order of progression. Thus, like other sets of directions, there is great potential within the syllabus for planning the learning process, particularly outside the classroom environment. For example, the assignment schedule can list the material to be covered and explain the import of the material, how it is to be covered, and why. Further, the syllabus can include the questions the teacher wants the students to consider while preparing for class. The explanations and questions can encourage students to focus on the larger perspective of the course and not just on the discrete chunks of substantive material covered each day.

3. Course Materials

There is perhaps no greater influence on the content of law school courses than that of the course materials, specifically the casebook. The design and substance of the casebook usually significantly affect the design and substance of a course. As teachers grow more comfortable with a subject area or a casebook, they often adapt it to include additional materials such as articles, videos, computer exercises, and documents (wills, pleadings, contracts, etc.). However, the casebook usually remains the primary resource, and the extra materials serve as a supplement.

The opportunity for planning in this context is to fit the materials of the course to the independently determined course objectives and methods, not vice versa. Planning thus may mean using only certain parts of a book or using the text in a supporting role to hypotheticals, role-playing, or other learning projects. It also means the professor communicates a bigger picture for the course than the book alone, connecting the material to lawyering skills, ethics, and the evaluation process.

4. Teaching/Learning Methods

The classroom dynamic in many respects can not be planned, since the conversation that develops is not rehearsed. It is unknown what students will say in response to questions, how they will interpret questions, and how exactly most questions will be phrased. Despite these inherent ambiguities in the classroom, there are many aspects of the classroom that can be the subject of planning.

a. Discussion and Debate

The nature, subject matter, duration, and other aspects of class discussion can be planned. A teacher can decide in advance to call on students in different parts of the room or on specific students, to ask a certain number of questions of each student, or to have a certain tenor of conversation. The teacher also can decide whether the questions will be fact-oriented, rule-oriented, rationale-oriented, or focused on something else altogether. There are also decisions to be made about whether to commence a discussion of a case with information, a statement of goals, or other prefatory material. Even the types of hypotheticals used can be planned. While a successful discussion might occur if the professor "wings it," teachers (just like talk show hosts) are invariably better off if they know who the guests are and what kinds of questions will be discussed.

b. Integrating Theory and Practice

In recent years, a considerable body of literature has accumulated advocating that legal education should combine legal theory with law practice skills. A particular impetus for fostering the coalescence of theory and practice was the MacCrate Report, which took law schools to task for not teaching students enough skills to promote lawyering competency.

Yet, even prior to the publication of the MacCrate Report, many professors had been utilizing lawyering skills in theory-oriented, basic courses. In large-group, traditional, first-year courses, some teachers had been regularly conducting negotiations, interviewing, counseling, writing assignments, and role-playing exercises.

Because the teaching of these skills often diverges from the usual "Socratic" dialogue, their planning may require additional and specific attention. For example, in a small-group exercise, it may be important to create an accompanying handout or to have instructions written on the board. If there is a role-playing exercise, it may be important to notify student participants about the exercise in advance and to discuss their roles with them, even to the extent of writing out scripts. In-class writing assignments require advance thought about how much time to allocate to the writing and how feedback on that writing will be provided—will it be peer review, teacher initiated, or a combination of both? These and other questions can be dealt with in the planning stage.

5. The Architecture and Environment of the Class

While classroom structure and configuration are often beyond the control of the professor, there are many aspects of the class environment that are within the professor's influence. Where students sit—whether they all vacate the front rows for the "cheap seats" in the back, for example—whether food and drink are permitted, whether students can tape the class, where students with computers sit, whether a podium is used, what colors of markers or chalk for the board will be available, and whether multimedia materials are used, are all questions appropriate to the planning of a course.

6. The Openings and Closings of a Class

The beginning and ending of a class are often omitted from the planning process. Like the opening statements and closing arguments of a trial, however, these can be crucial to the learning process.

a. The Opening

Just as the psychological literature talks about the importance of primacy or first impressions, the opening of a class can set the tone and the direction for the day. A professor can lead with a brief review, the objectives for the day, or simply dive right in to the cases assigned. Professors can experiment with the opening to determine its impact on the learning process. One professor, for example, routinely begins class by asking students, "Where are we?" to get them thinking about the nature of the subject matter. Other professors begin by taking care of "housekeeping" matters such as assignment reminders or by articulating the objectives for the class.

b. The Closing

Often, the closing of a class is marked simply by the completion of the time allotted. The class may end in the middle of a discussion or analysis of a case. Better alternatives exist. A class can be designed to conclude with a question that leaves the students thinking about what they have just covered or what they will cover in the next class. It also may consist of a brief summary of the important points covered in the class or may include student reactions to the material. In any event, the last memory of the class is often just as important as the first.

7. Evaluation Techniques

How students will be evaluated is an important planning issue. The teacher can consider a variety of types of evaluation methods — essay exams, multiple-choice tests, papers, drafting, class participation, etc. Evaluation can occur during the substantive part of the course and need not wait until a comprehensive final examination. The evaluation techniques could count as part of a student's grade or may be used for the primary purpose of providing feedback to students (and professors) during the course. To be used successfully and to maximize their pedagogical values, evaluation measures should be scheduled and planned.

It is often disconcerting for first-year law students to observe the apparent discontinuity between case analysis in class and the time-pressured final examination upon which their grade is based. Part of this discontinuity involves students not seeing what the evaluation process is like early and often in the legal education program. Without this connection, some students have a difficult time appreciating the relevance of classes in relation to evaluation. (Evaluation of students is discussed in detail in Chapter 11.)

References

AMERICAN BAR ASSOCIATION SECTION OF LEGAL EDUCATION AND ADMISSIONS TO THE BAR, LEGAL EDUCATION AND PROFESSIONAL DEVELOPMENT — AN EDUCATIONAL CONTINUUM. REPORT ON THE TASK FORCE ON LAW SCHOOLS AND THE PROFESSION: NARROWING THE GAP (1992).

BARBARA GROSS DAVIS, TOOLS FOR TEACHING 3–27 (1993).

James Eagar, *The Right Tool for the Job: The Effective Use of Pedagogical Methods In Legal Education*, 32 GONZ. L. REV. 389 (1996–1997).

JOSEPH LOWMAN, MASTERING THE TECHNIQUES OF TEACHING 193–224 (2d ed. 1995).

ROBERT F. MAGER, PREPARING INSTRUCTIONAL OBJECTIVES (2d. ed. 1975).

MARYELLEN WEIMER, IMPROVING YOUR CLASSROOM TEACHING 29–47 (1993).

Specific Course and Class Planning Ideas

#1: Using the Syllabus as Course Synthesis and Teaching Plan

The syllabus for any course can be a pedagogical instrument as well as a map of the course. The outline of the course can serve as a basis for asking questions and framing the subject matter for each class meeting.

For the past several years, I have worked on several projects related to learning and the law, including a Critical Thinking and the Law Project (see Holley and Ogilvy, *Critical Thinking and The Law*, 1 INTERN. J. OF LEG. PROF. 343 (1994)). I have tried to transfer some of the lessons learned in undertaking that work to the teaching of my traditional law courses. The idea expressed in the first paragraph is one of those lessons.

In my substantive criminal law course, I distribute to the students an eighteen-page syllabus. The bulk of the syllabus is made up of a series of approximately two hundred questions. The questions synthesize in sequence every topic covered in the course casebook (Dix and Sharlot), as well as seek to focus attention on the position taken on the topic in the Model Penal Code and the current majority view of the topic. For example, with regard to the topic of general principles of "culpability" (syllabus questions 50–70), question 58 asks: "What presumptions do most recently revised penal codes require that courts and other lawyers use to identify the requisite culpable mental state, when it is unclear, what, if any, culpable mental state is required for a crime or for a specific element of a crime?" Question 59 then asks: "What other evidence do courts and other lawyers employ to identify the requisite culpable mental state, when it is unclear, what, if any, culpable mental state is required for a crime or for a specific element of a crime?" The following are some of the key teaching techniques that can be employed once such a syllabus is created.

First, students are provided with a detailed "assessment" model to assist them in understanding what they are "reading." Students are told to review the sequence of topic questions prior to reading the casebook and other material, to look for answers to the questions as they read, and to mark in the materials when they find an answer to one or more of the questions. Students are also instructed that certain questions pose such complex issues (see question "59" above for example) that "answers" to them can be found in several of the sequential topics, perhaps in more than one chapter of the casebook.

Second, the bulk of class discussion focuses on the answers the students have prepared to these questions prior to class. Students are told to "answer" each question by converting the language of each question to a "law statement," with the authority for that statement. Hence the students receive repetitive practice in not only "reading" the casebook, penal codes, and other materials assigned, but in using them to create a work product that seeks to synthesize and provide perspective about those materials. Students are also asked to anticipate and revisit their answers to these questions during earlier and subsequent class sessions, which use them as part of the "Review/Preview" warm-up part of the class. Finally, students are provided a further incentive to do a good job in creating that work product, because they are told that it should serve as the only class outline they will have to prepare. The teaching of thinking literature recommends that students be afforded repeat opportunities to practice a thinking skill and related strategies.

Third, the sequential syllabus questions can be used to facilitate student understanding of the most complex conceptual problems presented in the course. For example, after asking students to identify the position taken by the common law, the Model Penal Code, and most revised penal codes with regard to the conduct element of attempt, a syllabus question then asks why most revised codes rejected the Model Penal Code position. The teaching of thinking literature recommends that students be taken through a subject matter area in sequential steps — with the progressive introduction of more complex thinking skills and concepts.

In summary, with a detailed sequential syllabus as an assessment model, students can repeat opportunities to practice a valuable lawyer thinking skill, prepare an accurate synthesis of all course material, and progressively experience increasingly complex and related doctrines. Although it takes several hours to construct, the long-term benefits for your teaching and student learning make it well worth the investment.

Dannye Holley
Texas Southern University

#2: The Ten Commandments of [The First-Year Course of Your Choice]

Students are aware that law school is a different ball game from undergraduate school before they set foot in the door. They have heard horror stories about the Socratic method and the immense workload. The problem is that they are familiar with these things only as abstractions. For example, they know it is important to be well prepared for class, but have no clue as to what "being prepared" means. As a result, new law students spend their first few weeks on the verge of panic attacks as they sit through classes speculating about what is going to happen and how they are supposed to behave.

Properly directed, a little anxiety can be a powerful motivational force. But when it is unfocused and consuming, anxiety interferes with learning. A simple and effective way to help alleviate this problem is to give beginning students some vital information up front about what they can expect in your course. I accomplish this with a protocol I call *The Ten Commandments of Torts I*, which is just a jazzy way of saying *Here Are Ten Important Things You Need To Know About This Course*. This protocol gives students a kind of blueprint to help them navigate through my course. Eventually, they would pick up this information on their own, but only inefficiently and after much wasted emotional energy. An abbreviated version of *The Ten Commandments* appears below. It can be adapted to any course.

1. *Thou shalt be prepared for class.*

It is extremely important that you always be prepared for class. "Being prepared" means that you must know: (1) the facts of the case; (2) the procedural history that resulted in the case being heard by an appellate court (*examples*: the trial court dismissed the complaint filed by the plaintiff and the plaintiff is appealing; or the trial court gave a legal instruction to the jury which the defendant asserts was incorrect and the defendant is appealing); (3) who won the case (the plaintiff or the defendant); (4) the substantive legal issue in the case; and (5) the court's reasoning. To be well-acquainted with a case, you usually will be required to read it at least twice. Briefing cases is essential for first-year law students. By "cases," I mean the principal cases that are set forth in the casebook. You are not required to look up the "note cases."

2. *Thou shalt be on time.*

It is rude and distracting to both your classmates and the professor to arrive late to class. Please make your best effort to be on time.

3. *Thou shalt not be afraid to ask questions.*

Most people do not know anything about the law when they get to law school. Even diligent studying and preparation are not going to answer many of your questions, particularly early on. Thus, I encourage you to ask questions. There is no such thing as a "stupid question." If you have a question about some aspect of a case, the chances are good that many others share your confusion.

4. *Thou shalt not be afraid to voice your opinion, even when it is believed to be contrary to the professor's.*

A law school class should be a vital and exciting learning environment. The most controversial issues of our time are rooted in the law (e.g., abortion, affirmative action, gun control). Law school can be an intimidating place, but I encourage you to come to class willing to discuss the material. Your thoughts and opinions are valuable and your contributions to class discussion will make Torts a more enjoyable course for everyone. Do not be afraid to disagree with me. So long as we all remain respectful of one another, hearty debate is something to be encouraged.

5. Thou shalt tolerate the professor's offbeat sense of humor.

Students learn better when they are interested and involved in what is going on in the classroom. Thus, I go out of my way to try to make classes interesting and entertaining. If I make a humorous remark at your expense, please take it in the spirit in which it was intended. I do not try to belittle students.

6. Thou shalt respect thy classmates.

You are all in this together and one of the most wonderful things about law school is the bonding that occurs among entering classes. Students come to law school from many different backgrounds, which affect their viewpoints. All views are entitled to respect. There is no such thing as an incorrect opinion.

7. Thou shalt understand that there is method in the madness.

Most first-year law school classes are conducted by the Socratic method. From a student's perspective, the Socratic method might be defined as follows: "The professor hides the ball and then tries to embarrass students who can't find it." I can appreciate this view, but embarrassment is not the purpose of the Socratic method. Students arrive at law school believing they are here to learn and memorize legal rules. That is certainly part of it, but not nearly all of it. You could memorize all the legal rules in the world, but still be a lousy lawyer. Good lawyering is about problem solving, and the Socratic method involves forcing you to apply legal rules to solve problems. That is why I use many hypothetical fact situations in the classroom. I am trying to enhance your ability to reason well. Unfortunately, true appreciation of this usually comes, if at all, only when it is all over. In the meantime, I ask you to just trust me that it really does work.

8. Thou shalt not be afraid to seek out the professor's office.

I encourage you to drop by my office to talk about Torts, law school, or anything else that is on your mind.

9. Thou shalt regularly attend class.

[I explain my attendance policy in detail.] Though you are allowed six misses, I strongly encourage you not to use them unless necessary. I can tell you from experience that rarely does a student who has missed several classes do well on the final exam.

10. *Thou shalt take a deep breath and prepare for a long, hard semester.*

Law school is not like undergraduate school. It requires a tremendous amount of work. You need to realize this at the *very beginning* so you do not fall behind. Over the years, many students who did not succeed in law school have told me they just did not realize how much work it required until it was too late. Do not let that happen to you. My goal is for all of you to succeed. I will do my best to assist you, but, ultimately, your success will depend primarily upon how hard you are willing to work.

Andrew J. McClurg
University of Arkansas at Little Rock School of Law

#3: Teaching Legal Analysis: An Inventory of Skills

It is unfortunate that many first-year courses are titled and organized as if their only objective were to impart legal doctrine. In my Contracts class, the teaching of substantive law is an important goal, but may be less important than teaching the skills of legal analysis.

Over the last few years, I have moved toward a skills-based approach to teaching Contracts. In part this reflects my orientation as a clinical teacher (my first few years in teaching were as a full-time live-client clinician), and in part it is a reaction to the apparent and expressed educational needs of the students in my Contracts class. Some students come into law school with intellectual skills that enable them to learn the complex skills of legal analysis with little explicit guidance. Most students, however, are better able to learn legal analysis and problem solving if they are not only asked to do it, but shown how and given opportunities to practice each of the component skills.

What follows is an inventory of skills that are necessary to do legal analysis. The development of this inventory helped my teaching, because it required me to articulate more precisely what skills I want to work on during class. This led me to focus more explicitly on skill development, to allocate more time to discussions focusing on skill development, and to talk with the students about the skills that I was trying to teach them. The students responded very positively to my increasing emphasis on Contracts as a "skills" course and to the road-mapping I offered them.

My suggestion to other teachers is not to use my inventory, but to make your own. The process of examining one's own teaching and identifying and refining one's goals is more useful than adopting the goals of another. If I have a clear idea of what I am trying to teach, and why I believe that my goals are worthwhile, and let my students know what my goals are, they are in a better position to learn effectively.

1. Prerequisites

I begin with a list of skills which each of us possesses in different degrees and all of which are necessary to do legal analysis. Weakness in one or more of these areas could present an obstacle to learning the skills of legal analysis.

a. Logical thinking
b. Organizing ideas
c. Oral expression (includes the ability to think and speak simultaneously, requires self-confidence)
d. Writing (basic skills in exposition, grammar, spelling, and punctuation)
e. Reading comprehension
f. Listening, attentiveness
g. Formulating questions (identifying what one doesn't understand and articulating it)
h. Figuring out what is being taught and what will be tested
i. Thoroughness and attention to detail
j. Judgment, common sense
k. Note-taking (making a good record of class discussion for future study)
l. Sensitivity to ethical dilemmas
m. Creativity, imagination
n. Ability to concentrate
o. Time management and planning (making and implementing decisions about what to study and how to study, and monitoring and adapting one's study plans as the semester goes on)

2. Comprehension of law and facts (presented in court decisions)

a. Understanding facts
  1) Understand what happened in a case or the facts of a problem
    a) Comprehend an unfamiliar context (e.g., disposal of spent nuclear fuel)
    b) Learn unfamiliar vocabulary
  2) Understand the legal importance of facts to:
    a) Distinguish those that are important from those that are not
    b) Recognize ambiguities and omissions in a statement of facts

    b.   Understanding a legal doctrine
       1) Understand the scope of the category of rules of which the doctrine is a part
       2) Learn what are the sources of law in that category
          a) How each source came into being
          b) How much authority each source has
          c) The relationship between the sources
       3) Understand the structure of the source of law in which a particular doctrine appears
          a) Recognize the parts of a rule
          b) Understand the meaning of each part
          c) Understand the relationship of the parts
          d) Distinguish the general rule from the exceptions
    c. Understanding a judicial opinion
       1) Discern how an opinion is structured and identify its parts
       2) Understand why and how the law and facts of other cases are used
       3) Understand why and how statutes are applied
       4) Understand why and how secondary sources are used
       5) Understand the non-law factors that contributed to the analysis
       6) Understand why and how an opinion departs from previous ones and how the departure is justified

3. Synthesis of multiple sources of law

    a. Explain the relationship between multiple sources of law on a particular topic
    b. Identify the concepts or elements that are common to the various sources
    c. Identify those concepts or elements that differ among the various sources
    d. If the synthesis is of case law, recognize these similarities and differences as to both facts and law
    e. Explain which similarities or differences are most important and why
    f. Explain patterns or trends that emerge from an analysis of the group of sources

4. Critical thinking about cases and statutes

Development of facility in recognizing and exploring:

    a. Why the rule is x rather than y
    b. Whether x is the best possible rule, or what would be a better rule

    c.   What is the relationship among a group of rules

    d.   What purposes are accomplished by particular rules

    e.   What interests are reflected in particular rules

    f.   What ambiguity exists in a rule, and what are the sources and consequences of that ambiguity

    g.   Whether the rule reflects an incorrect understanding of facts or false assumptions about a situation

    h.   What is the history of a rule, in what context has it been developed, and how has it changed over time

    i.   What is the economic impact of a rule

    j.   Does the rule have different impact on different groups (e.g., consumers, families, sellers, buyers)

    k.   What is the impact of the background, experience, social class, personality, sex, race, age, religion, marital status, sexual preference, education, intellectual ability, etc. of the decision-maker (judge, lawyer, legislator, etc.) and the parties or persons affected by the rule

5. Application of law

Students need to learn how to take a set of facts, identify the legal issues that are presented in those facts, identify the relevant rules of law, and figure out what result would be produced by applying the law to the facts. In each court decision judges identify and apply the law to reach a result. In class we use judicial decisions as models of analysis, and the students are often asked to do their own analysis of written problems assigned as homework and then discussed in class.

    a.   Application of a statute to a set of facts

        1) Overcome the foggy nauseous math-anxiety type of feeling that so often accompanies first encounters with statutes

        2) Determine whether the statute applies at all or whether it is binding or persuasive authority with respect to the matter at hand and, if so, identify the relevant section(s)

        3) Understand the relationship of different provisions in a statute

        4) Read the statute word by word and identify the questions that must be answered about the facts of the problem

        5) Distinguish the part of a statute that states a general rule, and the parts that state exceptions to the general rule

        6) Identify the relevant parts of any sources (commentary, precedent, scholarship) that help to understand what each word in the statute means and what questions it suggests

        7) Answer each question raised by the statute about the facts of the problem

8) Use the statute to understand the logical sequence between the answers to the various questions

9) Draw a conclusion from the sequence of answers to the questions

10) Recognize questions asked by the statute that can be answered in more than one way and follow through first one analysis and then another

11) Recognize the purposes of the statute and assess whether the analysis comports with its purpose

b. Application of a court decision to a new problem

This involves all the skills listed above and, in addition, requires the students to:

1) Draw analogies, or make distinctions, between the facts of a case and the facts of the problem

2) Construct arguments based on those comparisons or contrasts

c. Application of multiple sources of law

5a and 5b in this list look at what is required to simply articulate the relationship between a case or statute and a new problem. Another set of skills involves doing the synthesis described in section 3 above for a problem solving purpose. This would involve the additional skills of:

1) Constructing arguments for one or more parties based on the patterns identified in section 3

2) Determining the possible conclusions that might be drawn from the application of multiple sources to the problem

3) Evaluating which conclusion is most persuasive and why

6. Sensitivity to ethical issues

a. Alertness to and ability to analyze ethical considerations that are raised in judicial opinions

b. Recognition of ethical questions presented in the facts of a case but not addressed in an opinion

c. Sensitivity to ethical questions and constraints on the application of law to solve a problem

7. Problem solving

Essentially what lawyers do is solve problems by determining what legal constraints or tools exist that relate to the problem, integrating the legal and non-legal factors that affect the problem, and developing some advice, an argument, or a strategy. All of the above-listed skills are building blocks, the purpose of which is to enable legal problem solving.

Lisa G. Lerman
The Columbus School of Law, Catholic University of America

#4: Problem-Solving Curriculum

Law school curricula need a radical rethinking. Traditional legal education lacks a coherent underlying set of principles.

Problem solving, which is the core of lawyering, provides that set of principles. It includes all the other basic skills, and ought to be the basis of the curriculum. Problem solving involves five steps:

- identifying and diagnosing the problem;
- generating alternative solutions and strategies;
- developing a plan of action;
- implementing the plan of action; and
- keeping the planning process open to new data and ideas.

Inherent in these steps are the following skills: legal analysis and reasoning; legal research; factual investigation; communication; counseling; negotiation; litigation and alternate dispute resolution; organization and management of legal work; and recognition and resolution of ethical dilemmas.

The entire professional skills and professionalization curriculum should be built around students' learning to become increasingly adept at the five stages of problem solving to provide the base for future learning, and to help students retain what they learn.

The following is just one of an infinite possible number of first-year curriculum configurations. The same structure of integration of substantive law and policy with professional skills and professionalism issues in a transactional setting can be extended to the rest of the curriculum, too.

1. A contracts course focusing on transaction planning, document drafting, negotiation, and one or more ethical issues, such as taking a piece of a client's deal as part of the fee.
2. A torts course focusing on social policy as a generator of development of the law, law and economics, interviewing, drafting a settlement agreement and release, and one or more ethical issues.
3. A real property course focusing on legal history, drafting transaction documents, conducting a title search, and one or more ethical issues, such as confidentiality.

4. A criminal law course focusing on jurisprudence (exploring the nature of law, justice, and the like), counseling, persuasive writing (a motion to quash seizure of evidence), and one or more ethical issues, such as the limits on the duty of zealous representation.

5. A civil procedure course focusing on theories of dispute resolution (including ADR systems), drafting pleadings and motions, and one or more ethical issues, such as other aspects of limits on the duty of zealous representation.

Paul Ferber
Vermont Law School

#5: Student-Facilitated Seminars

Every year, I teach a seminar course on a topic in health care law. I have taught the following seminars: Death and Dying in America, Rationing in America, AIDS and the Law, and Genetics and the Law. Students are aware of the topic at the time of registration which helps assure "interested" students. The seminar size has ranged from as small as 12 to as large as 20. My role is to design the overall structure of the seminar. I select the materials to be used and outline the general pace. I evaluate student performance. However, after the first class, I do not conduct or facilitate the classroom discussion.

Facilitators

For each class, two or three students are assigned to facilitate the class meetings. Their role is to keep the class moving. If the group bogs down, it is the facilitators' role to help the group keep the discussion going by directing the class to questions, topics, or issues. Thus, they facilitate the group in deciding when a topic area has been explored enough. They help the group decide which topics to explore and in what order. They do not make presentations nor do they do a significant amount of the talking. In general, students are assigned to two or three classes to act as facilitator. The students select two topic areas they are interested in and, as much as possible, I try to assign the topics based on those choices. I also attempt to make sure that the same group of facilitators isn't always working with each other.

I am very clear about what is and is not expected of the facilitators: They are not responsible for the performance of the class; if their classmates are unprepared to fully participate, they are not to "act as teacher." I do not provide any other guidance to the facilitators on how to go about carrying out their role. Facilitators decide among themselves how they want to handle the responsibility. Some facilitators have met as a group and reorganized the questions. Some facilitators come to the class and "wing it." Some facilitators appoint a "head facilitator."

Student Questions

Students are required to turn in two questions on the readings the day before the class. The students are instructed to write questions which explore the underlying value implications of the reading; to write questions which explore the point at which a value important to them is violated; to write questions which challenge the desirable or undesirable consequences of a position taken in the reading; to write questions which make analogies to other things that they have learned; or to write questions which explore the priorities being set by some aspect of the reading.

I generally have to give some critique of the questions to help move students to jurisprudential inquiry type questions. After the first class, if only one or two students are having the problem, I talk to them outside of class about their questions, exploring with them how to generate more appropriate questions. If several individuals are having the problem, I ask for part of the class time at the end of a class to address the group as a whole. While I have helped students with their questions in every seminar, the problem is usually short lived. The overall quality of the questions is very high and students learn from reading other students' questions.

I organize the questions by topic and give them to the facilitators the morning of the class. No student names are connected with the questions.

Classroom Discussion

I always teach my seminars in two-hour blocks. (They are two-credit-hour courses.) I have found that 50 minutes usually cuts off discussion at a point where the students are just really beginning to get into it. At the first class, I usually start with an introduction to the class structure and my role. Students usually have a number of questions, such as "What if people don't come prepared?" or "What if they don't have anything to say?" I assure them everyone will come prepared and that everyone has something to say, even if they don't have something to say on every topic. I then give an introductory lecture to the course. I end the lecture with a statement that it is the last time that I will control class discussion.

The next couple of classes are usually painful for everyone. I come, take a seat, and wait. I sit off to the side. I found if I sit in front of the blackboard or what appears to be the head of the class it is harder to get students to take responsibility for the class. In fact, I try to arrive only a few seconds before the start of the class and I take whatever seat is available. The students come in and wait. After two or three minutes, one of the facilitators will read the first question at the top of the list and say, "Why don't we discuss?" There will be some discussion and then more waiting. It is important during that class that I say little if anything. To the extent that I participate, students become hopeful that I will save them. However, because I am very reserved in my class participation, students begin to get the picture that I really don't plan to conduct, lead, or facilitate the class.

By the third class, students begin to freely take responsibility for the classroom discussion. They will reorganize the questions or pose general broad questions. I begin, at that point, to model the kind of participatory behavior that I expect of them. That is, I begin to challenge things that I hear in class that I disagree with. However, this has to be done cautiously, especially in the first few classes. Too forceful or too frequent a challenge will lead students back to their hierarchical behavior of turning to the teacher for the answer. However, I have found by the last half of the semester I am able to fully participate as a member of the class without the danger of students reverting back to hierarchical behavior. The change occurs when they begin to challenge my input and find that I accept the challenge and respond to it. At that point, I can begin to model an additional skill, how to respond to a challenge.

Student Grades

Students are graded in a fairly traditional way: student papers (60%), student presentations (10%), and class participation (30%). Class participation includes turning in the questions, facilitating the group, and actively participating in the discussion. Students are advised that mere attendance is not enough.

Evaluation of the Method

My colleagues who have observed the seminar commented: Professor Randall's role [in the Health Care Law Seminar] was one of equal participant in the process.... [T]he seminar session [included] widespread and significant contributions by virtually all of the students in the course. This level and breadth of participating is commendable, and it reflects...leadership...and ability to engage the students in the process of learning."

But more importantly, all the students in the course have given high marks (3.6/4.0). They have commented: "Interaction between the students was great. This classroom situation was very conducive to learning and sharing." "This class encouraged discussion and thought like no other law school class that I've been in." "[T]he class caused all the students to talk at length about legal issues... I've never been in a law school class that stimulated so much thought and discussion." "I cannot overstate how much I have enjoyed this course."

I am confident that this method helps students learn the law and improve analysis. It also helps students understand themselves by helping them clarify their values. Finally, it helps students to step out of the traditional hierarchical approach to education and take responsibility for their own growth and learning.

Vernellia Randall
University of Dayton School of Law

#6: Four-Mat Learning

It is perhaps easy for veteran teachers to view the new "batch" of students as generic components of the educational process. It might be assumed that students learn when (1) teachers "fax" or "specially deliver" information to students; (2) the student digests the information; and then (3) the student organizes, stores, and recalls the information for examination purposes.

This generic vision of students, however, has been disputed by learning theorists who posit that students have different learning styles. Those theorists suggest that teachers who are able to identify the various learning styles or patterns of students will be better able to connect with and teach the individuals in the class. The key to this observation is making distinctions about the way students learn.

For example, it has been suggested that students have at least four dominant learning styles. These styles are characterized by the type of questions students tend to first ask about information presented to them. There are those people who first tend to ask the question "Why?", those who tend to ask "What?", those who tend to ask "How can that be applied?", and those who tend to ask "What if?" See B. McCarthy, FOUR-MAT LEARNING, and Professor Grayford Gray of the University of Tennessee Law School, who regularly focuses on these questions in teaching his classes. While one person may ask all four questions, this theory is premised on the belief that a person is inclined to emphasize one of the questions over the others, depending on the context. Thus, to truly maximize the communication of information and the learning process, an instructor should consciously try to utilize all four questions in teaching a class. Only then will the teacher have maximized the potential for learning. Similarly, the examination process should include all four types of questions to enhance the accuracy of the evaluation.

Steven Friedland
Nova Southeastern University Shepard Broad Law Center

#7: **Solomon and Civil Procedure**

My overall goals as a law teacher include instilling an ability to think critically about legal materials and teaching some of the substantive law necessary as a foundation for critical thinking. My perception of most first-year students is that they are ready to learn "the law," but overestimate the certainty of the law and underestimate the importance of learning critical thinking.

I have experimented with counteracting the students' initial emphasis on learning legal jargon by beginning the course with non-legal materials that encourage critical thinking. Because these materials do not involve legal language, they counter the students' rush to embrace the use of technical legal terms as a substitute for thinking. Moreover, non-legal materials provide a bridge from everyday experience to the study of law. That connection to pre-existing knowledge can make their learning of skills more effective.

I do this in a variety of ways in different courses, and an example may clarify my approach.

I begin Civil Procedure with Solomon's Judgment and the problem of cake division. (The assignment appears below.) You are probably familiar with one or both of these; certainly most of my students are. In Solomon's Judgment, Solomon is asked to decide which of two women is the real mother of the baby. In the cake division problem, two parents have to decide how to divide up a cake between two children.

I start by presenting Solomon as a conventional case by getting the students to go through the statements of both parties. I then ask them to decide the case on the basis of the information they think they have. The usual approach is to give the baby to the woman who has it. That leads to a discussion of the burden of proof, which I follow up by asking what advice they would give, were that the rule to be anticipated, to the woman who claims her child is kidnapped. In that case, I suggest that they advise the woman who *doesn't* have the baby. Eventually we work around to the idea of counter-kidnapping. Others suggest joint custody, but when we start to talk about how the two mothers will deal with one another, no one thinks that is likely to work.

Then we address Solomon's stated reason for decision and ask them to describe Solomon's reasoning. Eventually, we develop the idea that his major premise about reality is that the real mother wouldn't let her child be cut in two. At this point, the students are generally satisfied.

Then I ask them if they could present the case for the second woman better if they were her attorney. This took some work this last year, but when we staged a re-enactment, the students realized that the first woman's testimony implied that she saw the second woman's baby die, and that this is almost certainly false: if they were in different rooms, she would not have seen it, and even if the two women were in the same room, she would not have let the other woman crush her own baby.

At this point I say, "So it looks like Solomon awarded the baby to a perjurer. How many think he was right?" The split is usually close, with many now wondering if guilt, rather than love for the baby, influenced the woman to be willing to give her up. This brings out the importance of procedural rights; even with a judge as wise as Solomon, cross-examination could alter the result.

Then we talk about Solomon's result: even if you think he awarded the baby to someone who wasn't the true mother, is there anything to be said for the result? Many say that Solomon was right to give the baby to someone who wasn't the true mother, because she was the best mother. At this point, I ask them if that was what Solomon said he was doing. They realize that it wasn't, and then I ask them why he might have followed a rule different from the one he said he was following. The students quickly realize that a rule awarding custody on the basis of being the "best" parents would unsettle society by opening up litigation for any case in which someone wanted a child and claimed to be the better parent. I then follow up by asking them how they feel about Solomon's following a "rule" different from the one that he said he was following. This provides a reference point for legal fictions and judicial insincerity later in the course.

Finally, we discuss how lawyers should deal with women seeking legal advice in a similar case after Solomon's first decision. This brings up the ethics of witness coaching. I ask whether they would tell their client what to say when she gets in front of Solomon, and what they would say if their client asked them whether they are willing to tell everything they know about what will happen in front of Solomon. Once we get past that, we have to ask what Solomon will do when the two women before him each say, "Let her have the baby!" The difficulty of using Solomon's approach twice suggests that Solomon was more concerned than our system is with justice in the individual case and less concerned with general rules and procedures.

Then we get to the cake-splitting problem. Invariably the class suggests a rule whereby one child cuts and the other chooses. This seems so simple that it takes a bit of work to get to the underpinnings of that rule: reliance on the child's ability to protect herself, so we might not allow this between a three-year-old and a fifteen-year-old; reliance on the child's judgment, so that we might not allow a child to consume so much cake that she got sick; and reliance on a background allocation of entitlements or expectations so that we know the children will not fight to the death over the cake. We then discuss how procedural justice, particularly in the form of settlement, fits within the American judicial system.

We then look at other possible rules: having the parents award portions according to the arguments advanced, which leads nicely to a Lon-Fullerlike discussion of adjudication in terms of the presentation of reasoned proofs and arguments. Or, simply having the parents decide, to avoid the burden of their having to listen to arguments.

This will usually take two or three fifty-minute class sessions. The students are amazed at how much they got out of a brief problem, and that encourages them to read carefully in the future. In addition, deciding or nearly deciding that Solomon was wrong or not completely straightforward makes them much more willing to challenge the reasoning of the Supreme Court and other judges. I hope also that they have learned something about lawyering skills: scrutinizing facts critically and thinking about how to ask questions and present arguments.

At this point, we are ready to go on to the rest of the course. Because I use the Marcus, Redish & Sherman casebook, the Solomon and cake discussions set up the first standard case, in which an activist judge investigating municipal corruption in New Jersey is reversed for becoming too closely involved in the proceedings. The question I leave them with before getting to the New Jersey case is, "Would the New Jersey court of appeals reverse Solomon? If so, who is right?" I also ask them to compare the judge to the parent of the three-year-old: why can't the municipality protect itself?

When we get to discussing the case, we talk about the importance of legal rules in producing settled results, and the difference between Solomon's society and New Jersey society in their view of the judge and of the need for predictable rules. Excerpts from Max Weber on the various types of legal decision-making place this in context. The whole exercise allows them to see procedural rules as answering the procedural needs of the society in which they are used. They also see how our system has different characteristics in different places, so that juries function much like Solomon, rendering decisions without concern for precedent, while judges must provide reasons consistent with precedent, and statutes provide rules without including reasons. The discussion of judges and juries prepares them for the Seventh Amendment later in the course.

Professor Sergienko
Civil Procedure § 1B
First Assignment

Read the Judgment of Solomon and the Cake-Division Problem (both below) and Band's Refuse v. Fair Lawn, 1-18, and Kothe v. Smith, 18–25. Analyze the Judgment of Solomon as a case and prepare a solution to the Cake-Division Problem.

The Judgment of Solomon
1 Kings 3:16–26 (NIV).

[16]Now two prostitutes came to the king and stood before him. [17]One of them said, "My lord, this woman and I live in the same house. I had a baby while she was there with me. [18]The third day after my child was born, this woman also had a baby. We were alone; there was no one in the house but the two of us.

[19] "During the night this woman's son died because she lay on him. [20]So she got up in the middle of the night and took my son from my side while I your servant was asleep. She put him by her breast and put her dead son by my breast. [21]The next morning, I got up to nurse my son—and he was dead! But when I looked at him closely in the morning light, I saw that it wasn't the son I had borne."

[22]The other woman said, "No! The living one is my son; the dead one is yours."

But the first one insisted, "No! The dead one is yours, the living one is mine." And so they argued before the king.

[23]The king said, "This one says, 'My son is alive and your son is dead,' while that one says, 'No! Your son is dead and mine is alive.'"

[24]Then the king said, "Bring me a sword." So they brought a sword for the king. [25]He then gave an order: "Cut the living child in two and give half to one and half to the other."

[26]The woman whose son was alive was filled with compassion for her son and said to the king, "Please my lord, give her the living baby! Don't kill him!"

But the other said, "Neither I nor you shall have him. Cut him in two!"

[27]Then the king gave his ruling: "Give the living baby to the first woman. Do not kill him; she is his mother."

[28]When all Israel heard the verdict the king had given, they held the king in awe, because they saw that he had wisdom from God to administer justice.

Cake-Division Problem

Mom and Dad have brought home two pastries. One they propose to share themselves, and the other they want to divide between their two children. The children, ten and twelve, are reasonably well behaved, but perfectly capable of arguing at hideous length over the division of the pastry. How should Mom and Dad handle the problem?

Greg Sergienko
Southern Illinois University School of Law

#8: Methods Should Coordinate Form and Function

Much has been said lately of the "new" ways to teach. "Collaborative learning," "experiential learning," and "peer review" quickly have become familiar phrases in law teachers' vocabulary.

We have begun to understand that different people learn differently, and some of us have begun to teach differently. Especially in teaching writing, there are many opportunities to experiment with different types of teaching methods. However, before embarking on this experimental journey, we should think about the purpose of the teaching method.

Coordinate Form and Function

A teacher should spend time thinking not only about *what* she will teach but also about *how* she will teach it. The teaching method must serve a purpose. One should not do something "creative" in the classroom just for creativity's sake.

Sometimes, traditional lecture is the best way to teach something. For example, I teach a legal drafting course. In trying to teach students how to draft a will, I have to give an overview of estate law, just to provide the context students need to complete an assignment. Lecturing is the most appropriate method to teach this material.

Form should follow function. Lecture might be the appropriate method if you are trying to provide a context or background, or to make sure everyone understands basic concepts.

Balance the Methods

No one method is perfect or suitable for everyone. I balance the teaching methods I use by keeping a record of what I did in the previous class and what I plan to do in the following class. I like to follow lecture classes with either group or individual exercises. For instance, if I lectured in the last class on the principles of organizing a document, in the next class I have students review a sample document and evaluate it in terms of these principles. Sometimes, I team students up into small groups and have them review the document as a team. At the end of the class, all the teams present their opinions to the class as a whole. Other times, students review the document individually and complete a "critique" sheet that they turn in to me. I consciously vary the group and individual activities so that all students, whether they prefer to work with a group or by themselves, have a chance to maximize their learning.

Especially after a lecture class, I like to give quizzes to test students' understanding of the material. Sometimes I grade the quizzes or ask the students to exchange papers and grade someone else's work; sometimes we use the quizzes solely for discussion purposes. This variety keeps students on their toes and lets me track how well the class understood me.

Seek Student Comments

Although semester-end evaluations are helpful in assessing the course as a whole, they are not retroactive. I prefer to know whether my teaching methodology is working while the class is in session. I periodically ask students to write down what they have learned in the course so far and how they learned it. I then ask a student to share a "tip" with the class—the one thing that has helped her most so far. Mid-semester, I ask students to fill in an evaluation sheet for the course, in case I need to make any adjustments.

Most importantly, I try to really listen to what students are saying. I do not want to get so caught up in trying out a new teaching method in each class that I forget about the big picture—maximizing student learning.

Ruta Stropus
DePaul University College of Law

#9: Student Case Presentations

Beginning with the second class of first-year property, I assign cases to particular students in advance. In the next class students with assigned cases must stand in front of the class and present their case. They must then answer questions from their classmates and from me. The preparation is outstanding, though often overdone. The fear of speaking before a group of new people is overcome by the time spent in preparation. When the student finishes I give my analysis of the case. The students love it and soon try to "out-do" each other with charts, pictures, drawings, etc.

Twice during the semester I call on a student who was *not* assigned the case. If that student is not well prepared I immediately replace him with the person who was given the assignment.

I have been teaching for twenty-five years and this method has never failed to produce outstanding results.

D. Michael Featherstone
The University of Mississippi Law Center

#10: Coping Strategies for Research Seminars

I encounter three persistent problems in my research seminar, but I've developed some effective strategies for coping with them.

My seminar format is fairly standard: Twelve students complete research papers. For the first six weeks, I supply the reading. A two-week break from class meetings follows for completion of first drafts due in the eighth week. Two students present their papers in each of the final six weeks. A week before each class, students receive copies of the papers to be presented the next week; these papers are the reading assignment for the class.

The Problems

• *Procrastination.* Law school seminar students react quite predictably to the gauntlet of competing incentives they run. They resort to academic triage. The conventional strategy is to tread water in a seminar while devoting limited time and energy to more immediate pressures—job interviews, moot court and journal deadlines, daily classes. The semester ends with a research and writing binge fueled by caffeine and the adrenaline rush of a deadline and impending exams. My students' written work suggested procrastination was epidemic. First drafts reflected hours rather than weeks of work.

• *Inadequate thesis development.* My seminar students exhibited a near-primal attraction to the research memo as their model for legal writing. Page after word-processed page summarized and described cases, rules, statutes, articles, and opinions. Analysis and evaluation of these materials, much less advancing and supporting positions, seemed taboo.

In one-on-one sessions to review drafts, I cajoled and demanded. The students nodded and smiled. But their final papers provided little if any analysis or thesis development. Some would take positions, but simply tack them on as the last pages of their final papers, rather than supporting them throughout.

• *Lack of student engagement.* The third problem I encountered was the students' reluctance to invest time, energy, and interest in each others' work. Rigor mortis set in during student presentations. Class participation was weak. Responses to papers were superficial. In short, the student presentations often simply failed to spark the sort of exchange that marks a good class.

Procrastination and lack of thesis development were partly to blame for this lack of engagement. But it was an incentive problem, too. With no test on the material, there was no grade reward for investing in each others' work. And since the students often worked on unrelated topics, time and energy put into others' work may have seemed unlikely to bring tangible benefits for their own papers.

The Antidotes

These problems stemmed in part from my failure to communicate clearly enough to my students what I expected from them. In addition, I was working against an incentive structure that discouraged students from producing what I wanted. My strategies address both of these issues.

• *Thesis statement.* A good start in getting across the notions of analysis and thesis development is simply to emphasize and illustrate them. In the first class, I tell the students what I expect in their papers and that I will monitor their progress throughout the semester. A written statement of the seminar's requirements expands on these points. Reading assignments provide material for reinforcing analysis and thesis throughout the first six classes. These meetings focus on students articulating and evaluating each article's thesis and its support. Students also report briefly each week on the status of their papers with particular attention to thesis.

Blank stares at times leave me wondering if the message is getting through. Rather than waiting for first drafts to find out, I monitor their work on a thesis after the first four weeks. This allows time to remedy any misunderstandings prior to the first draft.

My monitoring device is one page from each student, due at the end of the fourth week, stating the student's thesis and how it will be supported. To illustrate what I am looking for, I suggest that students look at the precis used to introduce an article in many law reviews. The thesis statement allows me quickly to identify students who haven't gotten the message. I can easily require one or more rewrites of this statement in the weeks before the first draft until I am sure the student has the idea. To further emphasize the thesis point, a first draft that contains only a descriptive section with no thesis articulated or developed will not count as a first draft. In other words, no thesis, no credit on the first draft. And the first draft comprises 25% of the final grade. To ease the panic caused by the early deadline for the thesis statement, I emphasize that students are free to modify or jettison a thesis as their research and thinking progress.

• *Student editors.* My primary strategy for improving engagement in other students' work is to use students as editors for one another. This idea has two facets.

First, students are paired in editing teams, with the same two students working with one another throughout the semester. The students usually pick their own editing partners, and I do not monitor their work. I suspect the amount of work varies from team to team. From student reports, I know it is quite substantial for some.

The second aspect of the student editor idea requires each student in the class to edit *every other student's paper* once during the semester. This is accomplished as follows.

As I mentioned earlier, the last six class meetings are devoted to students presenting drafts of their papers. A week before each of these classes, I distribute copies of the drafts to be presented. Rather than simply requiring students to read these drafts, I require the students to *edit* them as well. Each student must turn in at the end of class a copy of the draft fully marked and edited for issues of both form and substance. Each student must also turn in a one-page sheet of written comments on the draft. I collect these at the end of each presentation.

Immediately after class, I quickly review the edited drafts and comment sheets. This review helps establish the 25% grading component for class participation. I then pass the marked drafts and comment sheets on to the student authors.

This editing requirement has greatly improved student presentation classes. They tend to run themselves, and I usually have to cut off discussion rather than try to resuscitate it. The editing requirement forces students to prepare for class and encourages active engagement with the topic. Reviewing their editorial work after class gives me a simple way to monitor and enforce class preparation.

This editing work also may pay dividends outside the classroom. My hope is that the students' editing improves their writing by enabling and encouraging them to bring editorial eyes to their own work. Also, each student author has the benefit of twelve edits—eleven from students and one from me—in preparing their final papers.

• *Grading.* Seminar grading that relies exclusively on the final paper severely tempts students to procrastinate. To encourage work early in the semester, I determine seminar grades by the following formula: (1) 25 % on the first draft; (2) 25% on performance in class; and (3) 50% on the final draft. The grading components based on the first draft and class performance provide obvious incentives for investing in the seminar earlier in the semester.

This approach also helps alleviate the problem of lack of engagement in the work of other students. The 25% component for class participation directly rewards their efforts in class. The 25% first draft component also improves class sessions. Because the drafts reflect more work and thought, they tend to be more engaging. Also, if students are more invested during the semester in their own seminar papers, they tend to be more involved in the seminar generally and in the work of fellow students.

Kevin C. McMunigal
Case Western Reserve University Law School

#11: Paying Respect to Law School's First Year

Given the importance we attach to the first year of law school, it is unfortunate we do not accord more dignity to its end. I remember being gravely disappointed on the last day of my first year. I had just completed the most arduous nine months of my life. My law professors had put me through hell. I worked my tail off for them. I suffered humiliation and terror at their hands. I endured! Now they wanted to end this grand and noble rite of legal passage with no more fanfare than a "Good luck on the exam." I felt cheated. I needed *closure*!

One constant in my approach to teaching is to avoid doing the things that irritated me most when I was a law student. To that end, I complete every first-year Torts course with a farewell address of sorts. Students appreciate this effort. Indeed, the feedback I have received suggests that these closing comments are the most important ten minutes of the first year for some students.

My farewell address covers a lot of ground, but has a definite "Follow your dreams" theme to it. I will describe the highlights below, but it is important to emphasize that closing comments need not be lengthy, dramatic, or adhere to any particular theme to be effective. Students are thankful for any effort to attach an ending to what will always be one of the most memorable chapters of their lives. My own teaching personality lends itself to a fairly theatrical approach with which many professors would be uncomfortable. Obviously, you need to be true to your nature.

However, you should not be unduly reticent about being a bit creative. Trying new ideas can be intimidating because of the risk of failure. For teachers it is even worse because when we fail there are many eyewitnesses. However, my experience has been that students recognize and appreciate any attempt to make their education more interesting and/or meaningful, even if it bombs. Remember: your students are *hungry* for a memorable closing experience. So go for it! The rewards can be great.

I set up my comments for the last day at the beginning of the year. I walk into the classroom on the first day, draw a large outline of a brain on the board, and ask: "Mr. Smith, what's a tort?" Assuming Mr. Smith gives me a satisfactory answer, I fill in a tiny corner of the large brain with: "*Knows What A Tort Is.*" Then I explain:

> This is Mr. Smith's brain. He knows what a tort is. That's good. But you can see that the rest of his brain is a dark void, a wasteland of unused mental space. The same is true for all of you. You know nothing about the law. Stop and appreciate that right now. Think how much you know about Tort law, about law school, about these people in here, about everything you're about to embark upon. I mean it. Lean back, relax, and think about it. Take in these strange surroundings. Look at that clock. Check out this blackboard. Look at all these strangers around you. Who are they? Why are they here? [Long pause.] Remember this moment. We'll repeat it on the last day.

Because these are the very first seconds of law school, students recall this incident vividly. I resurrect it for use in my closing comments, which may be compartmentalized as follows:

1. *Thanks for the memories.* We ask a lot from first-year law students and most of them deliver. I thank my students for their hard work and perseverance. I tell them how much I appreciated their thorough preparation, which made my job easier and more fun. I offer special thanks to those who participated in class discussion, saying they helped enrich the course for everyone. To give my students a sense of identity, I tell them every first-year class is different and memorable in its own way, and explain how their class fits within this principle.

2. *Congratulations!* Completing the first year of law school is a significant accomplishment. I congratulate my students on this major achievement.

> [Unless it's been a particularly wretched first-year class, students deserve at least this much. You could stop here and feel good about giving your students some meaningful closure.]

3. *"I'll be there for you."* Baptism under the fire of law school's rigors bonds people together. Making lifelong friends is perhaps the prime benefit of the first year. To allow students a moment to celebrate this important gift I reincarnate the opening-day scene discussed above. I remind them of the exercise and say it is finally time to repeat it:

> Stretch back. Look around. A lot has stayed the same. The old clock's still ticking away up there on the wall. God knows how many precious minutes of learning were wasted watching it. The blackboard's still here. Solid. Reliable. These things will never change. They'll be here for years after you're gone. But a lot *has* changed. Last August this room was filled with the faces of complete strangers. But who do you see now? *Friends*. That alone makes law school a worthwhile experience. A true friend is a rare and valuable thing indeed.

The room is now filled with beaming faces, some with tears staining their cheeks.

4. *Whaddaya know.* Another notable aspect of law school's first year is the tremendous amount of knowledge students acquire. Again resurrecting that first day, I ask my students to reflect on this fact:

> Remember Mr. Smith on that first day? He knew what a tort was, but that was about it. The rest of his brain was a vast empty chamber. But now it's standing-room only for concepts like *res ipsa loquitur* and *risk-utility balancing*. Think how much you've learned! You've acquired more knowledge in this first year of law school than you will in any other year of your life. More importantly, you've learned to use knowledge in a new way. You've learned to "think like lawyers," meaning you've learned to *reason well*, something most people never accomplish.

5. *Let's get personal.* The talk turns personal as I try to impart one of my most basic beliefs about life: that people should follow their hearts in making career choices. I tell my students how I arrived at law school as an idealistic young man intent on becoming a great civil rights lawyer but left as a brainwashed casualty of a flawed system that places the greatest value on those who are able to land high-paying jobs with prestigious law firms. I talk about money and how it can be a trap, how it can lock people into ever-spiraling obligations until there is no way out.

I then tell them a story about a pro bono case I handled as a young man and how it was the most rewarding experience I had practicing law. I conclude: "Life, as you'll find out soon enough, is short. It will race by leaving you wondering where it went. Don't find yourself regretting that you didn't make the most of it. When it comes time to choose your path, follow your heart, where it leads you."

Sappy? The sappiest. But it works. Many students make it a point to thank me for the comments. At a recent graduation ceremony, the student bar president devoted his comments to my "Farewell to Torts" speech, delivered two years earlier, explaining that it made a lasting impression on him. (Needless to say, I was surprised and deeply touched.) Most important to me, my *follow your dreams* advice has influenced several students in their career choices.

A recent graduate left Little Rock for Portland, Oregon. He had never been there and didn't have a job, but his heart told him that is where he wanted to be. His classmates scoffed. "You don't know anyone in Portland. You'll never make it." The student recently sent me a fax. He was excited about his new job with a firm representing indigent criminal defendants and loved Portland. The fax closed: "Keep telling your students to follow their dreams. I could not be happier. P.S. The beer here is excellent!!"

Andrew J. McClurg
University of Arkansas at Little Rock School of Law

Chapter 3

Questioning and Discussion Techniques

[T]he best wisdom cannot be communicated, [but] must be acquired by every soul for itself. — Emerson

For an observer, staying out of a discussion is almost as difficult as sitting through a lecture. — Eble

Discussion and questioning are teaching techniques aimed at eliciting student participation. The techniques feature two-way spoken communication between students and teacher and direct interaction among the students themselves. When using these techniques, teacher and students consider a topic, problem, or issue and exchange information, experiences, ideas, opinions, reactions, or conclusions.

A. Why Have Discussion and Questioning in Class?

Good discussions can be of great value to the learning process. Discussion helps students to retain information at the end of the course, to develop problem-solving and thinking skills, to change attitudes, and to motivate additional learning about a subject. In addition, discussion gives teachers feedback and ideas from their students.

Discussion allows students to "discover" ideas and knowledge which lead to deeper learning. Higher education research indicates that material learned through active discussion is better retained than material learned through lecture.

Discussion engages students in active learning. During discussion, students practice thinking through problems, formulating arguments, and dealing with counter-arguments. Good discussions result in students using higher-level thinking skills: applying information in new contexts, analyzing issues, synthesizing doctrines, and evaluating ideas.

Discussion not only helps students develop cognitive abilities, it has benefits in the affective domain as well. Through effective discussions, stu-

55

dents are exposed to diverse viewpoints, which helps students develop values and change attitudes. In addition, for many students, discussion makes learning more interesting and increases their motivation to work harder to learn more.

Finally, discussions provide teachers with valuable insights. Through student questions and comments, teachers get feedback about student learning, which effective teachers use to adjust their instruction. Further, given time to reflect and a safe environment in which to share ideas, students will express thoughtful views and creative approaches to problems which may not have occurred to the teacher.

B. Impediments to Effective Discussion

Although the benefits of effective discussions are significant, research shows that discussion makes up only a small portion of class time in college classrooms. In a study of 40 undergraduate teachers, the mean amount of class time spent on questioning and discussion was 4%. This finding was consistent from large to small institutions, from introductory to advanced classes, and from subject to subject.

What might explain the reluctance of teachers to allocate a larger amount of class time to discussion? There are several impediments to effective discussion. Discussion can get sidetracked or bogged down in irrelevant matters, leaving students bored and frustrated. Discussion can be dominated by a few students or simply fall flat, provoking little interest among students.

Student attitudes can be a significant obstacle to effective discussion. Some students believe that discussion is wasted time; they believe that they are not paying tuition to hear what other students think, but what the teacher thinks. These students fail to pay attention to what other students say. They take notes only on what the teacher says. Other students are leery of discussions because active participation entails the risk of being "wrong" in public or because they fear that their ideas will not be valued or taken seriously.

Discussions present risks for teachers as well. Questions the teacher intends to spark discussion can be met with silence from students. Further, discussion involves the loss of some of the teacher's control over the issues and ideas presented in the classroom. Students can take the discussion to places the teacher did not anticipate. Students can ask questions that the teacher can not answer. Moreover, discussions are time consuming and not well suited to extensive coverage of content.

C. A Guide to Effective Discussion and Questioning Techniques

There is a wealth of information about effective discussion and questioning techniques. Those techniques can be organized into four steps: (1) create a classroom environment conducive to discussion, (2) plan questions and discussion, (3) ask questions to initiate discussion, and (4) handle student responses and questions.

Step 1: Create a Classroom Environment Conducive to Discussion.

Because participation in a class discussion entails risks for students, the teacher must create an environment that encourages student participation.

a. Physical Environment

The physical environment matters. Thus, try to arrange seating during the discussion so that the students can see one another. Remove the teacher from the front of the room to encourage students to speak to one another and not only to the teacher.

b. Social Environment

Teachers need to establish a social environment conducive to discussion and rapport with their students to facilitate student participation. Teacher behavior that promotes rapport with students includes demonstrating an interest in each student and each student's learning, encouraging students to share their thoughts about class assignments or policy, and encouraging students to ask questions and to express personal views. Perhaps the single most important step that a teacher can take to improve the classroom environment is to learn the students' names.

Creating the social environment can be a cooperative venture between the teacher and students. Early in a course, teachers should have a conversation with the students about discussion as a learning method. Teachers should articulate the purposes and benefits of discussion. Likewise, teachers should explain why they expect students to prepare for and participate in discussions. Students take cues from the teacher, so the teacher should show enthusiasm for the discussion. The first few classes set a tone for the course, so the teacher should arrange for each student to speak early in the course.

c.   Teaching Students Effective Discussion Techniques

The teacher can teach the students how to participate in an effective discussion. The teacher can show a videotape of a good discussion — one in which a variety of viewpoints are expressed by a number of participants who are listening to what one another are saying. The teacher can explain to the class some principles of effective discussion:

> Focus on ideas rather than people,
> Practice listening — restate in your mind the point made by the previous speaker,
> Listen to others' ideas, even when you do not agree,
> Stick to the subject,
> Speak briefly,
> Seek out differences of opinion because they enhance discussion,
> Be open to changing your mind, and
> Respect other participants in the discussion.

Step 2: Plan Questions and Discussion.

Planning a discussion involves the same process as planning most other types of teaching and learning activities. The teacher needs to identify goals, materials, techniques, and appropriate questions.

a.   Identify Goals

When designing an entire course or a specific class, teachers should identify their goals. Discussion is appropriate to help the students achieve some, but not all, goals. For example, if the main purpose of the lesson is to convey information, lecture or demonstration may be more effective than discussion. On the other hand, discussion is particularly useful if the goals include problem solving and critical thinking. Likewise, discussion can provide the vehicle for the exploration of values and attitudes.

b.   Choose Materials

After identifying goals and deciding to use discussion, teachers must choose material that will form the basis for the discussion. Ideally, that material would be of interest to the students, be self-contained, and be complex enough to engender different points of view. Many types of material can fit the bill: a case, a legislative proposal, an essay, an article, or a videotape.

c. Choose Techniques

Teachers should consider the possible techniques or formats for discussion. Will the students discuss the material among the entire class, in small groups, or in pairs? Should the teacher assign roles to the students or ask the students to address issues from a certain perspective?

d. Prepare Questions

Teachers should identify in advance the critical questions they will use to start and guide the discussion.

(1) Question Types

Studies indicate that some forms of questions increase the number of student responses, the number of different students who respond, and the length of the responses. Those question forms include:

- Questions directed at a specific aspect of the material ("From reading Justice Smith's dissent, what do you think she believes are the purposes of peremptory challenges of prospective jurors?");

- Brainstorming questions that ask students to generate many ideas on a topic ("What factors should an attorney consider when deciding between state and federal court as the forum for a lawsuit?");

- A focal question in which students are asked to choose among a limited number of viewpoints and to support their views during the discussion ("Which of the three philosophies of law we covered in this unit most consistently explains the Supreme Court's opinions in search and seizure cases in the last five years?").

(2) Levels of Thinking

Teachers' choice of question type will depend on their goals for the discussion. For example, questions can be categorized by type of thinking skills: (1) cognitive memory questions ("What argument did the plaintiff make to the trial court? What are the factors the court applied when it reviewed the award of punitive damages?"), (2) convergent thinking questions ("How would the result of the case have been different if the court had accepted plaintiff's argument? What real-world effect would the punitive damages award have on the defendant?"), (3) divergent thinking questions ("What options could the parties have pursued in attempting to reach a settlement in this case? What other factors could the court have used to assess the punitive damages award?"), (4) evaluative questions ("Is the court's analysis in this case more or less persuasive than the court's analysis in the previous case? How could the legislature most effectively address this problem?").

Another categorization scheme for questions is Bloom's classic taxonomy of levels of thinking.

1. Knowledge—remembering previously learned material ("What are the elements of a civil claim for battery?").
2. Comprehension—understanding the meaning of previously learned material ("Explain what the Court means by the term 'sufficient minimum contacts'.").
3. Application—using information in a new context to solve a problem ("How could the National Environmental Policy Act apply to the proposal by the United States Forest Service reported in this morning's newspaper?").
4. Analysis—breaking a concept into its parts and explaining their interrelationships; distinguishing relevant from irrelevant material ("What are the major differences between negotiation and mediation as forms of dispute resolution?").
5. Synthesis—putting together the parts to form a new whole; solving a problem requiring creativity ("What changes would you suggest to make the discovery process less susceptible to abuse?").
6. Evaluation—using a set of criteria to come to a reasoned judgment ("What effects would the legalization of drugs have on the judicial, penal, and public health systems?").

Step 3: Ask Effective Questions to Initiate Discussion.

The ability to ask effective questions is one of the most basic and important skills for any teacher. Effective questioning has several components.

a. Questioning Components

The way the teacher poses the question ought to facilitate, rather than discourage, student response. For example:

(1) Questions should be clear. One way to improve the clarity of questions is for the teacher to write them out in advance. To increase student understanding of the question, prepare a visual aid by putting the question on the board, an overhead, or a handout.

(2) Questions should be open-ended. Questions that prompt "yes" or "no" answers stifle discussion.

(3) Ask one question at a time. Posing several questions tends to confuse, not clarify; they discourage, rather than encourage, participation.

(4) Pose a variety of types of questions to involve and interest all students, who have varying abilities and different levels of understanding of the material.

b. Planning

Teachers can improve the quality, quantity, and variety of student responses and student questions with planning. Teachers can give students the questions in advance and ask students to prepare to discuss them in an upcoming class. Likewise, teachers can ask each student to come to class with a relevant question to share with the other students.

c. Ask and Wait

Perhaps the most important attribute of an effective questioner is patience. After asking the question, the teacher needs to be silent and wait for students to process the question and formulate responses. Research reveals that most teachers wait less than one second after asking the question before answering it themselves, rephrasing the question, or calling on a student. However, research shows that if the teacher waits three to five seconds after the question is posed, more students will respond, the complexity of the responses will increase, and more students will ask questions. One way teachers can increase the "wait time" and make the silence less uncomfortable is to tell students to jot down notes of their responses and questions before taking oral responses.

Step 4: Guiding Discussion — Student Comments and Questions.

After the teacher poses a question and gives sufficient "wait time," the students usually respond with comments and questions. The ways in which the teacher responds to student comments and questions will shape the discussion and establish the learning environment.

a. Teachers' Nonverbal Behavior

Teachers' nonverbal behavior has significant effects on the discussion and learning environment. When a student responds, the teacher's eye contact with that student signals the rest of the class that they should listen to the student. At the same time, the teacher can move away from the respondent to draw the rest of the class into the conversation. Teachers must listen carefully to what students say, not only for the points teachers think are important but for new perspectives and ideas from students as well. Teachers can memorialize student contributions on the board, overhead projector, or computer. This visual tool validates and clarifies the comments, provides a summary of the discussion, and can illustrate the interrelationships among the ideas generated. Finally, by observing the nonverbal behavior of the rest of the class, teachers can decide when to expand, shift, or end the discussion.

b. Teachers' Verbal Behavior

The teachers' verbal responses to student comments guide the discussion and significantly affect student interest and participation. Teachers' responses to student comments should vary. These responses may invite elaboration, restate, emphasize, ask for clarification, expand on the response, praise the response, or use the student response to make a transition to another issue. Saying nothing while nodding and looking interested is another appropriate response. When the teacher is ready to close the discussion, announce that it is about to end so that students can make final comments. Then, the teacher can provide closure to the discussion by summarizing key points, comparing student ideas to the ones the teacher prepared before class, referring students to material that is on point for the key ideas discussed, and giving students a bit of time to add to their notes.

c. Increasing Student Participation

Teachers can use techniques to increase the number of students who make comments during the discussion.

(1) Employ the principles discussed above on creating an environment conducive to discussion and asking questions effectively.

(2) Give positive reinforcement for appropriate responses. If at all possible, find some positive aspect of the student's comment. Memorialize the contribution. Refer to the comment by the student's name ("Mary's idea" or "John's theory"). Acknowledge new ideas ("Gee. I never thought of that before. I appreciate the new way of looking at this problem.").

(3) Handle "wrong" answers tactfully. Focus on the answer not the student. See if the mistake is common to other students. Demonstrate that it is acceptable to make mistakes in the classroom because mistakes can lead to learning. Admit your own mistakes.

(4) Limit your own comments. Teachers need not respond to every student contribution. Otherwise the focus of the discussion rests on the teacher.

(5) Ask questions that encourage student-to-student interaction by asking students to respond or react to other students' comments or questions.

(6) Find opportunities for quiet students to contribute, such as prompting the student to repeat a comment the student made outside of class or using small-group discussion in which all students must participate.

(7) Discourage students who monopolize discussions. Assign that student a role. Don't make eye contact with that student but do so with others. Allow all students to jot down ideas before asking for volunteers. Wait till several hands are up before calling on a student.

d. Responding to Student Questions

Teachers guide a discussion not only by handling student responses but by dealing with student questions as well. Teachers should encourage students to ask thoughtful questions. Teachers can facilitate student questions by expressly asking for questions, by giving students sufficient time to formulate thoughtful questions, and by giving positive reinforcement to students who ask good questions.

When answering student questions, teachers can shape the discussion and create an environment that encourages student participation. Make sure the entire class can hear the question. If necessary, have the student, rather than the teacher, repeat the question so that students learn to listen to one another, not only to the teacher. Either the teacher or another student should answer the student's question directly—when students do not get direct answers, they quit asking questions. When the teacher is responding, talk to the entire class so that all students feel part of the conversation. Finally, check back with the student to see whether the question was addressed adequately.

e. Problem Spots

The higher education literature contains advice for teachers when handling troublesome questions. Some suggestions from the literature are:

1. Tangential questions—rephrase the question to be more on point or respond to the question outside of class;
2. "Stupid" questions—research shows that the other students generally empathize with the questioner, so be kind;
3. Overly complex questions—respond to the most important manageable part of the question or respond to the question outside of class;
4. Questions to which you do not know the answer—admit that you don't know the answer and offer to find the answer or explain why the question need not be answered in this class;

5. Repetitive questions—be patient because questions and answers make sense at different times for different students, depending on their changing understanding of the material.

References

CHARLES C. BONWELL & JAMES A. EISON, ACTIVE LEARNING: CREATING EXCITEMENT IN THE CLASSROOM 21–31 (1991).
BARBARA GROSS DAVIS, TOOLS FOR TEACHING 63–95 (1993).
PETER FREDERICK, CLASSROOM COMMUNICATION (Rose Ann Neff & Maryellen Weimer eds., 1989).
MARYELLEN WEIMER, IMPROVING YOUR CLASSROOM TEACHING 48–61 (1993).

Specific Discussion Techniques

#1: Using Video to Learn Students' Names

Several years ago while teaching a summer school tax class with 90 students, I realized that the session went by so quickly I didn't have time to learn many students' names. So I had the AV department come in and make a video seating chart of the students. I asked each student to say his/her name, undergraduate school, and major, so the picture wouldn't whizz by so quickly and also to learn a little about each student. I took the video home and with the use of the pause and reverse buttons, I learned the names of most of the students by the next class. It's more enjoyable to teach to 90 students with names than to 90 nameless faces, and the students appreciate being called on by name. I usually tape the students during the second class. It takes 10 to 15 minutes for a 90-person class, but I think the time is well spent.

Howard S. Chapman
Illinois Institute of Technology Chicago-Kent College of Law

#2: Lying Icebreaker

This is a very simple technique suggested to me by a colleague that has worked for me in a negotiations class with 24 students to break the ice at the beginning of the course. At the very beginning of the very first class, after the basic preliminaries, each student is told to stand up and introduce themselves by giving their name, what year they are in, and three things about themselves that others in the class don't know about them. However, one of the three things must be a lie. And the other students are to guess which is the lie and why they think so: the behavior of the student giving the information, the implausibility, etc.

It is a wonderful ice-breaker, but also leads into some fruitful discussion about the use of lying in negotiations.

Theresa J. Player
University of San Diego School of Law

#3: Thoughts on Questioning Students

By this time Gertrude Stein was in a sad state of indecision and worry. I sat next to her and she said to me early in the afternoon, What is the answer? I was silent. In that case, she said, what is the question?
— Alice B. Toklas, *What Is Remembered* (1963)

Questioning students, and addressing their questions, is a feature of the Socratic method of teaching law. It is a two-way process.

We Question Them

We often question students to get an immediate confirmation that they have received the information we think we have transmitted to them. All we are asking is the message be retransmitted. In this case, the student's mind may be no more than a reflector.

Other times, we question students to demonstrate the inductive or deductive propositions that flow from the material we have "taught." Or we may use the questioning to orchestrate conflicting interpretations of the material, to break the monotony of straight lecturing, or to maintain interest in the class or topic.

We should avoid using questions to punish or discipline students. If discipline is required, be direct in addressing the disruption rather than use the student's lack of knowledge as a weapon. Students always should have an "out." If they can "pass," or admit that they don't know, you still can call upon them at the next class so that they are not let off the hook.

We assume, in questioning students, that we should receive an immediate answer. Sometimes it is better to be prepared to allow them time to think about the answer. Students often give uncritical answers to questions posed by the lecturer, because they are not given enough time to produce a better one. Reflection time is valuable for understanding. Some strategies for giving students time to think about the ramifications of the problems posed are:

- Utilize "think-pair-share." Pair students or small groups of students with a view to requiring them to discuss the problem and opening up class discussion at the next session.
- Use follow-up questions. ("Why?" "Do you agree?" "Can you elaborate?" "Tell me more." "Can you give me an example?")
- Withhold your personal judgment. Invite other students to respond to the answer given by a student. Suggest they interrogate the respondent.
- Ask for a summary from another student. ("Could you please summarize John's point?") This promotes active listening.
- Survey the class. ("How many people agree with the author's/presenter's point of view?")
- Divide the class into plaintiff vs. defendant, prosecution vs. defense, etc., and set them against each other. Appoint a jury/judge to resolve the conflict of ideas.
- Allow the answering student to nominate the next student to respond. ("Will you please call on someone else to respond?")
- Require students to defend their reasoning against different points of view. Either play devil's advocate yourself, or ask the class to consider the question from the position of someone holding a particular point of view. ("What would the right-to-life people say about this?")
- Ask students to "unpack" their thinking. ("Describe how you arrived at your answer." "Think aloud.") Ask those who are making comments to their neighbors to share them with the class. Even half a thought will do for starters.
- Call on students randomly, not just those with raised hands.
- Let the students develop their own questions and answer them. If there is a flood of questioning, let the flood flow; tolerate what appears to be chaos. Let everyone have a go. Listen and summarize.
- Cue student responses. ("In answering this, I want you to think about (a), (b), (c)....")

They Question Us

Student questions to the teacher serve many different purposes. They come with different levels of confidence in their legitimacy. Questions serve the students' needs; they may serve or inhibit our objectives. They often need to be orchestrated in some fashion.

We should remember that students' questions are a window into the great unknown. Be alert to fundamental misconceptions that may underlie a question; those misconceptions may be more widely shared than you think.

A fool can ask a question which the wisest person cannot answer. We often have to answer questions by not answering them. Recognize that some "questions" never require an answer, but are rather in the form of a statement that invites a response. When a questioning student seeks a response, why do you have to be the one to give it? Ask another student to do so.

Be alert to the shy, diffident, and tentative questioner. Such a student may begin a question with "This will sound silly but...", or may question his or her neighbor rather than ask you directly. Reinforce these questioners by responding to them.

Then there are the confident, highly visible (front-row center), sometimes clever questioners (or show-offs). They seduce your attention. If allowed to dominate, they will provoke reactive non-cooperation from other members of the class. Take an active role in trying to prevent this. Invite questions from those who have *not* put up their hands.

Be aware that some questions may be deliberately diversionary, particularly if students know you are easily led off the topic.

While we ought to welcome questions, their timing and relevance often will not be appropriate to the topic under discussion, or will interfere with coverage of the material within the time allowed. Consider these strategies:

- Accept the question, but reassign it to a more relevant slot. ("That's a good question, but wouldn't it be better if we look at it when we get to the next issue?")
- Reinterpret a question. ("What I think you are asking is....")
- Ask stooge and phantom questions. Ask a student to ask a question in class (often because the student asked a pertinent question after class, but you would like the discussion shared with everyone else). Sometimes no one asked a question, but you can pretend someone did.
- When too many questions threaten continuity and timing of material, be up front: "I won't take any more questions for the moment. I need the last 15 minutes to complete the material I wanted to cover in this class. I will take questions after class."
- What if you don't understand a question? Consider: (1) asking the student to restate the question; (2) asking another student or students to explain what the question is; (3) reinterpreting the question so as to answer a question that you do understand which appears to be on the topic.
- What if you don't know the answer to a question? Consider: (1) saying you don't know; (2) discussing with the class the principles or policies that may provide an answer; (3) indicating you will look it up by the next class; (4) asking the class to look it up by the next class, and compare results; (5) indi-

cating what you think the answer might be, but qualify it by identifying what additional case law or legislative material would have to be checked in order to confirm your tentative conclusion.

- What if a question is explicitly or implicitly racist, sexist, or provocative (sometimes deliberately so)? Invite members of the class to make explicit the values or attitudes implicit in the question, rather than doing so yourself. Reverse roles ("How would you react if you were in this situation?") or appoint the questioner legal representative of a disparaged group and invite him or her to present the case for his or her clients; change or widen the context in which the attitude is being expressed in order to drive home its implications.

Richard G. Fox
Monash University Faculty of Law, Australia

#4: Leading Questions

The main purpose of law teaching, as I see it, is to get students actively involved in the learning process. One method that has worked in my classes is what I call the leading-questions discussion period.

It works like this:

One or two weeks before the discussion of a particular topic (arbitration as an ADR method, for example) I distribute the assignment sheet for the topic, containing the readings and a list of leading questions.

The questions serve as guidelines to the main themes in the readings, so that a student preparing for class can pre-test his or her knowledge. Examples are: What are the advantages of arbitration over litigation? Over other ADR methods? What are its disadvantages in contrast to mediation?

When the topic comes up for discussion in class, I distribute the questions among teams of students (three or four students to each team). Since no one knows beforehand which sub-topic his team will be handling, each team is given 10 to 15 minutes to share their thoughts on the particular questions assigned to them.

After this discussion period, a reporter from each team delivers and explains the answer agreed upon by its members. Time is also allowed for clarifying and for dissenting opinions.

I often add some prodding questions to each team's presentation and, after all the answers are in, I will interrelate the diverse answers and expand, as necessary.

The result: lots of lively group discussions among the students and real interest and involvement in the learning process. I also believe students come better prepared for class.

Eulalio Torres
Inter-American University of Puerto Rico School of Law

#5: Student Names and Backgrounds

I always teach the Clinical Law class. Our class-size is limited to 16, so it is important to learn everyone's name as quickly as possible. We also ask each student to fill out a student information sheet which includes questions about their undergraduate degrees, languages spoken, previous employment, and areas of interest in the law. This helps the seminar discussion in several ways. I often use students as experts during class discussions (i.e., a student with a degree in linguistics is able to provide extra information when I lecture on theories of communication or a student who has worked in the insurance industry can provide special insights), I can structure hypotheticals to appeal to their special interests and it helps me to know them more quickly. Students seem to be pleasantly surprised when I ask them to contribute based on their pre-law school experiences and try to respond in a more thoughtful way. It also demonstrates to students that almost every experience they have had will assist them in becoming an accomplished legal practitioner.

I think that it is easier to teach students when I know where they have been and am aware of their professional goals.

Mitzi M. Naucler
Willamette University College of Law

Know your audience. Especially in smaller section classes. Know student names, what students look like, and relevant biographical information. I ask students to provide me with information regarding their education, work, and life experience. I also attach student photos (provided by our registrar's office for this purpose) to my seating chart.

Asking a student a question in that student's area of expertise or addressing a student by name, without looking at your seating chart, usually brings a smile. I have found that smiling students are usually more receptive to learning.

Mark Broida
California Western School of Law

#6: Practicing Observation

Harry Lorayne, an author and authority on memory, suggests that people who claim that they forget things (such as others' names) often never really learned them in the first place. To learn, according to Lorayne, a person must not simply *see* things but *observe* them with a "clear mental picture." Once observed, the thing can then be remembered. Lorayne says observation can be accomplished by asking questions about the thing to be remembered, essentially cultivating curiosity. This approach can be practiced through specific methods, depending on the context. Certain methods are available to police investigation, for example, and other methods to individuals attempting to remember the names of people at a party.

Transposing Lorayne's approach to law teaching yields some interesting observations. In the "Socratic method," a teacher poses numerous questions to the students. Such questioning can be characterized as a very directed curiosity about the subject matter. In effect, the teacher is practicing his or her observation about the topic and mirroring Lorayne's suggestions regarding observation.

Under Lorayne's thesis, however, a Socratic format does not directly forward the students' own observation skills, but rather those of the instructor. To promote student observation, students can be asked to create their own questions about a subject or problem to generate their own curiosity about a subject. Students can create an examination question (usually multiple-choice) about a particular topic. These questions can be collected, typed, and then distributed for additional practice. (The students also can be informed that one of their problems will be placed on the final examination.) A less time-consuming alternative to this in-class exercise is for the students to write down five questions they have about a case, point, rule, argument, etc. The students can discuss their questions in small groups before or during class and come up with their three most difficult questions. In this way, the students learn to model methods by which they can practice their observation skills.

Steven Friedland
Nova Southeastern University Shepard Broad Law Center

#7: Talking in Circles

Each student participates actively in every discussion in my seminars. This is not accomplished by bribery, threats, or magic, but by our "talking circle" discussion format.

The format is simple:

- The professor articulates a question for discussion.
- Discussion proceeds around the room, with one person speaking at a time (the professor included) until each has had a turn.
- All participants listen respectfully.

While it is not essential, some semblance of a circular seating arrangement helps.

There are some additional implicit rules, which can be stated if the need arises. Law students (uncomfortable with the process) frequently ask for more "rules" in the first session. I usually suggest we try it first and clarify if we need to. We seldom need to, and the "rules" evolve out of the group's behavior rather than my having to lay them down. If I'm particularly interested in teaching about process, I may try to restate the unspoken rules which have evolved, but usually I do not. Typically, these "rules" include:

- If participants are sufficiently moved to break the circle by interrupting other speakers (either to ask clarifying questions or to interject comments), they may do so, and it is particularly worth listening to them because of the intensity of their need; when they are done, discussion reverts to the original speaker and thence to the next around the circle in order.
- If you don't have anything additional to say, you can affirm an earlier idea or "pass."
- It is not particularly helpful to repeat what somebody else has already said, except to note agreement or disagreement.
- It is frequently pertinent to have a second round, or even third round, of comments, and participants can begin or request them as they are moved. Part of my job as the teacher is to decide when further discussion is useful and when to ask a new question.

I begin each session with a quick round of short responses to a simple "grounding" question: "What has you most pressured right now?", "Where did you find parking today?", or "What would you be doing if you skipped class today?" I start promptly, and these take the place of the usual pre-class chit-chat while waiting for one more person. This gets strange looks in the first class session, but people catch on and it starts to feel less like group therapy.

This grounding is important. Each time, the circle and the notion of listening respectfully to each other are reintroduced experientially. Once listening is established in the room, it remains. Using the circle allows each person's voice to occupy the room, establishing a kind of territory. Participants find it easier to speak when others listen respectfully. The lack of immediate challenge (otherwise so prevalent in our lawyerly lives) helps to allay the fears of the apprehensive.

I do vary the format, sometimes giving a mini-lecture when there is a problem with material or a particularly complex setting. I sometimes jump to the board to record in tangible form a particularly productive or interesting line of discussion as it goes around.

There are several direct effects. Everybody talks. Participants pay attention. Thoughts are carefully marshaled. Contributions are concise, to the point, and mostly nonrepetitive. Ideas evolve and develop as the discussion moves around the room. Discussion tends to focus on understanding differences, stating alternatives, and constructing solutions, rather than attacking positions.

This approach appeals to me because it sets me in a particular role. I have knowledge and experience; I do not have "the answers." I am responsible for structuring a productive learning experience, for directing the discussion, and for seeing that some central questions are considered. Class is not a game; it is people working together to understand complex problems.

The format also conveys some important messages to students. They have knowledge and experience that they can apply to the problem at hand. What they say is intrinsically worthwhile. What their colleagues say is worth listening to. If they are not prepared and thoughtful, they will feel absurd. They can contemporaneously be learners and doers. Their analyses and insights are not the only possible ones. They can synthesize their ideas with other people's ideas and learn and grow in the process.

Students like it. While they are initially uncomfortable, they quickly adapt and have requested a return to the format when I depart from it. The biggest hurdle in getting used to the format is not running off at the mouth, but rather freezing up when others actually listen. The careful attention speakers get, and the respect and trust it implies, usually gives nervous speakers the strength to continue; and subsequent speakers somehow know when it is helpful to appreciate another's insight.

I like it, too. It renews my faith in human nature and the potential of lawyers. I get to teach by doing: articulating an analytical approach by modeling it (and frequently watching it evolve); teaching collaborative problem solving by creating a situation where it happens. The way I behave as teacher is consistent with behavior I want in my students' repertoire. I learn things. More often than not, I leave class drained, but excited.

Running a class this way feels no more forced than my seminars used to be, when I tried to run the discussion, muzzle the talkers, encourage the wall-flowers, and make sure the right things were said (by me if no one else). My job is to ask the right questions. This means that I can't get away with an outline of topics I want to cover. I have to actually anticipate how the discussion itself will run, and articulate questions that lead in the directions I want. If I misjudge, I have to be able to redirect discussion with well-placed questions or restatements. I need to know what the "take-home" points are, and to be prepared to reinforce them or make them in my turn, as part of the evolving discussion.

The format does not work as well for me on days when I'm a know-it-all and jump in to give "right" answers. Fortunately, the process itself works well enough that I feel silly, and students treat my intrusion as they would anyone else's. I also suspect that there is a limit on how big a class you can use it in without everybody getting bored. I have both participated in and facilitated use of the technique in dispute resolution with groups of up to 35; it can get tiresome at that scale. It works splendidly with 15 students in a seminar.

Trying this kind of process required me to give up certain assumptions about my role as teacher — particularly that I not only knew more, but knew better. It required trust in the capabilities of my students and intellectual honesty of a fundamental sort. Students have consistently and powerfully responded to that trust.

I have learned that, when people try to listen with respect, they can put their own assumptions on hold. They tend to hear, and understand, what is being said. When they understand, they tend to develop trust in the capabilities and insights of others. When they trust, they are open to learning themselves. As they learn, they reorganize information, grow, and change.

Maybe it *is* magic.

Paul Wilson
Northwestern School of Law of Lewis and Clark College

#8: Structured Debate

To spark discussion about the function of law in society, several St. Mary's University School of Law teachers distributed two hypotheses to first-year students midway through their second semester:

- Law is morally and politically neutral, and it provides an impartial method and forum for resolving disputes within our society.

- Law in our society is designed to preserve and protect the position and influence of those in power.

The project was part of a cooperative effort among four first-year professors (Amy Kastely, David Dittfurth, Doug Haddock, and Jeff Pokorak). Three of the four professors gave up one hour of class time for the project (the fourth agreed to serve as moderator).

The students were asked to divide themselves into groups of five or six, seeking to affiliate with like-minded colleagues. The formation of groups took place outside of class time. A few days after the groups were formed, one of the participating professors gave the student groups her scheduled class time to discuss the hypotheses. Each group chose one or two spokespersons.

About a week later, two of the other participating professors canceled their classes so that a two-hour discussion session could be scheduled. The spokesperson(s) for each student group were given the floor for five to eight minutes (time limits were strictly adhered to) to present the views of the respective groups. This consumed about two-thirds of the available time, and the remaining time was devoted to open discussion.

I was not directly involved in this project, but I had the pleasure of sitting in on the discussion. I have never been more impressed with the intelligence and thoughtfulness of a group of law students. I saw a side of the students I had never seen before. They showed remarkable levels of passion for their positions and sophistication about law and its function. Their use of specific examples from their substantive courses demonstrated far more appreciation for subtlety and meaning than I am accustomed to seeing. The students showed respect for each other and tolerance for each other's ideas.

Mark Cochran
St. Mary's University School of Law

#9: Interesting Questions to Start Discussion

I use two techniques for getting students interested in assigned reading. First, I begin a class or a case with a question designed to elicit from students an aspect of the reading that they find interesting—and particularly to circumvent the tendency of students to begin by reciting the facts. Examples:

- What makes this case interesting?
- What makes this case close?
- What makes this case worth studying?
- What makes this case wrong?
- What is the weakest aspect of the opinion(s) in this case?

Second, I assign students the role of counsel for one party to a case and ask them to discuss the case (or issue) on their clients' behalf. In the process, I pit student against student more often, intervening less often.

Michael Kelly
University of San Diego School of Law

#10: Classroom Configuration — The Circle

All too often, the classroom shape, size, and overall aesthetic are taken as given and ignored as superfluous to the learning process in law school. Yet, the location, size, shape, and nature of a classroom can make a considerable difference in the quality of the learning process.

The classroom's physical environment does more than act as a backdrop, but actually conditions both teacher and students. Much like Pavlov's famous experiments, teachers are trained to work from a podium at the front and center of the classroom. The podium contains the teacher's notes and appears to provide the security, elevation, and seriousness demanded of a law school professor. The position of the professor in the front and center indicates the relative importance of the teacher to the others in the classroom. It is the teacher's words that are the most important — all of the students are facing in a way that they can see and hear the teacher, not necessarily each other. The teacher has complete responsibility and control.

Students also are trained by the shape, size, and nature of the classroom. A student may often select the same seat in a classroom over and over again. It offers comfort and familiarity, as well as a particular perspective of the classroom. Where a student sits may indicate how willing the student is to engage and participate in the class. Sitting in the front row, for example, may indicate a certain comfort level with the material and/or the teacher or a desire to participate.

If, in a relatively smaller class (i.e., less than 25 students), the students and the teacher sat in a circle, this may radically change the class dynamic. In this configuration, all of the students and the teacher are on an even playing field. With everyone making eye contact, it is more difficult and less likely that a student can retreat and withdraw from the class. Interaction and participation are facilitated by the seating arrangement where the teacher can readily elicit comments around the circle or by making eye contact and drawing students out.

Of course, the teacher loses the security of distance and elevation, and even the comfort of the podium. Yet, students seem to enjoy being closer to "the action," once they get used to it, and the quality and quantity of participation seem to rise. In all, it is an easy way to promote active student learning.

Steven Friedland
Nova Southeastern University Shepard Broad Law Center

#11: Role-play to Discuss Controversial Topics

One technique I use occasionally to ensure participation in controversial or highly emotional subject matter areas is role-playing. For a period of time, our school, Windsor Law School in Windsor, Ontario, Canada, was embroiled in a chilly climate debate and many subject matter areas were "hot"—one area being the legal treatment of pornography. As a result some students refused to speak on the issue and others drowned out debate with the ferocity of their views. I assigned roles to the students before class. In class, they were to address the subject matter of the debate as the character they represented. The trick is to assign roles counter to the view that the student actually holds. For example, I give male students female roles: they are Gloria Steinem, Catherine MacKinnon, etc. Feminist women become the editor of *Playboy*, the Archbishop of Canterbury, etc. Quiet students become flamboyant local lawyers. Sometimes this works wonderfully; occasionally it flops! It depends on the good will of the class.

Leigh West
University of Windsor Faculty of Law, Canada

#12: Teaching Tips for Quiet Classrooms

Sometimes students are reluctant to speak in class. They may not volunteer comments. They may sit silently when a teacher asks a question. They may save their own questions about the assignments until after class, when they can ask privately. Some students may not ask questions because they feel isolated and unwelcome in the classroom for any number of reasons, including race, gender, sexual orientation, or their national origin. This essay deals not with factors that might affect individual students, but factors affecting the entire class.

Although all classes are quiet from time to time, some classes can develop a "Code of Silence" that continues for several sessions or even several weeks. This essay shares advice from colleagues who have found useful ways to stimulate discussion in classes. The ideas presented here are by no means comprehensive. They may, however, offer useful suggestions to those who find themselves standing in front of a quiet classroom.

Minimize Fear. Students undoubtedly have a great deal of anxiety in all of their law classes. Some students are afraid to ask "stupid questions" and to risk appearing foolish in front of classmates. They will not ask teachers to explain words they do not understand; they will not ask follow-up questions when they do not understand an answer to another student's question. I find that students will ask more questions when I treat each question with respect, just as I treat each student with respect. Sometimes I will rephrase the question before answering it, such as by saying, "if I understand what is behind your question, what you really want to know is...." I find that this approach is often appropriate for smaller classes. One colleague strongly disagrees with this approach, however. He would not rephrase the question but would instead keep asking the student to rephrase the question until the student "got it right." By forcing the student to rephrase the question, he hopes to help the student to develop skills that will be useful before judges and in other high-pressure situations.

Do Something Positive. A teacher can create a positive learning environment by saying something positive after a student asks a question. Professor Jan Levine suggests that the responses can range from a nod and a smile to saying "Yes, that's a great question!"

Minimize Competition. Some students will ask questions only after class because they are competitive. They do not want their fellow students to enjoy the benefits of the teacher's answers. I thwart this behavior in two ways. First, if I answer a question after class I will write down that question and repeat it at the start of the next class meeting. I might introduce the question by saying "someone asked me an interesting question yesterday..." or "you might be wondering whether...." By asking the question openly, no student obtains an advantage over others. Second, if a particularly competitive student will ask questions only after class, I will tell that student to ask the question at the start of the next class. By doing this once or twice, the particularly competitive student will learn to ask questions that will benefit the entire class. A particularly good question will often stimulate questions from other students (as will praise from the teacher for a particularly good question).

Maximize Opportunity. I begin each class with the words: "Are there any questions before we continue?" If students have questions from the previous lesson, the start of class is often the best time to answer them. If there are no questions, we continue with the assignment for that day. By inviting questions at the start of each class, students learn that they will always have an opportunity to ask what is on their mind. A regular time for asking questions may also minimize the "teacher's pet" syndrome, where one or two particular students ask so many questions that they may build resentment in other students. When there is a "teacher's pet," other students may refuse to ask questions lest they be similarly branded by their peers.

Refresh Memories. Professor Michael Closen suggested that the beginning of class also include a brief review of important points raised during the previous class. He found that this review helped to refresh memories and stimulate questions about the material from the previous class.

Try a Cliffhanger. Taking a cue from soap operas, Professor Susan Marie Connor suggested asking students a question at the end of class for students to consider and discuss at the start of the next class. She leaves her students in suspense: "What should the plaintiff's attorney do to save his client?" By informing students ahead of time that they must discuss a particular question, my colleague finds few problems with quiet classrooms.

Maximize the Environment. Sometimes students will fall into a midsemester lull. This may be attributable to the stress that many students experience under the unrelenting pressure of law school studies. In classrooms where I can move the tables, I sometimes find that merely rearranging the furniture will dramatically increase participation. Rather than have desks facing the blackboard, for example, we might push tables into the center of the room to form a giant conference table. Sometimes I can frame a research problem as if it were being discussed in a law firm partnership meeting. At other times, having one student start and then moving around the circle for additional comments will at least get every student talking. Rearranging the furniture improved class discussions for the remainder of the semester—even when we returned to the original placement of furniture in the room. In rooms where I cannot move the furniture, I may ask students to change their seats and to sit near someone that they do not know so well. This usually has the same ultimate effect as rearranging the furniture. The important factor is to change something in the atmosphere of the classroom. When a change is made it should signal to the students that silence is unacceptable and that you are imposing the change to increase the students' participation.

Try To Be Quiet. Professor Jan Levine notes that the hardest period for a teacher is the time between asking a question and getting the answer from a member of the class. It may feel like forever, he reminds us, but it seems far longer for the teacher than it does for the students. Professor Levine notes that often the silence may happen because the students are thinking (while the professor already knows the answers to most of the questions). Professor Levine also says that if we show students that we really want them to answer, and will wait for them, then they will speak. He believes that this tactic is most effective early in the semester, but it can work anytime. Professor Levine says that we can even tell our students that we will wait for as long as we have to, but they are the ones who must break the silence.

Rephrase the Question. Professor Elise Hiller of the Lawyering Faculty at Albany Law School reminds us that occasionally we at the front of the class need to rethink the questions we are asking. If our question is too open-ended or too vague, our students will have a difficult time answering us. She reminds us that often a single question, aptly phrased, may open a floodgate of discussion. Such discussions usually brand the classroom as one where open dialogue can occur.

Conclusion: Ask Others for Help. Because teaching styles and environments vary, the suggestions made here may not work for all teachers in all circumstances. Other teachers will have additional suggestions, although they may not share their suggestions unless specifically asked to do so. Any teacher who feels that a class is too quiet should ask colleagues for additional suggestions to improve student participation. Although you may get responses such as "who cares" from some colleagues, not to ask for help would make the teacher's silence an unlikely cure for the silence of the students.

Mark E. Wojcik
The John Marshall Law School

Chapter 4

Visual Tools

The inventor or introducer of the blackboard deserves to be ranked among the best contributors to learning and science, if not among the best benefactors of mankind. — Bumstead

A. What Are Visual Tools?

Visual tools are devices that allow teachers to engage students through their sense of sight. Visual tools include handouts, chalkboards, flipcharts, overhead transparencies, slides, videos, and computers. (Computers, the most modern visual tools, are the subject of Chapter 7.)

Visual tools can be divided into two categories according to their primary uses. The first category — handouts, chalkboards, flipcharts, overhead transparencies, and slides — is most useful for presenting graphics. Graphics are visual presentations that use a structure other than the sentence or paragraph to illustrate or analyze a concept or theory. Graphics include pictures, cartoons, diagrams, graphs, and charts. The second category, film and videos, allows students to experience a portrayal of real-life events or to view performances of themselves or others.

B. Why Use Visual Tools?

Research on cognitive learning theory suggests that people learn in different ways. Some learn best auditorally (listening and speaking), some experientially (simulations and field work), and some visually (graphics and videos). For many students, visual representations of concepts are more memorable than the spoken word.

Humans learn concepts best if they are connected in meaningful ways rather than isolated. The human memory is able to recall a small number of unconnected and unimportant items for a short time. However, we have a large capacity to learn concepts that are organized and connected. Organized cognitive structures are called schemata. For example, many legal educators have schemata for briefing a case or analyzing a statute; we understand the principles of statutory construction and the relationships between those principles.

Visual tools can help students create schemata. Graphics help students create cognitive structures by connecting and organizing concepts. For example, a flow chart of personal jurisdiction can depict the elements of analysis and the relationship between those elements. When students retrieve a graphic in their minds, they retrieve not only the information in it but the connections and organization as well. Students can then use the information and organization to solve problems in new situations.

Although film and video are not as effective as graphics in helping students create schemata, and research shows that TV or film is no more effective than live lecture to deliver content, video and film are important teaching/learning tools. Videotape has a significant positive effect when used to give students feedback on their performance as they attempt to acquire or refine skills. TV programs or films can give students a common experience which serves as an excellent trigger for class discussion. Moreover, visual images of actual events, places, and people can have a powerful effect on students' attitudes and understanding.

Visual tools have several other valuable uses in the classroom. First, visuals focus students' attention. When a teacher puts a transparency on the overhead projector, shows a slide, or writes on the board during class, all of the students concentrate on the visual. Second, when students create or manipulate graphics, they are encouraged to rethink concepts, rather than merely reread or restate them. Third, students' memories and notes are more accurate when the material is presented visually in addition to orally. Finally, visual tools can help teachers maintain high student interest in the course. Research shows that students' motivation and learning are enhanced when they experience a variety of teaching/learning methods in the classroom.

C. Designing and Using Visual Tools

Visuals, like all other materials and methods, are tools teachers can use in the classroom to help students achieve educational goals. The goals of the class should drive the teacher's choice of what type of visuals to use. For example, if the teacher wants to communicate clearly the directions and grading criteria for an assignment, a handout is more effective than other visuals. Likewise, if the goal of a portion of a class is to have students discuss an issue, a short film or video clip is an excellent way to spark the discussion. If the objective is to record key points students generate during a discussion, a chalkboard, flipchart, or overhead transparency will all work well.

The design of graphics also depends on their purpose. For example, if the purpose of the graphic is to give instructions to students for an activity to take place during class, such as problem solving in small groups, a handout or transparency should contain a clear, comprehensive list of the directions. The graphics will help insure that the students accurately receive the instructions, will save time in giving instructions, and will allow the students to refer to the directions throughout the activity. On the other hand, outlines or charts during class lecture or discussion may contain only major categories permitting students to engage in the activity of filling in the details during class. This activity of completing concepts during class helps students organize and understand key principles.

Just as the choice and design of visual tools vary based on the class goals, the ways to use the visuals in class depend on the teachers' objectives. For example, teachers can keep students' attention focused on one point at a time by revealing visual material gradually. Hence, the teacher can write one point on the board at a time or can cover the rest of an overhead transparency with a sheet of paper to keep students focused on the point at hand. Alternatively, visuals can be shown all at once to convey the "big picture" and the connections between concepts.

If teachers decide to use electronic visual tools, such as videos, slides, and overhead transparencies, preparation in advance is critical. Electronic visual tools can backfire on teachers when they do not operate smoothly. Nothing takes the wind out of teachers' sails and diverts students' attention like a malfunctioning projector or VCR. To avoid frustration for the teacher and students, the teacher should cue up videos and test all electronic visual tools before class begins.

1. Handouts

Although handouts are quite mundane compared to videos or multimedia presentations, they are valuable and versatile visual tools. Handouts can include outlines, instructions for assignments, chronologies, cartoons, charts, graphs, and diagrams. They have some advantages over other types of visuals. First, they convey exactly the information the teacher prepares in advance and can go directly into the students' notes, unlike items on transparencies or the chalkboard that students must copy accurately to keep in their notes. Second, handouts save class time because students need not copy the information off of the board or ask questions to ensure that they correctly heard items presented orally. Third, handouts are permanent. After teachers give handouts to the students, teachers can use them throughout the course and students can use them to review.

2. Chalkboards

Boards, whether black, green or white, are a nearly universal feature of law school classrooms. Although boards have been around for centuries, they remain excellent teaching and learning tools when used effectively. Teachers can use the board to do any of the following:

- Provide a preview by listing the goals and topics for class that day;
- Handle administrative details such as the reading assignment for the next day or due dates;
- Organize the class by listing major points either at the beginning of class or as they are developed during class;
- Record student comments during discussion;
- Summarize key ideas generated during class discussion;
- Present diagrams, graphs, and time lines; and
- Show steps in the analysis of a problem.

Research shows that students will try to copy into their notes virtually everything the teacher writes on the board. Chaotic board work confuses students. Teachers can maximize the effectiveness of their board work in a number of ways:

- As part of preparing for class, plan what will go on the board;
- Erase completely anything that is on the board from previous classes;
- Be selective—write nothing unimportant on the board:
- Visually highlight important points with a star or underlining;
- If using a diagram or chart that will expand during the class, let students know so they can leave room in their notes;
- Give students time to copy what is on the board;
- Write legibly—don't worry if that means writing slowly because students need the time to record the information anyway; and
- As a courtesy to your colleagues, erase the board completely before the next class.

3. Overhead Transparencies

Overhead transparencies are the most common electronic visual tool because they are so versatile and easy to prepare and use. Teachers can prepare transparencies before class by photocopying material from a printed page or by printing material from a computer file directly on the transparency. In addition, teachers can write on blank transparencies during class.

Teachers can use overhead transparencies to accomplish any of the tasks described above for chalkboards. In fact, overhead transparencies have a number of advantages over chalkboards.

- The projected image is often clearer and easier to see than material written on the board.
- Transparencies can be reused, so teachers can build up a collection of overheads for future classes.
- Teachers can write on the transparency during class without turning away from the students.
- Pens used to write on transparencies are less messy than chalk.
- Some material, such as cartoons and diagrams, are easy to copy on to a transparency but would be very difficult to recreate on the board.
- Teachers can turn off the overhead during class to refocus students' attention elsewhere.

On the other hand, projectors have limitations. First, like any other type of electronic visual tool, they can malfunction during class. Second, most projectors are noisy. Third, teachers must stand next to the projector when using transparencies.

A few guidelines can help teachers use overhead transparencies effectively:

- Before class, test the projector to be sure it is working, to focus it, and to find the appropriate light level in the room so the students can see clearly the projected images.
- Limit the amount of material on a single transparency. As a general rule, restrict each transparency to one topic.
- Be sure the typeface is big enough so all students can easily read the projected text. Twenty-four point type is usually sufficient, but the best way to know for sure is to test it in the classroom in advance of class.
- Use colored ink for emphasis on prepared transparencies or colored pens during class. Be aware that some colors (blue, purple) are much more visible than others (yellow, orange). It is best to test colors before class.
- Pause briefly after putting the transparency on the overhead so the students can scan its contents before listening to what you have to say.

- Give students time to copy the material on the transparency. If the transparency contains lots of information or complex diagrams, give the students a handout rather than have them copy the transparency.
- Be aware that pointer movements are magnified by the projector. Move the pointer or pen smoothly and slowly. Rapid movements are startling and small shakes look like major quakes.
- Turn off the projector when not using a transparency because the light and sound are distracting.

4. Flipcharts

Flipcharts are large pads of paper that sit on a display stand. Teachers can use flipcharts for any of the purposes described above for chalkboards. Many of the guidelines for effective use of the board or transparencies apply to flipcharts as well. Because of their size limitations, flipcharts are not as useful for large-group presentations as boards or overhead transparencies. On the other hand, flipcharts can be very useful in other settings. For example, small groups can each use a flipchart to record the key points of their discussions and then can use the flipchart to assist their presentation to the large group. In addition, sheets of paper from flipcharts can be taped to the walls around the classroom so they remain visible throughout the class period. Moreover, in rooms without a board or overhead projector, flipcharts may be the only visual tools, other than handouts, available to the teacher.

5. Slides

Teachers can use slides to present information or photographs. Slides can add interest, detail, and variety to the classroom. Perhaps the most effective use of slides in legal education is to show photographs of places, things, and people. Photographs can provide students with examples of general concepts, representations of abstract principles, and a real-life context for legal theory.

Slides do have certain limitations as visual tools in the classroom. Although almost any printed material can be photographed and developed as slides, the process is more cumbersome than creating a handout or an overhead transparency. Further, many slide projectors are trickier to operate than an overhead projector. Finally, for students to see the slides well, the classroom must be darkened, which makes it easier for students to doze off and hinders note taking.

6. Videotapes

Videotapes are powerful visual tools in the classroom. Videos can bring life to the classroom by presenting historic footage or documentaries of real events. In addition, many commercial videos demonstrate lawyering skills such as client counseling, negotiation, oral argument, and examination of witnesses. Clips from movies or television programs are effective devices to illustrate concepts, present problems, and provide a vehicle to start discussion. Finally, videos of students' performances, such as conducting a mock deposition, are important tools in helping them to acquire and refine skills.

The following principles can help teachers maximize the benefits of videos in the classroom.

- View the video before showing it to your class. Decide what objectives all or part of the video can help achieve. Take notes on possible discussion questions to use with the video.
- Practice operating the equipment and cue up the video before class. Be sure all students will be able to see and hear clearly.
- Prepare students to see the video. Explain why you are showing it and what you expect students to get out of it. Tell students whether they should take notes during the video.
- Help students view the video thoughtfully and critically. Give students a handout with several discussion questions before showing the video.
- Interrupt the video if it helps enhance learning. Pause the video to highlight points or conduct brief discussions. Of course, too many interruptions can be distracting.
- Conduct an activity after the video to maximize its effectiveness. A whole-class discussion, small-group activity, or short writing exercise may be appropriate.
- Include content or concepts from the video on exams. Let students know that if the video is important enough to show in class, it is a potential source of test questions.

References

Charles C. Bonwell & James A. Eison, Active Learning: Creating Excitement in the Classroom 33–35 (1991).
Corinne Cooper, Getting Graphic 2: Visual Tools for Teaching and Learning Law™ (Institute for Law School Teaching, 1994).

BARBARA GROSS DAVIS, TOOLS FOR TEACHING 177–202, 315–333 (1993).
JOSEPH LOWMAN, MASTERING THE TECHNIQUES OF TEACHING 145–154
(1995).

Specific Visual Tools

#1: Algorithms

Law teachers who use white boards, overhead projectors, or other visual aids know the value of using diagrams and flow charts as powerful means of conveying relationships between ideas.

Visual aids help students to see the components of a rule and the situations it is intended to cover. One sophisticated visual aid is the algorithm—a flow chart containing more specific instructions for the application of the rule to fact situations. It serves as a checklist indicating what is required by the rule at each step and what follows if that element is, or is not, satisfied.

Over the years, I have encouraged my students, particularly first-years, to adopt this technique to help them understand new and complex legal rules. I have been willing to accept student research papers in this form where the task I have set for them is to prepare an algorithm analyzing majority and dissenting judgments in some new and important case and to defend their diagram by providing accompanying notes explaining and critically evaluating the major choice points represented in it. A helpful discussion of the use of algorithms in this manner can be found in Twining W. and Miers D., HOW TO DO THINGS WITH RULES, (3rd ed.) London, Weiderfeld and Nicolson, 1991, Appendix II, p. 431–437.

Some years ago, in order to illustrate the merits of algorithms, I started to sketch out the class survival skills required of first-year students and invited members of the class to assist in finishing it. The algorithm on the next page is the product of successive generations of student inventiveness and the application of computer-aided design skills in law schools in both Australia and the United States. It is now distributed routinely to my first-year students during discussion of study methods in law. It serves both as an ice-breaker in the first week of classes and as an illustration of the value of diagrams in note-taking and briefing.

Teachers as well as students recognize themselves in the illustration, but it contains a troubling message for the teachers. I have taken both it and my *Thoughts on Questioning Students* (see Idea #3 in Chapter 3; also found in THE LAW TEACHER, Fall 1995, at 6–7) to discussion groups on teaching methods for new and experienced teachers in order to invite them to consider why there is such an apparent gap between what we think we are doing in the classroom with our Socratic methods of teaching and how the students view the process as revealed in this algorithm.

Richard G. Fox,
Monash University Faculty of Law, Australia

A DAY IN THE LIFE OF A FIRST-YEAR LAW STUDENT

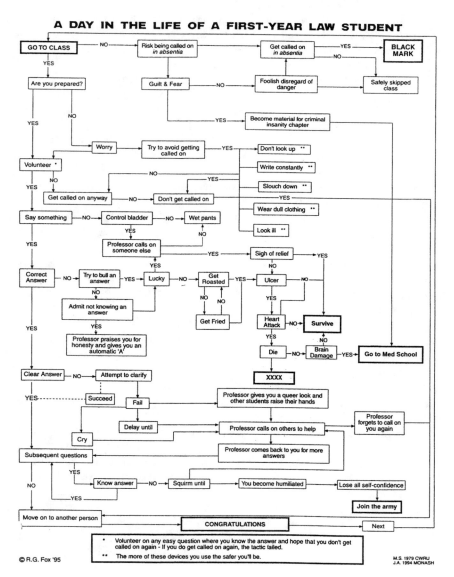

* Volunteer on any easy question where you know the answer and hope that you don't get called on again - If you do get called on again, the tactic failed.
** The more of these devices you use the safer you'll be.

© R.G. Fox '95

M.S. 1979 CWRU
J.A. 1994 MONASH

#2: Video Vignettes in Negotiations

I have had success in large-enrollment classes using short videotaped demonstrations showing aspects of a focused role-play that students have performed outside of class. These taped vignettes stimulate discussion on the points depicted, let students self-evaluate privately, and often generate questions and comments about identical or similar issues that arose in their role-play.

I use this approach in my civil procedure class where students do a focused discovery-negotiation simulation. This exercise lets students experience the adversarial tensions inherent in discovery and the close relationship between these processes and negotiation. [The course emphasizes roles procedure plays in negotiating settlement of civil disputes before trial with discovery supplying major bargaining chips.] The simulation is drawn from a clinic case I litigated involving a dog bite claim made against a company when one of its employees' dogs allegedly bit a bicyclist passing by on a public street.

All students get a summary of the pleadings and depositions in this case and then are paired with one representing the plaintiff and the other representing the defendant. Each side gets a seven-page set of confidential instructions which summarize case strategy, subtly hint what topics would be good ideas for further discovery, and provide negotiation authorizations. Each student must draft and respond to three requests for admission, and the negotiation authorizations are keyed to whether certain additional facts are discovered in this process. After the discovery segment, the students negotiate for no longer than an hour outside class and then submit a short written outcome summary if they settle or a much longer compliance with an order setting pre-trial if they do not.

The demonstration tape is used as part of the feedback process after the negotiation. [Data from the outcome summaries including highs, lows, and averages from both dollar amounts and an internal point structure which allows agenda expansion are also shared.] In addition to accomplishing the objectives listed in the first paragraph, this tape introduces topics that students can explore further in professional responsibility and skills courses. My tape runs about 12 minutes and shows clips demonstrating negotiation strategy-style differences, information bargaining [letting students see that negotiation and mediation are often important forums for informal discovery], and the ethical issues involving honesty in negotiation. A clip showing a defense lawyer lying about his negotiation authority and his knowledge of a prior incident where the dog bit a customer always sparks a lively debate about issues that arose in their role-play, and connects easily to issues of honesty in the discovery process which we have canvassed earlier.

Don Peters
University of Florida College of Law

#3: Fine Art Imagery

One of the challenges facing those teaching first-year students is how to help students learn to compare and contrast cases. The task involves multiple skills, including the ability to think critically about what one is reading. For many students, this is a very difficult task and takes considerable time (and many frustrating moments). In thinking about the difficulty of the task, it struck me that today's students are very visually oriented and fully capable of making comparisons of visual imagery. Indeed, visual comparisons are much easier for some students than word and concept comparisons. This led me to use fine art imagery in my first-year class.

I do this exercise about a month or so into the semester—long enough to have dealt with a small repertoire of cases and short enough to still be able to capture lost students. I show students two portraits, one by Picasso of Marie Therese (1937) and one by Dante Gabriel Rossetti called La Ghirlandata (1873). (Actually, any portraits by different painters would work assuming they had different styles and approaches.) I produce large color duplicates of each portrait. I put the portraits up side by side on large poster boards which I stand around the classroom. I put one set at the front of the room (where it is projected onto T.V. monitors that are permanently affixed in the classroom).

I begin by asking students what *similarities* there are between the portraits, and I put their findings up on the board. Students make the following kinds of observations: both portraits are of women; both are in color; both women are seated; both women are looking to the side; both women look distant and detached; both women have their arms near their faces. Then, I ask students to identify the *differences* between the portraits. They make the following kinds of observations: the styles are distinct—the Picasso is modern and cubist while Rossetti is more realistic and "old-fashioned;" the colors used by Picasso are primary and vibrant; Rossetti uses softer, natural color; Picasso's portrait seems harsh and hard; Rossetti's seems almost tender and appealing; Picasso uses straight lines and edges; Rossetti uses curves and shading; Picasso focusses on nails; Rossetti adds nature through flowers and birds.

I then talk to the students about what they have just done. (I deconstruct, in essence, the art comparisons.) At the simplistic level, they have found in art what I want them to find in cases. In comparing portraits, they have compared "cases" and have identified what in law we call "fact similarities and differences." I emphasize that cases, like paintings, tell a story, and each story is different. Reading cases, then, is searching for similarities and differences in a story—expressed in words, not paint.

I then move the analysis to another level. First, I talk about the artists. Both were painting women they knew; both had complex relationships with these women. Both had unusual lives (Picasso's life is known; Rossetti was also a poet and author, and I cite to some of his work). Picasso drew in the 20th century; Rossetti drew in the 19th century. I then ask the significance of these added observations.

From this added material, I talk about the importance of recognizing when cases were decided (like when paintings were painted). Many legal decisions are a product of their era and can be explained or justified based on the then-existing state of the law. I then discuss the idea of legal evolution, how the cases we read show movement (some would say progress). I alert students to think about cases as having a time and a place and to identify their context.

I then talk about the painters and their styles and approaches. I analogize this to judicial styles. I introduce students to the idea that judges bring to their decision-making certain judicial approaches. I talk about judicial activism and judicial restraint. I talk about judicial philosophy. I keep returning to the differences (visual) between Picasso and Rossetti. I ask students to pay attention to who wrote what decisions as they read cases.

I then explain that cases operate at many levels—like a multi-layered cake. They tell a story; they represent a particular time in legal development; they reflect a judicial philosophy. So, when reading cases, one needs to work at all of these levels.

In the past, I then had students compare and contrast two assigned cases in their text (involving the grant and denial of specific performance) with a previously handed out hypothetical I have given them (which asks whether specific performance should be granted in light of the two cases in the text). The idea was to allow students to apply the portrait exercise to case analysis. When I tried this all at once, it was too complex. So, the next time, I would break the exercise into more component parts. First, I would have students compare and contrast two cases from the text so we could then discuss them in class after the portrait exercise. Then, I would give them the hypothetical. I would break them into groups so they could compare and contrast the hypothetical with the two cases they had read and analyzed. Then, we could reconvene as a large group and talk about the hypothetical. This could take place over two classes rather than one.

There are always issues of time allocation in a class, and this exercise may seem like it would take too much time. But, for me, the value of the exercise is that it has a lasting benefit beyond the substantive material covered (granting and denying specific performance). Moreover, the use of art gives some students an ability to "see" what is happening in the law school classroom for the first time. While there are students for whom the art is largely meaningless or for whom the exercise does not work, for those who suddenly can see, the exercise is well worth the time and effort.

Karen Gross
New York Law School

#4: Use of Overhead Transparencies

I use an overhead projector and transparencies in my Civil Procedure class to help explain each concept — from the basics of the class syllabus to personal jurisdiction.

Why do I use visual aids? A "basic" of my litigation training was that visual aids are essential, both at trial and on appeal. Most people, including juries and judges, learn more when they can both see and hear the material.

Visual aids are of special benefit to law students who are learning not only new material but a new way of thinking. Through visual aids, the students can see and learn by example the types of analysis that will help them in law school and practice. Most students do not know even the most simple forms of analyses and data manipulation. By depicting these on overheads, I teach not only the ultimate rule of law but also how I got there. Once students see the different types of analyses, they can develop their own form, best suited for them. In addition, by using and explaining why I use visual aids, the students will learn this "basic" of effective litigation presentation.

Why do I use overheads (rather than other forms of visual aids)? In practice, I experimented with many forms of visual aids and concluded that the simpler way was the better way. Overheads are particularly useful in the classroom. Unlike "hi-tech" aids, overheads cost only pennies for each transparency. I can prepare them minutes before class with a standard copy machine. They are simple to use and do not divert attention. Overheads are easier to see than chalkboards, students can have their own copy, and I can use the same transparency again, tying together old and new concepts.

How do I use overheads? I use transparencies to help teach almost every element of the class. For example, I teach the students how to dissect the rules of civil procedure by going over each rule word by word with a student. My transparency is simply the rule itself, which I have typed on a single page.

I begin a discussion of cases by teaching students how to master the facts of complicated cases using a chronology or diagram of the case's procedural history or underlying facts. I often create these aids during class on a blank transparency using information given by a student. I also pull out and dissect key tests and quotations from the cases.

As the class progresses through a topic, I help students understand how it all fits together by using a variety of analyses and summaries, including flow charts, line drawings, and tables.

I do not consider myself ready for class until I have tinkered with different forms of visual aids for the day. Creating the overhead is a good check on my own preparation, and the visual aid gives structure to the class discussion (and my notes).

I distribute most pre-typed materials in hard copy to the students when I first use them in class. If I do not give copies, students spend class time writing down every word rather than listening. If I give copies out too early, students forget them or prepare for class by trying to figure out my materials rather than first attempting to analyze the cases or rules on their own.

Carol Rice
University of Alabama School of Law

#5: Videos in Evidence

One of the courses that I teach is Evidence. Litigators, of course, use the evidence rules regularly, on their feet in the courtroom. In the classroom, though, students only read about the rules, discussing them through cases and problems. To them, I fear, Evidence is just another heavily rule-based course.

In order to try to make the law of evidence more real (and more interesting), I have used several short videos which present particular evidence problems. Some of the videos that I use contain short excerpts from televised trials or courtroom scenes in movies. I also use several videos from the Evidence Film Series—produced by Charles Nesson and Eric Saltzman—which show reenactments of portions of real trials.

I use each video somewhat differently, depending on the issue that it presents and the materials that the students have read. But with each, I pause the tape regularly, to ask the students questions about what objection they would make, how the judge should rule on the lawyer's objection, or what the lawyer is trying to accomplish with a particular line of questioning. In this way, the students get a sense of how the evidence rules work in the courtroom, and how the lawyer goes about getting evidence in, making an objection, refreshing recollection, and so forth.

Some courses, like Evidence, lend themselves better to use of video materials. I also teach Remedies, and I have had less success in finding videos which are appropriate and useful. In most courses, though, videos can be used to illustrate and give perspective. I recommend them as a teaching tool.

Peggy Cordray
Capital University Law School

#6: Flow Charts

Visual learning can occur in different forms. Some students think and reason in a linear fashion. For them, an outline or stepped organization is most valuable. A study outline is just such a visual tool. As teachers, we use this technique when we list doctrinal tests on the blackboard. This is usually accompanied by oral elaboration (speaking is also linear). We use two-dimensional visual aids when we write components on the board showing their connection and relationship by lines, arrows, boxes, etc. This is useful for illustrating multilateral relationships, different analytical routes, competing doctrine, and other items which don't lend themselves to linear organization. For instance, a Venn diagram is useful for demonstrating the concepts of over- and under-inclusivenesss.

The problem with two-dimensional visual presentations is that they are often hard to reproduce in handouts and text. As a result, these visual tools are mostly ignored in books and in teaching methods. Most of us were taught in a linear fashion, so we teach that way ourselves. Yet, as two-dimensional visual input becomes dominant in everyday life (e.g., TV, computers), replacing linear input (radio, text) students may become more responsive to graphical depictions. The challenge is to present information using the same media as found in common experience.

Several years ago I found that flow charts were a good two-dimensional tool. They can illustrate doctrine in a way that outlined and oral presentations can not. They can present an entire (albeit often oversimplified) body of substantive law on one page, and can depict multi-level doctrinal relationships. This allows students to move laterally as well as progressively through rules and tests, and visually perceive logical flow.

My construction of flow charts became easier, and my use of them expanded when I discovered flow charting programs, such as ABC and Visio. These programs facilitate the drafting and production of visually appealing charts.

Students have responded positively. I caution them that the charts are crude and superficial in terms of substance. They are merely a guide to understanding, not a self-contained reference. Standing alone they may be undecipherable. Thus, I go over each one in class as its elements arise in text and discussion.

It takes several years of refinement for me to produce a good flow chart; early versions often don't work well, and I may go through several iterations in consecutive classes. Students often spot conceptual problems that I don't see right away. I hope the process is as useful for them as for me. I now have a repertory of about 75 for my Constitutional Law and Federal Courts classes.

I am now in the process of turning the flow charts into interactive computer teaching tools. I do this in the following steps.

1. Convert the proprietary flow chart format (e.g., .abc) into standard graphical format (e.g., .jpg or .gif).
2. Bitmapping the flow chart with a command overlay (Mapedit does a good job). This crates "hot spots" on the flow chart which can be clicked by mouse action.
3. Hyperlinking the "hot spots" to other flow charts, files, URLs, or text.
4. Writing text corresponding to each of the flow chart elements. This text is called up when a user clicks on a "hot spot."

This process creates a three-dimensional flow chart which many students find to be an effective learning tool. Examples of flow charts (some of which are interactive as described above) can be found on my Web course pages. These can be accessed through my home page (http://www.law.lmu.edu/manheim).

Karl Manheim
Loyola Law School (Los Angeles)

#7: Drawings and Props

I am a terrible artist. When my ten-year-old daughter came to watch me teach Remedies one day, she was mortified by my stick figures on the chalkboard. However, I have found that my students remember cases and points much better if I illustrate them freehand; possibly their memories bear an inverse relationship to the quality of my drawings.

I don't think that I draw the same things for the same cases each year, but class after class claims to be able to identify cases by facts and holding simply by looking at my drawings. For some reason, in the first semester of Civil Procedure, several of the Montana cases I use to illustrate particular rules involve cattle, and in two instances dead cattle. My dead cow drawings are infamous.

At the student smoker each spring, there are invariable references to my art. One year, two incredibly observant women actually conducted a mock retrospective, and had poster-sized reproductions of many of the drawings I had done that year. I retaliated by having a colleague who is a part-time professional artist do a detailed illustration, in color, of the facts of a farming case, the night before we discussed it. I slid a panel of the chalkboard in front of it and then drilled a student, at much more length than usual, about the facts of the case: "How big was their house? What kind of animals did they keep? How far away was the factory? What crops were affected?" Finally, with a flourish, I unveiled the drawing. I now do this every year, and I have never answered all the direct questions about whether I in fact did that drawing.

I also use more tangible props. For instance, one of the cases in Laycock's Remedies text involves the cancellation of a sale of a boat, and the issue of whether the seller is entitled to recover lost profit even though it in fact later sold the boat to someone else. Much of the holding centers on the possibility of the dealer having made two sales, if the boat is a normal factory-run type. I have found that bringing a couple of small plastic boats, as well as a model cigarette-type boat, from the wide selection of bath toys at my house, really helps the students understand that point.

These are ridiculously simple devices, which take almost no class time, but bear highly disproportional benefit. The only real downside is the loss of face, but I can stand that since I have little to lose anyway.

Cynthia Ford
University of Montana School of Law

#8: Visualizing the Consequences of Environmental Law

We law teachers and our students tend to lose touch with the environment which exists beyond the classroom walls. Naturally we focus on the law, but because our time is limited and environmental law so vast and detailed, the law tends to crowd out not only other perspectives on environmental issues, but even the environment itself. The law becomes the end, not the means to one or more ends, and the ultimate consequences of environmental law in the world are too often neglected.

To address in a small way the distance between law study and environmental concerns, I began showing slides to students in my course on the environmental law of natural resources. I took pictures of places which were the subject of some of the opinions we studied, locations affected by statutes we read, and areas which had generated a few of the controversies we examined. One purpose in showing them to my students was to give them a better sense of the resources at stake in such situations, and thereby begin to reconnect them to the real-world environment. But some slides do more, I think. They illustrate both significant environmental values and instances of environmental degradation, so students can see graphically both the successes and the failings of our laws.

After a few years of seeking out those locations which were related to my course and relatively accessible to me, I can now illustrate for my students implementation of the National Environmental Policy Act and a comparable state statute with slides of a completed project requiring a federal wetlands permit and state and local approvals for different phases. We may also read excerpts from an environmental impact statement on a proposed national forest timber sale and the class can "visit" the site of the proposed harvest through slides. Our understanding of the complex water dispute addressed by the Truckee-Carson-Pyramid Lake Water Rights Settlement Act of 1990 is enhanced by slides taken along the entire watercourse, including portions providing habitat for endangered species and the Indian reservation which asserted federal reserved water rights. The Rio Grande National Forest in Colorado was the subject of a leading case on the subject of national forest land management plans (*Citizens for Environmental Quality v. United States*) and I am able to provide students a visual overview of that forest, its vegetation and topography, and views of areas devoted to grazing, mining, and wilderness purposes. Other slides document the effects of recent logging in the Rio Grande, which can be compared to an area in the same forest harvested a decade ago. Depending on the topics to be covered in a particular semester, we can see the decline in environmental quality and restoration efforts in the Lake Tahoe Basin and restoration efforts or habitat for endangered wildlife on refuges in New Mexico and Colorado.

Showing slides in class may seem a step back to an old technology, but this medium has several advantages over videotape. First, the images are more impressive in the classroom. A typical video monitor is small by comparison to a projection screen. Slides may be static, but each commands the audience's attention for the short time it appears.

Second, you can take the slides yourself. Unless one is an experienced camera operator, many people find it difficult to make a quality video with a camcorder outdoors. Videotaping outside introduces the challenges of panning a scene at the right speed, zooming in on objects with some amount of skill, and deciding what to do about the recording of sound. The resulting tape, even if shot very well, will likely require some editing, which presents questions about who can do that and with what equipment. By contrast, taking slides does not require you be an expert photographer. Modern and fairly inexpensive "point and shoot" 35-mm cameras have automatic focusing and aperture adjustments and make good-quality images easy to obtain. A zoom feature, which gives you modest telephoto capability, is very helpful because you can frame your shot with the push of a button. And editing your presentation is simple: just select the slides you want to present and place them in whatever order suits you.

Taking the slides yourself is desirable because the images should be integrated into the course and not seem to be just an accessory. This means you should approach slide presentations with the same degree of planning and preparation you devote to other aspects of the course. Slides of an area taken for other purposes on last year's vacation will likely appear in your classroom to be an afterthought (although I admit to having made travel plans with the purpose of taking slides for my course well in mind). You need to know in advance of taking them just what you want to convey with your slides. For example, the oft-cited decision in *Sierra Club v. Morton* arose out of the proposal by Walt Disney Enterprises, Inc. to build a major-destination ski resort in the Mineral King Valley in the Sierra Nevada Mountains. In my course, we study the controversy as an instance of early environmental litigation and political effort by modern conservationists, not just for its contribution to the law of standing. My first visit to the area was for hiking, not to take slides for my course. When I thought of using in class the photos I did take on that trip (since a photo lab can make slides of reasonable quality from prints) they proved not to be useful. On a later trip to Mineral King, I took slides of the valley floor where the resort was to be located, slopes which would have been groomed for ski runs, and the hanging valleys where check dams would have been built to control debris flows. I also took slides of the narrow, winding road to the valley because the need to upgrade the road provided the basis for important causes of action in the Sierra Club's lawsuit and the cost of improving access played some role in Disney's ultimate decision to abandon its plans. None of these things appeared in my first set of photos of Mineral King.

In preparing to show your slides, an inexpensive slide sorter (essentially a piece of translucent plastic with a light behind it) will allow you to quickly select and organize them. The logistics of the presentation will depend to some extent on the audio-visual facilities built into your classroom and the support available from the university or law school audio-visual department. Consider, however, the advantages of a projector with a wireless remote that controls not only the direction of the slide carousel but focus as well. If you wish to refer to your notes during your presentation, you will need a small light for the lectern. Finally, identifying for your audience particular aspects of the image on the screen is best accomplished with a hand-held pointer using a laser beam.

My use of slides in the classroom has been very well-received by students. Since it takes very little time to show a good number of slides, and because they are directly related to the law we study, students do not consider them filler. Since they are taken by the teacher, the slides seem to demonstrate a greater involvement by the instructor in the subject, which students seem to appreciate. Many of my students in the natural resources law course also enroll in my seminar on local environmental issues, and quite a few make their own visits to nearby sites and take slides to use in their presentations to the seminar. For these students, their connection with the real-world environment has been strengthened, and I believe for others the distance between the law we study and the environment it affects is shorter.

Richard J. Fink
California Western School of Law

#9: The Video "Bite"

Good teaching involves capturing and harnessing the interest of students.

One technique that I use to generate interest is the video "bite." I avoid instructional videos, and turn instead to movies and television. My objective is not to use the video to instruct, but to illustrate. I look for short scenes that capture an issue. I then use the video to initiate discussion.

A perfect example is the opening scene from the movie, *The Star Chamber*. In the early morning hours, two undercover police officers observe a young man walking down the street. On a "hunch," one of the officers decides to talk to the man. The man flees. The chase is on. It ends with the man fleeing into his home, but not before he drops something into his garbage can. The police officers do not search the garbage can, but wait for the contents of the can to be dumped into a garbage truck that is just approaching. They find a handgun that connects the accused to several murders. Flowing from this discovery, the accused is questioned and fully confesses. Authorities search his home and find various items stolen from the murder victims.

The scene moves to the courtroom. All is for nought. The handgun and all evidence flowing from its seizure are ruled inadmissible. Why? The accused's Fourth Amendment right to protection from unreasonable search and seizure was violated. How? The accused retained a "reasonable expectation of privacy" in the contents of his garbage can.

"Garbage," you say. Not so. There is precedent, including the case of *People v. Krivda*, 486 P.2d 1262 (1971), which is mentioned in the scene, and *California v. Greenwood*, 486 U.S. 35 (1988), in which Justice Brennan provides an eloquent defense of the reasonable expectation of privacy in one's trash and the intimate secrets contained therein.

Where does this lead? It leads to discussion on the notion of "reasonable expectation of privacy"; it leads to discussion on the whole issue of exclusion of evidence flowing from a violation of the Constitution; and for my students, it leads to discussion of the Canadian approach under our Charter of Rights and Freedoms.

The video "bite" in a vivid and visual way acts as the standard law school hypothetical. Like most of our hypotheticals, it is extreme and exaggerated, but it serves as an excellent catalyst for discussion.

Next time you are watching a movie, think about the video "bite."

Lee Stuesser
University of Manitoba Faculty of Law

#10: Student-Created Graphics

Many students learn better visually than textually. To help those students, I use many graphics in my materials and in class. One of the most effective uses for graphics is to have students participate in their creation. This makes them more invested in the graphic and requires that they really master the material.

There are several ways to get students to participate in creating a graphic. Sometimes I produce a template and ask students—either in class or as part of their homework—to fill it in. For example, I ask them to map out the parol evidence rule of U.C.C. § 2-202 by filling in a chart indicating what types of evidence are admissible under what circumstances. Other times I ask students to create the graphic completely on their own. For example, in Contracts, after covering the contract policing doctrines (e.g., fraud, duress, unconscionability, mistake, and frustration of purpose), I ask students to present a one-page graphical depiction of how these doctrines interrelate. I then use their work to focus class discussion on the relationship of the various doctrines. For example, the Venn diagram below was submitted by one group of students. It demonstrates a great deal of high-level thinking about the material, and it also prompted an interesting class discussion about whether there is a greater relationship between the doctrines of concealment and mistake than the graphic suggests.

Students are often quite excited about these projects, and frequently exhibit a significant amount of insight into the material. Moreover, they often produce different types of graphics. For example, in addition to several Venn diagrams, I also received a wide assortment of flow charts, as well as the amusing illustration below (which was accompanied by text describing the attributes of the characters depicted).

There are at least two benefits to this. First, it is a helpful reminder that students may think about the material in a completely different way than I do. If I know that, I can be more sensitive to their learning styles and perhaps be more likely to disabuse them of any misunderstanding they may have. Second, and perhaps more important, it also may prompt me to think about the material in a new way.

Stephen L. Sepinuck
Gonzaga University School of Law

"A Picnic of Contract Elements"

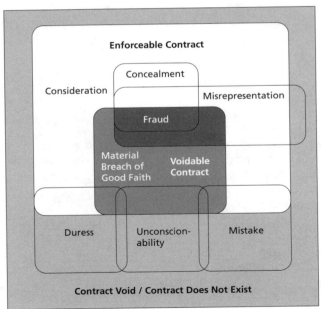

The Venn Diagram

#11: Concept Mapping

Because a common complaint in the educational arena is that many students learn only a little, a question often asked is how can students be taught to learn more? In a well-known study, a professor reported that the human mind structures information by relating it horizontally — e.g., in a sequence — and vertically — e.g., in a hierarchy. Thus, a constitutional law class on due process may include students linking due process horizontally with other rights such as equal protection and vertically with "lesser included" concepts such as basic due process or void for vagueness.

Teachers can use this study to encourage students to build their own internal "flow charts." One such technique is "concept mapping." This technique has been defined as "the identification of concepts...and the organization of those concepts into a hierarchical arrangement from the most general, most inclusive to the least general, most specific concept." (Novak, 1981 at 31, quoted in C. Rafferty and L. Fleschner, *Concept Mapping: A Viable Alternative to Objective and Essay Exams*, 1993 READING RESEARCH AND INSTRUCTION 25, 26.) "Concept mapping" promotes the use of diagrams, pictures, and maps to explain concepts. Maps of "due process," "freedom of speech," or "intestate transfers of property" may be difficult to visualize, but to many students, drawing and organizing a hierarchical picture help to clarify a doctrinal area more than an oral or written explanation.

This active learning technique asks students to create a "map" of a particular concept or principle. The map need not be restricted to flow charts, but can visually depict by words or phrases. For example, the due process doctrine of void for vagueness can center around a question mark to show reasonable people must necessarily guess as to the meaning and application of the law.

This approach is based on a belief that many people learn better by creating their own visualizations. There is at least one limitation, however. The drawing should be a visual description and thus a mere outline will not suffice. Further, the drawing should contain all of the nuances and subtleties of the particular doctrine; the more detailed the map, the more knowledgeable its creator.

Steven Friedland
Nova Southeastern University Shepard Broad Law Center

#12: "One Hundred and One" Torts Video

I like to use some seemingly unrelated aspect of popular culture, preferably a high-energy one, as the way of getting the attention of students and focusing that attention on a point of law to be learned. I have found this to be particularly useful at the beginning of the first class. It sets the tone at a "fun" level and really lets the students know that they have to think when they come to the class. And for first-years, it provides an additional icebreaker and relaxer when they are all wondering whether they should even be enrolled in law school.

For example, at the beginning of torts class, after intros and (hopefully) calming statements, I tell the students where we are going and briefly list and explain the elements of a tort. Then I show about ten minutes of the video from Walt Disney's animated version of "The One Hundred and One Dalmatians," beginning with Cruella's entrance on the night of the puppies' birth, and have them try to identify all of the torts that are occurring. There is a large number and quite a wide variety, from intentional torts, to trespass, to defamation, to negligence. This hopefully primes the members of the class to start looking for torts throughout their daily life and focuses their attention and understanding throughout the class.

Victor B. Flatt
Georgia State University College of Law

Chapter 5

Real-Life Learning Opportunities

Tell me, I forget. Show me, I remember. Involve me, I understand.
—Proverb.

A. What Is Experiential Learning?

The dominant mode of teaching and learning in most law schools occurs through students' reading cases and statutes. In class, the teacher and students analyze those sources and apply them to hypothetical questions and problems. However, other types of education, including experiential learning, take place inside and outside the law school classroom.

Experiential learning integrates theory and practice by combining academic inquiry with real-life experiences. Students can have real-life experiences with law outside the classroom in courts, agencies, and law offices. Teachers can arrange for students to encounter real life in the classroom through newspapers, videos, actual legal documents, and speakers. For effective experiential learning to occur, simply offering students the experiences is not enough. Students must engage in an accompanying reflective process in which they glean meaning and lessons from the experiences. Hence, for purposes of this chapter, experiential learning includes two elements—real-life experiences and reflection.

Experiential learning in various forms occurs in every law school. Examples include:

> *Clinics.* Many law schools have in-house law clinics in which law students represent clients under the supervision of faculty members. Most clinics include a classroom component designed in part to provide for student reflection.

> *Externships.* In a typical externship program, a faculty member places students in legal positions with agencies, courts, prosecutors, public defenders, law firms, citizens' groups, etc. Direct supervision of the students is provided by personnel at the placement. Often, the faculty member conducts a series of seminars to allow reflection by the students.

Service Learning. A relatively new format for experiential learning in law schools is service learning. Service learning combines public service and academics. It often occurs in conjunction with a course. For example, teachers in Women and the Law or Environmental Law courses may require that each student volunteer at a service agency or community group. Teachers then integrate student reflection on the connection between public service and the content and skills of the course.

Field Trips. A common type of experiential learning in all disciplines is the field trip. Field trips are extremely flexible. They can be for an hour or two in which students go on their own to view a hearing in a court or administrative setting. Other field trips can last for many days during which students travel with a faculty member to distant locations. Teachers then incorporate student reflection on the field trip into the course.

Real Life in Class. Many law teachers bring real life into their classrooms via newspapers, examples of legal documents, videos of events, and guest speakers. Student reflection on these experiences becomes part of the course.

B. Theoretical Bases for Experiential Learning

Three different theoretical bases support experiential learning: (1) holistic learning, (2) Kolb's cyclical model, and (3) reflection-in-action.

1. Holistic Learning

In recent years much research has been conducted on the evolution and functioning of the human brain. Modern research suggests that the human brain has three major components that evolved sequentially and have different functions. The reptilian portion of the brain, which developed 200 million years ago, plays an important role in aggression, territoriality, ritual, and social hierarchy. The old mammalian portion of the brain, which developed 60 million years ago, contains the pituitary gland and deals primarily with emotions. The new mammalian brain, which makes up about 85% of the modern human brain, is the site of most cognitive functions.

The three portions of the brain do not operate in a logical, rational, or linear manner. Instead, the brain works in a multilineal way, using all three portions and going down many paths at once. For example, we identify an object, usually in less than a second, by considering its size, shape, color, sound, smell, weight, location, surrounding objects, and how other people are reacting to it. What the brain does well is to create, store, recognize, and retrieve patterns. Thus, the strength of the human brain is its holistic, multipath ability to make sense of the world by generating and calling forth patterns to deal with experience.

Learning theorists believe that an understanding of the brain's functioning has significant implications for education at all levels. Instead of engaging students in linear, step-by-step learning of subject fragments arranged in a sequence that seems logical to someone, teachers should give students the opportunity to participate in holistic learning based on new experiences. Experiential learning involves the student's eyes, ears, touch, mind, emotions, and intuition.

2. Kolb's Cyclical Model

David Kolb is a contemporary learning theorist who has set forth a cyclical model of experiential learning: concrete experience—>reflective observation—>abstract conceptualization—>active experimentation—>concrete experience—>etc. Experiential learning begins when students have a concrete experience. The students reflect on what the experience means. Then the students formulate abstract conceptualizations of what has taken place. They then test the abstract conceptualization with active experimentation to see if the conceptualizations work. The cycle repeats as active experimentation creates another concrete experience.

Kolb views learning as a process rather than as a set of outcomes. Accumulations of facts, ideas, and behaviors will not serve learners well because they will become outdated. For Kolb, ideas are not fixed elements of thought but instead are formed and reformed through experience. Understanding is a process of continuous construction, built on the interaction of ideas and experience.

3. Reflection-In-Action

Donald Schon, in THE REFLECTIVE PRACTITIONER: HOW PROFESSIONALS THINK IN ACTION, goes further than Kolb by arguing that knowledge gleaned from experience is the most useful knowledge for professionals. Schon asserts that the education of professionals (lawyers, doctors, social workers, engineers, etc.) is dominated by the "Technical Reality" model. Technical Reality stresses the development of a standard body of information, principles, and theories that can be used to solve recurring professional problems.

Schon believes that actual professional practice does not fit well with the Technical Reality model. Modern professional practice is characterized by complexity, uncertainty, and value conflict. The heart of professional practice is not the ability to solve recurring problems with standardized knowledge and skills. Instead, modern professional practice requires the practitioner to identify problems out of unique and unpredictable events. Schon believes that modern professionals need a new way of knowing, which he calls "Reflection-in-Action." This is knowledge that grows out of experience and reflection.

C. Goals and Benefits of Experiential Learning

The three theories described above provide a basis for experiential learning in law school in any of its forms—clinics, externships, service learning, field trips, and real life in the classroom. Likewise, those forms of experiential learning share all or some of the following goals:

- To broaden, extend, and deepen students' understanding of concepts and principles;

- To help students integrate theory and practice;

- To increase students' motivation through the experience of working in the field; and

- To help students develop the knowledge, skills, and values they need as professionals.

Educational researchers report a number of benefits of experiential learning in higher education. These include:

- Students experience law as it is—complicated and imperfect—rather than the organized, packaged version of law from a textbook.

- Students get a real-life context in which they give meaning to the ideas, skills, and values explored in the classroom.

- Experiential learning gives students the opportunity to be actively involved in their own education.

- Experiential learning has positive effects on students' motivation, attitude toward the course, willingness to participate in class, ability to ask insightful questions, and acquisition of knowledge and skills.

- The teacher-student relationship and the relationships among students often are enhanced when they share the experience of law and the legal profession in real life.

D. Maximizing the Benefits of Experiential Learning

The following principles can help students and teachers make the most out of experiential learning:

1. *Make learning the primary objective of the experience.* Mere activity does not constitute experience and not all experience leads to educational growth. Student experiences are most likely to promote significant learning if they are carefully planned, monitored, and structured to achieve specific learning goals.

2. *Clarify the student's role.* The teacher, student, and field personnel (if applicable) should have a clear understanding of the student's role in the experience. Written guidelines could include:

The learning objectives of the experience;
The student's responsibilities;
How the student will integrate the experience with classroom learning;
How the student will receive feedback during and after the experience; and,
How the student will be evaluated.

3. *Give students explicit assignments.* Most students (and their teachers) perform best when they understand what is expected of them. Therefore, explicit assignments help students reach their potential. For example, an assignment that asks students working for an agency to "reflect on their experience" or to "critically evaluate their work for the agency" will leave many students unsure of what the teacher expects of them. More specific directions would help clarify the assignment for most students: "Describe the culture of the agency, its employees, and the people it serves." or "Articulate how your values conflict with or are in harmony with the values of the agency employees." or "Explain how the law (specify) we studied in the classroom differs from or is consistent with the law as applied at the agency."

4. *Make critical reflection part of the experience.* An important element of experiential learning is student reflection on the experience. Student re-

flection can take place in various formats, including journals, essays, and small-group discussions. What matters is that students think about their experiences; articulate their concerns, insights, and opinions; and share their thoughts with their teachers and their peers.

References

BARBARA GROSS DAVIS, TOOLS FOR TEACHING 166–172 (1993).

JAMES R. DAVIS, BETTER TEACHING, MORE LEARNING: STRATEGIES FOR SUCCESS IN POSTSECONDARY SETTINGS 299–341 (1993).

Michael F. Follo, *Field Trip as a Teaching Method,* in HANDBOOK OF COLLEGE TEACHING: THEORY AND APPLICATIONS 189–195 (Keith W. Prichard & R. McLaren Sawyer eds., 1994).

DONALD A. SCHON, THE REFLECTIVE PROFESSIONAL: HOW PROFESSIONALS THINK IN ACTION 3–69 (1983).

Specific Real-Life Learning Opportunities

#1: Hardhat Teaching

For the past five years, I have taught a Land Acquisition and Development Seminar. This upper-level course tends to attract the ten or fifteen students in each class who, like their teacher, cannot walk past a construction site without peering over the fence for a few minutes.

Several times in past years, students have suggested that it would be valuable to visit a construction site at some point during the semester; perhaps to meet with the owner, the general contractor, and the architect; and to get a sense from people in the business about how a project progresses. For some reason, I never followed up on their suggestions.

But an irresistible opportunity arose last year, when the University of Tennessee College of Law began a thirty-month renovation and expansion project.

Toward the end of the semester, the university's director of facilities planning, the general contractor's project manager, and the project architect met with the class and me. By this point, students had spent most of the semester representing the various parties involved in the construction of fictional Trumpet Tower. They had studied the intricacies of development financing and had drafted and negotiated construction and permanent loan documents. They had examined the American Institute of Architects' standard construction documents. But nothing that I did in class could simulate bargaining leverage, scheduling desperation, time pressure from actual clients (as opposed to a fictional client who grades students at the end of the term), sinkholes, unexpected aquifers, or heavy rains. In short, the students had been playing poker with chips not backed by cash, and I needed to bring in people not unlike their future clients to import some reality into the Trumpet Tower project.

I entered the special class session with some trepidation. Although I had practiced real estate law for four years and had been exposed to construction law, I had been teaching for five years and was increasingly worried that I had become rusty. Perhaps my background provided an accurate portrayal of the world of 1990, but was I hopelessly out-of-date? Perhaps the books and documents we had used in class were credible, but are the scholars who write in the field as knowledgeable about the construction process as I had always optimistically assumed? I was introducing experts to the class who could credibly dispute my knowledge.

The class went quite well, at least as best as I could judge. Nearly all of the students showed up for this optional session on a beautiful spring Friday at the peak of the dogwood season. I had asked each of them to bring in a short list of questions — in particular, questions about local practices that they had asked me during the year, and for which I had been able to offer only uncertain answers. Nearly all of the students asked pointed questions based on their increasing knowledge. They received straightforward responses from knowledgeable, skilled experts. They interacted, as professionals, with professionals.

The first hour of the two-hour session produced a few substantive law surprises. As it turns out, lien waivers, a topic on which we had spent a great deal of class time, seem to be infrequently used on projects in this part of the country. And the AIA form documents are only rarely negotiated in state projects — the state simply drafts supplementary conditions, attaches them to the commercially prepared form document, and seeks bids on the package. But all in all, the first hour of the class accomplished exactly what I had hoped, by adding the one missing ingredient — reality — to my simulation class.

The second hour of the session probably was less valuable substantively but far more memorable. It also was the hook by which I had enticed everyone to attend — a guided tour of the construction site, a journey inside the chain-link fence that had separated us from the various people doing mysterious and noisy things inside "the hole."

The architect led us through the building plans, pointing out some of the more subtle features. We learned that fire-prevention systems are among the most difficult to design, because they must be connected to so many of the other building systems. And we observed how the Americans With Disabilities Act has altered building design.

Based on my two-hour experience with hardhat teaching, I recommend it highly. While it may not work in some areas of the law school curriculum, in other areas the benefits seem incontestable. Thus, a Securities Law teacher might take her students to an all-night session at the printer's, or a Health Law teacher might visit the general counsel's office of a major hospital. And Real Estate professors need not wait for their own law school buildings to be renovated — any local construction project might work just as well.

The students benefited in several ways. They received more complete responses to some of the questions they had asked in class. They started to see how lawyers and business persons interact as useful members of a productive team. And they began to develop the confidence that they really knew more law than they thought they did, and that their own legal proficiency would continue to develop long after graduation.

I benefited, too. I was able to see students, who knew little about an area of law just fourteen weeks earlier, asking articulate questions and receiving answers from people who obviously respected their growing expertise. And, even as I increased my own knowledge, I was able to confirm that the teacher did, in fact, have something useful to offer.

Best of all, we were able to spend that second hour down in the red East Tennessee clay, watching the subs pour concrete, and crowding around the bed of the contractor's dusty red pickup to peer at the building plans that rippled gently in the spring breeze, on a warm Friday afternoon, at the peak of the dogwood season.

Gregory M. Stein
The University of Tennessee College of Law

#2: Service Learning — Housing for Single Mothers and Their Children

Last semester, the class and I agreed to incorporate "service learning" into our course on housing and community development.

We had a recent alumna who was interested in working in the public interest/housing area, but was unable to find a job. She decided to form her own nonprofit corporation and apply directly for funding for a home for single, unwed mothers. She had to develop a plethora of legal documents to support her application.

I originally planned the class as a traditional two-hour course with a three-hour final at the end of the semester. On the first day of class, I told the class I wanted to try something different, and proposed that we adopt the nonprofit corporation as our "client," write two or three papers each on different topics designed to help the alumna in her application, and still have a one-hour final at the end of the semester.

Because the registration material had listed the course as a non-paper course, I told the class I had to get the consent of each student to convert to a paper course. I then said that before we voted on the proposal, I wanted the class to meet the "client." The alumna stepped forward and spent the next hour setting out the dire need for safe housing for unwed mothers with small children that exists in south-central Los Angeles and her proposal to buy a boarded-up building and turn it into a mixed-use housing and training center for the tenants. By the end of the hour, the class had unanimously and enthusiastically adopted the proposal.

The service-learning component of the class really brought the class to life. I had the "client" come in several more times during the semester to update us on her progress. We took a field trip to the boarded-up building she had under contract to view the environment and to visualize her plans. We also were able to relate the materials in the course to her particular project. And by researching and writing papers on issues inherent in the start-up and operation of a home for unwed mothers, the class was able to contribute toward a project that will make a difference in the lives of the people selected as tenants and in the immediate community around the building. It is impossible to discuss in detail all the tangible and intangible benefits we received from adding the service-learning component of the class, but I can say without question it made the class the most meaningful class I have ever taught. Several students said it was the most meaningful class they took in law school.

Peter Wendel
Pepperdine University School of Law

#3: Ethics in the Clinic

To make ethics and ethical dilemmas more "real" to students, we have tied our Ethics seminar into the work done by the students in the Legal Aid Clinic.

The class is limited to approximately 12 students. The students and I meet once a week for two hours, basically to talk about ethical problems that the students or I have encountered in the cases that they work on in the clinic. I assign a reading for the students each week, and I require them to keep a journal containing their reflections. Their reflections may be on the reading and how it relates to their cases, or it may be on any matter that arose and that relates to ethics in any way.

Before class, I ask students' permission to talk about their journal entries in class or ask the students themselves to talk about their journal entries. Occasionally, we invite a guest speaker to participate. This has been helpful when the topic that we are discussing relates to a particular area of expertise such as representing children.

I have found that because the ethical dilemmas encountered arise in actual rather than hypothetical cases, students are more prone to seek solutions. This is not to say that one solution is prescribed or mandated, but the student who has the ethical problem actively seeks help from his or her peers; this encourages and stimulates group participation.

This method of teaching ethics is much more rewarding than teaching Professional Responsibility from the Model Rules. It encourages students to explore ethical and moral issues, and it also highlights the fact that the ethical rules and code may not always provide the answers.

Christine Venter
Notre Dame Law School

#4: Newspaper Stories in Criminal Law

As I was trying to develop a syllabus for a Criminal Law class, I remembered how dry and boring the course seemed when I was in law school. It was not until I had been practicing for several years that I stumbled into the exciting realm of criminal defense.

I am a chronic newspaper-clipper. In my apartment are withered snippets of articles going back for years. Many of those articles deal with the bizarre things people do that lead them to getting arrested and prosecuted. While looking through my collection, the germ of an idea began to crystallize. I decided to select what turned out to be three major stories involving different types of crime. Each news story formed a unit from which I developed three to four weeks of reading and discussion.

After some slight modifications, I gave the stories to the students. We spent the next class discussing what the students knew about the actual case; what they thought they needed to know about the crime, the victims, or the defendants if they were going to prosecute; and what they needed to know if they were going to defend the accused. Based on their discussion, I assigned readings from the casebook and supplemental materials if required. After discussing the assigned reading, we talked about what the principles in the reading meant to our unit case.

This approach allowed the students to learn about crimes, defenses, and theories of punishment in a real context. The level of discussion and participation in the class was outstanding. Having the context of the original news story before they did the reading allowed students to quickly decipher the significance of the cases and note material.

Michelle Jacobs
University of Florida College of Law

#5: Boring

Let us speak the truth. Law school is too often, er, you know, kind of, well, boring. Was it any different when you were in law school?

I have no answers, only a few suggestions. We must intersperse traditional legal education methods with media that are user-friendly for students. But the TV show, film, etc., must always be a supplement to, not a substitute for, traditional law school programming.

Every year, my most successful class transpires when I show the PBS video, *Eyes on the Prize, America's Civil Rights Years, Episode 2: Fighting Back (1957-62)*, to my Education Law Seminar students. They are assigned to read *Brown v. Board of Education* and its 1960's progeny prior to class. But they just don't get it. Then they see the National Guard with bayonets drawn at Little Rock's Central High and lawyer Thurgood Marshall and Old Miss ablaze and public schools chained shut by government decree. The reaction tends toward actual disbelief. It cannot be true; it can't have happened. Then I bring out my secret weapon: a black colleague who grew up in Alabama in that era, who calmly relates the conditions under which she fought for what every one of my students has always taken for granted, the right to attend high school. Her one-hour visit to my class, by the way, would dispel anyone's doubts about the critical need for multiculturalism in legal education. (The *Eyes on the Prize* series is generally available in public libraries, and I'm more than willing to act as an agent for my colleague.)

Another eye-opener for students is Frederick Wiseman's film, *Titicut Follies* (available through Zipporah Films, One Richdale Ave., Unit #4, Cambridge, MA 02140, telephone 617/576-3603), depicting conditions in a Massachusetts "correctional" mental institution. I show this to students in my Disability Law Seminar. I want students to feel what long-term institutionalization meant for mental patients. Then I take them on a field trip to a local state mental hospital. (Be careful. Hospitals often want to give students a sanitized tour. Insist on visiting locked wards and forensic units. At least one of our state hospitals has preserved an underground tunnel with rings fastened into the walls for chaining up the "patients.") Our local institution has a small, but excellent museum on site, with extensive photographs, electroshock paraphernalia, and—best of all—a log book of commitments, going back to the mid-1800s. Students are edified to see that one could be institutionalized for such aberrant behavior as reading novels or extensive studying.

Field trips can be enormously useful, although cumbersome for large groups and sometimes expensive. With the gracious assistance of Justice Blackmun, I once took a group of clinic students to the Supreme Court to observe the oral argument of a case that would affect a number of our clients.

Sometimes, however, if you can't take the students to reality, you can bring reality to them. One of our state appellate courts was happy to schedule a panel to hear a full week of argument on our school's premises. Students were in and out of that room all week long. Similarly, the Social Security Administration's Office of Hearings and Appeals has had a program—of which I've taken advantage—to hold administrative hearings at law schools. With the claimants' written permission, a local administrative law judge scheduled four hearings one morning at our school, and my entire Administrative Law class attended. As a double learning opportunity, the cases were presented by students in my Disability Law Clinic. (You can bet they were over-prepared when they had to represent clients in front of their peers!) Although the formal program apparently no longer exists, SSA continues to encourage its ALJs to perform such public service. As a practical matter, I suggest contacting your local OHA at least two months prior to the date that you would like to have the hearings.

John McCutcheon's brilliant song, *The Red Corvette* (from the *Water From Another Time* album, (Rounder 11555) Appalseed Productions, 1025 Locust Ave., Charlottesville, VA 22901, phone 804-977-6321, fax 804-977-9708 ($17 for cassette), Web site http://www.folkmusic.com), invariably brings the house down in Family Law. It also, I hope, teaches students, in a way they are not likely ever to forget, the need for both spouses to maintain reasonable control over the sale of marital assets. (Sorry, but I won't explain the song any more fully in print; you'll have to get it yourself.)

Finally, when all else fails, try doggerel. I have inflicted my own effort at verse, *The Cautionary Ballad of Susan M.*, 40 J. Legal Educ. 485 (1990), on an Education Law seminar to try to demonstrate the futility of educational malpractice litigation. The sequel, *Susan M. Reprised*, 43 J. Legal Educ. 149 (1993), maybe, just maybe, will illustrate the concept of *res judicata* to first-year Civil Procedure students, so that even if they don't remember the phrase, they still get the idea.

The point is that law school does not have to be as, well, you know, as it tends to be. With a little leavening, one can get a rise out of the students. And they just might learn, and remember, something valuable.

Robert E. Rains
The Dickinson School of Law

#6: Examples of Drafting Problems from Real Documents

Student motivation seems to increase the more you can show why the subject matter is worth learning. Showing the why seems to work best when related to experiences students readily understand. That's often hard to do in the first year or two of law school when the custom, language, and technique of legal education often are quite foreign and confusing for students.

This is a short (10-15 minutes), in-class cooperative learning exercise that instructors can use to show the "whys" of certain legal writing or document drafting principles.

Create a bank of examples of poorly drafted legal phrases or paragraphs culled from common, real-life sources most students are familiar with: newspaper or magazine ads, parking garage or laundry receipts (mostly legal disclaimers), product warnings and instructions, state and local property tax notices or assessments, employee handbooks, insurance and bank contracts or notices, contracts to purchase cars or houses, apartment rental agreements, etc.

Using an overhead projector, conduct or assign a student to conduct a cooperative editing exercise with the class or a pre-assigned group. You can edit the example in its entirety, tailor the editing exercise to focus on current topics or stylistic points being taught that week, or use it to introduce a new topic. Important to the exercise is discussing who may be affected by unclear or bad legal writing and the range of consequences to the potential parties.

After participating in a couple of these exercises, I find that students eagerly seek and easily find their own examples to share in class.

This exercise also might work well substantively for contracts, torts, and commercial law courses. I have used it in more limited ways to teach several topics in Health Law.

Bonnie Mitchell
University of Utah

#7: Current Events in the Classroom

One of the things that drives me crazy about (legal) education is the tendency for the classroom to be a cocoon out of time and out of place. My experience is that students make a transition when they enter the classroom to a place far, far away, a place that has little or no connection to the "real" world. Of course, teachers often contribute to this feeling by their constant reminders that what the student thinks or feels based on her/his life experience is irrelevant to the mastery of the law.

Since I believe that the law is a vibrant part of the mosaic of everyday life, I often chafe at the narrow version of life that is entailed by the ordinary classroom. So I try to liven things up a bit. (I am still responsible enough to know that I have a knowledge-transmitting job to do. I do publish a syllabus, do have a textbook, etc.) In trying to inject some reality into the class and yet not have a seminar in current news, I tried several approaches. One was simply to comment on the relevance of something I had read or heard around the time that a particular class was given. This usually met with polite boredom. That was not what I was after, so I escalated my efforts.

What I do now is find something in the news that is directly relevant (in my eyes) to all or part of the lesson for the day. I literally decide what the vehicle for my teaching is in some cases as I drive to school in the morning, having read the newspaper and listened to "Morning Edition." It helps that I teach classes (Professional Responsibility, Administrative Law, and Jurisprudence) that have plastic agendas. I now use a variation on this approach, at least in some classes. I ask the students if they have read or heard anything that pertains to the subject we are pursuing. This is a bit more risky, since their idea of relevance may not be the same as mine, but I am usually nimble enough to make their stories fit, and if not, at least "save" them until there is a better fit with the syllabus. In any case, I try to make clear at the outset that I am going to do this in the syllabus and with a short introductory talk at the beginning of the term. Ironically, I "discovered" this method by teaching a third-grade class the Bill of Rights. I was going to talk about parades. The students thought that was too boring and focused all of us on a then-current local controversy regarding an attempt by a park board to outlaw boom boxes on the beach.

Two Examples. One of my favorites was a story that appeared in the local paper regarding the efforts of the health district to shut down a "cookie and hot chocolate concession booth" at a little town's winter festival. The booth was run by the Boy Scouts, with goodies supplied by their parents. None had the proper food handler licenses, tax numbers, etc. The feature story cast the health district personnel as villains out to spoil a community's fun.

It so happens that this story appeared at the beginning of a term during which I was teaching Administrative Law, so I seized on it to discuss the tension between giving field personnel discretion and the rule of law, which then opens up the whole crazy fabric of administrative law. I continued to use the story that semester because, with a little imagination, it served as the vehicle for discussion of much of the doctrine in the subject.

A more recent example popped up during Jurisprudence this past semester. I was trying to develop a more multicultural perspective on philosophy of law, and so Michael Fay (of caning fame) served two purposes:

his situation generated discussion about the relationship between law and justice within a particular community as well as analysis of arguments about the role of external standards to judge the validity of a law.

This method of teaching is far from perfect. Let me point out some drawbacks. First, one has to be prepared to hit newsless days. They happen, not often, but they do. I think this may be a major problem for teachers of some courses: it probably isn't very often that UCC Article 3 appears in the news. (You can tell that I do not read *The Wall Street Journal*.) I revert to the syllabus at that point. Second, you have to read the newspaper, or at least news magazines, and listen to or watch the news. There are many days when I would prefer to pull the covers over my head. Third, you have to have the courage to think laterally to make connections between what you are reading and what you teach. Fourth, you have to assume that the students will pay as much attention to the news as you do, which in many cases is a faulty assumption. It helps to have handy access to a copy machine, and to be prepared to compose a summary of a news event that you heard on the radio or watched on TV. Fifth, you often have to work pretty hard to overcome student resistance and withdrawal. I can read minds, and so know that many think, "What the heck is he talking about? That wasn't assigned on the syllabus." or "I just don't see how cookie sales related in any way to the requirement that agencies comply with the APA in making policy." One of the ways that I deal with the latter problem is to ask leading questions to both draw the students into the problem and make connections to the doctrine.

Despite the drawbacks, it is a fun way to teach.

Jim Vaché
Gonzaga University School of Law

#8: The Ten Commandments: A Humble Offering at the Shrine of the Field Placement

I. Thou shalt love the externship, thy Program, with all thy heart, with all thy soul, and with all thy might.

> Create a program you can passionately believe in, and support/defend it without hesitation. Articulate and address directly any concerns that you have, including consultation with adult learning specialists if necessary. If you doubt your program, who won't?

II. Thou shalt bear no false gods before thee, but shall prosper in the Truth in all thy ways.

Be alert to recognize and address directly any biases and assumptions that suggest that externships are not responsible programs generally. If your program is designed and administered well, you will not have (long-term) problems. Avoid accepting negative stereotypes, and don't fall into the trap of defending apparent imperfections in externships. The best scholars and teachers have classroom students daydreaming in the back rows, and no in-house clinic is perfect either. Why apply the (impossible) standard of perfection only to field placements?

III. Yea, though thou walkest through the valley of the shadow of uncertainty, thou shalt not fear, for thy Program is with thee.

It is crucial to create a clear and descriptive set of educational objectives and methods, and have them approved by your Curriculum Committee or overall faculty. Live by them, and amend them as necessary to reflect the reality of your programs. The inevitable uncertainty of some field placements (and supervisors) is a reflection of the reality of law practice and real lawyers, and will not undermine the program if you have considered realistic imperfections in your program design.

IV. Thou shalt humbly render the regulators, thy dean, and thy faculty their due, but thou shalt not bow down before them. And through thy steadfast righteousness it shall come to pass that they also shall believe upon thee and upon thy Program.

Develop camaraderie with the faculty and work against any "we-they" attitudes. Generate an educationally responsible program that complies, at least largely, with the accreditation standards. Be consistent and confident in the administration of the program, and avoid reacting to negativity. People come around with time.

V. Let there be no wailing, nor gnashing of teeth, over thy status or thy rewards, for verily I say unto thee that thence shall be planted many dark seeds in thy heart, and they shall be as a blight upon thy Countenance and upon the Countenance of thy children.

Complaining can make you miserable, and is likely to affect your home life as well as your job satisfaction. Avoid comparisons—you'll always come out "better" or "worse" than someone else. Work for salary and status parity, but don't forget to appreciate the great job you have and your chance to shape skilled and decent lawyers. If that's not enough, try remembering how happy you were to leave the old job for this one; and if that doesn't restore a positive attitude, consider going back.

VI. Neither shalt thou bow down before the God of the In-house Clinic, for She is a True God, but She is not the One True God, nor is She thy God.

> One of the particular assumptions that creates a defensive posture for externships is that the in-house clinic is the superior (or, perhaps, only legitimate) approach to clinical training of good and decent lawyers. It is clearly the more established and accepted approach, but look out for the unspoken standard that a good externship must necessarily model a good in-house clinic. That is a setup for guaranteed stress, as you try to ignore, deny, or cover up the obvious differences between the two. The legitimacy of your program will depend only on its design, objectives, and conduct of the program responsibly to meet its objectives.

VII. Thou shalt teach Goodness, Self-Reflection, and all these Truths to thy students, and shalt prepare them well that they may go forth and prosper in the whimsical Land of Externship.

> Look realistically at the goals of your program, and the general level of reliability and expertise of your field supervisors; then decide how much preparation and relative autonomy your students will need to have a successful placement. Prepare them well with these factors in mind, and if you can't, amend the goals or structure of the program.

VIII. In thy dark moments quaver not before the plight of thy students, nor the fancy of their supervisors, but in all ways be true to thy Scriptures.

> Inevitably, some students will have problems with their supervisors. They may learn well from the experience if properly prepared, and/or they may need to be transferred to a new supervisor or even a new office. Work to amend the supervisor's approach (if errant), by reference to your published objectives, methods, and supplementary materials. If that fails, make the necessary changes to maximize the student's semester, and consider suspending the placement or amending the relevant objectives and credit award.

IX. Suffer not the little accreditors to come before thee, for theirs is the Kingdom of Power and Glory. Neither tremble nor prostrate thyself in fear before them, though their ways be vexatious and strange, for verily shall they lift thee up in thy time of travail, and shall anoint thee in righteousness before thy dean and thy faculty.

> Theirs is, indeed, a position of relative power, and unfortunately, different teams will have different approaches and attitudes. Try to learn the identities of the members early, and hope for someone with externship experience, or at least a minimum of biases. But remember a few things: if your program makes sense and you are convinced and passionate about its worth, the team is likely to see things clearly. And if you need resources, the team is likely to note that in the report, thereby encouraging the administration to give more support to your program. Few programs indeed have been closed as the result of accreditation visits. Approach the visit openly as a learning (and teaching) opportunity, in your own thinking and when interacting with the team. And communicate with the assigned visitor well before s/he arrives, to arrange for a cooperative and time-effective visit.

X. Go forth in Light, and joyfully sow the seeds of thy placements upon the fields. For though thou dwellest in toil with the doubtful and the weak of understanding, thou shalt be delivered mightily by the Light of thy Program, and thou shalt prosper in the Fields of Externship forever.

> This should be the natural result of creating an educationally responsible program, standing confidently behind it, and avoiding negative reactions to possible biases or negativity. The worth of your program will be well articulated and supported for you by your students, alumni, and at least some of your faculty. Additionally, quality clinical programs are increasingly demanded from outside the college — both by hiring attorneys and more skills-oriented regulatory standards. Stand clear and firm, approach difficulties honestly, care about your students, appreciate your work, stay positive,...and thrive.

Larry Krieger
Florida State University College of Law

#9: State Bar Association Meetings and Problems

I teach a seminar of twenty students in Problems in International Trade. Although I use a problem approach, I have been trying to develop a greater sense of real practice experience in this area of the law that our students are not likely to experience in clinic or any other skills course. I am attempting to do this in two ways.

The international law section of our state bar association meets once a month to discuss topics in international trade law. I am arranging with the section chairperson for my students to attend these meetings and for the topics discussed to track areas covered by the class during that month.

The second way of integrating problems actually encountered in the practice of international trade is to have members of the state bar association section develop, with my assistance, theoretical problems out of cases on which they are presently working. These problems will be assigned to a group of five students to research and to write a memo to me and to the practicing lawyer working on the case.

Eric C. Schneider
University of Baltimore School of Law

#10: Wills and Trusts Projects

Law students—and professors—often complain about second- and third-year courses. Typical complaints are: Teachers do all of the talking, the material is boring, and student interest in a particular subject varies widely from "All I want is to pass the bar examination," to "I plan to practice in this area."

I confront these problems in teaching a basic Trusts and Estates course, and have found that offering individual experiences, both in and out of the classroom, can stimulate student interest and learning. Here are my suggestions:

Law Reform: Help students to form interest groups to study various Uniform Probate Code proposals and make recommendations to the State Law Revision Commission, the Estates and Probate Section of the State Bar Association, the Real Property Probate & Trust Law Section of the American Bar Association, the American College of Trusts and Estates Counsel, or a state legislature.

Pro Bono Work: Encourage students to visit homes for the elderly and, under your supervision, help the residents to prepare simple wills, living wills, durable powers of attorney, etc.

Estate planning interview: Tell the students that they will get a lot more out of trusts and estates by talking to people about their experiences. Suggest to students that they find mock "clients" who will cooperate by allowing them to conduct estate planning interviews and to draft estate planning memos for them. Explain to the students that you will be available as a resource and that you will review their completed memos. If a student needs some guidance regarding how to go about making up an estate planning memo, consider providing supplementary materials or samples of memos done by other students.

"Invest a sum of money" project: Inform the students that trusts and estates attorneys need to be concerned with investment. To give them a feel for this, suggest that interested students pretend they have a certain amount of money to invest as a trustee. Have the students prepare a plan of investment.

Visit a probate court: Advise students to spend an hour or more at a local court. In addition to sitting at an actual hearing, the students might be able to arrange to interview court personnel or a judge.

Visit a bank trust department: Suggest that students visit a trust department and confer with a trust officer in order to gain a feeling of how the trust department operates.

Track the law of a state: Recommend that students follow the issues covered in class with research of the law in the state where the student plans to practice. Students will be able to compare more general materials with the more specific rules in their own jurisdictions. Urge students who are tracking individual states' laws to alert the class about local differences in the treatment of issues that arise in class.

Robert Whitman
University of Connecticut School of Law

#11: Using Doctors to Teach Law Students

Ten years ago, I left private practice as a trial lawyer to teach litigation-related courses such as Trial Advocacy and Evidence at the University of Arkansas at Little Rock School of Law. While I still teach those courses, I have added a Law and Medicine Seminar to my repertoire. I utilize physicians as expert witnesses in Trial Advocacy workshops to give my students an opportunity to examine real doctors in a simulated courtroom setting. My Law and Medicine students observe doctors at work and spend time communicating one-on-one with physicians.

The Philosophical Basis

The years I spent dealing with physicians as expert witnesses in bodily injury and medical negligence cases have given me some appreciation of the problems that physicians and lawyers experience when forced to communicate with each other. I have listened many times as lawyers attempted, without success, to elicit technical information from medical witnesses in a way that jurors could comprehend. Also, I have experienced firsthand the difficulty lawyers and physicians encounter when they are forced to converse across the chasm that separates the two professions' approaches to solving problems.

Each professional speaks its own peculiar dialect. Doctors and lawyers have different objectives. More significantly, the members of each profession are trained to approach problems in different ways. The physician seeking to diagnose and cure a patient's illness has no use for an adversary system of problem solving. The physician seeks data empirically and adopts no preconceived, desired diagnosis or treatment regime. The physician rejects no fact because that fact does not support a desired diagnosis. On the other hand, the lawyer-advocate always has a predetermined goal—the client's victory. The lawyer utilizes facts that support that result and rejects facts that do not.

The situation is complicated by the fact that lawyers and doctors often simply do not like each other. Many physicians believe that most of the problems with America's health care system can be attributed to lawyers who file frivolous suits against doctors. Conversely, some lawyers see physicians as overpaid, self-indulgent egotists, and virtually all lawyers agree that injured patients should have recourse against physicians' negligent blunders.

Despite these difficulties, doctors and lawyers are frequently thrown together in a courtroom, where it is critical that they overcome their inability to communicate and set aside their mutual aversion in order to convey vital information to a jury. One of the basic premises of my efforts to foster interaction between my students and practicing physicians is that medical evidence will be more effective—and further the goal of achieving fairer trial decisions—if the lawyers who ask the questions and the doctors who answer them have some elemental appreciation of the operational methods, the professional goals, and the semantic peculiarities of one another's professions.

Trial Advocacy

Our interdisciplinary efforts began when I telephoned the chairs of the Pathology and Psychiatry Departments at the University of Arkansas for Medical Sciences, seeking physicians to role-play expert witnesses in Trial Advocacy workshops. Much to my surprise, several residents and even some staff physicians volunteered. For a couple of years I continued that system of recruiting volunteer witnesses each year.

One day, the residency director in the Family Practice Department contacted me and suggested that UAMS require every Family Practice resident to participate as an expert witness in a Trial Advocacy workshop. This was music to my ears. I collaborated with a couple of UAMS physicians to develop a problem based on an actual patient's medical records. Since that day seven years ago, every Trial Advocacy workshop group has devoted a three-hour session to examining a "treating physician" in a mock bodily injury suit. The residents approach the experience eagerly, because they know it prepares them for the day when they will be called upon to serve as expert witnesses in real cases. These same residents later have an opportunity to show my Law and Medicine seminar students how they work in their natural habitat.

The next major step was when the director of Clinical Pathology Laboratories, a physician who has often testified as an expert witness, agreed to deliver a lecture to my Trial Advocacy class. After the lecture, he agreed to furnish pathology residents and staff physicians each year to testify as pathologists in Trial Advocacy workshops. He has continued to lecture to each Trial Advocacy class, and we have devoted one workshop session to the examination of forensic pathologists.

Law and Medicine Seminar

The Law and Medicine seminar is, on its face, a rather ordinary, two-credit law school elective. Enrollment is limited to twelve students in their final semester of law school. Each student is required to submit a paper for the final grade. There is no final examination.

However, our course is unique in that it allows each student to share in the working experiences of physicians. These field trips give my students an appreciation of the practice of medicine that no amount of reading or discussion could achieve.

One of our first field trips — not exciting, but essential to an understanding of the practice of medicine — is an afternoon each student spends in the Family Practice Clinic at UAMS paired one-on-one with a resident. The law student accompanies the resident, sitting in the room as the resident takes patient histories, performs physical examinations, and prescribes treatment. Of course, the clinic obtains prior patient approval of the law student's presence. Between patient appointments, students observe the physicians entering notes in patient records and also converse informally with the doctor to whom they are assigned. Each student then tours a hospital ward with the resident on call.

Another field trip requires students to visit the UAMS Gastroenterology Department for "morning rounds" and a roundtable discussion, at which the director of the department reviews cases with the attending physician, the residents, the fellows, and medical students. Afterward, the students observe an endoscopy procedure.

Students also spend a busy evening shift in the Emergency Room at University Hospital. The students often stay all night, and are sometimes pressed into service to help hold down violent patients, to wheel gurneys, or to sop blood. This experience gives students an appreciation for the sometimes heroic nature of a physician's work that no other experience imparts.

Students also spend a morning in the operating room observing surgery. After standing at surgeons' sides during operations, students typically emerge with a new understanding of the technical and physically demanding nature of surgery, as well as the high level of tension in an operating room.

Finally, I take the students in small groups to the state medical examiner's morgue to observe an autopsy. The medical examiner selects cases of suspected homicide or other particular interest to future lawyers. The students usually approach the morgue with some trepidation, expecting to undergo a grisly ordeal. They are frequently surprised by the clinical, non-gruesome atmosphere that surrounds post-mortem examinations.

Observation of an autopsy often is something of a metaphysical experience. These visits usually stimulate discussion, in and out of class, of the mystical nature of life, of the overwhelmingly obvious absence of the spark of life in corpses, of violence in society, and of the need to control the availability of guns. To see death helps us appreciate life.

Conclusion

My interdisciplinary efforts are based on an abiding belief that when lawyers and doctors have opportunities to meet and share experiences in nonadversarial situations, greater mutual understanding and respect usually result. Mutual understanding and respect can only benefit our patients and clients.

W. Dent Gitchel
University of Arkansas at Little Rock School of Law

#12: Motion Docket Observation and Evaluation

At the beginning of each new semester, the new interns for our real-client clinical program have an orientation period to familiarize them with the local court procedures, clinical program office procedures, and general family law statutes and mandatory, statewide forms. As part of that orientation, interns are required to observe four family law motion dockets.

The intern records the following information: (1) date of docket; (2) name of case; (3) commissioner hearing case; (4) respondent's attorney; (5) petitioner's attorney; (6) type of motion; (7) issues being argued; (8) decision; (9) your reaction to decision (i.e., fair and equitable?); (10) good points of the arguments and attorney styles; (11) aspects of the argument or style that were poor or ineffective; and (12) why they were ineffective.

This forces the interns to familiarize themselves not only with the local courtrooms and family law procedures, but also with the various court commissioners and their approaches to decision-making. The interns frequently compare notes and reach conclusions about members of the bench. They also begin to know the family law members of the bar who may well be opposing counsel at some future date.

Submitted Anonymously

#13: Administrative Hearings — Testimony and Reports

In this article, I describe what has now become a standard (and increasingly popular) assignment in my Administrative Law class: requiring students to attend an administrative hearing of a federal, state, or county agency during the course of the semester. In addition to attending the hearing, students must prepare and hand in written testimony at the hearing; giving oral testimony is optional, but I encourage them to do so. They must then turn in a copy of their written testimony to me, along with a written report. The report must include:

1. Name of agency and source of notice for the hearing.
2. Subject matter and purpose of the hearing.
3. Date, time, and place of the hearing.
4. Length of hearing, identity of person(s) presiding, and number of attendees and their affiliations.
5. Procedures used in the hearing, such as sign-in sheets and/or testifiers, order of testifiers, time limits on testimony, opportunities for dialogue with person(s) presiding, etc.
6. Student's observations of the hearing regarding its effectiveness in accomplishing the goals of public hearings in general and this hearing in specific.
7. Any other observations he/she wants to include.

The students are responsible for finding a hearing at which the agency accepts written public testimony. Their report and copies of their testimony are due the last week of classes.

This assignment is typically worth 30 percent of the final grade. I weight the assignment this way to let students know that I consider this experience an important part of the course and to discourage procrastination. Because agencies often hold hearings irregularly, I strongly suggest to the students that they start looking for hearings early in the semester; doing so also gives them adequate time to research and prepare their written testimony. I put on reserve in the law library a handout on drafting written testimony, as well as examples of sample testimony. (Student questions to me on drafting testimony decreased about 75 percent once I started making the handout available.) Also, at a student's request, I will read and critique drafts of written testimony prior to the hearing; however, few students take advantage of this opportunity.

As the semester progresses, I check their progress by asking what, if any, hearings they have identified and encourage oral reports to the class once the student has attended a hearing. These oral reports illustrate the variety of experiences that can occur at an administrative hearing. Some attend controversial hearings with hundreds of participants and hours of heated testimony; others find they are the only ones at the hearing other than the agency staff. In the latter case, the students often engage the staff in a discussion after the hearing to gain a better sense of whether their experience is typical for the agency.

By having to attend hearings, students experience firsthand the frustrations and the benefits of agency process. They discover that hearings are often held at inconvenient times and in inconvenient locations with limited parking. As one student reported: "I arrived at the office about ten minutes before the hearing began. (I would have been there earlier if not for the frantic minutes I spent searching for a legal parking space in that part of Kakaako)."

Some students are surprised to learn that between the time they picked up the material pertinent to the hearing and the hearing itself the subject matter of the hearing was amended. For example, last semester two students prepared testimony on a permit to place a particular cellular phone service antenna at one location. They discovered at the hearing that both the configuration of the antenna and the placement had been changed without notice to the public. What appeared from reading the statute to be clear, straightforward requirements of public notice and opportunity for comment took on new meaning for these students.

Students also learn which agencies are helpful in supplying information to prepare for the hearing and which seem to view the public as an annoyance. The following student received an important lesson in public information while completing the assignment:

> Getting the information necessary to write my testimony proved to be a very educational experience. At the DLNR, a secretary or receptionist standing near the counter immediately asked if she could help. I told her the date of the hearing, the application number, and asked to see the public record. Seeming completely surprised and confused, she disappeared into the abyss of cubicles located in the rear of the office. Just as I began to think she was lost forever, she returned and informed me that someone would be with me shortly. After about five minutes, I was told by a gentleman that the application had been assigned to a planner, I think her name is Eileen, who was at lunch. I should wait 15 minutes and then ask 'someone' if she had returned, he said. I was very surprised and disap-

pointed that information regarding the subject of a public hearing was not accessible during all business hours. Over the next 15 minutes, I saw two other women enter, stand at the counter, and wait to be helped. The three of us must have been invisible because neither the receptionist nor the other employees returning from their lunch asked if we needed assistance.

Not all students confront such uncooperative staff. Many are pleased when agency staff thank them for their testimony. Others would like to be more anonymous:

An administrator for the Liquor Commission told Kevin [another student] that we should sit in the front of the hearing room and submit our written testimony so it could be read into the record. The revelation that our written testimony would be read into the record sent waves of panic rippling through our group.[Six other law students attended the same hearing.]

Still others are dismayed when the agency makes a decision at the end of the hearing, obviously not having taken the time to read their testimony. As one student quipped: "So much for their responsibility to consider the whole record before making a decision."

All report that the experience, which some viewed with skepticism early in the semester, taught them valuable lessons that cannot be imparted in the classroom. I found the following comments by a student to be particularly compelling.

I learned that I should have been prepared to testify even though the outcome was decided and there was nothing at stake. I kicked myself all the way home for not taking Commissioner Jervis' somewhat personal challenge to testify. The more I thought about it, the more embarrassed I was. The lesson here was that I was sloppy and too reserved. Even with the [seemingly] predetermined outcome, I should have used my best efforts to represent my school and myself. Concerned about my future as a litigator, I promised myself that from now on I would be better prepared and eager to present my arguments when asked.

If you believe, as I do, that clinical experiences can be a valuable addition to a standard law school class, I urge you to find opportunities in your community for students to experience the living, breathing reality of the concepts they are learning in the classroom. If so, you will find, as I have, that your teaching, the student, the law school, and the wider community will benefit.

Casey Jarman
University of Hawai'i at Manoa
William S. Richardson School of Law

Chapter 6

Reconstructing the Classroom Through Collaborative Learning

Learning is something students do, not something that is done to students. — Johnson, Johnson, and Holubec

In law school, students primarily work alone. The students take tests alone, respond or ask questions in class alone, and participate in out-of-class assignments alone. The culture of law school is a competitive one, rewarding the victors of the grading system, law review, moot court and trial advocacy competitions. Competing successfully is taken as a measure of the competency level of the future attorney.

In legal education, cooperation tends to be unrewarded. While it is morally preferable, there are few incentives for students to cooperate, particularly when compared to the incentives to compete. Even the collaborative study group appears to have a short shelf life, used by students in the first year of school and then abandoned as unnecessary.

Given this background, it is not surprising that collaborative learning historically has not been a productive part of legal education. In addition to the perception that it is "soft" and "anticompetitive," the history and culture of legal education have relegated such a method to foreign status, certainly not readily assimilated into a "Socratic dialogue."

Yet, collaborative skills have been recognized as important to society and to lawyering. Lawyers often work in firms, try cases in teams, and work with other attorneys to achieve mutual ends. In other avenues of education, cooperation is recognized as a skill that can be learned and refined. Significantly, there is a growing belief that cooperation is a valued competitive skill, not, as many have believed, the antithesis of competition.

If knowledge is communicated and created through dialogue — Socratic or other — and is constructed through consensus, collaborative learning certainly would be helpful to individuals participating in a group process. Ironically, the Socratic dialogue is premised on a similar theory — through conversation, insight and knowledge will emerge.

There is significant support for this view of conversation as a progenitor of knowledge. To L.S. Vygotsky, for example, reflective thought is merely internalized conversation. In an essay titled "The Voice of Poetry in the Conversation of Mankind," Michael Oakeshott called education a "conversation in which we learn to recognize the voices, to distinguish the proper occasions of utterance, and in which we acquire the intellectual and moral habits appropriate to conversation." The cultural anthropologist, Clifford Geertz, has said that "human thought is consummately social: social in its origins, social in its functions, social in its form, social in its applications."

Applying this conceptualization to legal education, the conversation that is developed in the classroom is crucial to the learning that occurs. While the Socratic dialogue is one form of conversation, a collaborative conversation between students can be just as significant. Unlike the lecture format or even the Socratic questioning style, the collaborative method shifts to students in significant part the responsibility for furthering the classroom conversation. While other methods, such as writing exercises, also serve to transfer the responsibility of the classroom learning, the collaborative approach adds the dynamic of interpersonal skills.

In addition to its social benefits, collaborative learning can enhance the accuracy of the learning process. The individualistic approach to learning assumes that each individual hears what is said accurately, assimilates it as spoken, and then reconstitutes it in a meaningful and precise manner. If these assumptions are in error, however (and studies show they often are), collaborative learning can be used to correct any flaws in an individual's learning process. Collaboration can assist students in achieving a more accurate and more realistic understanding of what the subject matter means.

Hundreds of studies have demonstrated that collaborative learning is more effective than competitive or individualistic learning methods for a broad spectrum of cognitive, affective, and interpersonal goals. Collaborative learning is an efficient and effective method to achieve objectives central to legal education: critical thinking, reasoning, and problem solving. Learning in groups helps students understand, retain, and apply concepts. Well-run small-group activities increase students' motivation and lead to students' positive attitudes towards the subject matter. In addition, collaboration among students helps them develop skills such as listening, expression, conflict resolution, negotiation, and consensus building. Finally, collaborative learning in heterogeneous groups results in students expanding and deepening their understanding of different perspectives of students from various backgrounds.

A. Introducing Collaborative Learning

Collaborative learning is a strategy for learning that places students in teams to accomplish several structured tasks. Each of the students in a team has a specific role and assignment, so that the accomplishments are both individual and group-oriented. The basic elements involve interdependence among team members, face-to-face interaction between students, and individuated responsibility for the group's effectiveness. This "positive interdependence" is intended to produce a higher level of learning than if every member of the team acted alone.

Of particular significance is the creation of heterogeneous working groups, rather than groups that are organized homogeneously. For example, heterogeneous groups will have members of different gender, backgrounds, and abilities. The dynamics and process of the group matter as well as the outcome.

Collaborative methodology has been adapted to different goals and contexts. One such method involves divisions based on teams and goals, in which heterogeneous groups of students work together to achieve specific tasks. Other cooperative methods include: the "jigsaw," in which student-teams tackle only portions of assignments (much like junior attorneys working on a big case in a large firm), with all of the teams' work equaling the whole assignment; "teams-games-tournaments," in which team competitions replace quizzes as measures of performance; and group investigation, where the focus of the activity is cooperative group inquiry.

B. How Are Collaborative Techniques Constructed?

Collaborative techniques can be broken down into stages. These stages do not reflect either a group form of Socratic method or an uncontrolled cooperative session, but rather a thoughtful and deliberative learning program. One such framework for collaborative learning follows.

1. One Model: Classroom Consensus Groups

One form of collaborative learning endeavor is the classroom consensus group. This involves dividing up a class into smaller working groups to work on a limited but open-ended task, negotiating among themselves what they think and know in order to arrive at some kind of consensus or agreement, including, sometimes, agreement to disagree. The class is then reconvened as a whole to discuss what the small groups have done and to see if a larger consensus is possible.

a. Specify Task Objectives

It is important initially to specify precisely what performances are sought in the collaborative exercise. Studies have shown that the greater the detail in which students explain the relevant concepts, the more likely the exercise will succeed. Also, the description of the performance should be some sort of measurable competency, not an aspirational ideal. Instead of having students "understand" a concept, for example, they should be able to "recite" it or "write an answer to a problem" or the like. Furthermore, students ought to be informed about the expected nature and detail of their participation.

b. Creating Collaborative Groups

Several issues arise in the creation of groups. The first is the size of the group. As group size increases, the interpersonal challenges grow. Many researchers recommend groups of three to six students. The second issue is the selection of group members. It is generally recommended that the teacher choose the specific groups and not let students self-select. Self-selection usually leads to homogeneity and not the novelty of working with people with a variety of backgrounds. The third issue is the duration of the group. Some groups may be maintained for the entire course; other groups may have a short duration, working together only for a single doctrinal area or even one hypothetical.

c. Provide Group Instructions, Roles, and Individual Goals

It is extremely important to clearly communicate to the groups the kinds of behaviors that comprise the goals of the collaborative project. That is, what skills are being taught, what is their relevancy and how can those skills be practiced and mastered? Illuminating the relevancy of skills promotes interest and motivation on the part of the participants. Explaining how skills work means how to practice them and what mastery looks like. The conduct-oriented mastery can be observed through periodic demonstrations by various group members. Thus, in a contracts class that is participating in a drafting exercise, the class could be stopped periodically to illustrate how a particular provision could be written.

When the practice occurs through role-playing, it is important to assign roles with specific instructions. The role-playing allows students to adopt a particular perspective and to challenge the roles of others. The roles in a law class could be law firm oriented and include partner and associate. More generic roles could include a writer, editor, and presenter.

d. Create Monitoring and Intervention Plan

A monitoring and intervention plan is helpful in maintaining the desired course of action. Monitoring can occur from designated members of the groups or by the teacher. If the teacher is doing the monitoring, the observation should be focused on particular skills and data should be gathered on each group. This data should be used to check on the performances, but should also be offered to each group—or even the whole class—as feedback. Thus, the teacher can illustrate a point using the way one group has accomplished that point, or can inform a group specifically what is going wrong and work through how to correct the difficulty.

e. Provide for Closure and Feedback

It is essential that the students are given feedback on their performance. This feedback is best given on a periodic basis and not simply at the conclusion of an exercise. The feedback serves not only as a mirror for the student, but as a mechanism for improvement and accreditation for competent performances.

Closure, ironically, does not occur with the provision of feedback and is not provided by the teacher but by the students themselves. It may involve the students' explaining what they have learned to some other students or to actively reviewing the task at hand.

As part of or following the closure process, assessment and evaluation can occur. The evaluation can be self-determined (students rating their own performance) or determined by the teacher. Specific measurements are preferable to a general "grade" or cursory assessment.

2. Other Collaborative Learning Models

Collaborative learning in law school need not focus solely on solving hypotheticals. Instead, collaborative learning exercises can involve writing or formal peer tutoring. These models can be used to supplement or even supplant the traditional learning methods in the classroom.

a. Collaborative Writing

The value of collaborative writing is premised on the importance of writing to the construction of knowledge. It has long been advocated that writing is not just an extension of knowledge, but a reflection of analytical skills—specifically, how a student has learned and organized that knowledge. Thus, writing deficiencies suggest a discrete problem with a particular skill as well as a problem with the underlying analytical ability.

Writing exercises abound. Students could respond to hypotheticals as "law firm associates" or engage in the legal drafting of a document, such as a contract for a client. The premise of the collaborative writing model is that writing ability can be enhanced by editing or creating a descriptive synopsis of another's paper—providing feedback on what exactly is being communicated in the writing.

b. Tutoring and Feedback

Peer tutoring or peer review places students in a supportive yet hierarchical role—that of assisting another through feedback. Peer review can provide information and data to other students that they might not get in any other formal context. A peer review model first depends on students' preparing a writing assignment individually, either in class or outside of class. The peer tutoring or review then can occur in class, in teams, or in small groups. The peer review has two stages. It first requires the reviewing student to write out a descriptive outline of the other student's work. Then, in stage two, the reviewing student offers—verbally or in writing—a prescriptive evaluation of the work.

These are just some of the collaborative techniques that are being used in all levels of education. How these methods have been adapted to legal education by law teachers around the country follows.

References

Kenneth Bruffee, Collaborative Learning: Higher Education, Interdependence, and the Authority of Knowledge 28 (1995).

James Cooper, et al. Cooperative Learning and College Instruction, Effective Use of Student Learning Teams (1990).

David Johnson, Roger Johnson , Edythe Holubec, Cooperative Learning in the Classroom 4 (1994).

David Johnson, Roger Johnson, Karl Smith, Cooperative Learning: Increasing College Faculty Instructional Productivity (1991).

William M. Timpson & Paul Bendel-Simso, Concepts and Choices for Teaching: Meeting the Challenges in Higher Education 109–119 (1996) .

Specific Ideas for Cooperative Learning and Small Groups

#1: Structuring Collaborative Exercises

Collaborative learning exercises serve a variety of learning objectives. Because they provide an active learning experience and engage all students in the learning process, collaborative learning exercises help students develop their analytical, reasoning, communication, and interpersonal skills. Moreover, they help increase tolerance of difference because, in working in a more intimate environment, students learn to appreciate different points of view, learning styles, and approaches to problem solving.

Collaborative learning exercises benefit all students. Students who are strong in a given area benefit by explaining a concept they already understand or by explaining their reasoning because they have to articulate their ideas and respond to questions. Weaker students benefit because the stronger students will explain the concept or reasoning. Often, students are more effective in explaining a concept or reasoning because they have just recently figured it out for themselves, so they are much closer to the experience of not understanding. Because they are much closer to this experience, they may be aware of the steps they had to take in order to understand. Finally, weaker students must at some point articulate their own reasoning, and the smaller-group setting offers a much less threatening environment.

Common concerns about collaborative learning exercises are that they can be time consuming; some students may dominate the smaller group; the teacher has less control over the content of the session because he or she cannot listen in on every group at once; and students can get off track or fail to take the exercise seriously. However, these problems can be overcome by reviewing group process skills and expectations, selecting group composition appropriate for the particular exercise, setting up a specific and detailed agenda, building in some accountability for each individual group member, debriefing in a large group, and interacting with the groups.

Review Group Processing Skills

Because most students' prior learning experiences are primarily competitive, students need to know how to work effectively in groups. Thus, you should clearly explain the dynamics of group processing, discuss different learning styles, establish ground rules such as mutual respect, and teach active listening skills. This way, students will be able to more quickly establish rapport with each other and will create a safe learning environment within the small-group setting.

Select Group Composition

In selecting group members, you should consider the task at hand, the purpose of the exercise, and the ability of the students. Research indicates that the optimal number of students per group is three; however, depending upon the task, a group of five may be appropriate. Groups larger than five tend to get off track or have dominating members. Students can be grouped randomly, homogeneously by ability or learning style, or heterogeneously. Random grouping works well for introducing new topics and having the students brainstorm. Homogeneous grouping based on ability is useful for developing analytical skills when some students have mastered the topic or concept, but others are still lagging behind. In the homogeneous grouping, those students who have mastered the basics can advance to more sophisticated problems and challenges, while those students who are still struggling with the basics can continue to work on basic problems. The teacher can spend more time with the groups working at the basic level without slowing down the other students. The heterogeneous grouping works well when students are working on a new concept or topic. Some students may be further along than others, but the concept is still new enough that the stronger students would not be stifled by spending more time reinforcing their basic understanding.

Set a Specific Agenda

After determining group composition, you should develop a specific agenda and detailed tasks for the groups. Give an estimate of how much time they should spend on each specific task. Assign roles for each group member. For example, one member should be the recorder, one the reporter, and one the timekeeper or taskmaster. Other roles could be discussion leader, summarizer, assimilator, or conceptualizer. You could also assign students to play specific roles for a simulated client interview, oral argument, settlement conference, etc.

Give *written* instructions for what you want the group to discuss and what you want the group to produce from their discussion. Providing written instructions communicates your commitment to the success of the group process, gives students something to review to help them stay on task, and builds critical reading skills. Examples of effective collaborative assignments include having the group identify the main points of a reading assignment or argument, prepare a presentation to the class, analyze a hypothetical and then prepare an outline of their analysis, or critique a written answer and then revise it.

Sometimes it is helpful to provide the agenda and tasks in writing before you plan to use them. This allows students to prepare for the group exercise in a more sophisticated manner. Assigning roles and tasks in advance also allows for more creative and challenging exercises and reduces the amount of class time spent on setting up the exercise.

Build Accountability

While agenda and task setting helps to keep the group focused, building in individual accountability helps keep all the students engaged in the learning exercise. Some ways to hold students accountable include having each student summarize the group's discussion or outline the group's analysis in writing, respond to questions in the debrief, or change groups and exchange ideas generated from the previous group.

Debrief

Debriefing with the entire class, especially if you call on students randomly, can be another way of holding students accountable. But the more important reasons for debriefing are to reclaim some control over the content of the learning, to summarize major points, and to provide a check for students to evaluate their learning. Debriefing is especially important when students have engaged in role-playing exercises. This debriefing should include some discussion of how it felt to be in those roles as well as what they learned from the process itself.

Interact

Finally, be actively involved with the groups. Circulate among them to ensure that they stay on task and to help group members who are having difficulty. Such interaction communicates your commitment to the students, their learning, and the collaborative process.

I have used collaborative learning exercises in my classes for years. In my experience, it not only helps students learn but, more importantly, it helps them build community both within and outside the classroom, develop a greater sense of respect for one another, and keep them in touch with their own humanity. This is no small feat in law school.

Paula Lustbader
Seattle University School of Law

#2: Designing Cooperative Learning Experiences

Cooperative learning is a form of instruction in which small groups of students work together on an academic task. Cooperative learning focuses on structures designed to ensure student-student interdependence. I teach first-year Torts, and my sections have varied in size from forty-five to ninety students. I have successfully used cooperative learning as a teaching method in large classes.

Here's how I implement cooperative learning in a large class:

- Define objectives. I make course objectives, unit objectives, and lesson objectives. The cooperative learning technique that I decide to use is based on the objective I'm trying to achieve.

- Decide on how to structure positive interdependence. To create goal interdependence, I allow only one answer or work product from the group. To create resource interdependence, I sometimes assign group members responsibilities for reading different resources and for teaching the other members in the group about that resource. To create task interdependence, I sometimes assign each student a task that contributes to the group effectiveness. To create role interdependence, I often assign roles in the group; the most common roles are summarizer, recorder, and checker for understanding.

- Decide on size. Cooperative learning literature suggests that groups of three to six are best, with four recommended as the ideal number. I form the basic group around four for classroom work, since smaller groups require more individual interaction. However, sometimes I use groups of two for in-class activities. I use groups of six for written work, so I have fewer responses to read.

- Assign students to groups. I assign seats to provide for heterogeneous groups based on Myers-Briggs type, gender, race, age, and prior academic performance. I try to assure that in any group of four there are at least two women, two persons of color (preferably of the same ethnic/racial background), and two Myers-Briggs "feeling" types. After the first semester, I reassign seats to provide opportunity for students to work with different individuals and to provide diversity in performance.

- Arrange the room. Since furniture cannot be moved and time is limited, an important step is structuring the large class so students do not have to move to be in their cooperative learning groups. It is important that members of a learning group sit closely enough that they can share materials, maintain eye contact with each other, talk quietly, and exchange ideas in a comfortable atmosphere. While the room does get fairly noisy with twelve to twenty or more groups working, groups have never complained about that aspect of the process.

- Choose materials. I usually use materials that are part of the assigned reading for that day.

- Choose the cooperative learning technique. There are many cooperative learning strategies. I have tended to utilize the following three less-complex strategies:
  1. *Think-write-pair-share*: A question is posed to students before class. Students think about the question and a response before class. In class, students pair with a member of their group to discuss their responses and write a pair response. Students then share their pair response with the other pair in their group and refine a response for the group. The group shares its response with the whole class. The class critiques, analyzes, and discusses the group responses. I have used this technique in helping students analyze cases and for analyzing hypotheticals. I find that the caliber of the discussion is enhanced by this technique, and all students have an opportunity to learn by both reflection and verbalization.
  2. *Three-step interview*: Students interview one another in pairs, alternating roles. They then share in their four-member learning team the information or insights gleaned from the paired interviews. While I have used this as a team-builder, I have also used it to allow students to share ideas, hypotheses, or reactions to the assigned materials.
  3. *Numbered heads together*: Members of the learning team count off 1, 2, 3, and 4. I pose a question that involves some higher-order thinking skills. The students discuss the question, making certain that everyone knows the answer or the arguments. I call a specific number and the designated team members respond as group spokespersons.
- Do any necessary teaching. I package the cooperative learning strategies between other teaching methods. Consequently, I usually do a mini-lecture to explain concepts important to the exercise.
- Explain to the class the academic task and the criteria for success. My criteria for success are that everyone comes prepared to the group and that everyone participates in the group.
- Start the groups. I place my objectives, instructions, and time limits on the blackboard. If the activity is a short assignment—three to five minutes—I stay at the podium. If the activity is a longer one—fifteen to twenty minutes—I leave the room for four to five minutes to give the groups the opportunity to get started. When I return, I circulate among the groups to

monitor group effectiveness and to provide task assistance or cooperative skills assistance.

- Provide closure to the task. I have the class reunite. I have some of the groups report. I start a discussion and get reactions to the reports.
- Provide closure to small-group activity. The first several times that I use a cooperative learning technique, I ask the students to write down one or two things their group did well and one thing their group could improve on next time.

Vernellia R. Randall
University of Dayton School of Law

#3: Three-Minute Discussions

The most challenging pedagogical task in teaching classes with enrollment in excess of seventy-five is getting everyone motivated to participate in the discussions.

I have found that only about ten or fifteen students normally participate in the discussions in large classes. The rest of the students sit back and let the small cadre of students do the work for them. I wanted to turn this around; I wanted to be more passive and I wanted the entire class (not just the usual discussion leaders) to be more active. Here is my idea:

On the first day of class, I break the class into groups of three (e.g., in a class of ninety students, there will be thirty small groups). I tell these groups they are to work together throughout the semester. Each time the class meets, a different person in the small group acts as a reporter or spokesperson for the group.

From time to time, I will ask the groups to work on problems, hypotheticals, and doctrinal issues that come up in our large-class discussions. For example, I ask the groups to work on problems like the following: "The defendant in this case is arguing that Case X applies to the instant case. Give me three arguments the plaintiff would likely make in distinguishing Case X from the instant case. You have three minutes to come up with the three arguments. The spokesperson will report the results of your group output to the class. Okay, start!"

There will then be thirty small-group discussions taking place. The entire classroom is buzzing with discussion. At this point, I am watching the time, taking a break, and collecting my thoughts for the next topic of discussion. At the end of the *three* minutes (I am very strict about the time), I call the class back to attention and ask for hands of spokespersons. Everyone seems interested in learning what the various groups have come up with.

I have used small-group exercises in both upper-level and first-year classes in this way.

Gary Minda
Brooklyn Law School

#4: Cooperative Learning Groups in a Large Class

A cooperative learning technique I use is to divide a large class (up to approximately 70 students) into groups of five to seven students. Normally, I use this device in first-year courses, but it also works well in upper-division courses. The various benefits of this technique are outlined below.

The members of each group are chosen by me and follow the race and gender composition of the class to the extent possible. I try to designate the groups by the second class meeting. The group members must sit in designated seats, clustered around each other. The class breaks into groups when needed to examine concepts that have created difficulties for the students and to consider problems and hypotheticals. On many days, small-group discussion is unnecessary. However, in first-year courses small groups are particularly effective in the early weeks of the first semester. While engaged in group discussion, I am available only to clarify facts. The time spent in groups depends upon the topic considered, but in most instances I limit the time to approximately ten minutes. Usually, the group reports the essence of its discussion to the entire class. The group spokesperson changes with each report.

This technique helps achieve several goals:

1) I believe that it will aid students' understanding of the material for several reasons: the opportunity to hear another explanation of the material (sometimes a student will more readily comprehend an issue when it is explained by a peer); the opportunity to ask what a student might perceive as a "dumb question" (no matter how many times I stress that student questions are helpful, some students will be more comfortable asking them to a small group); and the opportunity to advocate one's own interpretation and test it in the group.
2) Breaking into small groups may actually free up class time since minor questions may be asked and answered in the group.
3) Group discussion gives each student an opportunity to be part of the discussion. In a large class it's easy for students to allow their more vocal colleagues to dominate the discussion. In a small group it is likely that all will engage in dialogue.

4) Students will learn to listen more closely to and value the opinions of their classmates. Some students believe that the important thoughts come only from the teacher. In the group, they have the opportunity to consider the views of each member in a setting where I do not contribute to the discussion.
5) Since the groups are diverse, I believe that group members will at least hear, and optimally contemplate, viewpoints to which they previously may not have been exposed.
6) The students learn that group problem solving is an efficient and effective way to address problems.
7) It helps keep students awake!
8) The difficulties of connecting with a study group are mitigated since each student now has a group for study and support.

Rick Nowka
Louis D. Brandeis School of Law University of Louisville

#5: Network for Cooperative Learning in Higher Education

The Network for Cooperative Learning in Higher Education is committed to disseminating information concerning research and practice relating to cooperative learning in higher education. Cooperative learning is a structured, systematic, instructional strategy in which small groups work together toward common goals. Research on cooperative learning indicates that it has a powerful effect on a number of student cognitive and attitudinal measures. The technique may have particular impact on women and minority students. The Network was founded in 1990 through a grant to California State University, Dominguez Hills from the Fund for the Improvement of Postsecondary Education (FIPSE) in the U.S. Department of Education.

The Network has co-sponsored a national conference dealing with cooperative learning and higher education and has affiliated itself with other groups attempting to foster active-learning strategies in higher education such as the International Society for Exploring Teaching Alternatives and the National Center on Postsecondary Teaching, Learning and Assessment.

Legal educators may contact the Network for information and materials on cooperative learning, including annotated bibliographies, research summaries, workbooks, videos, and other materials. Network personnel and consultants are available to answer questions relating to cooperative learning in higher education and to present workshops. The Network publishes a newsletter entitled COOPERATIVE LEARNING AND COLLEGE TEACHING which presents research and theory in cooperative learning but which focuses largely on applications of cooperative learning to the college classroom. Persons interested in subscribing to the newsletter should contact New Forums Press, P.O. Box 876, Stillwater, OK 74076 (tel. 405-372-6158, e-mail: NewForums@aol.com). Those interested in other services of the Network should contact its director, Dr. Jim Cooper, CSUDH, 1000 E. Victoria, Carson, CA 90747 (tel. 310-243-3961, e-mail: jcooper@dhvx20.csudh.edu).

Jim Cooper
California State University (Dominguez Hills)

#6: Pair Participation in Large Classes

Some students come to class to take notes. Others, who wish to participate, are reluctant to speak in a large class. To encourage all students to actively engage in a large class, exercises in pairs—groups of two—can be used. Students can first be asked to write down a response to a question and then to share their responses with their neighbor. (If the question is similar to an issue spotter, the neighbor also can be asked to edit and/or critique the writing as well.)

Another variation is to have one of the students in each pair play a witness, client, or opposing counsel. Then ask all of the pairs in the class to role-play a problem or exercise such as a client interview or witness examination. After a short period of time in which all of the students participate, a pair of students can be used in a demonstration to the entire class.

A third variation is a form of in-class study group. Based on the belief that repetition reinforces knowledge and promotes understanding, students can be asked to explain the meaning of a rule or principle to a partner in class. This is done to provide each student with feedback (from their neighbor) about whether they understand the rule and can communicate it well.

While these tools make for a noisy classroom (since all of the pairs are active simultaneously), the techniques promote participation and contributions from all of the students, do not result in a loss of control and do not take up a significant amount of time.

Steven Friedland
Nova Southeastern University Shepard Broad Law Center

#7: Think Group Share

The Bluebook can be boring. Discovering that my legal writing class had not a clue about Bluebook form and fearing the tedium of a conventional approach, I used the following one-hour lesson to teach the basics. It worked. Students were engaged throughout the lesson and (to my surprise) complimented me on it afterwards.

I asked each student to bring a copy of the Bluebook to class and passed out a problem set (eight problems) at the beginning of class. I allowed students thirty minutes to work individually on the problem set. I then divided the class into eight groups of three and asked the members of each group to spend twenty minutes coming to consensus on their answers. Finally, I asked each group to report one answer to the class as a whole for discussion. I allowed ten minutes for this portion of the lesson.

In the discussion, I asked whether the reported answer was correct and why, requiring the participant to cite to the appropriate provision in the Bluebook and inviting disagreement from other students. In all cases, someone had the correct answer with an appropriate citation supporting that answer.

Result: The class members taught each other the Bluebook and enjoyed doing so.

Theodore Seto
Loyola Law School (Los Angeles)

#8: Teaching Discovery Through Small-Group Discovery About the Final Exam

I have often used small-group exercises, but if no incentive is provided, some students will slack off, while those who participate will feel burdened and may even have their grades harmed by participating in an exercise when they could be studying graded material. If a grade is used to provide an incentive, students may be too competitive to get the benefits of talking through ideas with one another.

Another difficulty I have had is teaching discovery effectively. What the students need is experience in thinking about how to use discovery, and reviewing cases in the book doesn't provide this.

One of my exercises in Civil Procedure resolves both these problems: providing the practical exercises that I believe are necessary in teaching discovery, and providing the incentive necessary to encourage participation. I allow the students to use the discovery rules to discover information relevant to the final exam. The desire to do well on the exam creates its own incentive for participation. Because the students share all results, they think cooperatively, not competitively. Finally, they get to thinking about discovery as a related series of rules that they can use.

I try to have about fifteen groups and divide the class into groups of from two to four members, depending on class size, through the primitive device of drawing lines through the alphabetical list of class members. Each group must act unanimously and can request the production of documents, ask an interrogatory, or designate someone to ask a deposition question. Each "discrete subpart" of a discovery request counts as a separate request. There is no automatic disclosure under rule 26(a)(1) and no duty to supplement.

Discovery is in waves. I allow an initial deposition, followed by submissions of interrogatories and requests for production, followed by my reply to the interrogatories and requests for production, followed by a final deposition.

I encourage different groups to coordinate with others to eliminate duplicative questions and tell the students that ideally they will collaborate on an overall, class-wide plan for discovery and that they may want to select one member from each group to participate in an overall allocation of responsibility and then meet separately as groups for drafting. The exercise is preceded by a handout along the following lines:

> Most cases get resolved before trial. Thus, pre-trial discovery has become one of the most important skills for litigators. However, knowing the individual rules of discovery doesn't make someone good at discovery. Real mastery of discovery requires at least two additional skills.
>
> First, you need the ability to think strategically about how you can use combinations of the rules to have an overall plan for discovery. Thinking strategically requires you to consider the advantages of different types of discovery. Some types of discovery allow you more flexibility and surprise; other types of discovery make it harder for an opponent to keep information from you just because an individual doesn't remember things. I hope that the exercise will encourage you to develop this sort of thinking, not only in discovery, but elsewhere.
>
> A second additional requirement for being good at discovery is to use indirection to get what you want. Here's an example from our police-stop hypothetical [in which the students come up with class definitions for victims of alleged police brutality]: In pursuing the case, you want to discover instances of police brutality following a traffic stop. If you ask the police department, "Identify all instances of police brutality following a traffic stop," they will cheerfully reply, "There weren't any." (If there were cases where a jury awarded damages for police brutality, they'll tell you — but no gain to you, because you probably knew about them already.) That's probably a defensible position on their part, so you'll have used up one of your interrogatories to no effect.
>
> Many interrogatories I've seen in practice look like this example: They use loaded language, either because they want the party to build a case against itself or because they use language as one might in cross-examination, to suggest to the jury an answer even if the witness denies it. However, the loaded words often narrow the scope of the question, leaving a loophole for the other party.

Proceeding by indirection, you could ask for all instances in which an initial traffic stop led to an arrest of someone on charges of resisting arrest, which were later dropped. The fit between the cases you've identified with this question and your image of police brutality cases won't be exact, but it's a darn sight better than anything you're going to get out of the police department if you ask directly about police brutality. This question can be tinkered with at the margins: you might eliminate the requirement that charges be dropped, or say that you wanted to know about charges of resisting arrest that ended in acquittal, or ask about traffic stops where the police subsequently called for an ambulance. Answers to these questions will identify situations where no complaint was made, but where you might want to investigate further. Asking questions like this also tends to reduce objections on the grounds of irrelevance.

Here, you don't know if all of the final exam has been written yet. As a back-up to questions about the exam itself, you need to ask about information that indirectly informs you about the likely nature of the exam. I won't tell you what that might be—that's your job.

A subsidiary goal of the project is to give you experience working in groups. Here, you've all got to cooperate in doing this discovery, both within your small group and with the other small groups. At the same time, you may have slightly different ideas about the questions you want to ask. Practicing working with comparative strangers is one reason I assigned people to groups. (The others are avoiding the prom-date-anxiety phenomenon, and, I'll admit, administrative convenience.)

Greg Sergienko
Southern Illinois University School of Law

Chapter 7

Computers

Computers are useless. They can only give you answers. — Pablo Picasso

[T]he effectiveness of technology in education will depend upon what goes on in students' heads. If computers encourage more thought, they will be a great asset; if the student-computer interaction is mindless, the potential will be lost. — McKeachie

Personal computers have the potential to play a very significant role in teaching and learning in law school. Although computers present significant challenges for legal educators, computers can help teachers and students accomplish many of the major goals of legal education.

A. Legal Education Goals

In *Teaching Law With Computers,* which forms the basis for much of this introduction, Richard Warner, Stephen Sowle, and Will Sadler establish a baseline for the successful use of computers in legal education— "easy-to-use technology that serves clearly articulated pedagogical goals." Consequently, the discussion of the use of computers in law school should begin by attempting to articulate critical goals of legal education.

Higher education in general, and legal education in particular, seeks to have students achieve three types of goals: content goals, skill goals, and value goals.

Both undergraduate and graduate education, including law school, is intended to help students learn content. A major goal in legal education is that the students understand the content of the substantive law. To understand law, students must learn not only the legal rules, but also the structure of the rules, their development, their underlying rationale, and relevant legal theory, among other things.

While content is important, many legal educators, like many other higher education teachers, consider skill goals to be the most important goals for their students. Some of the skills concern critical thinking, such as the ability to perform analysis and problem solving. Other skills include effective oral and written communication. Legal education encompasses specific

149

professional skills as well, such as fact investigation, negotiation, client counseling, and advocacy.

The goals of professional education extend beyond content and skills to professional values. Legal education seeks to help students develop a set of healthy professional values, such as the obligation to do *pro bono* work and the need to balance the lawyer's multiple duties to self, client, the court, and society.

B. Benefits and Challenges of Computers for Teaching and Learning

A significant body of literature addresses the effects of computers on teaching and learning in higher education generally and in law school specifically. Researchers have identified a number of beneficial effects of computers in undergraduate and legal education.

- Students in courses taught in part through computer-assisted instruction (CAI) (for example, tutorial lessons or presentation graphics) retain more content than students in the same course taught without computers.
- Students in courses taught in part through CAI learn content faster than students taught without CAI.
- Teachers in courses taught in part through CAI were able to devote more class time to goals other than teaching basic legal rules, such as the underlying rationale for the law or analysis skills.
- Students in courses taught in part with computers improved their attitudes towards computers.
- Many students in courses which include an electronic forum (for example, an e-mail or Internet discussion list) are more likely to participate in the course by asking questions or expressing their views than in courses without the electronic forum.
- Computer-assisted methods such as tutorials and electronic forums help teachers respond to varying student learning styles; for example, some students learn more comfortably and effectively in the electronic environment than in the classroom.

Like any other tool or method for teaching and learning, the benefits of computers can be offset by potential drawbacks. First, computer hardware, software, and their support are expensive. Some of the beneficial computer uses require that each student own or have easy access to a computer, which raises equity issues. Other uses require a well-functioning local network, which has technical and financial implications for law schools. Second, computers are sophisticated electronic tools that can, and do, malfunction. Third, the computer abilities of students and faculty range from very adept to novice. Consequently, some students and faculty will need to invest time in learning the technology before it can be useful as a teaching and learning device.

Teachers should balance the benefits and burdens of computers when deciding whether to use them in their courses. Warner, Sowle, and Sadler offer six questions to guide teachers' decisions.

(1) Is there a clear pedagogical rationale for using the technology?
(2) Is the technology integrated into an overall pedagogical plan in a way that avoids information overload?
(3) Can the teacher master the technology to use it easily and without distraction?
(4) Is the failure rate low enough so that the technology is relatively trouble-free?
(5) When the technology fails, can the teacher quickly and easily compensate for the failure?
(6) Does the school have a reliable computing environment, including a competent, available support staff?

With those questions in mind, teachers can evaluate the various uses of computers in legal education.

C. Effective Uses of Computers in Law School

During the 1980s and 1990s, innovative law teachers and legal publishers developed many uses and products for computers in legal education. Undoubtedly, legal educators will continue to explore and develop creative uses for technology in teaching and learning. Currently, five of the most effective and promising applications of computers in legal education are (1) the computer as a visual tool in the classroom, (2) electronic lessons, (3) electronic discussion and supplements, (4) the Internet, and (5) electronic casebooks.

1. Computers as Visual Tools in the Classroom

Visual tools have significant benefits in the classroom (discussed in more detail in Chapter 4). For many students, visual representations of concepts are more memorable than oral communication. Visuals also help students connect and organize related concepts. Moreover, visual tools help teachers focus students' attention and maintain their interest in the classroom. Finally, visual displays of information lead to more accurate note taking by students.

A laptop computer with a projector can be a powerful visual tool in the classroom. It allows students to view anything that teachers can display on a computer screen. The potential uses of this computer version of the blackboard or overhead projector are extensive. Three of the most successful teacher-tested uses of the computer as a visual tool in the classroom are (a) to show key portions of cases, statutes, and regulations; (b) to display problems, questions, and hypotheticals; and (c) to present outlines or frameworks. These uses are discussed in more detail below.

a. Show key portions of cases, statutes, and regulations.

The projection of portions of the law on a screen visible to the entire class has several benefits. It focuses the attention of each student on the key portion of the case, statute, rule, or other authority. The teacher can highlight critical language or rearrange the text to help students understand the material's structure. Also, the teacher and student can easily refer to the key part of the law during class discussion.

b. Display problems, questions, and hypotheticals.

A rather obvious, but significant, advantage of displaying questions, problems, and hypotheticals for the class is that each student will know exactly what the query is. Most teachers will be more precise in questions or hypos reduced to writing than those presented orally, and students are much more likely to take in all of the problem or question presented visually rather than orally. When a query is presented visually, students can focus their efforts on thinking about their responses and analysis rather than straining to make sure they know what the teacher is asking. Another advantage is that teachers can record student responses to the query and project them to the class.

c. Present an outline or framework.

An outline or framework for analysis helps students to understand the relationships among concepts and apply those concepts in new situations. Teachers can present outlines on a computer with presentations software. Teachers can focus students' attention by revealing the steps in the analysis or outline one at a time with the touch of a key or the click of a mouse.

Many of the guidelines for the effective use of computers as visual tools are similar to the guidelines for overhead transparencies described in Chapter 4.

- Before class, test the computer and projector to be sure they are working. Focus the projector and find the appropriate light level in the room so the students can see clearly the projected images.
- Limit the amount of material on a single screen. As a general rule, restrict each screen to one topic.
- Be sure the typeface is big enough so all students can easily read the projected text. Twenty-four point type is usually sufficient, but the best way to know is to test it in the classroom in advance of class.
- Use color for emphasis. Be aware that some colors (blue, purple) are much more visible than others (yellow, orange). Test colors before class.
- Pause briefly after projecting text so the students can scan it before listening to what you have to say.
- Give students time to copy the material on the screen. If the screen contains large amounts of information or complex diagrams, give the students a handout rather than have them copy the screen.

2. Electronic Lessons

Computer-based lessons are designed to provide individualized instruction to students outside the classroom. These interactive, electronic lessons can help students learn both content and skills. Three types of electronic lessons are common in law school: (1) commercial text-based lessons, (2) customized text-based lessons, and (3) commercial video-based lessons.

a. Commercial text-based lessons.

Commercial publishers produce numerous electronic lessons designed for legal education. The largest vendor of electronic lessons for law school is the Center for Computer-Assisted Legal Instruction (CALI), which sells CDs with over 100 lessons in more than 25 subject areas. Many electronic lessons are designed to teach content—legal rules, the structure of the rules, the rationale behind the rules, and application of the rules. For example, electronic lessons include tutorials on personal jurisdiction, hearsay, perfecting security interests, Title VII of the Civil Rights Act of 1964, and the Code of Professional Responsibility. Other lessons aim to teach skills such as contract drafting, legal analysis, and fact investigation.

b. Customized text-based lessons.

Teachers can create their own electronic lessons. One way is for legal educators to learn programming or to hire a programmer to create the lesson. A much more feasible way for most law teachers is to create the lesson using CALI's free authoring software—CALI-IOLIS. That software is designed to allow law teachers to create electronic lessons without knowing how to program. CALI-IOLIS is Windows-based and can be used effectively by anyone who can do word processing in a Windows environment.

c. Commercial video-based lessons.

The CLE Group produces The Interactive Courtroom, a series of video-based lessons suitable for law school. The Interactive Courtroom, available on laserdisc or CD, focuses primarily on skills, such as client interviewing, direct examination, cross-examination, and taking and defending depositions. The lessons give students instructions from renowned experts, allow students to play a role as an attorney (interviewing a client, conducting a deposition, or participating in a trial), and provide immediate feedback on students' performance.

3. Electronic Discussion and Supplements

Teachers can extend the physical classroom into an electronic classroom through the use of e-mail or electronic classroom platforms available from law publishers. The primary feature of the electronic classroom extension is an electronic discussion forum, to which both teachers and students can contribute. An electronic discussion forum can facilitate the following:

- Teachers and students can continue class discussion by posting their thoughts to the list. Sometimes the most profound comments occur after everyone has a chance to reflect on issues raised in class.
- Teachers can pose questions, problems, and hypotheticals for students to consider for the next class meeting or for students to discuss online outside class.
- Teachers can give quizzes online to find out what students know, so class can focus on the troublesome areas or so students can assess their own level of understanding.

- Teachers can post material, such as syllabi, new cases, or handouts to the list either in addition to or in lieu of distributing the material in class.
- Students can pose questions to the teacher or their fellow students. Some students who are not comfortable asking questions or making comments in class are eager to do so online.

4. The Internet

Teachers and students can use the Internet as an extension of the classroom or as a substitute for it.

As an extension of the classroom, the Internet can accomplish the same functions as electronic discussions and supplements discussed above. The difference is that rather than conducting discussions and posting material on the school's local e-mail system or on a commercial platform, the forum is a Web site created by the teacher. Advantages of the Internet as a forum are that teachers and students can create links to the vast resources on the Internet, which can be accessed from anywhere.

The Internet can be a substitute for the classroom and allow distance learning. Teachers can create virtual courses that students can take from anywhere. All or some of the material for the course (cases, statutes, articles, handouts, syllabus, etc.) can be available at the course Web site. Teachers can pose questions, problems, and hypotheticals at the site and students can post their responses. Discussions can occur either over time in a discussion list format or in "real time" via video, audio, or text-based conferencing. The Internet can facilitate collaboration on projects by students in different locations. Law schools are just beginning to explore the possibilities of virtual courses.

5. Electronic Casebooks

Beginning in the mid-1990s, legal publishers began offering electronic casebooks. Each year more titles are available in increasingly sophisticated electronic versions. Students can use electronic casebooks to do everything they can do with a print version and more. Students can read the book on their computer, highlight text, place notes in the material, search for words and phrases, create links to materials in the book and online, cut and paste materials to a word processing program, and create outlines. Thus, the potential uses of electronic casebooks are significant. Although many students have not used most of the potential of the early versions of electronic casebooks, as the publishers improve the books and students become more comfortable in the electronic environment, teachers should expect that more students will take advantage of the benefits of electronic casebooks.

References

Diane Balestri, *Silicon Basements and the Liberal Arts,* in Teaching and Technology: The Impact of Unlimited Information Access on Classroom Teaching 99-107 (1991).

Charles C. Bonwell & James A. Eison, Active Learning: Creating Excitement in the Classroom 41-42 (1991).

Barbara Gross Davis, Tools for Teaching 177-202, 334-341 (1993).

James R. Davis, Better Teaching, More Learning: Strategies for Success in Postsecondary Settings 119-122 (1993).

Wilbert McKeachie, *How Teachers Teach, How Students Learn,* in Teaching and Technology: The Impact of Unlimited Information Access on Classroom Teaching 1-13 (1991).

Warner, Richard et al., *Teaching Law With Computers,* 24 Rutgers Computer & Tech. L.J. 101 (1998).

Specific Ideas on Using Computers

#1: Electronic Classroom

E-mail and threaded discussion groups can expand the walls of the classroom by facilitating continuing contact between professors and students. This article discusses several of the most common uses of these devices, but many more are possible, depending on the nature of the course and the teacher's instruction style and goals.

Using E-mail

1. Continuing Discussion Outside Class

Every professor has experienced the frustration of having to stop discussion of a topic in class before it has been fully aired. E-mail can provide an effective means for you to continue these discussions without taking up additional class time. You can use e-mail to pose additional hypotheticals, to address policy considerations or doctrinal subtleties, or to clarify areas students seemed to misunderstand.

You can use e-mail to create a virtual classroom by encouraging students to respond to your postings with comments and questions, as they would if you were presenting the material in the classroom. You can then forward to the entire class the comments or questions that you find particularly perceptive or useful, along with your responses. If you decide to use e-mail in this manner, consider whether your "default rule" will be to identify the students whose messages you forward, or to keep their identities confidential. Students are more likely to participate in e-mail discussions if they are assured anonymity, unless they explicitly authorize use of their names.

If you use the Socratic teaching style, you may view e-mail discussions as either boon or bane. On the plus side, you are more likely to receive considered responses to your questions because students have more time to think, which allows the dialogue to move quickly to a more sophisticated level. On the negative side, the immediacy of direct interaction is absent, and students are not challenged to think on their feet in a focused exchange, which many instructors see as the main advantage of the Socratic method.

2. Answering Student Questions

Students often have questions that cannot be addressed in class because of limited class time, because the question is tangential to the issues you want to emphasize in class, or because the student fails to raise his or her hand due to shyness or a sense of intimidation. E-mail can provide a useful means for answering these questions.

Some instructors believe that encouraging students to use e-mail for questions and comments signals that the instructor does not welcome office visits. In our experience, exactly the opposite seems to occur—as long as you clearly communicate to students that you welcome office visits and view e-mail as a complement instead of a replacement.

Many students are too shy to visit their professors, even during set office hours, and e-mail provides a means for these students to express their thoughts in a way that seems more anonymous. These students are more likely to visit you in person once they have broken the ice via e-mail. For less timid students, your willingness to address their questions by e-mail may help convince them that you are serious in encouraging them to come see you in person.

3. Conducting Short-Answer Quizzes

E-mail can be an efficient means of conducting optional or graded quizzes on class material. One of our colleagues (Ralph Brill) has used e-mail to pose short-answer questions in his first-year Torts class, distributing the questions by e-mail and asking that students submit their e-mail responses by a designated date. He then uses e-mail to draft and return comments on each student's answers. The entire process can be done from the professor's and students' computers.

4. Administrative Use

For many professors, the first several minutes of class are frequently devoted to administrative matters: what the students should read for the next class, rescheduling a canceled class, announcing an upcoming event, etc. Over the course of a full semester, these minutes can add up to a significant amount of time. Addressing such matters in e-mail can both save these precious minutes and contribute to an atmosphere of studiousness in class.

Threaded Discussion Groups

Threaded discussion groups are electronic bulletin boards that use Internet technology. When you access a discussion group, your screen will display all of the messages that have been posted by participants in the group to date. Typically, messages are listed, or "threaded," by topic and, within topics, by date. You can read an existing message by clicking on it with your mouse and can add a new message either by replying to an existing message or by creating a message with a new topic. All messages posted to the group can be read by all participants and retained indefinitely.

Discussion groups can be used for all of the purposes discussed above, with the exception of short-answer quizzes. Because postings to such groups can be viewed by all members, they can be used to post questions, but in most cases are inappropriate as a method for students to post their answers.

Comparative Advantages of E-mail and Discussion Groups

Assuming you have the technology to support both e-mail and discussion groups, which should you use? It depends. For many instructors, an important advantage of e-mail is that it allows them to control discussions by acting as the gatekeeper for everything distributed to the class. With discussion groups, by contrast, students can post anything they want for all members of the class to read. For some instructors, this feature may be an advantage rather than a disadvantage. It may be particularly well-suited to smaller seminar-style classes. E-mail lists can also be set up to allow students to post messages to the entire class.

Another potential advantage of e-mail is that students are more likely to see (and, one can only hope, to read) your messages. With discussion groups, you may find it hard to persuade students to access the site regularly, and participation in discussions may suffer. We have had noticeably more success using e-mail than discussion groups.

One of us (Richard Warner) is experimenting with using class credit as an incentive for students to access and participate in a discussion group set up for class discussion. The results so far are encouraging — significantly more students are participating as compared with a similar discussion group set up for the same course a year ago.

Threaded discussion groups have one distinct advantage over e-mail groups: Because messages appear in threaded form and all messages can be accessed from a single screen, it is much easier for students to follow the flow of particular discussions and to comprehend the development of concepts and arguments, especially during the first year, when students are struggling to learn basic legal concepts and styles of legal reasoning.

During this time, threading can be a considerable advantage in helping students understand the material. A compromise solution is the threaded archiving of e-mail discussions on a Web server through commonly available free programs such as Mhonarc and Hypermail.

Effects on the Classroom

As noted above, you can save classroom time if you make announcements or give quizzes electronically. More important, using e-mail or a discussion group to continue classroom discussion and to answer student questions allows you to devote more time to expand issues discussed in class or to clarify areas of confusion; you no longer need to worry that spending additional time addressing a particular topic will be at the expense of an equally important (or more important) topic later in the course.

One consequence of this is that using e-mail or discussion groups to supplement classroom interaction frees up additional classroom time for delving more deeply into theoretical and policy considerations, exploring hypothetical applications of the legal rules under discussion, and so on. Classroom time can thus be reserved for discussion of difficult or sophisticated issues that are best taught in direct exchanges with students.

Another benefit is that students who lack the confidence to participate actively in class may feel more comfortable taking part in online discussions, particularly if they can be anonymous. This helps counteract the unfortunate tendency for classroom discussion to be dominated by a few students.

Making It Work: Final Thoughts

To use e-mail effectively, all of your students must have e-mail accounts and must be persuaded to consult their accounts on a regular basis. This task is greatly aided if your school has an ingrained "e-mail culture." At Chicago-Kent, for example, students are given e-mail accounts when they arrive, and they quickly realize that the administration and their professors rely on e-mail heavily to make announcements and communicate information on a wide range of academic and administrative subjects.

Use of e-mail and discussion groups will work effectively, of course, only if students have reasonable access to your school's computer network from lab computers, their own laptops, or through dial-in access from home computers.

Stephen D. Sowle and Richard Warner
Illinois Institute of Technology Chicago-Kent College of Law

#2: Electronic Supplements

Computer technology is more than just an efficient way to manage data. It also enables us to apply principles of learning theory more effectively than ever.

Authorware designed for law teachers makes it possible to employ electronic mechanisms to give effect to learning theories. I attempted to bring technology and learning theory together in an electronic supplement, titled *Tortorial*, for my Torts course.

The last 75 years have seen little change in legal education and its twin defining attributes: the study of appellate opinions to discover the law, and the Socratic classroom in which the teacher's skillful questions guide the student to these discoveries. Those attributes will not continue to be the lynchpins of legal education because they frequently operate in counterproductive ways.

Students—even very bright ones—struggle to master the legal method as well as the substance of their courses in the first year. They suffer unnecessary anxiety that further reduces their ability to study effectively. With little feedback from professors, students take a three- or four-hour exam at semester's end that determines their course grade and whether they rank high enough for job interviews with top firms. Under these stressful circumstances, it is surprising that students learn as much as they do.

What law professors know about learning theory is more likely to be the result of intuition than formal education. For example, we know that repeated exposure to material enables students to learn, though we may not apply the term "associative learning" to the phenomenon. A more conscious application of learning theory will permit law teachers to reach their students more effectively.

This led me to write *Tortorial*. The software I used was FolioVIEWS 3.1. I divided the law of torts into 18 topics arranged under six primary subjects. Each interactive topic contains a narrative explanation of the law followed by two practice sections. The narrative contains pop-up links and jump links that appear as brightly colored hypertext on the computer screen. When students place the cursor over a hypertext word, the cursor changes to an icon of a hand with a pointing finger. Double-clicking on the icon activates one of two functions:

Pop-up Links: A smaller box pops up on the screen with additional information. It may be a question and answer, a definition, or a citation to a case. The students read the information and return to the main text by closing the box.

Occasionally the pop-up will close a question and there will be a lighter question mark at its end. Students who double-click on the question mark will retrieve an answer in a pop-up within the primary pop-up. The students then back out of both pop-ups by closing each one in turn. I included as many as five pop-ups within a primary pop-up.

Jump Links: When students double-click on a jump link, the program takes them to another part of the supplement, which may be to another, more detailed narrative or to a relevant section of the Restatement (Second) of Torts or other supporting documents. The students can return to the original narrative by clicking on "backtrack" in the margin.

At the end of each topic are the practice sections, "Preparation" and "Test Yourself." By double-clicking either of these brightly colored words, students will access either questions that will help in preparation for class discussions or hypotheticals, many with pop-up sample responses. These exercises enable students to gain immediate feedback regarding their ability to understand foundational principles.

An electronic supplement employs the efficiency and excitement of interactive computer technology. More important, it uses that technology to serve essential pedagogical purposes: to enable students, inundated with new material, to connect pieces of relevant information and to assess their ability to apply the law intermittently.

At any point in the course, students can use *Tortorial* in various ways:

To Preview a Topic Before Reading the Case

Only practice can help first-year students to overcome the difficulty posed by reading and understanding cases. Practice is more productive when students have some advance notion of what they are expected to get out of the case and how it connects with the rest of the course. Previewing the topic helps students to recognize the rules and exceptions.

To Review and Relate Topics to Upcoming Material

For example, in the topic entitled "Consent as a Defense to International Torts," the students encounter jump links that take them forward to "Defenses to Negligent Torts." This informs them that more defenses will be covered and that some defenses to intentional torts differ from defenses to negligent torts. The students may wish to read the material to preview, to reinforce previously covered principles, or to acquaint themselves with those that will be covered in the future.

To See Graphic Depictions of Legal Principles

Tortorial contains illustrations and graphs relating to such things as case analysis and synthesis, the role of judge and jury, defenses and privileges, allocation of damages among multiple tortfeasors, damages, and recovery for emotional distress. Many of these focus on the connections among various legal concepts.

Learning Benefits of Electronic Supplement

On a more general level, students who use an electronic supplement will reap additional benefits. Many of these benefits will manifest themselves in the classroom as well. Besides demystifying law school to some degree, *Tortorial* may reduce entering students' stress by providing immediate feedback. Professors benefit because they can teach more effectively if students are better prepared and less stressed.

An electronic supplement can be useful to students at all levels of performance. High achievers will be engaged by challenging hypotheticals. On the other hand, the interactive links and the practice exercises can be particularly helpful to students who do not learn as quickly as their classmates.

Additionally, electronic supplements are useful to students with different learning styles or modes of cognition. People tent to favor one of two primary modes of cognition: analytic or synthetic. Analytic thinkers tend to reduce new information to its smallest component, while synthetic thinkers tend to relate new information to the larger whole.

An electronic supplement utilizes both. Some people receive information best auditorially while others learn best visually. An electronic supplement adds an important visual component to the study of law. Moreover, it adds a tactile dimension to learning because it is interactive.

Students' reactions to *Tortorial* were very positive. They liked the way it gave them access to the law and direction in their studies. Some were initially reluctant, but most students were pleased once the program was up and running. Complaints centered on technical problems and dissatisfaction with the degree to which *Tortorial* repeated materials discussed in class. (Because the basis of *Tortorial* was my class notes, it is not surprising that the material overlapped.) Other students complained that I did not give enough class time to discussion of *Tortorial* hypotheticals. Responses on my course evaluations were overwhelmingly positive and employed such praise as "very helpful," "great," "wonderful," and "awesome."

In class, I noticed that we moved more quickly past the fundamentals (covered in *Tortorial*) and spent more time on advanced discussion than in previous years.

I found the experience worthwhile. I intend to continue to use *Tortorial* in class and am working on an electronic supplement for an advanced course.

Victoria J. Palacios
Southern Methodist University Law School

#3: Enhanced Learning Through Supplemental Computer Programs

The growth of continuing legal education requirements throughout the United States has spawned an educational industry which produces on disk or CD-ROM practical educational programs for attorneys to use for CLE credits. Many of these programs are sophisticated, challenging, and user friendly. These programs also provide an advantage to law school teaching because they permit the teacher to assign to the students practical legal education exercises in conjunction with the traditional classroom education. Certain law school subjects benefit from coordinated practical education and the practical-based CLE programs provide a significant enhancement to student learning. In particular, Evidence and Trial Advocacy classes benefit from a number of programs: *Objection!3.1©*, *Civil Objection!3.1©*, and *ExpertWitness1.1©*, produced by TransMedia, Inc. (Suite B-2, 2735 North Holland-Sylvania Road, Toledo, OH 43615-1844, (800) 832-4980), and *The Interactive Courtroom®*, produced by CLE Group, now a division of Practising Law Institute (695 Oak Grove Avenue, #2C, Menlo Park, CA 94025, (800) 373-1829). Both programs are available with a multi-user license for use by a law school class.

The first set of programs, *Objection!3.1©*, *Civil Objection!©*, and *ExpertWitness1.1©* are DOS-based programs that install from a 3.5 inch disk. They include a courtroom scene with some video graphics, but primarily operate from questions flashed on the screen which require the student to determine whether or not the question is proper or objectionable. To respond, the student presses the appropriate key, such as "*Q*" for a proper question, "*A*" for argumentative, "*H*" for hearsay, "*V*" for vague, etc. If the answer is incorrect the objection is overruled and the student has the option of looking up the evidence rules from on-screen prompts. A distinct advantage of this program is that it gives the student only a certain amount of time during which to answer before providing prompts, such as the judge scowling or checking his watch. Additionally, the student must get a certain number of points in order to advance to the next level and the point determination in the program is done by both correct answers and time. This ensures that the students understand the necessity for quick thinking and timing in making objections, often a difficult process to simulate in the classroom. Learning is also enhanced because groups of students will compete with each other to get the highest score. In the program *Objection!©*, a final score is provided after all of the levels have been successfully reached which can be turned in by the student to the instructor to show the skill level obtained and final score.

The comparable program, *Civil Objection!©*, is more complex in that it goes through a full trial, and it requires students to answer questions and to provide information regarding the direct examination and cross-examination of the plaintiff, the plaintiff's medical expert, the defendant, and the defendant's reconstruction expert. The program begins with opening statement by the plaintiff, which interjects facts and issues that must be carefully listened to for use in the examination questions. If your reflexes were instantaneous and you hit every question correctly, the participant could conceivably reach a civil verdict of $1.2 million. Certainly an interesting challenge for the law student. Both of these games provide a low-cost and low-tech way to provide some realistic courtroom training as part of an evidence or trial advocacy class.

Another interesting program on the market, also available with a multiuse license, is *The Interactive Courtroom®* by the Practising Law Institute. This program is produced on CD-ROM and involves full-motion video of a lawsuit, pre- and during trial. The CD-ROMs available are for client interviewing; direct examination; cross-examination; programs titled *You Be the Judge, Preparing For Depositions, Defending Deposition Experts*; and a program for preparing the client for his or her deposition. Of particular usefulness in trial advocacy are the programs *Direct Examination* and *Cross-Examination*. *You Be the Judge* is very useful for evidence classes. An advantage of these programs is the use of full-motion video which permits the student to see lawyering skills done very professionally and competently. In the direct and cross-examination programs it is the student's role to make the objections to the questions asked. Once the objection is made, the student has to give a basis for the objection and the score is tabulated based on correct and incorrect answers. At any point in the program the student can receive additional assistance on an issue by looking up on-screen the rule of evidence involved or reviewing "teacher's notes" which explain aspects of the rule and procedure. An innovative and useful feature is a video window that is called *Tips from the Expert*, where the student is also provided practitioner tips from legal experts on how to handle a trial situation. This provides the student with practical legal training in conjunction with the trial advocacy class, and also provides the teacher with a different perspective for teaching trial tactics.

In an age when more and more students are learning through television and computer displays, as opposed to books, the use of programs that fit a new style of learning enhances the traditional classroom teaching. These programs are educational, are fun to play, and have met with high student acceptance. They enhance learning and they provide a valuable supplement to the teacher's teaching tools.

Speedy Rice
Gonzaga University School of Law

#4: Computer-Assisted Legal Instruction

For law teachers who are beginning to venture into the world of computer-assisted instruction, a valuable resource is the Center for Computer-Assisted Legal Instruction (CALI). CALI is a consortium of over 160 law schools. It was formed in 1982 by the University of Minnesota Law School and Harvard Law School to coordinate the distribution and use of computerized instructional materials. CALI's materials make it easy for law teachers and law students to begin using computers to teach and learn law.

The CALI library of exercises is a collection of over 100 interactive, computer-based lessons covering more than twenty subject areas. The lessons have a variety of formats, from straightforward drill and tutorials to elaborate games and simulations. Most lessons are designed so that students can complete them in one to two hours. CALI has exercises available for Accounting, Administrative Law, Arbitration, Civil Procedure, Commercial Transactions, Contracts, Corporate law, Criminal Law, Employment Discrimination, Environmental law, Evidence, Federal Courts, Insurance Law, Intellectual Property, Labor Law, Legal Research and Writing. Professional Responsibility, Property Law, Sales, Securities Regulation, Taxation, Torts, Trial Advocacy, and Wills and Trusts.

Student access to CALI exercises at the member schools can usually be accomplished in several ways. Most member schools have the entire CALI exercises library available in the computer lab so that students can do the lessons in the lab. Further, students can download exercises to a disk so that they can work on the lesson at home. Finally, CALI sells to students at a reasonable price the entire library on CD-ROM.

Teachers can use CALI exercises to accomplish a variety of goals. For example, I have used the Civil Procedure lessons in four different ways. I used the Drafting a Complaint exercise to introduce students to the process of preparing a complaint. The Waiver Under Rule 12 exercise has become my primary teaching/learning device for that material, replacing a set of problems that I formerly used in class to explore that topic. Any of the four discovery games require students to apply the discovery rules and to use strategy and good sense in a realistic simulation of the discovery phase of a civil lawsuit. Finally, I recommend that my students use some of the lessons, such as Judgment as a Matter of Law and Analysis of a Diversity Jurisdiction, for purposes of review and exam preparation.

My students' reactions to CALI lessons have been mixed. Most students reported that the Rule 12 lesson was effective. One year the students raved about a discovery game and the next year they thought it was so-so. Some students are simply not comfortable learning at the computer, but my sense is that fewer students are put off by the technology each year. On the other hand, some students say that CALI exercises were critical to their understanding of portions of the course. My reaction is that any method that meets the learning needs of some of the students is worthwhile.

For law teachers who are confident in their own computer use, CALI has software to help teachers write their own computer lessons. The software, CALI-IOLIS, is designed specifically for law teachers. Those who have tried the software (I have not) such as Professor William Andersen, University of Washington School of Law, report that the program handles the design, screen layout, and other technical details. The law teacher adds the questions, problems, and responses to student input and the program assembles it into an attractive computer-based lesson. The CALI-IOLIS software is available to law teachers at member schools from CALI free of charge.

Gerald F. Hess
Gonzaga University School of Law

#5: Electronic Newsgroups: Discussion After Class

Some of the best learning occurs after class. Discussions I have had immediately after class or during office hours have been my most productive. In order to try to promote these types of conversations, I recently have experimented with Internet newsgroups.

Internet newsgroups are akin to the old-style, push-pin, bulletin boards. People "post" messages of general interest, and others respond. There is an opportunity to exchange views, ask questions, or quickly disseminate general-interest information. I have used newsgroups in two classes: Contracts and Advanced Bankruptcy. The results so far have been generally favorable.

In both classes, I use the newsgroup to quickly distribute general information. In Contracts, for example, I often have the students go through a problem that highlights issues we have just studied. After going through the problem in class, I post my answer (which is often informed by class discussion) to the newsgroup.

Students can also post messages and questions. Although I could screen the postings, I choose not to.

So far, I have not had any problems with the tone of the messages or with "flame wars" (an Internet term for a no-holds-barred, in-your-face, insult-laden diatribe). In fact, the student messages have been courteous and in many cases thoughtful. They have ranged from general inquiries (how do courts decide who will write the opinion) to specific inquiries about something we discussed in class. These later posts often draw responses—again uncensored—from other students. I add my two cents only when useful to focus the discussion.

How many students use the group? In Contracts, I have a class of 74. During the first semester (it is a full-year course), there were 42 messages posted, 28 from students. Ten students accounted for these 28 messages. Several messages were part of a coherent "thread." We had one extended discussion on promissory estoppel and bid practices in the construction industry, which I think many students found helpful. Although only ten Contracts students posted messages, many more read them. In my first-semester evaluations, for example, some 40 students mentioned that they liked the newsgroup concept and read the postings regularly.

How do students read or post messages? To answer that question, I first have to resort to a little technobabble. Newsgroups are technically part of something called "Usenet." Usenet, in turn, is a worldwide discussion system. It is available on many computer systems and networks, but the bulk of modern Usenet traffic is transported generally over the Internet. It consists of a set of "newsgroups" with names classified hierarchically by subject. There are over 7,000 newsgroups, ranging from the serious to the silly to the obscene.

People with the appropriate computer software post "articles" or "messages" to these newsgroups, and these articles are then broadcast to other interconnected computer systems via many networks. Some newsgroups are "moderated;" in these newsgroups, the articles are first sent to a moderator for approval before appearing in the newsgroup. (I use the unmoderated format.)

To use newsgroups, your university must have a Usenet server. The administrator controls both how the system is set up and who has access. He or she also controls what newsgroups can be read through that server.

Once the newsgroup is set up, how do students gain access? At Indiana, they can use the law school's computers, which are set up with software called "newsreaders" that enable students to reach the newsgroup postings, or they can use a modem to reach a central computer from their homes. Both methods require some instruction, although I did not spend more than ten minutes explaining the concept in either class. I did, however, prepare a fairly extensive handout giving them access instructions and leading them through a hypothetical newsgroup session.

As more students receive some form of computer-aided instruction at their undergraduate institutions, I think most present and future law students will welcome the opportunity to "chat" electronically. Indeed, many students seem almost grateful for an alternative method to ask questions which allows them to reflect and measure their responses.

Reading the messages has also given me an added opportunity to measure the temperature and temperament of the class. This feature alone makes experimentation with newsgroups attractive.

Bruce A. Markell
Indiana University School of Law — Bloomington

#6: Computerized Essay Exams

Electronic essay exams can make it easier for law teachers to recognize differences among students who completely miss issues, but who may understand the topic.

My project at Villanova began with a colleague's complaint that traditional law school exams do not allow the teacher to make these distinctions. My colleague, Villanova law professor Frederick Rothman, pointed out that in a typical exam, *all* students who completely fail to address an issue get no "points" for that issue, even though it is possible, and perhaps even likely, that some students would get differing amounts of credit if they had spotted the issue and addressed it.

Professor Rothman came up with the concept of a "layered" exam. The idea was that for each fact pattern, the first question would be very broad, such as: "What are the rights of the parties?" Each question that followed would focus on a narrower issue, such as: "Did you address issue X in your answer to question 1? If not, address it now." Students who addressed issue X in question 1, of course, got more credit than students who addressed it only after prompting.

To administer this exam, we needed a system that: (1) precluded students from seeing a question until they had answered all of the questions that preceded it, and (2) precluded students from changing their answer to a question after they had seen a subsequent question. That's where the computer came in. I designed an exam, using the Toolbook authoring software, that met these requirements. Students typed responses into a box, and then clicked on a "Submit" button, which saved their answer to a file on our network. Students couldn't see a question until they had "submitted" all previous answers. While they could return to previous questions to see their answers, they couldn't modify answers that they already had submitted.

Two other features are worth noting. First, the course used a Folio Views electronic casebook. Throughout the semester, Professor Rothman encouraged students to take detailed notes in their shadow files, because they would be permitted to cut and paste from the shadow files, and from the book itself, into their exam answers. Second, the exam had a timer on it. The computer automatically saved the students' answers when time expired.

The exam worked just fine. Students seemed to overcome their initial fear of the computer (we had given them a practice computer exam earlier in the semester), and gave generally positive feedback. We intend to try it again this semester in two more classes.

If there's interest, I hope to create a program that will allow other teachers to easily build their own electronic exams similar to the one we've developed at Villanova.

Brett Amdur
Villanova University School of Law

#7: Washburn Law School Internet Services and Discussion Groups

Web Servers

WashLawWeb provides users with links to all known law-related materials on the Internet.

Generally speaking, the information is arranged by subject, by geographic location, and alphabetically. All links on the main WashLawWeb menu are maintained by full-time staff members. Many pages have full-text searching of local as well as distant resources. Information is added on a daily basis.

Washburn also hosts a large number of law-related listserv discussion groups. Users can access the archives of those listservs, as well as other legal discussion groups and mailing lists at this Web site. The WashLawWeb "starting point" is at:

> Legal Research:
>   Web: http://washlaw.edu, or http://lawlib.wuacc.edu
> Law School:
>   Web: http://washburnlaw.edu
> Library Catalog:
>   Web: http://lib.wuacc.edu

The Law School hosts several law-related sites:

>**Kansas Supreme Court and Court of Appeals:**
> Web: http://lawlib.wuacc.edu/kscases/kscases.htm
>**10th Circuit Court Decisions:**
> Web: http://lawlib.wuacc.edu/fedcases/ca10
>**Topeka Area Bankruptcy Council Decisions:**
> Web: http://lawlib.wuacc.edu/bankrupt/bankrupt.htm
>**American Association of Law Libraries:**
> Web: http://www.aallnet.org

All Washburn Law School Internet services are free. To facilitate continued growth, the Law School is always seeking partnership opportunities with organizations that have similar interests. Contact Mark Folmsbee, zzfolm@acc.wuacc.edu for details.

Highlights of WashLawWeb include:

*Directories
> http://lawlib.wuacc.edu/washlaw/directry/directry.html

Includes connections to more than 50 legal directories and covers law schools, law firms, and law-related organizations.

*Federal Law and Government Documents — DocLaw
> http://lawlib.wuacc.edu/washlaw/doclaw/doclaw5m.html

Provides access to all known federal law in the United States as well as law-related government document resources. It is arranged by subject and agency.

*Foreign and International Law — ForIntLaw
> http://lawlib.wuacc.edu/forint/forintmain.html

Provides comprehensive Internet access to foreign, international, and United Nations legal materials. This Web site contains links to primary and secondary sources in many countries.

*Kansas WEB
> http://lawlib.wuacc.edu/washlaw/kansas.html

Offers links to Kansas information including historical materials, state colleges and universities, cities, area business information, and entertainment opportunities.

*Law Firms
> http://lawlib.wuacc.edu/washlaw/lawfirms.html

A growing list of all law firm Web sites.

*LawJobs
> http://lawlib/postlaw/postlaw.htm

A source for anyone seeking information about careers and education after the completion of law school. Includes bar preparation, seminars, continuing legal education, post-law school opportunities, and job opportunities.

*Law Journals
    http://lawlib.wuacc.edu/washlaw/lawjournal/lawjournal.html
A comprehensive list of all law-related electronic law journals. Includes some full text searching.
*Law Library Catalogs
    http://lawlib.wuacc.edu/washlaw/lawcat/lawcat.html
Provides connections to over 100 law (or law-related) library catalogs. Includes descriptions of special collections, telefax numbers, phone numbers, street addresses, and ariel (a type of special file transfer) addresses.
*Law Schools and Legal Organizations
    http://lawlib.wuacc.edu/washlaw/lawschools.html
A list of all law school and legal organization gopher and Web sites. Includes addresses.
*Listserv Information and Archives
    http://lawlib.wuacc.edu/washlaw/listserv.html
This includes access to all law-related listservs maintained at Washburn University School of Law (lawlibdir-l, lawlibref-l, privatelawlib-l, statecourtcountylawlib-l, lawclinc, familylaw-l, lawdeans-l, and many others).
*State Law, Government, and Legislative Information — StateLaw
    http://lawlib.wuacc.edu/washlaw/uslaw/statelaw.html
A comprehensive set of state law links in the United States.
*Subject Index/Access to Law related materials
    http://lawlib.wuacc.edu/washlaw/subject/subject.html
Includes links to all law specialty sites and is organized according to the "section" breakdown for the American Association of Law Schools (AALS).

FTP (File Transfer Protocol) Site 198.252.9.248

If you have information about your bar association, AALL, law-related chapter, consortium, association, committee, or special interest section, and do not have a location to make the data available to the association (or your group) on the Internet, feel free to put the data at the FTP site.

Once the data has been transferred to the FTP site, it can be moved to the Web. Please allow 48 hours to make the basic link and set up your Web site. Since the data will be loaded as Web data, your members will be able to go to it directly.

How to put data at this site?

You will need to use the FTP command. FTP stands for file transfer protocol and provides you with a way to transfer data from one computer to another. There are many FTP programs available on the Internet; you will need to check your site to see which one you use.

One example using WIN95 is below:

1) At the MS DOS prompt "command line" window using WIN95, after you have connected to the Internet through your Internet provider, type the following command within the sub-directory that has your file
Type: ftp 198.252.9.248 and press ENTER
2) Next you will be asked for a username or login:
Type: anonymous and press ENTER.
3) Next you will be asked for a password:
Type: your@email.address.com and press ENTER.
4) Now you are connected.
Type: put filename.txt and press ENTER.
The file should transfer.

More Advanced Commands

A) **How to transfer a file from a specific subdirectory or disk drive (and not "clog" your FTP software directory)?**
1) When you are connected to the FTP site, but before you use the "put" command:
Type: lcd c:\wp\doc (for example) and press ENTER
This will cause the "put" command to "look" to the c:\wp\doc subdirectory for your documents.
B) **How to transfer an image?**
1) To do this, you must change the transfer setting to "bi-nary." After you are connected to the FTP site, but before you use the "put" command:
Type: binary and press ENTER
Then use the "put" command to transfer the image.
C) **How to transfer many documents (all at once)?**
1) Make sure you have loaded all the documents to be trans-ferred into a separate subdirectory on your local com-puter. Once you are connected to the FTP site, but before you have used the "put" command:
Type: prompt and press ENTER
2) Then, use the lcd command (above) to direct your FTP software to the particular subdirectory you are interested in.
3) Then:
Type: mput *.* or mput *.txt or mput *.gif (as the case may be) and press ENTER.

Washburn Listservs

Washburn Law School discussion groups are intended to provide a scholarly forum for the exchange of ideas, opinions, and information relevant to law professionals. When you join a discussion group, you will receive e-mail from others who have also joined the group. Some groups are very active, while others are inactive. Generally speaking, it is not appropriate to send "spam" or marketing material to a discussion group. Each group is focused on a specific topic.

When you post a message, even though the membership is intended to be limited, it MAY be read by many people on the Internet (not just those on the list). In some cases, the message archive is public.

Post only if you intend your views to be widely read.

Some discussion groups are completely unmoderated. Washburn University does not endorse *any* message posted by *any* subscriber and does not control what is posted. Join and participate at your own risk.

Some lists are fully moderated and post additional instructions about the list, as well as the specific groups they seek to serve. You may see these additional joining instructions when you subscribe. If you are not a member of the intended group and can not join, please do not be offended. We are merely trying to focus the discussions.

Other groups are partially moderated and work more on an "honor" system. If you are not a member of the intended group, you may be removed from the discussion group.

Members of the legal community are invited to join most of the discussion groups. Please join under the *group names* listed. Valid group-names are: *lawyer, lawprofessor, lawstudent, lawlibrarian, legaladministrator, paralegal*, and *other*. Additionally, please list your *area of interest* in your subscription request. You must describe your area of interest in one word in your subscription request.

If you have joined a group and are experiencing problems unsubscribing, send e-mail to:
manage@lawlib.wuacc.edu

For e-mail listserv "unsubscribe emergencies" contact the Law School computer help desk at:
(785) 231-1010 ext 1088.

Please read the following document for terms and conditions to participate:
http://lawlib.wuacc.edu/liability.htm

INSTRUCTIONS:

To subscribe:

1) Send a message to the **specific discussion group server:**
   Example: listserv@lawlib.wuacc.edu

2) Message says: subscribe listname yourname groupname areaofinterest
   Example: subscribe familylaw-l markfolmsbee lawlibrarian legislation

To unsubscribe:

1) Send a message to the **specific discussion group server:**
   Example: listserv@lawlib.wuacc.edu

2) Message says: unsubscribe listname
   Example: unsubscribe familylaw-l

NOTE: Some listservs are named with the -l (L) at the end. This was merely the naming custom used to describe the list. Many sites no longer follow this custom.

Other commands (e-mail messages) sent to the listserv server will generate responses below.

EXAMPLES:	(using listserv server listserv@lawlib.wuacc.edu)
Send message to:	listserv@lawlib.wuacc.edu
Message:	set lawlibref-l mail postpone
Purpose:	Stops incoming listserv messages
Message:	set lawlibref-l mail ack
Purpose:	To resume postponed mail
Message:	set lawlibref-l mail digest
Purpose:	Digest will contain the postings for a week (or several days) with summaries listed
Message:	recipients
Purpose:	Gets you a list of subscribers to the listserv

Listserv Servers

The listservs or discussion groups that follow are located on one of the servers below. You can tell which listserv is on which server by noting what follows after the "@" symbol in the list of listservs.

listserv@lawlib.wuacc.edu
listserv@aall.wuacc.edu
listserv@assocdir.wuacc.edu
listserv@law.wuacc.edu

listserv@hein.wuacc.edu
listserv@ftplaw.wuacc.edu
listserv@topeka.wuacc.edu
listserv@lawdns.wuacc.edu
listserv@lawlibdns.wuacc.edu

List of Listservs:

AALL Committee Chairs (moderated)
Name: aallcommitteechairs
Post to:
aallcommitteechairs@aall.wuacc.edu
Server: listserv@aall.wuacc.edu

AALL Public Relations (moderated)
Name: chapterpr
Post to: chapterpr@assocdir.wuacc.edu
Server: listserv@assocdir.wuacc.edu

AALL Asian American Law Librarians
Caucus
Name: aallc
Post to: aallc@ftplaw.wuacc.edu
Server: listserv@ftplaw.wuacc.edu

AALL Members (moderated)
Name: aallmembers
Post to: aallmembers@aall.wuacc.edu
Server: listserv@aall.wuacc.edu

AALL Executive Board (moderated)
Name: aalleb
Post to: aalleb@aall.wuacc.edu
Server: listserv@aall.wuacc.edu

AALLNET (moderated)
Name: aallnet
Post to: aallnet@aall.wuacc.edu
Server: listserv@aall.wuacc.edu

ABA Questionnaire (moderated)
Name: abaquestionnaire-l
Post to: abaquestionnaire-
l@ftplaw.wuacc.edu
Server: listserv@ftplaw.wuacc.edu

ABA Law Student Division
Name: aba-lsd
Post to: aba-lsd@ftplaw.wuacc.edu
Server: listserv@ftplaw.wuacc.edu

Adoption
Name: adoptlaw
Post to: adoptlaw@law.wuacc.edu
Server: listserv@law.wuacc.edu

African Law
Name: africanlaw
Post to: africanlaw@topeka.wuacc.edu
Server: listserv@topeka.wuacc.edu

ALL-SIS (Academic Law Libraries Special
Interest Section–AALL)
Name: all-sis
Post to: all-sis@assocdir.wuacc.edu
Server: listserv@assocdir.wuacc.edu

Agricultural Law
Name: aglaw-l
Post to: aglaw-l@lawlib.wuacc.edu
Server: listserv@lawlib.wuacc.edu

Alabama Attorneys
Name: alabamaattorneys-l
Post to:
alabamaattorneys-l@topeka.wuacc.edu
Server: listserv@topeka.wuacc.edu

Alaska Attorneys
Name: alaskaattorneys-l
Post to:
alaskaattorneys-l@topeka.wuacc.edu
Server: listserv@topeka.wuacc.edu

Alla (Atlanta Law Library Association)
Name: alla
Post to: alla@aall.wuacc.edu
Server: listserv@aall.wuacc.edu

Alluny (Associaton of Law Libraries of
Upstate New York)
Name: alluny
Post to: alluny@aall.wuacc.edu
Server: listserv@aall.wuacc.edu

Alternative Dispute Resolution-Law
Clinic
Name: adrclinic
Post to: adrclinic@assocdir.wuacc.edu
Server: listserv@assocdir.wuacc.edu

AMPSC (moderated–AALL)
Name: ampsc
Post to: ampsc@aall.wuacc.edu
Server: listserv@aall.wuacc.edu

Announce New Law Web Sites
Name: announce-new-law-websites
Post to: announce-new-law-websites@
assocdir.wuacc.edu
Server: listserv@assocdir.wuacc.edu

Appellate Practice
Name: appellatepractice-l
Post to:
appellatepractice-l@topeka.wuacc.edu
Server: listserv@topeka.wuacc.edu

Arizona Attorneys
Name: arizonaattorneys-l
Post to:
arizonaattorneys-l@topeka.wuacc.edu
Server: listserv@topeka.wuacc.edu

Ariel Project Discussion
Name: lawariel-l
Post to: lawariel-l@lawlib.wuacc.edu
Server: listserv@lawlib.wuacc.edu

Arkansas Attorneys
Name: arkansasattorneys-l
Post to:
arkansasattorneys-l@assocdir.wuacc.edu
Server: listserv@assocdir.wuacc.edu

Attorneys
Name: attorneys-l
Post to: attorneys-l@lawdns.wuacc.edu
Server: listserv@lawdns.wuacc.edu
List Owners: Mark Folmsbee,
zzfolm@acc.wuacc.edu

Automation and Scientific SIS (Computer
Services Special Interest Section)
Name: cs-sis
Post to: cs-sis@assocdir.wuacc.edu
Server: listserv@assocdir.wuacc.edu

Awards
Name: awards
Post to: awards@aall.wuacc.edu
Server: listserv@aall.wuacc.edu

Azall (Arizona Association of Law Libraries)
Name: azall
Post to: azall@aall.wuacc.edu
Server: listserv@aall.wuacc.edu

Bankruptcy
Name: bankruptcy
Post to: bankruptcy@law.wuacc.edu
Server: listserv@law.wuacc.edu

Bar Associations
Name: barassociations
Post to: barassociations@lawdns.wuacc.edu
Server: listserv@lawdns.wuacc.edu

Bio-Ethics Law
Name: bioethicslaw-l
Post to: bioethicslaw-l@lawlib.wuacc.edu
Server: listserv@lawlib.wuacc.edu

ByLaws
Name: bylaws
Post to: bylaws@aall.wuacc.edu
Server: listserv@aall.wuacc.edu

California Attorneys
Name: californiaattorneys-l
Post to:
californiaattorneys-l@assocdir.wuacc.edu
Server: listserv@assocdir.wuacc.edu

Call (Chicago Association of Law Libraries)
Name: call
Post to: call@aall.wuacc.edu
Server: listserv@aall.wuacc.edu

Canada Lawyers
Name: canadalawyers-l
Post to:
canadalawyers@topeka.wuacc.edu
Server: listserv@topeka.wuacc.edu

CaseBase User Discussion
Name: casebase-l
Post to: casebase-l@lawlib.wuacc.edu
Server: listserv@lawlib.wuacc.edu

Citation
Name: citation
Post to: citation@aall.wuacc.edu
Server: listserv@aall.wuacc.edu

City Attorneys
Name: cityattorneys
Post to: cityattorneys@topeka.wuacc.edu
Server: listserv@topeka.wuacc.edu

City MIS Managers
Name: city-mis-managers
Post to:
city-mis-managers@topeka.wuacc.edu
Server: listserv@topeka.wuacc.edu

Civil Procedure
Name: civprocedure-l
Post to:
civprocedure-l@lawlibdns.wuacc.edu
Server: listserv@lawlibdns.wuacc.edu

CLE Index
Name: cleindex-m
Post to: cleindex-m@lawdns.wuacc.edu
Server: listserv@lawdns.wuacc.edu

Clark Law Society
Name: clarklaw-mw
Post to:
clarklaw-mw@assocdir.wuacc.edu
Server: listserv@assocdir.wuacc.edu

Coall (Colorado Association of Law Libraries)
Name: coall
Post to: coall@aall.wuacc.edu
Server: listserv@aall.wuacc.edu

Collection Attorneys
Name: collectionattorneys-l
Post to:
collectionattorneys-l@lawdns.wuacc.edu
Server: listserv@lawdns.wuacc.edu

College Bound
Name: collegebound
Post to: collegebound@topeka.wuacc.edu
Server: listserv@topeka.wuacc.edu

Colorado Attorneys
Name: coloradoattorneys-l
Post to:
coloradoattorneys-l@assocdir.wuacc.edu
Server: listserv@assocdir.wuacc.edu

Communication Law
Name: comlaw-l
Post to: comlaw-l@lawlib.wuacc.edu
Server: listserv@lawlib.wuacc.edu

Conference of Law Library Educators
Name: lawlibed
Post to: lawlibed@aall.wuacc.edu
Server: listserv@aall.wuacc.edu

Conflict of Law
Name: conflicts-l
Post to: conflicts-l@lawdns.wuacc.edu
Server: listserv@lawdns.wuacc.edu

Connecticut Attorneys
Name: connecticutattorneys-l
Post to:
connecticutattorneys-l@assocdir.wuacc.edu
Server: listserv@assocdir.wuacc.edu

Continuing Legal Education
Name: lawcontinuinged-l
Post to:
lawcontinuinged-l@lawlib.wuacc.edu
Server: listserv@lawlib.wuacc.edu

Copyright (moderated–AALL)
Name: copyright
Post to: copyright@aall.wuacc.edu
Server: listserv@aall.wuacc.edu

Council of Chapter Presidents (AALL)
Name: councilchapterpresidents-l
Post to: councilchapterpresidents-l@
assocdir.wuacc.edu
Server: listserv@assocdir.wuacc.edu

Courts
Name: courts
Post to: courts@lawdns.wuacc.edu
Server: listserv@lawdns.wuacc.edu

Court Public Information Officers
Name: courtpio
Post to: courtpio@topeka.wuacc.edu
Server: listserv@topeka.wuacc.edu

CRIV (moderated–AALL)
Name: criv
Post to:criv@aall.wuacc.edu
Server: listserv@aall.wuacc.edu

CS-SIS (Computer Services Special Interest Section)
Name: cs-sis
Post to: cs-sis@aall.wuacc.edu
Server: listserv@aall.wuacc.edu

CUSEEME Law (Videoconferencing)
Name: cuseeme-law
Post to:
cuseeme-law@assocdir.wuacc.edu
Server: listserv@assocdir.wuacc.edu

DALL (Dallas Association of Law Libraries)
Name: dall
Post to: dall@aall.wuacc.edu
Server: listserv@aall.wuacc.edu

Death Penalty
Name: deathpenalty
Post to:
deathpenalty@assocdir.wuacc.edu
Server: listserv@assocdir.wuacc.edu

Delaware Attorneys
Name: delawareattorneys-l
Post to: delawareattorneys-l@topeka.wuacc.edu
Server: listserv@topeka.wuacc.edu

Deltathetaphi
Name: deltathetaphi
Post to: deltathetaphi@topeka.wuacc.edu
Server: listserv@topeka.wuacc.edu

Diversity (moderated–AALL)
Name: diversity
Post to: diversity@aall.wuacc.edu
Server: listserv@aall.wuacc.edu

Domestic Violence
Name: dvclinic
Post to: dvclinic@topeka.wuacc.edu
Server: listserv@topeka.wuacc.edu

Donative Transfers
Name: donativetransfers
Post to: donativetransfers@aall.wuacc.edu
Server: listserv@aall.wuacc.edu

DWI and DUI Attorneys
Name: dwiduiattorneys-l
Post to:
dwiduiattorneys-l@lawdns.wuacc.edu
Server: listserv@lawdns.wuacc.edu

Evidence
Name: evid-l
Post to: evid-l@lawlibdns.wuacc.edu
Server: listserv@lawlibdns.wuacc.edu

Environmental Law
Name: envirolaw
Post to: envirolaw@hein.wuacc.edu
Server: listserv@hein.wuacc.edu

Expert Witness
Name: expertwitness
Post to:
expertwitness@assocdir.wuacc.edu
Server: listserv@assocdir.wuacc.edu

Family Law (Lawyers, Law Professors, Law Students, Law Librarians only)
Name: familylaw-l
Post to: familylaw-l@lawlib.wuacc.edu
Server: listserv@lawlib.wuacc.edu

Family Law Faculty
Name: familylawprof-l
Post to: familylawprof-l@assocdir.wuacc.edu
Server: listserv@assocdir.wuacc.edu

FCIL (moderated–AALL)
Name: fcil
Post to: fcil@aall.wuacc.edu
Server: listserv@aall.wuacc.edu

Federal Caselaw Index
Name: federalcaselawindex-m
Post to:
federalcaselawindex-m@lawdns.wuacc.edu
Server: listserv@lawdns.wuacc.edu

Feminist Jurisprudence
Name: femjur
Post to: femjur@assocdir.wuacc.edu
Server: listserv@assocdir.wuacc.edu

Fire Chiefs
Name: firechiefs
Post to: firechiefs@topeka.wuacc.edu
Server: listserv@topeka.wuacc.edu

Florida Attorneys
Name: floridaattorneys-l
Post to:
floridaattorneys-l@assocdir.wuacc.edu
Server: listserv@assocdir.wuacc.edu

Foreign and International Law
Name: forintlaw
Post to: forintlaw@law.wuacc.edu
Server: listserv@law.wuacc.edu

Georgia Attorneys
Name: georgiaattorneys-l
Post to:
georgiaattorneys-l@topeka.wuacc.edu
Server: listserv@topeka.wuacc.edu

Government Relations (moderated–AALL)
Name: government-r
Post to: government-r@aall.wuacc.edu
Server: listserv@aall.wuacc.edu

Grants (moderated–AALL)
Name: grants
Post to: grants@aall.wuacc.edu
Server: listserv@aall.wuacc.edu

Hawaiiattorneys-l
Name: hawaiiattorneys-l
Post to:
hawaiiattorneys-l@topeka.wuacc.edu
Server: listserv@topeka.wuacc.edu

Health/Legal Issues
Name: healthlaw-l
Post to: healthlaw-l@lawlib.wuacc.edu
Server: listserv@lawlib.wuacc.edu

Hein Subscribers (restricted)
Name: hein-subs-l
Partner: Hein Publishing
Post to: hein-subs-l@lawlib.wuacc.edu
Server: listserv@lawlib.wuacc.edu

Human Rights Issues
Name: humanrights-l
Post to: humanrights-l@lawlib.wuacc.edu
Server: listserv@lawlib.wuacc.edu

Humanities and the Law
Name: humlaw-l
Post to: humlaw-l@lawlib.wuacc.edu
Server: listserv@lawlib.wuacc.edu

Idaho Attorneys
Name: idahoattorneys-l
Post to:
Idahoattorneys-l@topeka.wuacc.edu
Server: listserv@topeka.wuacc.edu

IFLP (moderated–AALL)
Name: iflp
Post to: iflp@acc.wuacc.edu
Server: listserv@acc.wuacc.edu

Illinois Attorneys
Name: illinoisattorneys-l
Post to:
illinoisattorneys-l@assocdir.wuacc.edu
Server: listserv@assocdir.wuacc.edu

Indiana Attorneys
Name: indianaattorneys-l
Post to:
indianaattorneys-l@topeka.wuacc.edu
Server: listserv@topeka.wuacc.edu

IPL (moderated–AALL)
Name: ipl
Post to: ipl@aall.wuacc.edu
Server: listserv@aall.wuacc.edu

Intellectual Property Law Librarians
Name: iplawlib-l
Post to: iplawlib-l@law.wuacc.edu
Server: listserv@law.wuacc.edu

International Law Professors
Name: intlawprofessor-l
Post to: intlawprofessor-l@law.wuacc.edu:
Server: listserv@law.wuacc.edu

Iowa Attorneys
Name: iowaattorneys-l
Post to:
iowaattorneys-l@assocdir.wuacc.edu
Server: listserv@assocdir.wuacc.edu

ITIWG (moderated–AALL)
Name: itiwg
Post to: itiwg@aall.wuacc.edu
Server: listserv@aall.wuacc.edu

Jewish Law Professors
Name: jewishlawprof-l
Post to:
jewishlawprof-l@lawlib.wuacc.edu
Server: listserv@lawlib.wuacc.edu

Judges
Name: judges
Post to: judges@assocdir.wuacc.edu
Server: listserv@assocdir.wuacc.edu

Judges (Kansas District Court–restricted)
Name: KDJA
Post to: kdja@lawdns.wuacc.edu
Server: listserv@lawdns.wuacc.edu

Juvenile Law
Name: juvenilelaw-l
Post to: juvenilelaw-l@lawlib.wuacc.edu
Server: listserv@lawlib.wuacc.edu

Kansas Attorneys
Name: kansasattorneys-l
Post to:
kansasattorneys-l@lawlib.wuacc.edu
Server: listserv@lawlib.wuacc.edu

Kansas CINC Judges (moderated)
Name: kansascincjudges-m
Post to:
kansascincjudges-m@lawdns.wuacc.edu
Server: listserv@lawdns.wuacc.edu

Kansas CINC Attorneys (moderated)
Name: kansascincattorneys-m
Post to:
kansascincattorneys-m@lawdns.wuacc.edu
Server: listserv@lawdns.wuacc.edu

Kansas City Area Law Librarians
Name: kcall-l
Post to: kcall-l@aall.wuacc.edu
Server: listserv@aall.wuacc.edu

Kansas City Attorneys
Name: kansascityattorneys-l
Post to:
kansascityattorneys-l@assocdir.wuacc.edu
Server: listserv@assocdir.wuacc.edu

Kansas Libraries Paraprofessional Staff
Name: kanlibparaprofstaff-l
Post to:
kanlibparaprofstaff-l@assocdir.wuacc.edu
Server: listserv@assocdir.wuacc.edu

Kansas Trial Lawyers Association
Name: ktla_ct
Post to: ktla_ct@lawdns.wuacc.edu
Server: listserv@lawdns.wuacc.edu

KBA Net Managment
Name: kbanetmanagment
Post to:
kbanetmanagment@law.wuacc.edu
Server: listserv@law.wuacc.edu

Kentucky Attorneys
Name: kentuckyattorneys-l
Post to:
kentuckyattorneys-l@topeka.wuacc.edu
Server: listserv@topeka.wuacc.edu

Kids Voting Program
Name: kidsvoting
Post to: kidsvoting@assocdir.wuacc.edu
Server: listserv@assocdir.wuacc.edu

Land Use Law
Name: landuselaw-l
Post to: landuselaw-l@aall.wuacc.edu
Server: listserv@aall.wuacc.edu

Law Deans
(restricted- subscription request to
zzfolm@acc.wuacc.edu)
Name: lawdeans-l
Post to: lawdeans-l@lawlib.wuacc.edu
Server: listserv@lawlib.wuacc.edu

Law Discussion Group Owners
(Moderated–Washburn only)
Name: lawdiscussionowners-m
Post to: lawdiscussionowners-m@
lawlibdns.wuacc.edu
Server: listserv@lawdns.wuacc.edu

Law Discussion Group Owners
Name: lawdiscussionowners-l
Post to:
lawdiscussionowners-
l@lawdns.wuacc.edu
Server: listserv@lawdns.wuacc.edu

Law Firm Administration
Name: lawfirmadmin-l
Post to: lawfirmadmin-l@lawlib.wuacc.edu
Server: listserv@lawlib.wuacc.edu

Law Students
Name: lawstudents
Post to: lawstudents@law.wuacc.edu
Server: listserv@law.wuacc.edu

Law Teaching
Name: lawteach
Post to: lawteach@assocdir.wuacc.edu
Server: listserv@assocdir.wuacc.edu

Law Teaching Technology
Name: lawteachtech
Post to: lawteachtech@assocdir.wuacc.edu
Server: listserv@assocdir.wuacc.edu

Law Journal Index
Name: lawjournalindex-m
Post to:
lawjournalindex-m@lawdns.wuacc.edu
Server: listserv@lawdns.wuacc.edu

Law Library Education
Name: lawlibed
Post to: lawlibed@aall.wuacc.edu
Server: listserv@aall.wuacc.edu

Law Subject Index
Name: lawsubjectindex-m
Post to:
lawsubjectindex-m@lawdns.wuacc.edu
Server: listserv@lawdns.wuacc.edu

Legal Clinic Educators
Name: lawclinic
Post to: lawclinic@lawlib.wuacc.edu
Server: listserv@lawlib.wuacc.edu

LHRB-SIS (moderated–AALL)
Name: lhrb-sis
Post to: lhrb-sis@aall.wuacc.edu
Server: listserv@aall.wuacc.edu

Libfest-l
Name: libfest-l
Post to: libfest-l@law.wuacc.edu
Server: listserv@law.wuacc.edu

Library Buildings
Name: library buildings-l
Post to:
librarybuildings-l@lawlib.wuacc.edu
Server: listserv@lawlib.wuacc.edu

LISP-SIS (moderated–AALL)
Name: lisp-sis
Post to: lisp-sis@aall.wuacc.edu
Server: listserv@aall.wuacc.edu

LLAA (Law Library Association
of Alabama)
Name: llaa
Post to: llaa@aall.wuacc.edu
Server: listserv@aall.wuacc.edu

LLAGNY (Law Library Association of
Greater New York)
Name: llagny
Post to: llagny@aall.wuacc.edu
Server: listserv@aall.wuacc.edu

LLOPS (Law Librarians of Puget Sound)
Name: llops
Post to: llops@aall.wuacc.edu
Server: listserv@aall.wuacc.edu

LLSDC (Law Librarians Society of
Washington, D.C.)
Name: llsdc
Post to: llsdc@aall.wuacc.edu
Server: listserv@aall.wuacc.edu

Louisiana Attorneys
Name: lousianaattorneys-l
Post to:
louisianaattorneys-l@topeka.wuacc.edu
Server: listserv@topeka.wuacc.edu

Imaging and Electronic Publishing
Name: lawimaging-l
Post to: lawimaging-l@lawlib.wuacc.edu
Server: listserv@lawlib.wuacc.edu

Legal Employment
Name: lawjobs-l
Post to: lawjobs-l@lawlib.wuacc.edu
Server: listserv@lawlib.wuacc.edu

Law Review/Law Journal
Name: lawjournal-l
Post to: lawjournal-l@lawlib.wuacc.edu
Server: listserv@lawlib.wuacc.edu

Law Library Directors (Academic Law
Library Directors only–Moderated)
Name: lawlibdir-l
Post to: lawlibdir-l@lawlib.wuacc.edu
Server: listserv@lawlib.wuacc.edu

Law Publisher Announcements
Name: law-publisher-announcements
Post to: law-publisher-announcements@
aall.wuacc.edu
Server: listserv@aall.wuacc.edu

LCCLASS-K
Name: lcclass-k
Post to: lcclass-l@assocdir.wuacc.edu
Server: listserv@assocdir.wuacc.edu

Legal Reference
Name: lawlibref-l
Post to: lawlibref-l@lawlib.wuacc.edu
Server: listserv@lawlib.wuacc.edu

Legal Ethics
Name: legalethics-l
Post to: legalethics-l@lawlib.wuacc.edu
Server: listserv@lawlib.wuacc.edu

Lexis Users
Name: lexisuser-l
Post to: lexisuser-l@lawlib.wuacc.edu
Server: listserv@lawlib.wuacc.edu

Little-Brown (moderated–AALL)
Name: little-brown
Post to: little-brown@aall.wuacc.edu
Server: listserv@aall.wuacc.edu

LRENET
Name: lrenet
Post to: lrenet@aall.wuacc.edu
Server: listserv@aall.wuacc.edu

MA-SIS (moderated–AALL)
Name: ma-sis
Post to: ma-sis@aall.wuacc.edu
Server: listserv@aall.wuacc.edu

Magistrates
Name: magistrates
Post to: magistrates@lawdns.wuacc.edu
Server: listserv@lawdns.wuacc.edu

Maine Attorneys
Name: maineattorneys-l
Post to:
maineattorneys-l@topeka.wuacc.edu
Server: listserv@topeka.wuacc.edu

MALL (Minnesota Association
of Law Libraries)
Name: mall-1
Post to: mall-1@aallwuacc.edu
Server: listserv@aall.wuacc.edu

Maryland Attorneys
Name: marylandattorneys-l
Post to:
marylandattorneys-l@topeka.wuacc.edu
Server: listserv@topeka.wuacc.edu

Massachusetts Attorneys
Name: massachusettsattorneys-l
Post to: massachusettsattorneys-l@
topeka.wuacc.edu
Server: listserv@topeka.wuacc.edu

Matthew-Bender (moderated–AALL)
Name: matthew-bender
Post to: matthew-bender@aall.wuacc.edu
Server: listserv@aall.wuacc.edu

Mayors
Name: mayors
Post to: mayors@topeka.wuacc.edu
Server: listserv@topeka.wuacc.edu

Mentor (moderated–AALL)
Name: mentor-ret
Post to: mentor-ret@aall.wuacc.edu
Server: listserv@aall.wuacc.edu

Mexican Attorneys
Name: mexicanlawforum
Post to:
mexicanlawforum@topeka.wuacc.edu
Server: listserv@topeka.wuacc.edu

Michigan Attorneys
Name: michiganattorneys-l
Post to:
michiganattorneys-l@topeka.wuacc.edu
Server: listserv@topeka.wuacc.edu

Midwest People of Color (moderated)
Name: midwstpocconf
Post to:
midwstpocconf@assocdir.wuacc.edu
Server: listserv@assocdir.wuacc.edu

Minnesota Attorneys
Name: minnesotaattorneys-l
Post to: minnesotaattorneys-
l@topeka.wuacc.edu
Server: listserv@topeka.wuacc.edu

Mississippi Attorneys
Name: mississippiattorneys-l
Post to:
mississippiattorneys-l@topeka.wuacc.edu
Server: listserv@topeka.wuacc.edu

Missouri Attorneys
Name: missouriattorneys-l
Post to:
missouriattorneys-l@assocdir.wuacc.edu
Server: listserv@assocdir.wuacc.edu

Montana Attorneys
Name: montanaattorneys-l
Post to:
montanaattorneys-l@topeka.wuacc.edu
Server: listserv@topeka.wuacc.edu

NALP
Name: lawrec
Post to: lawrec@lawlibdns.wuacc.edu
Server: listserv@law.wuacc.edu

Needs and Offers for Library Acquisitions
Name: needsandoffers-l
Post to: needsandoffers-l@law.wuacc.edu
Server: listserv@law.wuacc.edu

Nevada Attorneys
Name: nevadaattorneys-l
Post to:
nevadaattorneys-l@topeka.wuacc.edu
Server: listserv@topeka.wuacc.edu

New Law Book Notice
Publishers are encouraged to publish
notices of new books
Name: newlawbooks-l
Post to: newlawbooks-
l@lawlib.wuacc.edu
Server: listserv@lawlib.wuacc.edu

New Hampshire Attorneys
Name: newhampshireattorneys-l
Post to: newhampshireattorneys-l@
topeka.wuacc.edu
Server: listserv@topeka.wuacc.edu

New Jersey Attorneys
Name: newjerseyattorneys-l
Post to:
newjerseyattorneys-l@assocdir.wuacc.edu
Server: listserv@assocdir.wuacc.edu

New Mexico Attorneys
Name: newmexicaattorneys-l
Post to:
newmexicoattorneys-l@topeka.wuacc.edu
Server: listserv@topeka.wuacc.edu

New Orleans Law Librarians
Name: noall
Post to: noall@assocdir.wuacc.edu
Server: listserv@assocdir.wuacc.edu

New York Attorneys
Name: newyorkattorneys-l
Post to:
newyorkattorneys-l@assocdir.wuacc.edu
Server: listserv@assocdir.wuacc.edu

National Network of Law School Officers
Name: nnlso
Post to: nnlso@law.wuacc.edu
Server: listserv@law.wuacc.edu

National Network of Law School Offi-
cers–Executive Bd
Name: nnlso.bd
Post to: nnlso.bd@law.wuacc.edu
Server: listserv@law.wuacc.edu

Nebraska Attorneys
Name: nebraskaattorneys-l
Post to:
nebraskaattorneys-l@assocdir.wuacc.edu
Server: listserv@assocdir.wuacc.edu

NJLLA (New Jersey Law Librarians
Association)
Name: njlla
Post to: njlla@aall.wuacc.edu
Server: listserv@aall.wuacc.edu

Nominations (moderated–AALL)
Name: nominations
Post to: nominations@aall.wuacc.edu
Server: listserv@aall.wuacc.edu

North Carolina Attorneys
Name: northcarolinaattorneys-l
Post to: northcarolinaattorneys-l@
topeka.wuacc.edu
Server: listserv@topeka.wuacc.edu

Non-Profit Organizations
Name: nonprofitorganizations
Post to:
nonprofitorganizations@aall.wuacc.edu
Server: listserv@aall.wuacc.edu

North Dakota Attorneys
Name: northdakotaattorneys-l
Post to:
northdakotaattorneys-l@topeka.wuacc.edu
Server: listserv@topeka.wuacc.edu

Northeastern Kansas Library Association
Name: nekls-l
Partner: Northeastern Kansas Library
Association
Post to: nekls-l@assocdir.wuacc.edu
Server: listserv@assocdir.wuacc.edu

Northern California Association of Law
Libraries
Name: nocall
Partner: Northern California Association
of Law Libraries
Post to: nocall-list@assocdir.wuacc.edu
Server: listserv@assocdir.wuacc.edu

OBS-SIS (moderated–AALL)
Name: obs-sis
Post to: obs-sis@aall.wuacc.edu
Server: listserv@aall.wuacc.edu

Ohio Attorneys
Name: ohioattorneys-l
Post to:
ohioattorneys-l@topeka.wuacc.edu
Server: listserv@topeka.wuacc.edu

Oil and Gas Law
Name: oilgaslaw-l
Post to: oilgaslaw-l@lawlib.wuacc.edu
Server: listserv@lawlib.wuacc.edu

Oklahoma Attorneys
Name: oklahomaattorneys-l
Post to:
oklahomaattorneys-l@assocdir.wuacc.edu
Server: listserv@assocdir.wuacc.edu

ORACLE
Name: oracle
Post to: oracle@lawdns.wuacc.edu
Server: listserv@lawdns.wuacc.edu

ORALL (Ohio Regional Association
of Law Libraries)
Name: orall
Post to: orall@aall.wuacc.edu
Server: listserv@aall.wuacc.edu

Oregon Attorneys
Name: oregonattorneys-l
Post to:
oregonattorneys-l@topeka.wuacc.edu
Server: listserv@topeka.wuacc.edu

Patents (unmoderated)
Name: patent-l
Post to: patent-l@ftplaw.wuacc.edu
Server: listserv@ftplaw.wuacc.edu

Patents (moderated)
Name: patentpractice-l
Post to: patentpractice-l@hein.wuacc.edu
Server: listserv@hein.wuacc.edu

PDC (moderated–AALL)
Name: pdc
Post to: pdc@aall.wuacc.edu
Server: listserv@aall.wuacc.edu

Pennsylvania Attorneys
Name: pennsylvaniaattorneys-l
Post to: pennsylvaniaattorneys-l@
assocdir.wuacc.edu
Server: listserv@asssocdir.wuacc.edu

Placement (moderated–AALL)
Name: placement
Post to: placement@aall.wuacc.edu
Server: listserv@aall.wuacc.edu

Police Chiefs
Name: policechiefs
Post to: policechiefs@topeka.wuacc.edu
Server: listserv@topeka.wuacc.edu

Poverty Law Discussion
Name: povertylaw-l
povertylaw-l@lawlib.wuacc.edu
Server: listserv@lawlib.wuacc.edu

Prelaw Discussion List
Name: prelaw-students
Post to: prelaw-students@lawlib.wuacc.edu
Server: listserv@lawlib.wuacc.edu

Preservation (moderated–AALL)
Name: preservation
Post to: preservation@aall.wuacc.edu
Server: listserv@aall.wuacc.edu

Private Law Librarians SID Executive
Committee
Name: privatelawlibexeccomm
Post to:
privatelawlibexeccomm@aall.wuacc.edu
Server: listserv@aall.wuacc.edu

Private Law Librarians
Name: privatelawlib-l
Post to: privatelawlib-l@lawlib.wuacc.edu
Server: listserv@lawlib.wuacc.edu

Product Liability
Name: productliability
Post to: productliability@assocdir.wuacc.edu
Server: listserv@assocdir.wuacc.edu

Professional Development
(moderated–AALL)
Name: profdevelop
Post to: profdevelop@aall.wuacc.edu
Server: listserv@aall.wuacc.edu

Publications Policy (moderated–AALL)
Name: pubpolicy
Post to: pubpolicy@aall.wuacc.edu
Server: listserv@aall.wuacc.edu

Public Relations (moderated–AALL)
Name: pubrelations
Post to: pubrelations@aall.wuacc.edu
Server: listserv@aall.wuacc.edu

Publications Review (moderated–AALL)
Name: pubreview
Post to: pubreview@aall.wuacc.edu
Server: listserv@aall.wuacc.edu

Public Utilities/Telecommunication
Name: pubutilstelecom-l
Post to: pubutilstelcom-l@hein.wuacc.edu
Server: listserv@hein.wuacc.edu

Puerto Rico Attorneys
Name: puertoricoattorneys-l
Post to:
puertoricoattorneys-l@topeka.wuacc.edu
Server: listserv@topeka.wuacc.edu

Recruitment (moderated–AALL)
Name: recruitment
Post to: recruitment@aall.wuacc.edu
Server: listserv@aall.wuacc.edu

Research (moderated–AALL)
Name: research
Post to: research@aall.wuacc.edu
Server: listserv@aall.wuacc.edu

Rhode Island Attorneys
Name: rhodeislandattorneys-l
Post to:
rhodeislandattorneys-l@topeka.wuacc.edu
Server: listserv@topeka.wuacc.edu

RIPS (moderated–AALL)
Name: rips
Post to: rips@aall.wuacc.edu
Server: listserv@aall.wuacc.edu

Securities Law
Name: securitieslaw-l
Post to: securitieslaw-l@aall.wuacc.edu
Server: listserv@aall.wuacc.edu

Scholarships (moderated–AALL)
Name: scholarships
Post to: scholarships@aall.wuacc.edu
Server: listserv@aall.wuacc.edu

SFALL (South Florida Association
of Law Libraries)
Name: sfall
Post to: sfall@aall.wuacc.edu
Server: listserv@aall.wuacc.edu

SIS Council (Special Interest Section
Council–AALL)
Name: siscouncil-l
Post to: siscouncil-l@aall.wuacc.edu
Server: listserv@aall.wuacc.edu

Snella (Southern New England Law
Librarians Association)
Name: snella
Post to: snella@aall.wuacc.edu
Server: listserv@aall.wuacc.edu

SR-SIS (Social Responsibility Special
Interest Section–AALL)
Name: sr-sis
Post to: sr-sis@law.wuacc.edu
Server: listserv@law.wuacc.edu

Southern California Association of
Law Libraries
Name: scall-list
Post to: scall-list@assocdir.wuacc.edu
Server: listserv@assocdir.wuacc.edu

South Carolina Attorneys
Name: southcarolinaattorneys-l
Post to: southcarolinaattorneys-l@
topeka.wuacc.edu
Server: listserv@topeka.wuacc.edu

South Dakota Attorneys
Name: southdakotaattorneys-l
Post to:
southdakotaattorneys-l@topeka.wuacc.edu
Server: listserv@topeka.wuacc.edu

Spectrum (moderated–AALL)
Name: spectrum
Post to: spectrum@aall.wuacc.edu
Server: listserv@aall.wuacc.edu

State and County Court Librarians
Name: statecourtcountylawlib-l
Post to: statecourtcountylawlib-l@
lawlib.wuacc.edu
Server: listserv@lawlib.wuacc.edu

State Caselaw Index (moderated)
Name: statecaselawindex-m
Post to:
statecaselawindex-m@lawdns.wuacc.edu
Server: listserv@lawdns.wuacc.edu

State Law (moderated)
Name: statelaw-l
Post to: statelaw-l@hein.wuacc.edu
Server: listserv@hein.wuacc.edu

Statistics (moderated–AALL)
Name: statistics
Post to: statistics@aall.wuacc.edu
Server: listserv@aall.wuacc.edu

Tailored Solutions Users
Name: tailoredsolutionsuser-l
Post to:
tailoredsolutionsuser-l@lawlib.wuacc.edu
Server: listserv@lawlib.wuacc.edu

Teach Legal Writing and Research
Name: teachlawres-l
Post to: teachlawres-l@lawlib.wuacc.edu
Server: listserv@lawlib.wuacc.edu

Tennessee Attorneys
Name: tennesseeattorneys-l
Post to:
tennesseeattorneys-l@topeka.wuacc.edu
Server: listserv@topeka.wuacc.edu

Texas Attorneys
Name: texasattorneys-l
Post to:
texasattorneys-l@assocdir.wuacc.edu
Server: listserv@assocdir.wuacc.edu

Trademarks
Name: trademarks-l
Post to: trademarks-l@lawdns.wuacc.edu
Server: listserv@lawdns.wuacc.edu

Trial Lawyers
Name: trial-lawyers
Post to: trial-
lawyers@assocdir.wuacc.edu
Server: listserv@assocdir.wuacc.edu

TS-SIS (Technical Services Special Interest
Section–AALL)
Name: ts-sis
Post to: ts-sis@aall.wuacc.edu
Server: listserv@aall.wuacc.edu

Uniform Commercial Code
Name: ucclaw-l
Post to: ucclaw-l@assocdir.wuacc.edu
Server: listserv@assocdir.wuacc.edu

Utah Attorneys
Name: utahattorneys-l
Post to:
utahattorneys-l@topeka.wuacc.edu
Server: listserv@topeka.wuacc.edu

Vermont Attorneys
Name: vermontattorneys-l
Post to:
vermontattorneys-l@topeka.wuacc.edu
Server: listserv@topeka.wuacc.edu

Virginia Attorneys
Name: virginiaattorneys-l
Post to:
virginiaattorneys-l@topeka.wuacc.edu
Server: listserv@topeka.wuacc.edu

Washington Attorneys
Name: washingtonattorneys-l
Post to:
washingtonattorneys-
l@topeka.wuacc.edu
Server: listserv@topeka.wuacc.edu

Washburn Admittees
Name: washburn-law-admittees
Post to: washburn-law-admittees@
assocdir.wuacc.edu
Server: listserv@assocdir.wuacc.edu

Washington DC Attorneys
Name: washingtondcattorneys-l
Post to: washingtondcattorneys-l@
assocdir.wuacc.edu
Server: listserv@assocdir.wuacc.edu

West (moderated–AALL)
Name: west
Post to: west@aall.wuacc.edu
Server: listserv@aall.wuacc.edu

West Virginia Attorneys
Name: westvirginiaattorneys-l
Post to:
westvirginiaattorneys-l@topeka.wuacc.edu
Server: listserv@topeka.wuacc.edu

Westlaw Users
Name: westlawuser-l
Post to: westlawuser-l@lawlib.wuacc.edu
Server: listserv@lawlib.wuacc.edu

Wisconsin Attorneys
Name: wisconsinattorneys-l
Post to: wisconsinattorneys-
l@topeka.wuacc.edu
Server: listserv@topeka.wuacc.edu

Women in Legal Education
Name: antigone
Post to: antigone@assocdir.wuacc.edu
Server: listserv@assocdir.wuacc.edu

WPLLA (Western Pennsylvania
Law Library Association)
Name: wplla
Post to: wplla@aall.wuacc.edu
Server: listserv@aall.wuacc.edu

Wyoming Attorneys
Name: wyomingattorneys-l
Post to:
wyomingattorneys-l@assocdir.wuacc.edu
Server: listserv@assocdir.wuacc.edu

NOTE: All of the AALL discussion groups (American Association of Law Libraries) are limited to AALL members. Not all of the AALL regional discussion groups are active at this time. It was simply easier for me to create them all at once. Most of the lists described as "moderated-AALL" are standing AALL committees.

Mark Folmsbee
Washburn University School of Law

#8: Lists for Law Professors

The following list is an excerpt from my "Law Lists" guide to Internet mailing lists and Usenet newsgroups related to law at http://www.lib.uchicago. edu/~llou/lawlists/info.html and http://www.lib.uchicago.edu/cgi-bin/law-lists. This sub-list includes discussion groups specifically for law professors as well as other scholarly and professional electronic mailing lists on legal topics. The URL for this sub-list is http://www.lib.uchicago.edu/~llou/lawlists/lawprof.txt.

These lists can be used to exchange information with other professors about syllabi, class materials, recommended casebooks, approaches to teaching particular courses, current issues related to an area of law, recent cases and statutes, and legal education, and to find solutions to common problems (see, for example, the LAWPROF, E-TEACH, CRIMPROF, IMMPROF, ECONLAW, AALSMIN-L, LAWCLINIC, CYBERPROF, and LAWCOURTS-L lists). Some of them can also be used to announce new or forthcoming publications, conferences, job openings, etc. (e.g., NEWLAWBOOKS-L). Other lists are for distribution of tables of contents, abstracts, book reviews, case summaries and updates, or full texts of legal articles, and news items (see LIIBULLETIN, SciB, LAWOBSERVER, WEBJCLI-NEWS, UNTT-LPBR, etc.). And some lists are useful for on-line and off-line legal research (see NET-LAWYERS, CLNET, and INT-LAW). I have also included scholarly research sources such as LSN, JURIST, Counsel Connect, and TWEN which support electronic discussion groups or law professor networks.

Detailed instructions on how to subscribe and unsubscribe from the lists below are provided in my "Law Lists" guide. The basic protocol for subscribing to most lists, though, is to send an e-mail message to the address of the software that runs the list, with the following in the body of the message: subscribe [listname] [Your Name]. So, if Allison Payne wanted to subscribe to the CIVILRTS list, she would send e-mail to:

> LISTPROC@CHICAGOKENT.KENTLAW.EDU with only the following words in the body of the message (and leave the subject line blank):
> subscribe civilrts Allison Payne

To unsubscribe, she'd send the following message to:

> LISTPROC@ CHICAGOKENT.KENTLAW.EDU:
> unsubscribe civilrts

Note that MAJORDOMO and MAILBASE lists have slightly different commands for subscribing, so check my "Law Lists" for more information (or if you have problems subscribing to any of the lists below). Additional resources to check for lists of interest to law professors include: Regent University School of Law (http://www.regent.edu/lawlib/lists/ll-lwsch/html#lawprof); American Bar Association (http://www.abanet.org/discussions/open.html); Counsel Connect (free membership for law faculty—http://www.counsel-connect.com/); The West Education Network (discussion forums for instructors and students—http://twen.com/); the Institute for Global Communications (PeaceNet, LaborNet, WomensNet, EcoNet, ConflictNet—http://www.igc.org/igc/); and JURIST ("virtual classroom"—http://jurist.law.pitt.edu/). Please contact me at llou@midway.uchicago.edu if you have any questions concerning lists for law professors.

LISTS FOR LAW PROFESSORS
(as of 4 May 1998)
Compiled by Lyonette Louis-Jacques (llou@midway.uchicago.edu)
(http://www.lib.uchicago.edu/~llou/lawlists/lawprof.txt)

LIST NAME	SUBSCRIPTION E-MAIL/WEB ADDRESS	BRIEF DESCRIPTION
3DT	listserver@abanet.org	Deals/Dirt/Death/Taxes
AALS-FAMILYLAW	majordomo@uidaho.edu	Family Law List
AALSCONF	listserv@listserv.syr.edu	New Ideas/Exp. Teachers
AALSMIN-L	listserv@ube.ubalt.edu	Minority Law Professors
ABA-PTL	listserv@home.ease.lsoft.com	Probate and Trust Law
ABA-TAX	listserver@abanet.org	Tax Law
ACALI	majordomo@law.usyd.edu.au	Australasian CALI
ACUNS-IO	listserv@brownvm.brown.edu	International Orgs.
ADMINLAW	listproc@listproc.kentlaw.edu	Administrative Law
ADMLPROF	listserv@uofrlaw.richmond.edu	Admiralty & Maritime
ADRCLINIC	listproc@assocdir.wuacc.edu	Alternative Dispute Res.
AFRICANLAW	listproc@topeka.wuacc.edu	African Law
AGLAW-L	listproc@lawlib.wuacc.edu	Agricultural Law
AIL-L	listserv@austin.onu.edu	Artificial Intelligence
ANTIGONE	listproc@assocdir.wuacc.edu	Women in Legal Education
ANTITRUST	tdsl-l@dsl.edu	Antitrust & Trade Reg.
ANTITRUST POLICY	http://www.antitrust.org/onldtoc.htm	Antitrust Policy
ASIL-INNOVATIONS	majordomo@mail.law.vill.edu	Teach/International Law
ASILIEL	listproc@u.washington.edu	Int'l Environmental Law
ASILIELG	listproc@listproc.kentlaw.edu	Int'l Economic Law
ASP-L	listproc@chicagokent.kentlaw.edu	Academic Assistance
ASYLUM-L	majordomo@ufsia.ac.be	Asylum and Refugee Law
BANKRLAW	majordomo@polecat.law.indiana.edu	Bankruptcy Law
BIOETHICSLAW-L	listproc@lawlib.wuacc.edu	Law/Medicine/Health Care
BIOLAW	listserv@yu1.yu.edu	Biology and Law
BIZLAW	listserv@law.ab.umd.edu	Business Associations
BLUESKY	majordomo@mail.law.vill.edu	State Securities Law
CALI-L	listproc@listproc.kentlaw.edu	Computer-Assisted LI
CCGROUP	majordomo@sunsite.wits.ac.za	South African Const.
CFO-LAW	listproc@email.unc.edu	Chief Financial Officers
CHIFEMS	listproc@chicagokent.kentlaw.edu	Feminists/Law/Chicago
CITES-L	listproc@wcmc.org.uk	Trade/Endangered Species
CIVILRTS	listproc@chicagokent.kentlaw.edu	Civil Rights/Liberties
CIVPRO	owner-civpro@law.wisc.edu	Civil Procedure
CIVPROCEDURE-L	listproc@lawlibdns.wuacc.edu	Civil Procedure
CLA	owner-cla@law.wisc.edu	Contract Law in Action
CLNET	listproc@u.washington.edu	Chinese Law Net
CLPNET	majordomo@mark.geneva.edu	Christian Law Professors
CLSPEECH	listproc@ftplaw.wuacc.edu	Free Speech/1st Amend.
CNI-COPYRIGHT	listproc@cni.org	Intellectual Property
COC-L	listserv@ube.ubalt.edu	Clinicians of Color
COMLAW	majordomo@majordomo.srv.ualberta.ca	Computers/Legal Ed.
COMLAW-L	listproc@lawlib.wuacc.edu	Mass Communication Law
COMPCONS	listserv@uofrlaw.richmond.edu	Comparative Constitutions
COMPLAW-L	listproc@usc.edu	Comparative Law/Courts
COMPUTERSUPPORT- LAW-SCHOOLS	mailbase@mailbase.ac.uk	Computers/Law Schools

CONFLICTS-L	listproc@lawdns.wuacc.edu	Conflicts of Law
CONLAW	listproc@ssiinc.com	Constitutional Law
CONLAW-ABSTRACTS	listserv@lawlib.slu.edu	Con Law Articles
CONTRACTS	listserv@austin.onu.edu	Contract Law
CRIMPROF	listproc@chicagokent.kentlaw.edu	Criminal Law/Procedure
CTI-LAW	mailbase@mailbase.ac.uk	Info Tech/Law Teaching
CYBERIA-L	listserv@listserv.aol.com	Internet Law Issues
CYBERPROF	mlemley@mail.law.utexas.edu	Cyberspace/Internet Law
CYBERSPACE-LAW	sandy_barnes@ssrn.com	Cyberspace Law Abstracts
DATA-PROTECTION	mailbase@mailbase.ac.uk	Personal Data/Protection
DEANTECH	majordomo@law.uoregon.edu	Deans/Law School Tech.
DEATHPENALTY	listproc@assocdir.wuacc.edu	Capital Punishment
DER-INT	listserv@listserv.rediris.es	International Law (Spain)
DIRT	dirt+request@umkc.edu	Real Estate Law
DISPUTE-RES	listserv@listserv.law.cornell.edu	Dispute Resolution/ADR
DNSLIST	listproc@chicagokent.kentlaw.edu	Law School Deans
DONATIVETRANSFERS	listproc@aall.wuacc.edu	Donative Transfers
DVCLINIC	listproc@topeka.wuacc.edu	Domestic Violence Clinic
E-TEACH	listproc@chicagokent.kentlaw.edu	Electronic Law Teaching
ECONLAW	listproc@gmu.edu	Law and Economics
EDLAW	listserv@ukcc.uky.edu	Law and Education
EDUPAGE	listproc@educom.unc.edu	Computer/Internet News
ELAW-J	majordomo@cleo.murdoch.edu.au	Australia e-journal/law
ELDERLAW-L	listproc@topeka.wuacc.edu	Aged Persons
ELECTION-LAW	listproc@chicagokent.kentlaw.edu	Election Law
ENVLAWPROFS	majordomo@lists.uoregon.edu	Environmental Law
ERN	sandy_barnes@ssrn.com	Economics Research Net
ESL-LAW	listserv@vm.temple.edu	English/Second Language
EURO-LEX	listserv@listserv.gmd.de	European Law/Sources
EVID-L	listproc@lawlibdns.wuacc.edu	Evidence Law
EVIDENCE	listproc@chicagokent.kentlaw.edu	Evidence Law
EXTENSION-L	listserv@olemiss.edu	Copyright Term/Extension
FAC_RECRUIT	listproc@assocdir.wuacc.edu	Faculty Recruitment
FAMILYLAW	majordomo@uidaho.edu	Family Law
FAMILYLAW-L	listproc@lawlib.wuacc.edu	Family Law
FAMILYLAWPROF-L	listproc@assocdir.wuacc.edu	Family Law
FEDSEC	listserv@mail.law.vill.edu	Federal Securities
FEDCOURTS	owner-fedcourts@law.wisc.edu	Federal Courts
FEDTAX-L	listserv@shsu.edu	Federal Taxes
FEMJUR	listproc@assocdir.wuacc.edu	Feminist Jurisprudence
FEN	sandy_barnes@ssrn.com	Financial Economics
FIREARMSLAW	listproc@ssiinc.com	Firearms/2d Amend.
FORENSIC-LINGUISTICS	mailbase@mailbase.ac.uk	Language/Courts/Law
FORENSICECONOMICS	listproc@acc.wuacc.edu	Forensic Economics
FORINTLAW	listproc@law.wuacc.edu	Int'l Business Law
GAYLAW	listserv@unc.edu	Nat'l J. Sex. Orient. L.
H-DIPLO	listserv@h-net.msu.edu	History of Diplomacy
H-LAW	listserv@h-net.msu.edu	History of Law
HAYEK-L	listserv@maelstrom.stjohns.edu	Law/Political Economy
HEALTHLAW-L	listproc@lawlib.wuacc.edu	Health Law
HISLAW-L	listserv@ulkyvm.louisville.edu	History of Law
HUMLAW-L	listproc@lawlib.wuacc.edu	Law and the Humanities
HUMANRIGHTS-L	listproc@lawlib.wuacc.edu	Int'l Human Rights Law
IMMPROF	listproc@lists.colorado.edu	Immigration Law
INT-LAW	majordomo@listhost.ciesin.org	Int'l Law Research
INT-LAW-DIGEST	majordomo@listhost.ciesin.org	1 message a day=all msgs.

INT-TAX	listserver@abanet.org	International Tax Law
INTLAWPROFESSOR-L	listproc@law.wuacc.edu	International Law
IPPROFS	tfield@fplc.edu	Intellectual Property
IRISHLAW	listserv@irlearn.ucd.ie	Irish Law
IRTHEORY_LIST	mailserv@unimelb.edu.au	International Relations
IUSROMANUM	majordomo@jurix.jura.uni-sb.de	Roman Law
JEWISHLAWPROF-L	listproc@lawlib.wuacc.edu	Jewish Law Professors
JURIST UPDATE	jurist@law.pitt.edu	Law Professors' Web News
JUVENILELAW-L	listproc@lawlib.wuacc.edu	Juvenile Law
LABOR-EMP	listproc@willamette.edu	Labor/Employment Law News
LANDUSELAW-L	listproc@aall.wuacc.edu	Land Use Law
LATINO-LAW-PROFS	listproc@ucdavis.edu	Latino Law Professors
LAW-AI	mailbase@mailbase.ac.uk	Artificial Intelligence
LAW-DEPT-HEADS	mailbase@mailbase.ac.uk	Deans/UK Law Schools
LAW-FRANCE	law-france-request@amgot.org	French Law
LAW-WWW	mailbase@mailbase.ac.uk	World Wide Web/Law
LAWAID	listserv@rutvm1.rutgers.edu	Law School Financial Aid
LAWAND	majordomo@polecat.law.indiana.edU	Law and Society
LAWCLINIC	listproc@lawlib.wuacc.edu	Clinical Legal Education
LAWCOURTS-L	listproc@usc.edu	Law and the Courts
LAWDEANS-L	zzfolm@acc.wuacc.edu	Deans of Law Schools
LAWDEVEL-L	majordomo@law.uoregon.edu	LS/Development Officers
LAWLIBDIR-L	listproc@lawlib.wuacc.edu	Law Library Directors
LAWOBSERVER	listserv@maelstrom.stjohns.edu	Computer Law Observer
LAWPROF	listproc@chicagokent.kentlaw.edu	Law Professors/Lecturers
LAWREL-L	mailserv@lists.cua.edu	Law and Religion
LAWTEACH	listproc@assocdir.wuacc.edu	Law Teaching
LAWTEACHTECH	listproc@assocdir.wuacc.edu	Law Teaching Technology
LEA	sandy_barnes@ssrn.com	Law/Economics Abstracts
LEGAL-METHODS	listserv@listserv.temple.edu	Legal Methods Teaching
LEGALETHICS-L	listproc@lawlib.wuacc.edu	Legal Ethics
LEGALSTUDIES	listserv@listserv.law.cornell.edu	Undergrad Legal Educators
LEGPHIL	majordomo@lists.lrz-muenchen.de	Legal Philosophy/Theory
LEGWRI-L	listproc@chicagokent.kentlaw.edu	Legal Writing
LIIBULLETIN	listserv@listserv.law.cornell.edu	U.S. Supreme Court Cases
LNET-LLC	listserv@usa.net	Limited Liability C/Ps
LSN	sandy_barnes@ssrn.com	Legal Scholarship Network
LWSCHOLAR	majordomo@cwsl.edu	Scholarship/Law Reviews
MBTI-LAW	listproc@chicagokent.kentlaw.edu	Myers-Briggs/Law Schools
MKTREG	listserv@law.ab.umd.edu	Market Regulation
MIDWSTPOCCONF	listproc@assocdir.wuacc.edu	Law/Professors of Color
NET-LAWYERS	listserv@peach.ease.lsoft.com	Lawyers' Use of the Net
NLRB-WEEKLY	listproc@willamette.edu	Labor Decisions Summaries
OILGASLAW-L	listproc@lawlib.wuacc.edu	Oil and Gas Law
PAIDEIUS	listserv@listserv.rediris.es	Teaching Innovations/Spain
PATENT-L	listproc@ftplaw.wuacc.edu	Patent Law
POVERTYLAW-L	listproc@lawlib.wuacc.edu	Poverty Law
PROF-TXLAW	listserv@stcl.edu	Texas Law Professors
QI	majordomo@abacus.oxy.edu	Queer Immigration
QUEERLAW	majordomo@abacus.oxy.edu	Sexual Orientation/Law
QUEERLAW-DIGEST	majordomo@abacus.oxy.edu	Sex. Orient. Law/Digest
QUEERLAW-EDIT	majordomo@abacus.oxy.edu	Sex. Orient. Law/Moderated
RACE_AND_CRIME	lists@spclists.spc.uchicago.edu	Race and Crime Issues
REGIS-PROF	majordomo@cwsl.edu	Legislation
RELIGIONLAW	listserv@listserv.ucla.edu	Law and Religion
RESTITUTION	majordomo@maillist.ox.ac.uk	Restitution/Unjust Enr.

RISKWEB	http://www.riskweb.com/	Risk/Insurance
SciB	faris3-request@farislaw.com	Sup. Ct. Int'l Bull.
SECURITIESLAW-L	listproc@aall.wuacc.edu	Securities Law
SPTL-EC	majordomo@warwick.ac.uk	UK EU Law Profs List
TAXPROF-L	listproc@taft.law.uc.edu	Tax Law
TEACHLAWRES	listproc@lawlib.wuacc.edu	Teaching Legal Research
TORTPROF	listproc@chicagokent.kentlaw.edu	Tort Law
TRADEMARKS-L	listproc@lawdns.wuacc.edu	Trademark Law
TRIBALLAW	listserv@thecity.sfsu.edu	Tribal Law
TWATCH-L	listserv@listserv.acsu.buffalo.edu	War Crimes Tribunals
TWEN	http://twen.com/	West Education E-Forums
UCC2B	listserver@abanet.org	Uniform Commercial Code
UCCART2	listserver@abanet.org	Uniform Commercial Code
UCCLAW-L	listproc@assocdir.wuacc.edu	Uniform Commercial Code
UNT-LPBR	listserv@unt.edu	Law/Politics Bk. Revs.
USCOPYRIGHT	listserv@loc.gov	Copyright Office NewsNet
WEBJCLI-NEWS	mailbase@mailbase.ac.uk	E-J Current Legal Issues
WORKLAW	listproc@chicagokent.kentlaw.edu	Labor Law
YLOPEARL	listproc@seattleu.edu	Asian/Pacific American

Lyonette Louis-Jacques
University of Chicago Law School

Chapter 8

Simulations and Role-Playing

See One, Do One, Teach One. — Anonymous

[N]egotiation workshops, legal clinics, and computer simulations have broadened legal education to produce lawyers more highly trained and sophisticated than ever before. — Justice Ruth Bader Ginsburg

Simulations and role-playing are techniques that fall somewhere between doctrine-oriented hypotheticals and live-client clinical programs. Simulations in legal education include writing a contract, interviewing a client, or arguing in moot court. A simulation is an indirect, vicarious experience, like doctrinal hypotheticals in a casebook, but is often modeled to resemble direct, live-client situations. Simulations often involve fact-oriented, ethics-oriented, and client-oriented problem solving. In this manner, simulations are more directly concerned with the attorney's role in practical contexts.

A. The Argument for Using Simulations and Role-Playing

Law students provide these glimpses of students' experiences in simulations and role-playing:

> "In my Administrative Law class...and it was a huge class, we did role-playing and there were several issues that I didn't understand or doctrines that I didn't understand, but it all became clear during that day because it all became personal...[I]f you have to get up and play a part, be the victim, be the prosecutor, be the defense attorney, then it really becomes personal and those doctrines...take on a whole new life."

* * *

> "[S]he divided the class of about forty people into groups of four and everybody was going to pretend that they were making recommendations to a congressional committee about how to change the statute...[W]e had to read the statute the night before. We sat in our group and one group would be representing the workers' association; one group might be representing the manufacturers' association....And you had to argue

193

with other people in your group how the statute should be changed: you had to redraft it. You had to come up with a presentation to make to Congress, and then one person from that group had to make the presentation. Now you think about what you did in that thing. You had to read; you had to interpret a statute. You had to present and persuade to other people in your group, argue effectively, and then you had to stand up and make a presentation and you had to write a statute. Those are five incredible skills that you need to have as a lawyer that you had to practice in one hour. It was fabulous."

The theory behind simulations and role-playing is that these techniques promote interest in the subject matter, motivation to learn, better knowledge retention, and better understanding of how to apply the knowledge. It is also grounded in the old adage that people learn not by what they see or hear, but by what they do.

Simulations are consistent with adult learning theory. According to Professor Frank Bloch, adult learning requires: mutual inquiries by both teacher and students; an emphasis on active, experiential learning; students who are ready to learn; and a learning process presented in a useful context. Students who participate in simulation techniques are actively involved in an educational experience and are less inclined and less able to coast along as passive observers of education like passengers in a car, taking notes but lacking real engagement.

Simulation techniques are commendable because they encourage the use of the material, not just its memorization. In Benjamin Bloom's famous taxonomy of learning, the possession of knowledge constitutes a more basic level of learning than applying that knowledge. In law school, for example, while the class focus may be on the delivery of knowledge, unless concepts can be actively used—through clear writing, creative problem solving, in a final examination, on a term paper, or in demonstrating a legal skill—the student is not really learning effectively. This application component, in law school and elsewhere, provides students with feedback about what they understand and, more importantly, what they don't understand. Simulations help students to integrate theory, rules, and practice.

Simulations' benefits can not be cabined to active learning alone. Simulations can help deal with student anxiety over the unknown and ambiguous world of law practice, can improve both the quality of the work of students and their judgment skills, and can enhance students' cooperative abilities if they are working with other student-lawyers. Importantly, simulations can enhance a student's appreciation of and skills relating to fact-gathering, a useful part of many lawyers' practices.

Simulations have other special benefits for law practice. They give students insight into how a particular practice area may work, which in turn may help students make more informed decisions about jobs after graduation. Simulations can promote many personal traits that carry over into law practice. These include time-management, assertiveness, ethics, fortitude in making mistakes, accepting and giving constructive feedback, and dealing with the emotional aspects of a situation with legal implications.

B. Problems with Simulations and Role-Playing

1. Institutional History

As helpful as simulations and role-playing can be, these techniques are often relegated to advanced courses, particularly those with a "practitioner's" orientation. In many law schools, for example, simulations have become identified with courses such as Trial Advocacy and moot court. Thus, a school's culture and history may limit the use of simulations and cast an imprimatur on these techniques as not being worthy of displacing traditional methods. Further, the ease with which simulations may be adopted also may depend on the school's curriculum. Some schools have many "nontraditional" courses, or traditional courses with nontraditional orientations, that may more readily accommodate simulation techniques.

2. Resources

Even if the curriculum and culture of a school are both predisposed toward the use of simulations, a school's resources may provide another limit on their use. As Justice Ginsburg noted above, computer simulations are a terrific learning tool. If the school is not equipped with the proper technology, however, computer simulations will not occur.

3. Course Coverage

Simulations sometimes diminish the amount of doctrine that can be covered. This fact provides a deterrent to the use of this technique in many first-year and other basic courses where doctrinal coverage is often an overriding objective.

4. Preparation Time

Simulations take time to prepare and plan. Because there are often several people playing roles and because there is often acting involved, simulations may ask a professor to take on a role equivalent to that of a director. This takes time and deliberative thought.

5. The Hybrid Nature of Simulations

As a cross between doctrinal hypotheticals and live-client clinics, simulations also miss the distinctively conceptual or practical flavors of its component parts. For example, without live clients, the simulation may omit the irrationality and unpredictability of clients, de-emphasizing the important need for judgment as a legal skill. Similarly, simulations may deemphasize complex doctrinal theory.

C. Overcoming Problems with Simulations and Role-Playing

The problems posed by simulations are not insurmountable. Creative planning and the reallocation of resources should go a long way toward minimizing objections to the use of simulations, even in first-year courses.

Rejoinders to specific objections are readily made. While institutional history may serve as an obstacle, institutions change over time. Even the Socratic method has evolved in its delivery and status. The impetus for utilizing simulations may come from institutional or individual sources. Both the MacCrate Report, suggesting a greater focus on skills, and student interest in experiential learning may promote the institutional acceptance of simulations. Further, the stimulus for change may even be more localized, initiated by a teacher's interest in trying something new.

A lack of resources may provide an additional obstacle. Yet, simulations require primarily human resources, which cost little or no money if students and staff perform the roles. Even simulations using computers and other high-tech equipment will not increase costs for most law schools, which already have that hardware. Consequently, the costs of simulations can be manageable.

Allegations of diminished course coverage are often made when assailing alternative teaching-learning techniques. However, these alternative techniques, including simulations, need not sacrifice coverage. Indeed, simulations provide a rich environment for the discussion of a variety of issues, theories, concepts, and subject areas. For example, the simulation of the Bernhard Goetz case, the so-called "N.Y. subway vigilante," raises doctrinal issues of self-defense and justification, the question of race in a criminal case, the procedural matters of indictments and appeal, and much more.

The initial construction of a simulation may take additional time because simulations have more component parts than lectures or Socratic techniques. But preparing a simulation should not be significantly more arduous than preparing well for a more traditional class. In addition, well-constructed simulations can be used in future years with a little fine-tuning.

The addition of simulations to a course does not mean abandoning traditional teaching techniques such as lecture, discussion, or the Socratic method. Instead, simulations can be one of a variety of teaching techniques to help students achieve the course objectives. What simulations provide is an additional way for students to learn traditional substantive materials and a wide variety of lawyering skills.

D. Designing Simulations and Role-Playing Exercises

In an excellent article on the use of simulations in law school, "Simulations: An Introduction," Professor Jay Feinman described the creation and design of successful simulations. This section on how to design simulations borrows from some of the helpful insights offered by Professor Feinman.

According to Professor Feinman, when creating an effective simulation, teachers must determine the size and nature of the simulation, identify objectives, and choose its format.

1. The Size of the Simulation

"Size" of the simulation indicates its nature and type. A "small" simulation would be a one-time single exercise of fairly short duration. This exercise might involve writing an opinion letter, a brief, or a complaint. The small simulation could be used as a component in a doctrinal first-year course, in an upper-class doctrinal course, or in a seminar. It is a very flexible device.

A "larger" simulation includes longer and recurring exercises, often based on more complex facts that are elicited over time by the students. These exercises may include interviewing clients, engaging in negotiations that occur throughout a course, or drafting a contract. Of course, the subject matter is not dispositive of the nature of the simulations — what counts is the length and complexity of the simulation.

2. The Objectives of a Simulation

The objectives of a simulation should be planned and developed in advance. It is not enough for the teacher to provide a conclusory goal, such as relating law school to the real world of legal practice; specifically articulated goals are much more useful. These goals should clearly relate to one or more of three major educational objectives: the cognitive (analytical) abilities of students, the performance (activity) skills of students, or the affective (emotive) qualities of the lawyering experience.

In the cognitive domain, the students would increase their doctrinal problem-solving talents. In the performance area, skills, such as those discussed in the MacCrate Report, would be emphasized and practiced. Students would become aware of what is required for competency in legal practice and not focus solely on the criteria for exam performance. Finally, affective learning focuses the student attorney on the dynamics of the attorney-client relationship and the dimension of dealing with the needs and interests of live clients.

3. The Simulation Design and Format

To implement the objectives of a simulation, the professor must choose a particular format—how the simulation will occur in or outside of the class. A simulation is generally built around a set of facts. So what the facts include and how they are presented provide the initial design decision. The facts provide the students not only with legal issues, but also with ambiguity in terms of what was omitted and how given facts are to be interpreted.

Once the facts are constructed, the various participants must be assigned roles and cues, much like the presentation of a play. In fact, the creation of a simulation often parallels that of other types of performances, such as plays or movies. The teacher should give students written descriptions of their roles.

While role-playing is the second major piece of the simulation construction, it should be coordinated with a determination of whether this will be a team effort or an individual performance. If it is a team effort, the size of the teams and the relationships within the teams also should be dealt with in advance.

A simulation should have a final product in addition to the experience of participation. This product can be a contract, a set of interview notes, or even a description of the simulation experience by each of the participants. The creation of a product helps students to focus on the purposes of the simulation.

Other factors in preparing for a simulation include how much time will be allocated for the simulation experience; where the simulation will take place; whether teaching assistants or outside attorneys will assist in the process; whether the simulation will require research by the participants; and how the simulation will be critiqued and reviewed.

References

Gerald Hess, *Listening To Our Students: Obstructing and Enhancing Learning in Law School*, 31 U.S.F. L. Rev. 941 (1997).

F. Bloch, *The Andragogical Basis of Clinical Legal Education*, 35 Vand. L. Rev. 321, 323 (1982).

Barbara Gross Davis, Tools for Teaching 159–165 (1993).

James Eagar, *The Right Tool for the Job: The Effective Use of Pedagogical Methods in Legal Education*, 32 Gonz. L. Rev. 389 (1996–1997).

Jay Feinman, *Simulations: An Introduction*, 45 J. Legal Educ. 469 (1995).

Ruth Bader Ginsburg, "Remarks at the Rededication Ceremony, University of Illinois College of Law, September 8, 1994," 1995 U. Ill. L. Rev. 11 (1995).

Keith W. Prichard & R. McLarren Sawyer, Handbook of College Teaching: Theory and Applications 171–178 (1994).

Specific Ideas for Simulations

#1: Diverse Views and Values Through Role-Play

Trying to bring out diverse views or values regarding a particular issue is sometimes very difficult. When the issue is especially controversial, some voices are more easily heard than others. Dominant ideologies, cultural biases, social class, power relations, and, more recently, political correctness might hinder the fullest consideration of divergent views.

Some topics might come to mind. Consider, for example, obscenity, race relations, sexual harassment, same-sex marriage, abortion, and the like within Constitutional Law. In my particular context, I might add the colonial relations between the United States and Puerto Rico. Is it possible to "force free speech," so to speak, to make sure that divergent views are exposed in class?

Take, for example, the discussion of obscenity and indecency in a Constitutional Law course. Needless to say, an actual obscene or indecent showing or performance might very well do the trick. But of course, not even tenure might shield you from some very embarrassing accusations.

Still, role-playing might be useful. I have designed an exercise which works most of the time. In the class, before the students do their reading of the traditional material (*Roth, Miller v. California, Paris Adult Theater, Ferber v. New York, Cohen v. California, Pacifica Foundation,* and the like), I assign several roles to volunteer students. They don't actually know what they're getting into when they volunteer. They are asked to maintain their "secret identity." The roles are:

- a very conservative politician running for office,
- a fundamentalist preacher,
- a married couple that enjoys watching pornography as part of their sex life,
- a homosexual who hasn't "come out" and watches pornography regularly,
- a feminist activist,
- a college professor of art,
- a representative of the A.C.L.U.

The students are asked to study the materials and to come prepared to react to them in the next class within their assigned role, regardless of their personal views and beliefs. Then, as the materials are presented in class, the volunteer students make up a "panel of experts" and take turns presenting their reactions to the case law. Sometimes they actually get carried away and I must intervene to control what becomes an actual debate. Somewhere along the line, I (as moderator) open the discussion to the rest of the class.

In the process, not only do the relevant doctrines get explained and criticized, but the most varied views are laid on the table for the benefit of the whole class (and for my own, I willingly admit). And since it is only "a show," it's also a lot of fun.

Carlos I. Gorrin-Peralta
Inter-American University of Puerto Rico

#2: Year-Long Simulation in Civil Procedure

As part of a two-semester, six-credit, first-year civil procedure course, I have developed a simulation involving a water pollution problem that can be characterized as a nuisance or a violation of the Clean Water Act (CWA). I use it as a hypothetical to explore course material in both semesters, as a vehicle for drafting, and to give the students some "hands on" experience using civil procedure. The problem is patterned after *International Paper Co. v. Ouellette*, 479 U.S. 481 (1987) and *Gwaltney of Smithfield v. Chesapeak Bay Foundation, Inc.*, 484 U.S. 49 (1987). It involves a paper mill in New York State which discharges treated effluent into the Susquehanna River. Mary and Peter Jackson live downriver from the mill in Pennsylvania and object to the pollution. So far, I have made the simulation exercises closed-universe for time control and focus purposes. Accordingly, I give the students additional facts, statutes, and case law when needed for a given assignment.

We begin the year with a brief introduction to subject matter and personal jurisdiction which we study in depth during the spring semester. The students then interview Mary Jackson, the client. Following the interview we discuss case planning, legal research, alternate dispute resolution, ethical issues, statutes of limitations, and anything else that comes up. We also review subject matter and personal jurisdiction.

During the unit on pleadings, the students draft a federal complaint for Mary and Peter Jackson alleging a nuisance, a CWA violation, or both. After they finish their complaints, they critique a defective complaint. I give them a sample nuisance complaint and a sample CWA complaint. The students then answer the CWA complaint and receive a sample answer. The class also prepares arguments for and against a 12(b) motion to dismiss and a Rule 11 motion. I choose several volunteers to argue the motions before the class, to serve as the judge's law clerks, and to act as the bailiff. In addition to forcing the students to work with the federal rules and cases that they have been studying in class, these exercises allow them to struggle with some fairly complex statutory language in order to use the citizen suit provision of the CWA.

The class then studies discovery. We discuss discovery planning using the Jacksons' case. Working in small groups, the students draft sample interrogatories, requests for documents, and requests for admissions. We also discuss whom they would depose. If there is time, I sometimes have them draft a discovery plan. The students choose which side they wish to represent. Class discussions generally raise all sorts of interesting ethical issues as well as explore discovery strategy, devices, and policies.

When the class examines summary judgment, the students discuss possible arguments for and against summary judgment or partial summary judgment in the Jacksons' case. They also discuss what evidence should be submitted in support of and in opposition to the motion. This allows review of discovery as well as summary judgment.

When we get to trials, the students pick a jury in *Jackson v. Century Paper Corp.* The students volunteer to play the attorneys and jurors. For the jury panel I try to select volunteers who did not enter law school immediately after college (i.e., those who have had a "real life" before law school).

I tell them to answer the "attorneys'" questions during voir dire truthfully except that they are now citizens of the forum state. I do, however, slip several potential jurors additional facts to create grounds for causal challenges and to induce the "attorneys" to use their peremptory strikes. After the jury is selected, we discuss the students' strikes. This class is fun for the students and provides a nice break toward the end of the fall semester. For this reason, I have kept it in the syllabus even though I am generally running out of class time for more important material at this point in the semester.

I use the *Jackson* fact pattern as a regular hypothetical for the rest of the fall and spring semesters although less often to prevent "overkill." By manipulating the facts in the spring, the students can explore jurisdiction, service, venue, joinder, and *Erie* conflicts issues.

This simulation can be easily adapted to a one-semester course and seems to work equally well whether you begin with jurisdiction or the litigation rules. At the end of the year, I post on my office door an obituary of a Mary Jackson from the local paper. The students who have suffered through my Civil Procedure course and the upper-class students and faculty who have played Mary Jackson for me seem to take morbid delight in seeing Mary Jackson's death notice.

Katharine F. Nelson
Widener University School of Law

#3: Skills Lab

In 1992 an ABA task force on legal education and professional competence concluded that law schools and bar programs often fail to provide practical training for beginning lawyers. The report issued by the task force (MacCrate Report) urged both law schools and the practicing bar to work jointly toward improving the skills training of young lawyers. With the assistance of a FIPSE grant from the United States Department of Education, Gonzaga Law School has put the principles of the MacCrate Report into action. Our program is easy to implement, cost-effective, and popular with both students and faculty.

What We Did

In our program law faculty and practicing attorneys who are experts in a particular field jointly plan a one-credit skills lab that is taught in conjunction with a doctrinal course. For example, I teach a course in wills and trusts. My practitioner/partner and I decided that our skills lab would require the students to work on three different problems during the semester.

In the first problem, students interview clients and prepare all necessary papers to probate the estate of a person who dies without a will. The second problem is an interviewing and drafting problem involving preparing a will and trust for a couple with minor children. In the third problem, students explore ways to settle a will contest involving allegations of undue influence. In this way, students gain valuable experience in three aspects of a probate attorney's practice: the attorney as counselor and adviser who helps clients plan and draft wills and trust, the attorney as procedural specialist who assists clients deal with court, and the negotiator/litigator who helps clients resolve conflicts with others. This lab focuses on interviewing, counseling, and drafting, but the skills are taught in the context of a real-life probate practice.

My partner and I worked closely to plan the skills we wanted to emphasize, the assignments students would complete, and the ways we would assess student progress. We also structured the labs so that assignments would build on the content offered in the large doctrinal course. My partner was given adjunct status and actually taught the lab. I sat in and was impressed. In addition to emphasizing essential skills, the lab format promoted active learning. Students applied theories learned in my class to identify problems, suggest solutions, and set goals. In addition, my partner served as a powerful model of a compassionate, ethical, and tough-minded professional.

Gonzaga has offered skills labs in Family Law, Professional Responsibility, Environmental Law, Taxation, Business Associations, and Creditors' Rights.

How We Did It

First, all skills labs are electives. We realize students take courses for a variety of reasons. For example, some take my wills and trusts course to gain enough theoretical knowledge to pass a bar exam. Others may be motivated to take the course for personal reasons (i.e., family currently involved in a probate matter), while others may plan to make estate planning their life's work. We believe students are in the best position to decide if a skills lab would benefit them. Second, each skills lab is limited to 16 students. We want to make sure students get individual attention from the instructor. Finally, our skills labs are all graded pass/fail. We wanted the students and the instructor to focus on practice and improvement rather than grades.

Why You Might Want To Do It, Too

We think the skills labs make a lot of sense from both the student's and the institution's perspectives. Student response to the skills labs has been very positive. Students uniformly report increased competence in skills areas and increased confidence in their ability to handle legal work. They appreciate the practical advice and "modeling" done by the practicing attorneys. They overwhelmingly endorse the skills lab concept and call for more labs in future semesters.

Skills labs also work well from an institutional viewpoint. Besides being easy to implement, labs require no major changes in the existing curriculum or structure of the academic program. They are proposed, planned, and approved like any other new course. In addition, our eight labs provide an opportunity for over 100 students to practice legal skills under the close scrutiny of attorney/experts at a very modest cost. Labs improve students' substantive knowledge by creating an active learning environment that emphasizes student-centered activities. Finally, labs bring the students into close contact with ethical, competent attorneys who model professionalism.

Conclusion

Skills labs are an excellent way to meet the goals set forth in the Mac-Crate Report. They provide a cost-effective way to make skills training broadly available. They recognize the need for academics and practitioners to work together to improve legal competence, and, best of all, the students and teachers think they are a lot of fun!

Kay Lundwall
Gonzaga University School of Law

#4: Simulation Led by Practicing Lawyers

In first-year Torts, I spend approximately three weeks teaching products liability. In the last class session devoted to the topic, I engage the class in an extended hour-and-a-half role-play. The students are designated as associates in a law firm that has been asked to represent a plaintiff in a complex design defect case. The class is divided into law firms of approximately seven students. Each law firm has two "senior partners" assigned to it: one a plaintiff's attorney and the other a defense attorney specializing in products litigation.

Each law firm is charged with the task of conducting the initial meeting of the "litigation team" assigned to this case. They are (1) to determine whether or not the firm should undertake representation in the case and, assuming that it does, at least for the purposes of further investigation into the viability of a claim, (2) to plan the investigation and discovery of the case. The students met outside of class to prepare as a group.

The students begin with a written case hypothetical that includes the kind of sketchy facts that an initial client interview and some cursory product exploration would provide. With the hypothetical, the students receive directions as to the format of the class and the goals of the simulation they will conduct. Finally, I provide "Skills Information," a brief description of the practical aspects of planning investigation and discovery and some cursory insights into the methods of discovery most conducive for developing certain types of information. I then suggest a format for planning investigation and discovery that moves from the elements to be proven, to the facts necessary to prove each, to the method(s) of fact-gathering to be used to learn those facts; I tell the students to create a flow chart with those items and bring it to the simulation class.

The attorneys receive copies of all the materials the students have. In addition, I speak with each on the telephone to describe the exercise, their role, and my objectives. The letter I send confirming their participation is quite detailed, laying out my expectations and objectives. I include a fact sheet of additional information that can be provided to the students once they identify a certain avenue of investigation (e.g., contacting the federal agency that regulates the product whose design is in question), which information can then generate further inquiry. Finally, I provide a relatively detailed outline of the topics to be covered, with suggested times to devote to the discussion of each topic. Experience has proven that the attorneys appreciate a seasoned teacher's suggestions as to format and time expenditure.

During the class itself, each firm acts as the litigation team. They explore the facts they need to learn, the methods they would use to uncover them, the practical ways they would pursue those methods, the anticipated costs and time expenditures involved, how to identify and work effectively with experts, strategic and tactical considerations, alternatives for relief the client should explore, and ethical considerations. The senior partners, being litigators from both sides, provide the students with insights from both plaintiff and defense perspectives. (Incidentally, this opportunity to observe the "other side's" perspective attracts the attorneys, who believe they benefit from this insight into each others' camps.) They serve as "reality" checks for the students and discuss the pragmatic limits of certain ideas and tactics.

My students have always responded very positively to this class. They are paradoxically impressed by how much they *do* know and understand about products liability and litigation and by how much more they have to learn and consider in order to be able to solve problems for clients effectively. They feel tapped in to the professional community, getting to see attorneys at work and watching the way they relate to each other. I believe this understanding of the relationship between "adversaries" as both respectful and cooperative in many ways is one of the more important things the exercise teaches the students. They get an understanding of professionalism and civility that most students lack and that only example can convey. The attorneys, who raise and confront the ethical issues of client representation, also teach the students that ethics is a constant in practice — something else that I find students generally believe is not true. Providing role models of ethical attorneys is a valuable objective of the exercise. I find that the students begin to understand the complex relationship between law, theory, facts, and practice by having to do it themselves.

Student evaluations of the exercise indicate that many of them believe they learned more in this class than in any other. (One needs a healthy ego to do this!) They also almost universally wish for more time to be devoted to it. Although the students really appreciate what the attorneys tell them about what they do, and how things are done, they are also disappointed by (even resentful of) the rare lawyer who monopolizes the discussion and does not give them a chance to express and explore their own ideas and respond to questions and challenges from the attorney. I inform the lawyers that the students should do most of the talking, with the lawyers entering in with their opinions and ideas after the students have tried themselves. By having evaluations of the exercise and attorneys, I am able to learn who might pose a problem and either educate or avoid using him or her in the future.

Elizabeth Reilly
University of Akron School of Law

#5: Case Arguments in First-Year Classes

One device which I have used with some success in my Contracts classes, especially after the middle of the first semester and in the second semester, is forcing the students to adopt the role of lawyer for one of the parties and argue the case which we are examining. For example, after briefly mentioning the facts, I call on a student and ask her to explain the plaintiff's theory of her case and to argue it.

Objectives of this type of exercise in class are: (1) to accustom students to arguments as early as possible in their career; (2) to accustom students to use cases as tools, that is, to argue application of the cases; (3) to help the first-year students to see the use of cases as precedent; (4) to help first-year students perceive the effect of the rationale (or of various rationales) on the use or value of a case as precedent; (5) to force the students to integrate prior cases into the case study.

One situation where the technique is helpful occurs where the case being covered in class has been preceded by a case which is similar, and the second case changes the law or reaches a different result. In that situation, after briefly going over the facts of the case, I will say to one of my students: "All right, if you had been the lawyer for the plaintiff in this case, and you had in your jurisdiction only the law which had developed up to the previous case (not the one at bar), how would you have argued *this* case; what would have been your theory?" One way or another, I will make clear to the students that, given preexisting law, they are to put themselves into the shoes of the lawyer arguing the present case. Then the class and I can ask what was different about the case at bar? The facts? The arguments of the lawyer who actually argued it (and perhaps added something to the prior case or cases)? The judges? Thus, it leads into a discussion and argument about how to distinguish one case as precedent from another.

This device has several effects. This question forces the students to use the holding and rationale of the previous case and apply them to the present case. It forces analysis and application in relating the previous cases to the present case. And it does this while forcing students to practice thinking and argument.

There are several variations which have worked well in particular situations. One is to use the "lawyer role" device following a case in which a court has used multiple rationales. Frequently, a student will argue only one. Then, the teacher can argue the other rationales, or argue hypos which will force the student to consider the other rationales. Another use is, when covering contentious material (e.g., in the contracts area, portions of unconscionability), have one side of the classroom argue the plaintiff's case or theory and the other side the defendant's. The faculty member helps to keep the argument at a high level and helps the students tie their arguments into approaches taken in the cases.

John Gedid
Widener University School of Law

#6: Early Introduction to Judicial Decision-making

Typically, law students are trained to be advocates who owe their ultimate allegiance to an individual client to the exclusion of duties owed to others. Consequently, most of the simulated exercises in law school place students in the role of partisan advocates. Students in such roles often provide answers that resolve issues in their client's favor even when the law and facts clearly support the other side. It may be true that effective advocacy requires a partisan approach to issues. However, such an approach should not be myopic and ignore the larger concerns of the court.

An exercise that permits students to divorce themselves from the role of partisan advocates and places them in the role of decision-makers would help them focus on those factors other than the law that influence judicial decisions. If they are exposed to this process early in their legal education, it may prevent the formation of bad habits (i.e., excessive partisan advocacy) that may compromise their effectiveness as advocates for future clients.

Implementation—This is a group discussion/drafting exercise. Students are divided into mock appellate courts with five, seven, or nine members. Students are given briefs of a case previously decided or a case that is before the court (all identifying information removed) with instructions to decide the case. It is also possible to create a mock case and briefs in order to focus the issues in accordance with course objectives. In any event, the case should present some close legal issues or present an issue of first impression. Student courts should read briefs, confer, decide the case based upon a majority vote, and collaborate on the drafting of the opinion. Dissents will be permitted and encouraged. The student draft opinion will be presented to the class and compared with the actual opinion in the case or a suggested opinion that resolves all the issues.

Target Group—Students who have completed the first semester of law school would derive the most benefit from this exercise. The exercise presupposes some familiarity with case analysis and issue spotting, and should be introduced early in the student's legal education.

Expected Student Outcomes—Students will

- learn to integrate substantive and procedural aspects of a case.
- have a broader view of the decision process.
- have the opportunity to evaluate the logic of their own and others' positions.
- learn to work better in group settings.
- develop better exam taking skills.

William H. Hanson
University of Colorado

#7: Mock Supreme Court Arguments

In teaching criminal procedure, I occasionally set up the classroom as a moot courtroom and have students argue opposite sides of a criminal procedure case that the Supreme Court has agreed to review but has not yet decided. (This works better in the fall semester before the Court has decided many of its cases, and better in those years in which the Court agrees to hear several Fourth Amendment or confession cases.) Other students play the role of Justice and question the advocates. (In some years, I have asked the students to play the role of particular Justices.) The students are chosen for these roles on a voluntary basis several weeks in advance of the arguments (which occur in the week in which the particular subject—e.g., consent searches, automobile searches, etc.—is discussed in class). After the argument, I open up the discussion to the entire class, in order to address, e.g., how the Court ought to rule, how the Court is likely to rule, what additional arguments could have been made by the student-advocates, etc.

Bruce Green
Fordham University School of Law

#8: Students as Judges

One of my classes is a first-year property course with about 85 students. There was an important case on a topic that was only cited in the notes following the selected edited cases. The reading assignment was already heavy, and a supplemental assignment of the case would have raised howls of protest by the students. A "mini-lecture" on the case would have been efficient but boring.

Instead I tried this: I selected three students (back row, center) and appointed them appellate judges. I told them that I would present short arguments to them and they would not only have to decide the issue, but explain to the class why they decided as they did. I formally presented an argument for one side, then for the other. In the arguments, I was able to emphasize the important policy and substantive law that I wanted them to know from the case. The arguments were no longer than a lecture would have been.

I let them confer with each other a few minutes, then they gave their decision and supporting rationale. I quickly polled the class to see how many students were in agreement with the judges' decision. Because there were compelling arguments for both sides, there was substantial disagreement. I asked all students to predict the effect—in the real world—of the law which was just "made" in the classroom. After that, I told them what the U.S. Supreme Court had decided in the real case.

This short exercise has several advantages. First, it sparks interest because it is a change from the usual class format. Second, the students (first-semester, first-year) get a glimpse of formal oral argumentation—which they must undertake in their second-semester advocacy class. Third, the students look at the case from the perspective of one who must decide, rather than the perspective of an advocate (or worse, an indifferent student). Last, it drives home the points that real people—with differing but reasonable views—decide cases and that the decisions matter in the real world.

Eileen Gauna
Southwestern University School of Law

#9: Negotiation Exercise

This exercise allows first-year law students to use the legal writing, research, and analysis skills they have developed in creating an office memorandum in another practice context. After completing the office memorandum, students negotiate a resolution to the client's legal problem. Students are assigned to represent both sides of the conflict and receive special instructions concerning the need to resolve the conflict. (Since students have written an objective memorandum, they should understand both viewpoints.) The students are placed in groups of four, with two students working as co-counsel on each side. The exercise has two steps: first, the students draft a demand letter to the opposing side; and second, the students negotiate a settlement for their clients.

During step one, I take a group of students to the computer lab where they work on drafting their demand letters. The students in the lab all represent the same side and each team of two students uses one computer. Each team is instructed to draft a demand letter to the opposing side, which they will deliver before the negotiation. This step results in an excellent collaborative writing exercise. The students compare each other's work and discuss appropriate tone and the merits of their client's case. Students complete their letters within the class time and print them out in the lab. The students then distribute the letters to their assigned opposing team. Each team, therefore, writes and receives a demand letter.

During step two, the negotiation, students meet in an assigned location and have one hour to negotiate a settlement. Each side receives special instructions explaining why their client wants to settle the matter and the client's settlement range. As the negotiations unfold, students receive an early lesson in the power of words. The tenor of the demand letters they send and receive has an impact on how the sides approach each other in the negotiation. Students do not have to resolve the conflict. At the end of the hour, they complete a "Negotiation Progress Report" and discuss the success or failure of their negotiation.

This exercise is a valuable component within our curriculum. As students work on their demand letters and engage in the negotiations, they choose very different approaches. It is interesting to note the "professional voice" that they choose. Since the exercise is collaborative, students are exposed to the different approaches fellow students use. This exposure to different, yet equally effective forms of professional communication, helps the students see that although they are part of a distinct discourse community, they can still develop their own individual professional voice in both written and spoken communication. Through their choice of words, the inclusion of legal jargon, and the tone they establish in their negotiations, students take a step, albeit small, in their development as a legal professional.

An additional benefit in the exercise is its ability to link skills taught throughout the semester. The exercise gives students an opportunity to present the same legal arguments they had grappled with in a written context, in a spoken context. Some students that had struggled with legal writing had an opportunity to shine in another context. This "linkage" between written and spoken communication is an added bonus in this exercise. Since the exercise is done during the last week of classes, it provides an excellent closure to the semester. It also lets students explore their own perception of what it means to be a lawyer.

Maria Perez Crist
University of Dayton School of Law

#10: Negotiation Problems

The American Bar Association's Task Force on Law School and the Profession: Narrowing the Gap (MacCrate Report) urged that law schools pay more attention to the teaching of skills. Similarly, the Executive Committee Regulations of the American Association of Law Schools urge member schools to offer additional instruction in dispute resolution, planning, problem solving, drafting, and counseling. Faculty members teaching a traditional law school course using a casebook are faced with the following question: How and when, if at all, can such skills training be integrated into such a course?

One possibility of integrating skills into a traditional course is to assign a negotiation project for completion outside of class. Students benefit from a practical application of substantive law and also learn some insights into the dynamics of negotiation. A good source for negotiation problems is former problems used in the American Bar Association Law Student Division's Negotiation Competition. This competition has been held annually since 1984. The subject areas have been family law (1984–85), personal injury (1985–86), contracts (1986–87), health care (1987–88), children in the law (1988–89), business (1989–90), employment discrimination (1990–91), real property (1991–92), emerging issues in family law (1992–93), small business ventures (1993–94), contracting across national borders: international small business ventures (1994–95), sports and entertainment law (1995–96), health law (1996–97), and education law (1997–98). Within each subject area, there is a related series of negotiation problems. The problems drafted in the later years tend to be better ones.

These problems would fit in well with many substantive courses. The students can be asked to keep a log showing their planning, strategy, and progress, or the students can be asked to prepare a report of the results of the negotiation. Specific problems can be obtained from American Bar Association Law Student Division, 750 North Lake Shore Drive, Chicago, IL 60611.

Larry Teply
Creighton University School of Law

#11: Negotiation, Drafting, and Argument Regarding Prenuptial Agreements

Objectives

1. Expose the students to case law from various jurisdictions that describe differing rules for determining enforceability of prenuptial agreements.
   - The cases appear to establish different standards for validity. The students will be able to find the common elements.
   - There may be different standards, depending on the situation, i.e., divorce v. death, or property division v. spousal maintenance. The students will identify the differences.
2. The students will learn various drafting measures that can be used to protect the contract.
3. The students will evaluate or explore the ethical and practical difficulties of attempting to meet the client's wishes when some of the client's demands are controversial, probably unenforceable, or appear unfair.
4. The students will better appreciate the unpredictable impact of language when the contract is interpreted under factual patterns they never anticipated.
5. The students will be reminded of rules learned in a prior section of the course on the duties and expectations of marriage.

Methods

Brief Description. The students are told to read assigned cases illustrating five differing statements of rules for determining validity of prenuptial agreements. The cases are not briefed in class. Each student, with a partner, represents the male or female client described in a fact scenario. All the initial descriptions are the same. The partners negotiate with partners representing the other client, and draft a prenuptial agreement. The contracts are then subject to interpretation in a divorce or probate type action that occurs approximately ten years after the marriage. During that class session, each student judges one contract, using one of five different fact scenarios I have drafted. The attorneys who drafted the agreement are allowed to argue their particular position, but do not know what the ten-years-later scenario will be when they draft the contract. The judge drafts an opinion interpreting and determining the validity of all or parts of the contract. I organize the class session so each contract is "judged" by four different judges (or under four different factual scenarios).

Wrap-Up General Class Discussion

- Discussion of the experience. (Objectives 3, 4, and 5 are usually initiated by the students at this point. If they are not, I initiate the discussion.)
- Discussion of Objective 1.
- Discussion of Objective 2 if not already covered.

Comments

- The sessions take at least two to three classes. (The negotiation and drafting are done outside class time.)
- The logistics can be confusing for the professor the first time. Generally, it is better to have a larger number of small groups than a smaller number of large groups.
- There is never enough time to do justice to the choice of language used in particular contracts. I try to balance that by having each contract evaluated four times by different student judges under four varying scenarios.

I am willing to share my factual descriptions and scenarios and my logistical plans if you are interested.

Helen Donigan
Gonzaga University School of Law

#12: Negotiation and Drafting in Contracts

When I graduated from law school I had never reviewed a contract, let alone drafted one. When I began teaching Contracts I decided that was one omission I would correct with my students. To do this, I developed a simulation in which the students, working in four-person teams, would negotiate and draft a contract. The exercise centers on the negotiation of a personal services contract under which an athletic shoe company wants to hire a marathon runner as its spokesperson. I schedule the simulation during the middle of the second semester to assure that the students had sufficient grounding in basic concepts. Because my classes had approximately 100 students in them, this simulation was logistically challenging. However, with the assistance of other faculty members I have successfully carried it out for the last three years.

Format

The exercise takes three one-hour class periods and requires the students to turn in two documents. The week before the exercise I spend 10 minutes in class explaining the simulation and giving the students the team list and other materials. The teams consist of four students each—one student assigned to act as the client and three student attorneys. Half the teams are assigned to represent the shoe company and half the runner (I have developed two pages of information about each "client" for the teams, which is to be kept confidential). I then pair the teams and the game's afoot.

During the simulation week, we spend the first class session discussing negotiation strategy and methods. After this session the student teams meet, interview their client, and prepare a two-page document identifying their strategy and goals. I give the "client" information that the rest of the team does not have with instruction to tell the "lawyers" whatever s/he feels comfortable sharing. I tell the students to act as they imagine real clients would.

During the second class period the students meet for a negotiation session. For many of them this is the first such session. Since I have ten different groups meeting, I schedule them in rooms all over campus. In addition, a faculty member observes each group (I call in a lot of favors and engage in shameless begging to accomplish this part). I instruct the faculty member to observe approximately 35 to 40 minutes of negotiation and then spend a few minutes discussing the session with the students and making suggestions without divulging any "confidential" information. Once this step is completed, the students can resume the session and then meet as many times as necessary to complete the negotiation.

The third class session is a lecture on drafting contracts. I give the students approximately five days to complete negotiations and draft a final contract which all the members of each negotiating team must sign. I have so far successfully avoided impasses by requiring teams which cannot reach agreement to each draft what they consider to be a reasonable agreement. In order to keep the excess verbiage at a minimum I impose a five-page limit for the contracts (double-spaced).

During the next week of class I spend some time discussing the exercise and asking the students for their observations. I also ask them to anonymously complete a short evaluation form concerning the simulation. Finally, I critique the contracts and return them to the teams.

Results

The evaluations of this simulation have been consistently very good. The students like having the opportunity to do "real work" and to apply the concepts they have been learning all year. Many students express their appreciation for the faculty participation in the exercise. Even though this is an ungraded exercise, the documents the teams prepare are well done and complete; they obviously take the exercise seriously. Finally, I think this exercise is also valuable for the unanticipated lessons it teaches: ethical issues have arisen each year, students have been disappointed when others didn't live up to their bargains, clients have "forgotten" important facts until the middle of a negotiation session, and so on. I approached this exercise a little bit fearfully the first year, but am now absolutely sold on it.

Karen Harwood
Gonzaga University School of Law

#13: Trial Advocacy Evidence Simulation

Trial Evidence Advocacy is a one-unit simulation course designed to teach students to apply evidentiary principles and to resolve ethical, procedural, and tactical issues arising during the advocacy process.

The course methodology is to teach each area of evidence through performance. The course objective is for the students to be comfortably able to determine what it is they wish to accomplish in a courtroom with respect to specific evidentiary questions, and to be able to structure the most logical, persuasive, ethically sound, and trouble-free means to that end. I have written problems that address a specific evidentiary point and teaching notes for the course based on two case files.

In general, the class focuses on one or two areas of evidence each week. The class uses a problem format. Each student is assigned a number from 1 to 4 for the semester. Each problem involves a proponent, opponent, witness, and judge. Students are assigned a role in each problem by number, and are responsible for performing that role in class. Each student performs one or two problems each week. I, and ultimately the non-performing students, critique each simulation. Each student rotates role each week. I have found that while the simulations are critical to a mechanical understanding of how the rules of evidence function in a courtroom, the roles of judge and witness are particularly valuable as tools to increase the students' comprehension and utilization of advocacy skills.

My role expectations are:

The witness must be familiar with the testimony involved in the problem assigned, and should have thought about the problem sufficiently to be able to add reasonably foreseeable testimony during the course of the examination.

The proponent is responsible for preparing the witness before class for both direct and cross-examination, giving some thought to that witness's credibility. The proponent is responsible for structuring the direct examination and for anticipating responses to potential objections.

The opponent is responsible for anticipating the nature of the direct examination, for structuring an appropriate cross-examination, and making timely, articulate, and correct objections to the direct examination.

The judge must analyze the problem sufficiently to rule on the evidence and any objections, and to give a sound factual and legal basis for that ruling.

Laura Berend
University of San Diego School of Law

#14: Focus on Facts

When I was in law school, most of the critical thinking I did involved analyzing and synthesizing appellate court decisions. Many law school classes require students to understand and apply *facts* only on a final exam. But after law school, I quickly learned that reading cases and statutes was only part of what a lawyer does. After all, knowing what the law is (or may be) often doesn't tell you much about how the law will affect a particular client's position.

I like to give students these kinds of realistic experiences throughout the semester. One simple and engaging way to do that is to create a factual scenario for a fictitious client, then let a student (or a group of students) interview this client in class. Then the students can see how the law they've been learning would apply in a typical case.

This idea works particularly well in my Research & Writing class. Rather than drafting a dry fact scenario (which students could easily copy verbatim or with only minor changes for a research memo), I require them to research an area and prepare to interview a mock client. They then use the facts generated from the interview as a basis for a writing assignment. It is relatively easy to make sure the mock client gets across the essential basic facts, and the non-essential background information can come from the mock client's imagination. I'm frequently amazed and amused by the differences in students' perceptions of the "facts" that these interviews generate.

This same idea would work in doctrinal classes, too. For example, after exploring a particular area of law, you could bring in a mock client whose story raises a typical issue in that area. After the in-class interview, you could ask the students (either individually or as part of a class discussion) to apply the law they've learned to the client's circumstances. It's a simple and instructive way to give students a taste of what they'll be doing after graduation.

Lee Fellows
Gonzaga University School of Law

#15: Estate Planning — Interviewing and Drafting

I teach a seminar on drafting estate planning documents for small estates. In addition to drafting skills, I focus on interviewing and counseling skills. The students are required to prepare five drafting assignments over the course of the semester and to participate in a number of mock interviews.

In practice, I found that many attorneys who were excellent technical drafters had several deficiencies when explaining documents to clients. First, some had difficulty explaining how provisions operated in language that clients could understand. Second, some had difficulty relating why certain provisions were included in documents. Based on my experiences, I tried to design a seminar that would teach students not only the technical aspects of drafting estate planning documents, but also the drafting skills necessary for client communication.

For the final project, I ask the students to prepare a complete will package for a hypothetical client. The project tests all of the skills learned in the seminar. Thus, the assignment requires the students to use their interviewing, counseling, drafting, and communication skills.

I ask the students to hand in: (1) the will, (2) a memorandum to the assigning partner explaining any matters that the student feels should be brought to the partner's attention, and (3) a transmittal letter to the client explaining the will. The grade for this project, which counts for fifty percent of a student's semester grade, is based forty percent on the will, forty percent on the letter to the client, and twenty percent on the memorandum to the assigning partner. I grade the project based on execution of the client's objectives, clarity, and organization.

The students gather the necessary information for this project by interviewing someone (usually me) portraying the client. Before the interview session, which they engage in as a class, they are told a few facts about the potential client. Their task during the interview session is to obtain all necessary information about the client's personal situation and wishes.

Usually, when they begin to draft, the students find that they have forgotten to obtain some piece of information that would be helpful in completing the client's will. In that situation, they are to use their judgment when drafting to attempt to best carry out the client's objectives. I also expect them to explain to the client what they have done and why.

Carolyn L. Dessin
Widener University School of Law

#16: Mooting for Clinical Teachers

Many teachers in law school client services clinics prepare their students for specific case events—be they client interview, negotiations, or in-court examinations or arguments—through mooting. Since these moots involve many of the real-life situations for which the students will need to be prepared, they are often the perfect solution for supervisor, student, and client.

In many instances, mooting resolves important dilemmas for clinical teachers seeking synergy between their twin duties to provide excellent service to the clients as well as excellent education to the students.

Some teachers may worry that an overreliance on simulated experiences based on facts unrelated to the students' clients' cases may send students a message that lawyering is about lawyer performance rather than service to clients; mooting for an event important to an actual client, however, keeps the client at the center of the endeavor.

Others fret about throwing students into real-life lawyering without the benefit of adequate training. Mooting can offer the students a safe forum for education as well as experimentation, in a context narrowly tailored to equip students for a future important event. Thus, this relatively simple device promotes excellence in both client service and professional training, and it does so in a constructive and time-efficient context. What a useful teaching mode we have created!

Unfortunately, the carelessly structured moot can also hinder client service and student learning by panicking or traumatizing the student, compromising the supervisor-student relationship, confusing the student, or failing to help the students keep a clear perspective on what is most important—the client's stake in the whole process. It is high time then that we paid proper respect to mooting; at the same time, we need also to identify both the useful components of the constructive moot and the pitfalls of careless mooting.

The principles and 10 tips below offer some ideas that can be implemented easily and can dramatically improve our use of mooting. These ideas will be offered in the context of mooting for judicial arguments; keep in mind, however, that students and clients can be mooted for any case event.

Three Central Principles of Excellent Mooting

Consider what is at stake for the client.

First and foremost, all preparation should include as much information as the supervisor and student know about the client's subjective understanding of the event. How important is this event to the client? How does the client perceive this event?

This ongoing attempt to understand the case as well as possible *from the client's point of view* should color all other planning.

Consider how the issues raised relate to the lawyer's theory of the client's case.

As in all trial work, the lawyer's theory of the case — that is, his or her publicly announced understanding of the facts in the client's world relevant to the legal issues raised — must drive all actions in the case. Therefore, all performance events must act either to enhance the lawyer's understanding of the theory of the case (as in private conversations with the client or important witnesses) or showcase the lawyer's theory of the case (as in negotiation or trial strategies). In their preparation, supervisors and students must be careful not to sacrifice their overall strategy and vision of the case merely to gain short-term logistical victories.

Focus on your theory of the case. Mooting that ignores this precept, or that focuses on too many details, may teach students to ignore the big picture in case preparation.

Decide what structure of mooting will best prepare *this* student for *this* event.

Students approach any moot for a real event in particular contexts: the context of the client's case; the context of student-supervisor relationship; and the context of the students' own personal and professional development. For this reason, each mooting experience should be designed fresh for these students. The supervisor should avoid deciding that a certain kind of mooting would be excellent for student X because it worked two years ago for student Y. Every series of moots must fit its own particular circumstances, and teachers should be careful to structure the moot in ways that create a constructive educational and professional experience for *this* student and *this* client alike.

Ten Planning Tips

1. Start with a baseline moot.

An initial moot should establish the baseline: how a student would do if forced to perform without further preparation. This moot can be held immediately. In my experience, these moots usually show that students already know most of what they need, which allows them to focus on what could be critical at the final event. This first moot should be the length and expected timbre of the real event. If the judge is known to allow students ample time to speak, then students should be prepared to speak at length; if the judge will be all over students from the start, then students should be prepared with questions from the first moment.

The baseline moot should also target foundational parts of the case. In the context of a judicial argument, students should be asked to refer to the record, to summarize the holding of a case, and state the facts of a critical precedent.

This baseline moot will establish the agenda for further moots. Sometimes it is best to plan the series after a baseline moot has been completed; later moots can then target only what is absolutely necessary.

2. Decide how many mooting sessions to conduct.

Although in many cases a single moot may suffice, it is always preferable to leave adequate time for a second moot if possible. This leaves students time to regroup before final preparation. If necessary, leave time for a series of moots.

If you are mooting your students for real-life court experience, schedule the moot with a distinguished stranger playing the judge before whom the student is to appear. Mooting for federal appellate arguments has provided me a terrific opportunity to involve my colleagues.

Moots should be as real as possible as the series progresses. An early moot might be designed to be longer than the expected argument. Students should train specifically for the event by honoring strict time constraints and the smallest logistical matters—podium height, room lighting, how to dress, and the management of documents.

Trips to the exact forum or courtroom can ease the student's nerves. When students know where to put their Kleenex and their glass of water, and where to find the bathroom, they are apt to be better prepared to handle the inevitable stress and, thus, be in a better position to learn from the experience.

3. The supervisor should attend all moots.

I have found that most "judges" who take time to do a moot are eager to offer the student feedback and advice. It is disconcerting for students to hear contradictory advice, or to change their style after an initial moot only to be advised later that their initial style was preferable. The supervisor, by attending all moots and by taking careful notes, can help the student sort out contradictory feedback.

4. Try the lecture-in-disguise moot.

Use the moot as a "lecture in disguise." For instance, if the student and the supervisor have discussed the way in which a procedural point jeopardizes a substantive point of the argument, the supervisor can organize this moot to show through judicial argument the necessary links and contradictions between those two points.

5. Try the "workings of the judicial mind" moot.

Arrange for a judge to explore with students how an argument can affect the judge's sense of how to decide a case. For instance, a judge could ask, "If I rule with you on Part A, doesn't that mean that I have to rule against you on Part B?" In this way, students can track how their arguments might affect one practical judicial thinker. It will also help students get away from the abstract issues in the case and realize that certain judges will always be focused on the decision at hand.

6. Try the moot of complete silence.

As students deliver their spiel, simply remain silent. This teaches students the importance of being prepared to meet a judge's stony gaze, of how to keep the floor when it is given to them, and of how to figure out a way to make a lively, useful presentation.

7. Try the worst-case scenario moot.

Encourage your students to articulate their most fearful scenarios and then help the students act them out. This moot invariably goes better than the student expects. It typically gives students new confidence. In the rare case, the supervisor and student may reconsider whether the student can handle the case event; in such situations, this moot may provide the occasion when the supervisor and student decide that the supervisor should handle the actual event.

8. Consider the reverse moot.

It often is useful for students to moot their supervisor. Seeing the supervisor argue the case may provide students some useful ideas. Students can also use this as an opportunity to ask the supervisor difficult questions and have the supervisor help work out possible answers. Putting the student in the position of a judge also increases the student's empathy with the decision-maker. Doing a reverse moot also helps teachers express solidarity with the students (as well as helping supervisors work through their own latent desires to do the argument themselves!).

9. Help the student design the best written instrument.

As the moots progress, students will increasingly refine their written aids. Some students prefer voluminous outlines; some might prefer to go with no notes at all. In my experience, using a single-page crib sheet is an important complement to other student aids. The crib sheet should contain the argument in brief and the theory of the case, and it should pinpoint citations to key documents.

10. Don't forget the principle of the 30-percent jump.

Because of the adrenaline flowing during the actual event, most students and clients improve on their best moot performance by a substantial margin. Knowledge of this may soothe the nerves of jangled supervisors and students during the inevitable lowest moment.

It is common to follow an excellent moot or an excellent first attempt with a dismally bad second attempt, but supervisors can avoid conveying an air of panic by remembering that students, through experience and applied practice, perform significantly better in real-life situations.

Jean Koh Peters
Yale Law School

Chapter 9

Writing Exercises

Good assignments elicit good work; bad assignments, bad work. —Elbe

A. Why Use Writing Exercises?

Writing assignments have been championed by many individual teachers as well as a national movement in higher education, Writing Across the Curriculum. This movement encourages teachers in all disciplines to incorporate a wide variety of writing experiences in their courses. Underlying this movement is a considerable body of research documenting the benefits of writing.

Writing exercises, whether done in or out of class, whether graded or not, whether formal or informal, help to develop thinking skills. As students explain or explore an idea in writing, their understanding and misunderstanding of concepts become clearer. For example, when students draft legal documents such as a will or a complaint, they discover the limits of their knowledge and they develop a deeper understanding as they apply abstract principles to a life-like situation.

Writing in class gets students actively involved in learning the subject matter and skills of a course and can focus students' attention. For example, at the beginning of class, students could write for several minutes on the essence of a major topic to be covered in class that day. Likewise, writing briefly at the end of class can help students to solidify the major points from that day's class. Writing exercises also help generate thoughtful class discussion. By writing on a topic for several minutes, students have time to organize and develop their thoughts much more thoroughly than when responding immediately to teachers' questions in class.

Writing not only helps students learn content and skills, it is an excellent vehicle for students to explore and articulate their values. Through writing exercises such as journals or reflective essays, students take abstract principles and give them personal meaning. By exploring how concepts fit into their own lives, students develop a deeper understanding of their own perspectives and are better able to apply ideas in new personal and professional situations.

223

Writing exercises provide teachers with a window into their students' thought processes and into the students' levels of understanding. Teachers can use the information they get about their students' learning to refocus and revise their instruction to meet students' needs.

Writing assignments are often used as all or most of the means of determining students' grades. Those assignments are addressed in Chapter 11—Evaluation of Students.

B. Types of Writing Exercises

The types of appropriate writing exercises in legal education are limited only by the creativity of legal educators. The examples of writing exercises briefly described below only scratch the surface of the productive written work teachers can devise for their students. The examples are organized in two categories: (1) Out-of-Class Writing and (2) In-Class Writing.

1. Out-of-Class Writing

- Term Papers, Seminar Papers, and Law Review Articles, Comments, and Notes. These are formal, lengthy, extensively researched, and carefully revised. They usually represent a significant portion of the grade for a course.
- Legal Memoranda, Briefs, Letters, and Documents. Examples include the office memo, trial and appellate arguments, settlement and demand letters, motions, discovery papers, wills, and pleadings.
- Admit Slips. These are short pieces of writing that students turn in at the beginning of class. Examples include responses to problems, answers to questions raised at the end of class, and questions about the material covered during the previous class.
- Dialogues. Students can create imaginary conversations on course concepts between two people; for example, Justice Brennan and Justice Scalia on judicial activism.
- Outlines, Timelines, and Flow Charts. These devices can help students organize concepts and explore the connections between ideas.
- Journals. These can include students' reflections on course material, class discussion, clinical experiences, field trips, etc.
- Book Reviews and Letters to Authors. These projects can require students to evaluate strengths and weaknesses of texts.

2. In-Class Writing

- Focus Pieces. Short writing at the beginning of class can focus students' attention on a major topic for that day's class. Or, writing during class can concentrate on analysis, argument, or values.
- Discussion Previews. Students can write for several minutes in response to questions, hypotheticals, or problems raised in class. Then the class as a whole or in small groups can discuss the responses.
- Exit Slips. Short pieces of writing collected at the end of class. Examples include a summary of the three important points from that class session, analysis of a hypothetical, and questions about the material covered that day.

C. Planning Writing Assignments

One key to enhancing student performance is to focus the writing assignment sufficiently so that students know what teachers expect of them. To provide that focus, teachers must first articulate for themselves the objectives they hope to achieve with the writing assignment. Then, teachers should expressly inform the students of those objectives. For example, "Students will use the elements of statutory analysis (list the elements here) to make an argument in favor of the plaintiff in problem __." or "Students will describe the operation and evaluate the effectiveness of (identify a legal doctrine here) in a real-life dispute."

Teachers must determine the size and number of the writing assignments. Several short papers provide more opportunities for students to develop their skills, provided they receive useful feedback. Thus several short papers are often appropriate for first-year students. Many students find several short writing assignments less stressful than one large writing assignment because the stakes are so high with one large assignment. However, multiple writing assignments can increase the teacher's grading and feedback burden. Longer papers allow students to develop more sophisticated, higher-level thinking skills such as analysis, synthesis, and evaluation. Hence, longer, more traditional term papers work well in upper-level courses.

Writing exercises can take place inside or outside of class. Traditional term papers and written responses to homework problems are typical of writing assignments outside of class. These assignments give students the time to do research and to refine their thinking before writing. Writing exercises in class help students learn concepts as they actively work on them. For example, by spending three minutes outlining their analysis of a problem, students may clarify their understanding of the applicable concepts.

Teachers need to decide whether and how the writing assignment will be graded. Grading schemes run the gamut from formal (A,B,C), to informal (+, OK, –), to ungraded. Students tend to feel more stress and exert more effort on writing assignments that are graded formally and constitute a significant percentage of their grade in the course. Ungraded writing assignments, on the other hand, can help students understand content, practice skills, and prepare for later formal evaluation.

If the written assignment is to be graded, students need to know the grading criteria. Teachers must decide the extent to which writing quality and content matter in the evaluation of the students' written work. Teachers should provide students with clear grading criteria in writing at the time the assignment is given. The more specific the criteria communicated to the students, the more likely that the students will be able to meet the criteria. Then, teachers should spend a few minutes in class answering questions about the assignment and the criteria to maximize the students' understanding of the teacher's expectations.

For writing exercises that students will complete outside of class, teachers should distribute a handout that contains all of the essential information for the assignment. The handout can help ensure that the teacher has thoroughly thought through the assignment and can minimize later misunderstandings. Although the precise contents of the handout will vary depending on the assignment, it should include the following:

- The objectives of the asignment,
- The type of paper (memo, brief, letter, article),
- The specific task (compare and contrast, argue, analyze),
- The audience (law firm partner, judge, legislative committee),
- The contents (issues, cases, statutes, policy, analysis),
- Format (paper size, spacing, type size, margins, stapled, exam number),
- Length restrictions (words, pages),
- Sources (limited, unlimited),
- Grading criteria if applicable (see discussion above),
- Deadline (due date, time, and place; consequences of missing the deadline),
- Collaboration policy.

D. Feedback to Students on Their Writing

Students need specific, concrete feedback on the strengths and weaknesses of their written work. The burden of providing individualized feedback to each student deters many teachers from using writing exercises. While teachers can respond to individual students on their writing, it is not the only way for students to get valuable feedback. Teachers can provide feedback to the class as a whole and students can provide useful feedback to one another and to themselves.

One way for teachers to provide feedback to individual students is through written comments and questions on their papers. It is important for teachers to remember how invested many students are in their writing, which communicates who they are and what they think. Teachers need to help students understand that the feedback is on the students' performance, not on their personal worth. Comments that are a good balance between encouragement and criticism are most likely to help students understand their strengths and weaknesses and to motivate students to try their best next time.

Another way for teachers to provide feedback to individual students is to meet with them to review their written work. Individual conferences are an excellent venue for teachers to answer students' questions, to reinforce what students did well, to provide detailed guidance for improvement, and to get to know students better. Individual conferences are often a required part of a writing course or a seminar. In other courses, teachers can reduce significantly the burden of providing individual feedback on student writing by offering to meet with any student, but not requiring conferences. Although only a small percentage of students are likely to make an appointment for a conference, most will appreciate the offer.

After reviewing a set of student papers, teachers can take a few minutes in class to let the class know in general terms the strengths and weaknesses of the papers. A dramatic way to give excellent feedback to the class is for the teacher to put a sample paper on the overhead projector and grade it in front of the students, speaking aloud the teacher's thoughts and comments about the paper. This feedback not only helps students to understand the assignment being reviewed, it demystifies the grading process as well.

Students can provide each other with valuable feedback on their writing. For example, after students spend several minutes in class drafting a response to a problem, they can trade papers and discuss the strengths and weaknesses of each other's analysis. Students can meet in small groups to review first drafts of short writing assignments prepared outside of class. Students can use a checklist prepared by the teacher to provide consistency in peer edits of each other's work. For example, when examining a draft of a research paper or law review article, the following instructions could guide the peer review:

- State the main point of the paper in a single sentence;
- List the major subtopics;
- Identify any word, phrase, sentence, paragraph, or section that is unclear;
- Evaluate whether each subtopic is supported with sufficient research, evidence, and discussion;
- Identify the major strengths and weaknesses of the paper.

With a bit of guidance from their teachers, students can evaluate much of their own writing. For example, after students complete short writing exercises in class, they can assess their own performance by comparing their work to the analysis developed in class. Teachers can facilitate students' self-evaluation of writing completed in class by listing the critical points on the board or an overhead projector during class. For writing completed outside of class, many students benefit from comparing their papers to model answers or scoring checklists. Another way for students to gather their own feedback is to review samples of other students' papers. This type of review is most helpful if students can compare copies of excellent, average, and below-average papers.

References

CHARLES C. BONWELL & JAMES A. EISON, ACTIVE LEARNING: CREATING EXCITEMENT IN THE CLASSROOM 35–38 (1991).
BARBARA GROSS DAVIS, TOOLS FOR TEACHING 205–235 (1993).
JOSEPH LOWMAN, MASTERING THE TECHNIQUES OF TEACHING 239–247 (2d ed. 1995).
Duane H. Roen & Kenneth J. Lindblom, *Using Writing as an Active Learning Tool*, in UNIVERSITY TEACHING 68–87 (Leo M. Lambright et al. eds., 1996).
MARYELLEN WEIMER, IMPROVING YOUR CLASSROOM TEACHING 109–111 (1993).

Specific Writing Exercises

#1: Short Writing Assignments in Large Classes

I was determined to make short writing assignments work in large classes. My goals were to have a way of individually evaluating each student, in addition to the final examination, and to get more feedback on the student's progress. I also wanted to give the students a response to their individual work during the semester. Another benefit, I discovered, was that overall the students did learn the concepts more thoroughly when they wrote about them. My reading on learning lead me to expect this and it was gratifying.

For Wyoming, a big law school class is 70 to 80 students. A problem, of course, is the time and effort involved in grading this many papers. In the spring of 1994, I assigned six one-page papers to the students in Contracts II. I picked my first-year course, believing the regular feedback throughout the semester was most important to the first-year students. I graded each paper "+", "√", or "-". I found this was a relatively easy grading method. It took me about one day to grade each set of papers and I was able to work this reasonably into my other responsibilities for the semester. I created a curve with the grades on the papers, and the resulting grade was 20% of each student's course grade. I pointed out to the students that the paper could easily determine the difference between a "B" and "C". (Wyoming did not have "+" or "-" letter grades at that time.)

Each assignment asked a question, and limited the authority to be used in the answer to a case, statute, restatement, and/or text note. I chose the subject of each assignment so that we were discussing it in class soon after the papers were turned in. This timing improved the class discussion, particularly because many of the reticent students then participated. Also, reviewing papers allowed me to see where the students were having problems with a particular principle, and I used that information to plan the class on the subject.

For the assignments, I often used fact patterns in the text. Most textbooks contain plenty of fodder for short writing assignments. For one of the assignments, I asked the students to use the facts of an old case in the text and apply the holding of more recent cases in the text to those facts. (The instructions for this assignment are reproduced below.)

I was persuaded to allow the students to discuss with each other the issue presented by the assignment, because of the learning value of the discussions themselves. However, I required that each student work alone when writing the paper. This structure worked well for all but one assignment. In that assignment, I had them calculate the allowable damages in a case and explain their result. The students discussed the assignment extensively among themselves. We had an excellent class discussion about it, and the students were not reluctant to challenge my conclusions. However, many of the papers were virtually identical.

Overall, I felt I achieved my goals with the paper assignments. I heard no complaints from other faculty teaching first-year classes that students were not attending class, or being unprepared, when my class had an assignment due. I think this bonus in faculty relations was due to the one-page limit on the assignments and the narrow focus of authority to be used for them.

One caveat—I got annoyed and frustrated with all the issues that came up about fonts and lines per page, with a one-page limit. No matter how specific the instructions were, a nuance or ambiguity was raised. In retrospect, providing samples of excellent student papers that did not reach the one-page limit might have helped.

ASSIGNMENT 1
CONTRACTS II

Question for legal analysis: If the *Laidlaw* case (Note 1, pg. 640–41) arose today, would the seller have a supportable claim to rescind the contract because of nondisclosure?

Authority: For the current law, use the law as stated in the *Hill* case and in Restatement (Second) of Contracts § 161. For legal analysis, remember that primary authority is better than secondary authority, and that Restatements are usually viewed as a more significant form of secondary authority than general commentary. Use only the material about the Restatement that appears in your textbook and rules supplement. Use only the facts about *Laidlaw* that appear in the note. (I realize that in our electronic age, it is unlikely that both parties would not know that a war had ended, but try to ignore that.)

Length: If your answer is typewritten, it must be double-spaced and no longer than one page. The page must have no more than 26 lines and no more than 12 characters per inch, or 27 lines and no more than 11 characters per inch. If you turn in a handwritten answer, it must have no more than an equivalent number of words to the typewritten limits just stated. All answers must have right and left margins of at least one inch. You need to reach a conclusion, and defend it. You do not need a question presented or other formalities of a memo. Do not use abbreviations. The answer needs to be in narrative form, with complete sentences and paragraphs.

Due: The answers are due at the beginning of class on Friday, January 21. If you do not attend class, your answer needs to be in my box in the front office before class. You need to make arrangements with me in advance if you are not going to meet the deadline. Otherwise, you will receive no credit for the exercise.

Evaluation: The criteria that I will use to evaluate your answer are:
1. Is it clearly stated and focussed?
2. Is your conclusion adequately supported, including authority for the principles applied and all of the steps in your reasoning?
3. Is it persuasive?

Other general instructions appear in the course outline.

Please retain this as it contains the instructions for length, missing deadlines, use of authority, and basis for evaluation, that will be used in future assignments.

Ann Stevens
University of Wyoming College of Law

#2: Writing to Analyze Facts

At bottom, the work of a practicing attorney consists in applying relevant legal rules to a specific set of facts. Yet this is a skill that we often take for granted and fail to teach in law school. Over and over again I see students struggling to tease from an appellate opinion a tidy rule of law that can be memorized with ease. The facts of the case are recited as mere background material; and if the instructor varies the operative facts, this is usually seen as a way of clarifying the all-important rule of law. Unless coerced, students do not focus on facts. They do not understand that the facts recited in an opinion may not comprise all the important factual information relating to the case.

On exam day, of course, application of the rules may be required. "Issue spotting" we call it. We evaluate students on the basis of their ability to apply legal principles in real-life settings, but what training have we provided to prepare our students for this awesome task? In the typical Socratic classroom we teach our students to analyze the law but rarely to analyze the facts.

Clinical courses try to remedy this shortcoming, and they seem to do so with very considerable success. But clinics are time consuming and expensive, and they have limited enrollments. By using fiction—that is, by creating facts that simulate the real world—we can help a larger number of students to acquire essential fact-analysis skills. Drafting problems present an ideal opportunity to assist students in working with facts. Drafting projects are appropriate in many different types of classes: e.g., contracts, property, civil procedure, trusts and estates, domestic relations, professional responsibility, and the like. Preparing "necessary instruments" for a client is real lawyer work, and most students love doing it.

Two factors may discourage instructors from using simulation projects in the classroom. First, giving adequate feedback in a large-class setting may be difficult; and second, creating a relevant imaginary world may prove challenging. One approach to the feedback problem is to devote enough class time to give a detailed group critique of the problem. In a large class, I use "Good," "Pass," or "Redraft" as grades for drafting projects and give individualized comments only if requested (which is usually not necessary after the class discussion). Group projects are also valuable, as they provide peer teaching and cut down on the instructor's burden.

Simulation projects are most successful if the fictional world is colorful, apropos, and reasonably true to life. How does one create interesting life-like situations? Garrison Keillor, one of America's finest story tellers, suggests that you start with people you know and love and then tell lies about them. If you begin with real people — your friends, neighbors, family members, or actual clients — the reality of their humanity will survive whatever alterations you must impose to illustrate important legal issues. Newspaper clippings, also, can be wonderful sources for fact analysis. I encourage students to bring in real-world stories that are related to our course.

Many kinds of stories make good teaching tools: stories buried deep in an appellate opinion, stories headlined in news magazines, stories invented by fiction-writing law professors. A good set of facts provides an excellent basis for comprehending, as well as applying, abstract rules of law. My students tell me that they understand "the rules" much better after making practical use of them. In addition, rules are more memorable when presented in a dramatic setting. Why do you suppose the Bible is a book of stories?

Joan Ellsworth
University of Baltimore School of Law

#3: Editing On An Overhead Projector

In large classes, I am often concerned about how to give personalized feedback. I commonly assign hypotheticals to be resolved in writing and brought to class for a group discussion. While I review the hypotheticals in class, this did not always serve to "correct" common errors. I tried having students turn in the essays and then marked them with a plus, check, or minus. While that gave students some sense of where they stood, it was still not a concrete and directed critique. So, I turned to the overhead projector.

I assign a short writing project that can fit on one page (typed). A letter to a client, an introductory paragraph to an essay, and a short answer to an exam question all work well. I usually try to do this as a way of summarizing or reviewing a substantive unit we have just completed. Sometimes, I have students do this project in pairs. Then, students hand in the written assignment to my office several days before class. I ask them to identify their papers by name. I then read through a sample of the responses to get a sense of the common strengths and weaknesses. That usually involves reading 30 out of 110 papers. I then pick three or four papers which contain the types of mistakes (and good points) I want to emphasize. These papers are then duplicated directly onto transparency paper for immediate use on an overhead projector. I always delete the student names. I correct nothing beforehand. The transparencies are a replica of what the students produced.

I come to class with my transparencies and several overhead projector pens. I then put the first transparency up on the screen, and I begin editing with my special colored pens. I discuss as I edit. I pause and ask for suggestions. I change colors for different kinds of edits—language (spelling, sentence structure), organization, legal analysis. By the end, the single sheet is filled with color and significantly marked up. Then, we proceed to the next transparency. (For those professors with laptop in-class capability, one can use the computer screen for this (projecting it onto a screen or into each student's computer) but editing would be done using the keyboard without the benefit of handwritten notations.) After class, I give students copies of what was up on the overhead projector so they can fiddle with the writing on their own.

The overhead projector approach has certain benefits. First, since I've picked papers with common errors and strengths, each student feels some personalized benefit. Second, the students actually get to *see* my thought process. The questions I ask about what is written alert them to what they should think about when they write. Third, the feedback on the writing is almost immediate—several days after the project has been completed. Fourth and finally, the exercise emphasizes the importance of good writing in a substantive class as opposed to leaving writing to writing courses.

Karen Gross
New York Law School

#4: In- and Pre-Class Writing Assignments in Property

In my first-year Property class I use some informal written assignments to get students to consider reasons behind rules, to consider alternative approaches to problems, to be prepared for questions I may ask, to look at things other than cases, to consolidate an area, and to consider the broader implications of a rule of law. Briefly the assignments are:

1.   Abolish Adverse Possession — Students are asked to complete the following: "Adverse possession should/should not be abolished because..."

2.   Cave Law — Students are asked to evaluate and choose among three approaches to the ownership of caves.

3.   What is this? — Students consider a document that might be either a lease or a license and think about the choices the drafter of the document may have made consciously or unconsciously.

4.   Eviction or Abandonment — Based on a case in the text the students consider alternative approaches to explaining the result and think about why the court chose the approach(es) it did.

5.   Residential Landlord Tenant — The students read cases and an article on residential landlord tenant law and then talk in small groups about changes that could be made and the results of those changes. The assignment ends with a general discussion of the effect of changes they may suggest.

6.   In-class Covenants — Students are asked to explain why some covenants "run" and others don't and then to formulate a test and apply it to new situations.

I use these assignments for different purposes:

1 and 6 are used in-class to let students look at the reasons behind the rules they have developed and perhaps modify the rules in light of the reasons they have for them. They are used to end a particular unit of study and give some closure to the area. I usually ask the students to do the writing in class and then work in pairs or triples to discuss the answers they have before we begin a more general class discussion. These are not turned in.

2 and 5 are specific to particular cases that I have in the textbook I use. Cave law is *Edwards v. Sims*, 232 Ky. 791, 24 S.W. 2d 619 (1929); Eviction or Abandonment is *Kulawitz v. Pacific Woodenware & Paper Co.*, 25 Ca.2d 664, 155 P.2d 24 (1945). I designed these because I had a particular question I wanted to ask in each case and when I just gave the question in class students hadn't really thought about it. So I handed the question out and told them to write an answer and turn it in. The class discussion has been much better since then.

3 and 5 are designed to add something different to the usual first-year case discussions. What is this? is designed to get them to begin with a document, not with a court's analysis. In the process of dissecting the document I also try to make some points about drafting. Residential Landlord Tenant is intended to let students see case law and statutes as different ways to solve problems and to see that some problems may be more difficult to solve. I have since added another (not necessarily writing exercise — though I may add some writing to it) involving interpretation of a

residential landlord tenant statute as applied to a person who is operating a business in residential rental property.

I don't grade the assignments, though with 2 and 4 I require that they be turned in. I do try to ask a question on my final exam that has some attributes of one of the exercises. I think of it as a thought question rather than a traditional fact-pattern question.

I have found that perhaps the most difficult task in preparing these short writing problems is framing questions that are narrow enough to focus student responses, yet admit of some discussion. I think forced choices (always including "none of the above") and requiring an explanation of the choice have served well.

I think the student response has generally been good and I think that some students are more willing to participate if they have had a chance to write out something before the class discussion begins and in some cases perhaps test it out in a smaller group. I have found that some students who haven't previously participated are more willing to volunteer after we've used some small-group exercises.

I'd like to share experiences with others who are working on these sorts of exercises. I can be reached at Seattle University School of Law or at jwweaver@seattleu.edu.

John Weaver
Seattle University School of Law

#5: Graded Problems: Benefits and Burdens

Grading is not fun. However, I recently decided that it might be worth some extra work to improve students' preparation for class and to give them some feedback before the final exam, so I began experimenting with using graded assignments in my classes.

Although I have tried various methods to improve class preparation, I decided that I needed to try something new last spring when I taught the Basic Federal Tax class to first-year students. I decided to have the students turn in homework assignments which I would then grade and return to them.

During the first week of class, I announced that I would adjust a student's grade on the final exam a maximum of one grade step up or down (for example, from a B to a B+) based on the student's class participation, preparation, and attendance. In order to evaluate the students' preparation, I graded their answers to the problems.

The students wrote out their answers to the assigned problems, as if they were writing exam answers. A day or two before we covered a given problem in class, I collected the students' answers to the problem, graded them, and returned them before the class in which we discussed the problem. The students prepared their answers without knowing whether I would ask them to turn them in on the day they were due. I asked the students to turn in their answers about two-thirds of the time.

I evaluated the answers using a "no credit," "check minus," "check," or "check plus" standard. Using this format, the grading was much quicker than exam grading, although I did take time to write comments on papers when they were warranted.

Not surprisingly, giving the students feedback seemed to greatly facilitate their learning. The students' attempts to analyze statutes, regulations, cases, administrative pronouncements, and policy considerations progressed dramatically over the course of the term. At the end of the semester, the students wrote terrific exams.

Although I had anticipated that the students would benefit from receiving feedback throughout the term, I failed to anticipate the benefit to me of reading the students' answers before we discussed a problem in class. Usually, we teachers have little idea of what goes on in the heads of most of our students until the final exam. For the most part, we are forced to read the faces of our silent students, like tea leaves, for signs that they either understand or are lost.

Although I have, in the past, thought that I was a pretty good judge of the level of comprehension in a class, I will never again trust my view of what is going on in my students' heads unless I read what each one thinks. Reading the students' answers was an eye-opener, and frequently led me to add material to my class notes that I never would have thought to add without the feedback from students. I know that I taught my students better as a result of receiving feedback from them throughout the term.

In addition, using graded assignments fostered a good student-teacher rapport. I admired the students for their consistent and considerable efforts to master the material. They appreciated the fact that I took the time to give them feedback on their work.

Using graded assignments also improved class participation. Having already attempted to answer an assigned problem on their own, the students were quite enthusiastic about solving the problem in class. Although class participation improved overall, I especially noticed increased participation by women in the class. Research indicates that male students are more likely to speak in class than female students, especially if the student is unsure of the answer. Taunya Lovell Banks, *Gender Bias in the Classroom*, 38 J. LEGAL EDUC. 137, 141–143 (1988). Perhaps having a prepared answer to the problem boosted the confidence of the women students in my class, prompting them to speak more often.

Requiring advance preparation of the problem also encouraged the students to learn actively. They were forced to learn the material as best they could on their own, in order to answer the problem. This active preparation allowed the students to understand and retain more of what went on in class. Several students remarked that tax was surprisingly easy to review because they had learned the material the first time they had studied it.

In addition, requiring advance preparation of the problems helped to mitigate any differences in intellectual ability in the class. Some students no doubt had to work harder than other students to prepare the answers before class, but by the time we began to discuss a topic, everyone had achieved a basic level of understanding of the topic at hand. Instead of feeling as though I had to choose between boring some students or proceeding too quickly for others, we all proceeded together from a common starting point.

What are the potential drawbacks of using graded problems, other than the obvious one of needing to write the problems and grade the assignments? Using graded problems raises certain ethical issues. If students may not work together on the problems, how do you enforce that rule? Do you treat violation of this rule as an instance of cheating? If students are allowed to work together, how do you know that an answer is a student's own work? I allow my students to discuss the problem in a group, but each student must individually draft his or her own answer. Several students told me that they had enjoyed discussing problems with a group of students and had benefitted academically from the experience.

Using graded assignments produced many more benefits than I had anticipated. Although I share your distaste for grading, in my view the benefits far outweigh the burden of grading assignments.

Katherine Pratt
Loyola Law School (Los Angeles)

#6: Book Critique Assignment

From time to time, law professors have been encouraged to use writing assignments in their teaching. *See, e.g.,* Kathleen Bean, *The Use of Writing Assignments in Law School*, 37 J. LEGAL EDUC. 276 (1987). We have had good success in using a twelve- to fifteen-page book critique as a writing assignment in small classes for law students.

Law students are expected to digest an incredible number of appellate opinions, a fair number of substantive notes, and small dollops of law review articles in the typical law school course. They are almost never expected to read entire books, and certainly never given the opportunity to relate such reading to their core assignments. The book critique is useful as a guided exercise, which enables the students to focus their thoughts about a subject through the prism of describing and reacting to an author's complete presentation in a book.

In our teaching, we have handed out a list of "approved" readings from which the students may choose a book for this exercise. Of course, we have also allowed the students to select their own book, with permission. We hand out a critique guide with the list of books. In order to enable students to benefit from the reading that others in the class have done, we require students to turn in the critiques about one month before the end of the term. We find that students then refer to their particular books in class discussions.

A Guide for the Writing of Critiques

A critical book review should be an evaluative assessment of a book. The following list provides a framework for such a critique. You should cover these points in a clear, interesting expository style. You may find it helpful to read book reviews in several law journals first.

Remember, you are always writing for the next reader. Books are an important part of the "tools of the trade." How good is this tool? That is the overall question you attempt to answer with a critique.

1. *Bibliographic information.** What book is under discussion? The reader may want to locate the book and will need complete information.
2. *Author's qualifications.* With what authority does the author speak? What is the author's institutional affiliation?
3. *The sponsorship of the study.* In what ways does the sponsorship influence the study? E.g., does it influence the *kind* of questions, or *how* they are asked? Does it influence the findings or conclusions? Be aware of the possible influences on the author.
4. *The overall purpose of the study.* What are the major themes? Examples: To study appellate opinions related to mental illness. To examine the dissenting opinions of one Supreme Court Justice.
5. *Major questions for examination or research.* Examples: Are judges capable of analyzing scientific testimony related to mental illness? How do dissenting opinions affect the development of the law?
6. *Specific hypotheses being tested.* Examples: Judges do not make appropriate use of inferential statistics as proof in employment discrimination cases. The original intent of the

framers of the Fourteenth Amendment was not to apply the Bill of Rights to the states.

7. *Method*. How was the study done? How was the information or data collected? Who collected it? For instance: Are people answering questionnaires? Are researchers observing behavior or reading records? Is the author analyzing Supreme Court opinions or legislative debates?

8. *The unit of study*. Who or what is being studied? Examples: 75 seniors in suburban high schools; 14 medium-sized communities; 7 important school desegregation suits.

9. *The findings*. What was discovered? If there are many themes or questions, focus on the one or two most important and summarize the others. Guide the reader through your discussion of the book by referring to specific page numbers.

10. *The author's conclusions*. This is the point where the author goes beyond the descriptive level. The author might offer an explanation, make inferences from data, answer the original major questions, suggest further research, or offer a new synthesis of the case law.

11. *Your discussion*.
    a. *Did the author fulfill the purpose of the book?* Base your decision on an examination of points 1–10. For example, consider the following:
       - do the interpretations or explanations seem reasonable to you?
       - do the inferences follow from the data or the case analysis?
       - were the specific hypotheses confirmed or not?
       - were the methods reasonable ones in terms of the questions under consideration?
       - was it possible to derive the necessary information by the methods used and from the sources studied?
       - do the auspices of the book, or the author's qualifications, or the time the study was done make you doubt the soundness of the research and/or conclusions?
    b. *"Place" the book generally.* Of what use is this book to others? Consider:
       - who would benefit from reading this book? (Scholars, lawyers, judges?)
       - where does it fit into the area of study as far as you can tell?
       - what particular information is found here?
       - what is unique about the book?

- is there anything particularly useful or detrimental about the presentation, writing style, footnoting, bibliography, etc.?

c. *"Place" the book specifically.* How does the book fit in with the themes presented in this course?
- does the book illuminate, support, contradict, or disprove particular themes?
- what would various authors and judges we have read for this course say about the book?

In the discussion portion of the critique, don't just say "yes" or "no" in response to the questions. Illustrate your points with analysis based upon specific examples from the book. Empty phrases such as "It is interesting," "I like the book," etc. should not be used. You wouldn't bother to say "I like using a tape measure" or "I like using a tape measure because it is green." However, you could say "I liked using the tape measure because I could measure more precisely than by using my thumb" or "The green color of the tape measure made the numbers stand out clearly." That is, make pertinent comments.

12. *Citations.* The problem of describing the source of ideas is always important. *First* of all, you must use complete footnotes as indicated above to enable the next reader to refer to specific matters which may be of interest. *Second,* when you are describing major ideas, such as the methods, the findings, and the author's conclusions, indicate precisely where the concepts are coming from. For instance, at the end of a paragraph in which you describe the author's chief findings, you can put a citation within parentheses indicating the general area of the book: e.g., (Chapter II) or (pp. 23–45). *Third,* if you use the author's exact words you MUST put them in quotation marks, and you MUST follow the quote with a footnote indicating the source or with a citation indicating the source. It is strongly recommended that you try *not* to use quotations at all, but rather put the ideas in your own words (and cite the author). Generally, there are only two times when quotations are useful in this type of writing. One is when the author says something in such a way that you cannot capture the spirit, the flavor, unless you use the precise words. The second time is when you want to specify that *this* person said the words, no matter what the words are. These events ought to occur rarely. Relying upon the author's words often prevents you from thinking through your own paper.

13. *Other References.* If you refer only to the book being critiqued, one full footnote will suffice. If you use other references, follow the rules of the BLUE BOOK. References to course material should be footnoted or put in the text parenthetically.
14. *Style.* Type double-spaced. Number your pages. Absolutely correct grammar and spelling are essential. Dot-matrix computer printing is *not* acceptable, unless your machine prints in "correspondence" or "letter" quality. If you have any doubt, show the professor a sample of the print quality well in advance of the due date of the critique.

* Author, *Title* (City: Publisher, Edition, Publication Date).

This full footnote should appear at the bottom of page 1, or the full information should appear on a bibliography page at the end. If you use but *one* book, you can simply refer to various pages, by putting the page number(s) in parentheses at the conclusion of the appropriate sentence or phrase in the body of the paper.

David I. Levine
University of California Hastings College of the Law

Adeline G. Levine
(Emeritus Professor of Sociology)
State University of New York at Buffalo

#7: Scrambled Sentences

Midway through the first semester of Legal Methods, my students seemed overwhelmed. I was demanding corrections on a closed-universe memo and a start on the open memo; other professors had accelerated the pace of classes to make up for holidays; exams loomed in students' peripheral vision.

We needed a respite. We had worked earlier in the semester on a "Lisa-Lenny" annulment problem, which I had used to teach case briefing, synthesis, and client counseling. Now I called on the "Lisa-Lenny" problem again. I wrote a 12-sentence paragraph. Then I scrambled the sentences, putting a number 1 through 12 next to each sentence and leaving space between the sentences. I then copied these scrambled sentences for each member of the class. I also took four copies and cut them apart, separating each sentence. I put each cut-up copy in an envelope labeled Group 1, 2, 3, or 4.

When students arrived, I divided them into four groups and explained that they were going to solve a puzzle. I reminded them of Lisa and Lenny. After giving each student a copy of the scrambled sentences, I gave one envelope to each group. The assignment was to take the cut-up sentences and put them in order. As a further incentive, I told the students that if their group succeeded in laying out the cut-up sentences in the correct order before class ended, that group could leave.

As I moved among the groups, my modest expectations grew. One group reviewed the substantive material, trying to find the elements necessary for an annulment. Another group searched for the topic sentence of the paragraph. Yet another argued which sentences comprised the middle of the paragraph. I critiqued as I moved from group to group. If, for example, two sentences were in the correct order or the topic sentence and conclusion were correct, I would tell the group. If a group foundered or meandered, I gave support or directions.

With about seven minutes left, one group solved the puzzle. With gleeful smiles the group members swung their backpacks onto their shoulders and departed. The other groups continued to shift the sentences, calling me to check whether they had solved the puzzle. When class ended, the other groups continued to work until finally they had to go to their next class.

"Scrambled sentences" was a big hit. It provided a respite, and much more: a review of substantive material and the opportunity for heated discussions on paragraph organization, logic, flow, transitions. It even lingered; in the next class, students argued that the order I had created in the puzzle was flawed.

I used the exercise again the next semester, but for a different purpose. I used substantive material from a brief we were writing. This time, I numbered the sentences in their correct order and cut them apart. What students received, therefore, was a copied sheet with a paragraph "correctly" ordered and numbered and a cut-up sheet for the groups to reassemble. Only one small group concluded early that the order was correct. Other students thought the order might be correct, but did not argue their convictions or yielded to assurances by more vocal classmates that I could not possibly have given them the correct order.

Part of what I had hoped to demonstrate this second time was that while collaboration could be very helpful, students must ultimately make their own decisions and must believe in their own theories and research. It was a gamble. I knew some students might be angry and feel "tricked," but I was bothered by the wholesale acceptance of theories expounded by some of the more boisterous members of my class. Although a few students muttered, others felt validated. Because the material provided insights into the brief required at the end of the semester, I believe all students forgave me for "tricking" them.

I used scrambled sentences again when teaching the summary of an argument for a brief. I wrote two summaries of fifteen sentences each, one for each side. Then I divided the class into petitioner and respondent groups and made each group unscramble the summary for the opposing side. I had several purposes in mind:

1) to force students to anticipate the opponent's argument and to prepare strong counter-arguments
2) to help struggling students with the substance of the problem
3) to model a summary related to their problem

The technique worked well, as it has every time I've used it.

This "scrambled sentences" exercise could be helpful in teaching thesis paragraphs, rule proof, elements analysis, and exam answers. Or perhaps it could simply provide that needed respite for shell-shocked students.

Brannon Heath
Touro College Jacob D. Fuchsberg Law Center

#8: Giving Students an Appreciation of Real-World Issues and a Global View of the Law in First-Year Courses

It is important to mix teaching basic legal knowledge and skills with an understanding of real-world issues. Students need to develop an appreciation of the real-world context in which the law is practiced. This is particularly true of first-year students who spend a large percentage of their time learning basic legal rules.

In our first-year legal writing program at Gonzaga we assign a complex memorandum at the end of the spring semester. I gave my students a complicated political asylum problem involving a woman facing serious discrimination and hardship in her native nation. Students found themselves confronted with a difficult dilemma in which U.S. law left the desperate asylee in a gray area, probably unable to obtain asylum.

The students had to deal with the socioeconomic, political, and emotional aspects of a difficult asylum case along with the legal issues. Many students commented that resolving the frustration of dealing with the political and emotional realities of the problem was an eye-opening experience for them.

The asylum problem also allowed students to utilize virtually every research resource in the library including international law materials. Student reaction to the asylum problem was very positive. Students enjoyed the challenge of working on a research problem that encompassed a multitude of legal, socioeconomic, political, and emotional issues. Students also found it interesting to work with international legal materials and issues in the first year of law school. The growing interdependence of nations makes it important to teach some international law early in the law school curriculum. The mixture of a challenging problem and the opportunity to work with an international problem made this an interesting and enjoyable experience for students. This was reflected in the intense amount of time and energy students spent on the problem and the good quality of the final memorandums.

Jared Levinson
Gonzaga University School of Law

#9: Reading Aloud to Illustrate Excellent Writing

I have used the following technique in a legal method and writing course to counteract boredom, provide context, and expose students to a different, and often finer, discourse than many casebooks provide.

I read out loud for up to five minutes at the beginning, or sometimes at the close, of many (but not all) classes from a fine piece of writing (fiction, non-fiction, or journalism) on a topic relevant to that day's lesson. In addition to your favorite op-ed pages and magazines for choice bits, law and literature bibliographies can be a wonderful source of ideas. See Gemmette, *Law and Literature: Joining the Class Action*, 29 VALPARAISO L. REV. 665, 795–895 (Spring 1995) and Gemmette, 20 LEGAL STUDIES FORUM 421–439 (Fall 1996), for a huge list of fiction ideas.

After a few demos on my side, I invite students to bring their favorite short works to read. Students can become very engaged in this activity, and it can get out of control, so I have explained that we only have time for one reading per class, and I ask students to give me a copy of what they propose to read at least one hour before class. I follow a first-come, first-read policy, with the exception that students who have already read must cede to those who have not. I put copies of readings for which we lack time on reserve in the library.

This exercise is fun and interesting (probably justification enough for doing it) but, in addition, it seems to have two practical effects. It enriches students' legal analysis by exposing them to data and reasoning freed from the confines of appellate opinions. It particularly benefits students in the first year of law school who have difficulty perceiving "issues" or critiquing arguments. In addition, it helps students grasp, through contrast with different rhetorical forms, the particular qualities (and limitations) of effective "legal" writing. In particular, it sensitizes students to the differences between arguments grounded in fact, reason, or emotion and arguments grounded in appeals to authority.

Kate O'Neill
University of Washington School of Law

#10: Peer Editing

Peer editing can improve your life. Additionally, it increases your students' learning. No matter what courses you teach, peer editing can work for you and those in your classes.

You know from your reading that students learn more when they personally apply principles, rather than just take notes on them. But you're a busy person. Do you want to take the time to read a set of assignments, knowing that commenting on and evaluating them will take you many hours? Or should you just rely on your usual semester exam? Or maybe you already have the students do an assignment for you, but you're less than happy with the work product you receive.

The common writing process without peer editing goes something like this: you outline the relevant law, explain the assignment, perhaps give the students a model, and set a deadline. Students individually prepare a written document: a trust indenture, a complaint, a settlement agreement, a will, an opinion letter, an appellate brief, an independent contractor agreement, a lien—whatever falls within your course. You evaluate the final product. It takes a lot of time, and you find that while some of the students did an excellent job, many students did only mediocre work, and some handed in an embarrassingly poor product.

When you add peer editing to the process, you and the students will both benefit. The process is inherently simple: students give each other structured, detailed feedback before an assignment reaches you for evaluation. (More on the specific process in a moment.)

One benefit for the faculty member is obvious: the work product you evaluate is nearly always much improved, so it takes you less time to read it, and you get to write more positive comments on each paper. Additionally, since the goal is that your course will encourage student learning, you are much closer to achieving that end.

The students' benefits are several, and apply to "real life." First, they learn the specific legal concepts sufficiently so they can recognize a problem and correct it. Second, they learn to give and receive constructive criticism. (I discuss this specifically in class, giving examples of comments attorneys may use in practice, some constructive and explanatory, others too general or purely pejorative. I also stress the importance of making at least one specific positive comment on each paper edited.) Next, they benefit from hearing other students' viewpoints and questions on issues they might not have considered or thoroughly understood. (This occurs more comfortably and openly in small groups, especially if students become used to working in such groups over the course of the entire semester, as opposed to the dynamic of discussions involving the entire class.)

Additionally, students improve their organizational skills with feedback. Finally, they begin to recognize the importance of process: outlining, drafting, and redrafting important documents, rather than cranking everything out in one sitting.

Comments from students about the peer editing process are almost uniformly very positive, assuming you take the time to structure it well and prepare students for the process. Their work product is indeed improved, and their understanding of the legal issues greater.

Fine. You think this sounds like an okay idea. But how do you get your students to succeed at peer editing?

Students' complaints are the same every year when confronted with this process for the first time: How can I edit something when I don't know anything about it? Are we doing this just to save you work? Why don't *you* read the first draft and the final draft? Can't I just do it myself? (Implication: I don't trust anyone else and don't want anyone else to have the benefit of my work.)

My answers are consistent each year, too: I will give you the tools with which to edit. Yes, this saves me some work because the product I eventually read will be better than if you did it all by yourself. I don't read both drafts because I don't have time to evaluate the assignment twice; instead, I will be available to answer your questions as you peer edit. Everyone must participate; I don't want to see any new concepts in the final product that you haven't discussed when peer editing (in other words, no holding out). My goal is to have everyone learn to do this particular thing well, and if everyone succeeds, I am happy to give everyone good grades, so competition shouldn't come into play here. (Unfortunately, not everyone gets great grades even when I use peer editing. However, it is rare that anyone receives grades as low as I end up giving when students work independently. For substantive courses, assignments which use peer editing may constitute only a small portion of the final grade, allowing the professor to maintain a curve, if necessary, when computing final grades.)

Peer editing is great; however, for its success you must put in some advance effort. Presenting peer editing as a part of your course by listing it in your syllabus gives the students notice of its value as a planned event. I list the specific dates on which peer editing will occur in class, and include a statement of exactly what work product, and how many copies, the students must bring to class for editing. By planning this in advance, I can also make sure the students will have time following the editing process to mull over the comments, react to them, and revise their drafts before the final deadline.

When you are planning, the particulars of the process you decide you will use are variable, but should include at least the following details: (1) the size of the student groups (I have tried pairs, triads, and groups of four and five; my sense is that students have the best experience with triads.);

(2) whether the students will self-select their groups (Allowing students to arrange their own peer editing groups may result in disparity in abilities among the groups, but allows for potentially greater comfort in working together.) or you assign them to groups (You might group students to include a mix of men and women, a variety of ages, a range of abilities, and a blend of other characteristics, but be aware of the potential concerns of isolating any person by making him or her the "token X" in the group.); (3) whether students will work within the same group the entire semester; (4) the tools you give your students, whether written or oral; and (5) the format of the peer editing process. (One option is to have everyone trade papers, so that A reads B's, while B reads C's, and C reads A's; A then discusses with B what she thought of B's paper. This seems to be less efficient, as A won't hear B's comments about C's paper and learn from them. Additionally, A can't listen to C and talk to B at the same time, requiring more time for feedback. A better alternative is to have everyone read A's paper simultaneously, then talk about it together, then move on to B's paper. I explain this process to the students before they embark on reading.)

Students' first inclination in peer editing is to look only for grammar and spelling errors, rather than confronting larger issues of organization, development, and substance. To prepare students to be effective peer editors, I provide a formal checklist and go over it in class in detail, giving examples. Sometimes, early in the semester, the checklists are more detailed. I explain in class that this checklist is closely correlated with the evaluation of the product. (In fact, I also give the students the evaluation sheet I use for the project prior to the assignment. They can see how the checklist mirrors the evaluation sheet yet develops the individual criteria in greater detail.) In the checklist, I break down what I want to see in each part of the document, and how it generally should be presented. The students use the checklist to go over the work product of their peers, using the format and structure you have chosen and explained to them. (One sample checklist is provided below.)

While the students engage in the editing process, the room is sometimes silent while everyone reads and makes written comments. At other points, the noise level is high, while different groups discuss the work products of individual students. While this uproar initially caused me some discomfort, I now recognize it as a sign of mental activity. As I circulate around the room, listening to different groups, I have found that nearly everyone stays on task the entire time, and everyone contributes comments in writing and orally. (This is especially true when everyone in a group reads the same person's work simultaneously. Then, when they are done reading and making written comments, A will discuss her concerns and questions, then B, then C. This way everyone has a chance to both give input and respond to that of others.) As the students discuss an individual product, they sometimes struggle painfully to express themselves, but gain conviction in their understanding as they communicate their thoughts to others.

Following the editing process, students in my classes must then work alone on the final product without commentary from others. This limitation provides them incentive to use the editing time wisely.

That's peer editing in brief. For more information, talk with me or any legal writing teacher!

LEGAL RESEARCH & WRITING
Professor Magone
MEMO REVISION CHECKLIST

	OK	Rev. Nec.

Overall Appearance

1. Does the memo include all necessary sections? (Heading, Question Presented, Brief Answer, Statement of Facts, Discussion, Conclusion)   ___ ___
2. Are the typing and physical presentation neat?   ___ ___
3. Did the writer number the pages?   ___ ___
4. Did the writer use appropriate font, double spacing, and 1" margins?   ___ ___
5. Did the writer de-justify the right margin?   ___ ___

Other:

Question Presented

6. Does the writer ask a question that can be answered yes or no?   ___ ___
7. Does the question identify the legal theory upon which the suit is based?   ___ ___
8. Does the question focus on the narrow problem(s) within this general legal area?   ___ ___
9. Did the writer include legally significant facts which show the case's unique character?   ___ ___
10. Did the writer use descriptive terms such as "purchase," "employer," or "minor," rather than terms such as "client," "defendant," or "appellant," or proper names such as "Mrs. Jones"?   ___ ___
11. Did the writer use active, rather than passive, and positive, rather than negative, language?   ___ ___
12. Did the writer state the question as clearly and simply as possible?   ___ ___

Other:

Brief Answer

13. Does the brief answer cogently and concisely respond to the question(s) presented?   ___ ___
14. Does the brief answer set out the standards, tests, elements, or issue relevant to the question presented?   ___ ___
15. Does the writer "plug in" specific facts for the tests/elements/issues in responding?   ___ ___
16. Does the brief answer provide a road map for the discussion?   ___ ___

Other:

	OK	Rev. Nec.

Statement of Facts

17. Does the writer identify the parties and the nature of the dispute? ___ ___
18. Has the writer included all legally significant facts, including all facts on which the writer relies in the discussion? ___ ___
19. Does the writer include background facts? ___ ___
20. Does the writer indicate the location of the incident at issue so the reader can determine the appropriate jurisdiction? ___ ___
21. Can the writer omit any facts in this section without confusing the reader? ___ ___
22. Can the writer omit any facts which, if they had not occurred, would not have changed the result in this case? ___ ___

Other:

Discussion

Organization

23. Can the reader use the first sentence of each paragraph to prepare an easily understood formal outline of the paper? ___ ___
24. Does such a formal outline make sense logically? If not, how would you revise it? ___ ___

Other:

Development

25. Does each paragraph have a topic sentence? ___ ___
26. Do the remaining sentences in each paragraph "prove," illustrate, or help explain the topic? ___ ___

    If not, can the writer omit that sentence? ___ ___

    Should the writer place the information elsewhere in the paper? ___ ___

    Could the writer add transitional words to the beginning of the sentence or otherwise change the sentence to make it more relevant to the topic? ___ ___
27. Did the writer say enough about the topic to convince the reader that his attitude about the topic is correct? ___ ___
28. Are the paragraphs too long (three-quarters of a page or longer)? ___ ___

    If so, can the writer divide any of them into two paragraphs? ___ ___

    If split into two paragraphs, does each have a topic sentence? ___ ___

Other:

Analysis

29. Does the writer analyze the problem completely and thoroughly, with no loose ends or unanswered questions? ___ ___
30. Does the writer support every legal statement with a citation to legal authority? ___ ___
31. Does the writer include all relevant legal authority in the discussion? ___ ___
32. Does the writer compare specific case facts to the specific facts of the problem? ___ ___
33. Does the writer use the IRAC method consistently and completely, setting forth rules, applying the rules, and coming to a conclusion for each issue? ___ ___

Other:

	OK	Rev. Nec.

Style

34.	Does the writer usually use short- and medium-length sentences?	___	___
35.	Does the writer use active voice, unless he uses the passive for a specific reason?	___	___
36.	Does the writer use strong verbs?	___	___
37.	Does the writer usually place the subject and verb together near the beginning of the sentence?	___	___
38.	Does the writer use simple, familiar words rather than archaic legalisms? (Could your mother understand?)	___	___
39.	Did the writer review the paper for spelling, grammar, and typing errors?	___	___

Other:

Citation

40.	Did the writer begin any sentences with citations?	___	___
41.	If so, can the writer shift the cite to the end of the sentence?	___	___
42.	Are the citations correct according to the blue book?	___	___
43.	Does the writer cite to authority whenever necessary?	___	___

Other:

Conclusion

| 44. | Does the writer in the conclusion answer all question presented clearly and succinctly by outlining the elements/tests/issues and explaining our specific facts in relation to each? | ___ | ___ |
| 45. | Does the writer set forth questions and recommendations, if any, for the senior partner or the client? | ___ | ___ |

Other:

LEGAL RESEARCH & WRITING
Professor Magone
MOTION AND SIMPLE BRIEF REVISION CHECKLIST

	Good	OK	Rev. Nec.

MOTION

Format

1.	Does the motion include all necessary sections (attorney's address and phone number, court caption and cause number, date, attorney's signature, certificate of service) and use the format specified by the Uniform District Court Rules?	___	___	___
2.	Are the typing and physical presentation neat?	___	___	___
3.	Did the writer number the pages at the bottom?	___	___	___
4.	Did the writer use appropriate font, double spacing, and 1" margins?	___	___	___
5.	Did the writer de-justify the right margin?	___	___	___

Other:

	Good	OK	Rev. Nec.

Content

6. Does the writer clearly identify the relief sought? (Order stating/precluding/limiting...)   ___ ___ ___

7. Does the writer identify the legal basis for the relief sought? (i.e., rule of civil procedure X, rule of evidence Y)   ___ ___ ___

Other:

Writing

8. Does the writer avoid legalese and the passive voice?   ___ ___ ___

9. Does the writer use simple sentences?   ___ ___ ___

10. Has the writer edited for spelling, punctuation, and grammar?   ___ ___ ___

Other:

BRIEF

Format

11. Does the brief include all necessary sections (attorney's address and phone number, court caption and cause number, introduction, argument, conclusion, date, attorney's signature, certificate of service) and use the format specified by the Uniform District Court Rules?   ___ ___ ___

12. Does the writer use point headings and subheadings persuasively and appropriately, including law and relevant facts?   ___ ___ ___

13. Could the writer use more point headings and subheadings to keep the reader on track?   ___ ___ ___

14. Are the typing and physical presentation neat?   ___ ___ ___

15. Did the writer number the pages at the bottom?   ___ ___ ___

16. Did the writer use appropriate font, double spacing, and 1" margins?   ___ ___ ___

17. Did the writer de-justify the right margin?   ___ ___ ___

Other:

Content

Introduction

18. Does the writer include legally significant facts for this particular issue?   ___ ___ ___

19. Does the writer cite to the record after each factual statement?   ___ ___ ___

20. Does the writer present the facts in chronological order?   ___ ___ ___

21. Does the writer include procedurally significant facts?   ___ ___ ___

22. Does the writer specify the relief sought?   ___ ___ ___

Other:

Argument

23. Does the writer set out the standards, test, elements, or issues relevant to the issue?   ___ ___ ___

24. Does the writer discuss the issue completely and thoroughly, with no loose ends or unanswered questions?   ___ ___ ___

	Good	OK	Rev. Nec.

25. Does the writer support every legal statement with a citation to legal authority? ___ ___ ___

26. Does the writer include all relevant legal authority in the discussion? ___ ___ ___

27. Does the writer compare specific case facts to the specific facts of the problem, and apply the reasoning of each case as appropriate? ___ ___ ___

28. Does the writer use the CRAC method consistently and completely, setting forth a persuasive statement and the rules, applying the rules, and coming to a mini-conclusion for each issue? ___ ___ ___

Other:

Conclusion

29. Does the conclusion include a recap of each mini-conclusion made in the brief, integrating facts and law? ___ ___ ___

30. Does the conclusion include a specific request for the Court to act upon? ___ ___ ___

Other:

Writing

Organization

31. Can the reader use the first sentence of each paragraph to prepare an easily understood formal outline of the paper? ___ ___ ___

32. Does such a formal outline make sense logically? If not, how would you revise it? ___ ___ ___

Other:

Development

33. Does each paragraph have a topic sentence? ___ ___ ___

34. Do the remaining sentences in each paragraph "prove,"illustrate, or help explain the topic? ___ ___ ___

    If not, can the writer omit that sentence? ___ ___ ___

    Should the writer place the information elsewhere in the paper? ___ ___ ___

    Could the writer add transitional words to the beginning of the sentence or otherwise change the sentence to make it more relevant to the topic? ___ ___ ___

35. Did the writer say enough about the topic to convince the reader that his attitude about the topic is correct? ___ ___ ___

36. Are the paragraphs too long (three-quarters of a page or longer)? ___ ___ ___

    If so, can the writer divide any of them into two paragraphs? ___ ___ ___

    If split into two paragraphs, does each have a topic sentence? ___ ___ ___

Other:

Style

37. Does the writer usually use short- and medium-length sentences? ___ ___ ___

38. Does the writer use active voice, unless he uses the passive for a specific reason? ___ ___ ___

39. Does the writer use strong verbs? ___ ___ ___

		Good	OK	Rev. Nec.

40. Does the writer usually place the subject and verb together near the beginning of the sentence? _____ _____ _____

41. Does the writer use simple, familiar words rather than archaic legalisms? (Could your mother understand?) _____ _____ _____

42. Did the writer review the paper for spelling, grammar, and typing errors? _____ _____ _____

Other:

Citation

43. Did the writer begin any sentences with citations? _____ _____ _____
44. If so, can the writer shift the cite to the end of the sentence? _____ _____ _____
45. Are the citations correct according to the blue book? _____ _____ _____
46. Does the writer cite to authority whenever necessary? _____ _____ _____

Other:

ORDER

Format

47. Does the order have the proper format (no attorney's name in the upper left corner) and caption, including a date and signature line for the judge? _____ _____ _____

Other:

Content

48. Does the order refer to the motion and its basis, the appearances of the parties, and the hearing? _____ _____ _____
49. Does the order, in its body, specifically grant or deny the motion? _____ _____ _____
50. Does the order provide a legal basis for the decision (the court's rationale)? _____ _____ _____
51. Does the document conclude with a specific sentence ordering the motion granted or denied, including a specific time for a party to act, if appropriate? _____ _____ _____

Kathleen Magone
University of Montana School of Law

#11: The Use of Journals

I recently incorporated a service-learning component into my Women and the Law course. Twenty-six students were placed as volunteers in 15 different agencies that provided services to women or girls. The primary purpose for the volunteer activity was to heighten student awareness of women's issues generally and the problems faced by women in transition and low-income women in particular. I had planned to use questionnaires to the students and to their agency supervisors to get feedback at the end of the semester. But I was uncertain how to monitor student involvement on an on-going basis. Journaling seemed a natural way to receive periodic input.

To formalize the project and differentiate student journaling from the keeping of a personal diary (and stave off the inevitability of my getting bifocals), I requested that the journal entries be typewritten. In addition, I asked the students initially to address three basic questions: (1) What new information have you acquired as a result of your volunteer experience? (2) How do you feel about your volunteer experience? (3) Have you had any specific problems in your placement? (I added the third question so I could make adjustments if needed.) For the final submission I asked students: "What changes would you make in the availability of services or the way services are delivered to the specific population with whom you are working?" The journal entries were not submitted anonymously, although students used exam numbers on the other two graded papers.

Students submitted their journals for my review every three weeks. The first submissions varied greatly in terms of format, content, and length. Because I did not dictate the use of a particular format, some submissions read like stream-of-consciousness musings; others resembled legal briefs. The individual personalities of the students emerged in a way that is uncommon in the law school setting. I would urge others to be loose about format requirements to allow student creativity to surface. At the same time, content—apart from the manner of presentation—was important to me. I received a detailed log of activities from some students that really did not speak to any of the questions I asked. It was difficult for some students to get in touch with their feelings about their experience, while others emoted on each page. I hoped for a balance and indicated such in my comments. Although I had heard some horror stories about teachers receiving 400-page journals, I did not set a page limit. Most students wrote about 10 pages, although I did receive a few in excess of 20 pages, and a couple of students wrote four or five pages the first time. In retrospect, it seems reasonable to set limits on length from the very start. I did provide comments at the end of each submission that ranged from making suggestions about ways the student could better answer my questions to brainstorming about how the students might handle a difficult situation.

Due in part to the nature of the student placements, I encountered a few problems. Two of the agencies were concerned about confidentiality issues. I assured them that the journals would be read only by me and that students would not reveal anything that would compromise client confidentiality. Other agencies experienced changes in personnel between the time the placement was established and the time students began volunteering. As a result, a handful of students did not get started in a timely fashion, so adjustments had to be made in the due dates for their journal submissions.

The other dilemma I faced was how to handle writing problems such as poor grammar, sentence structure, and the like. I was apprehensive about correcting these mistakes, particularly where the content was good. I mentioned specific writing problems in a brief comment at the end of each student's work. I indicated my willingness to assist, but I decided to allow the student to make the call whether additional input from me was desired. Only one student took me up on my offer.

The overall journaling experience seemed to work well, both for me and for the students. For me, it was a welcome change from reading the same hastily-scribbled exam response for the 125th time. For them, it was a rare opportunity to escape from the IRAC format in a time-pressured exam setting or from obsessing about proper citation form. Most of the submissions I received were thoughtful and reflective. Some were quite amusing. Many were extremely heartfelt and touching. I would definitely do it again.

Mary Pat Treuthart
Gonzaga University School of Law

#12: Memoranda Reveal Bias

Criminal Law at Emory is a first-year course. In addition to teaching substantive criminal law, I want students to understand that our criminal justice system is a series of decisions by individuals which greatly affects the lives of other individuals. I also want students to begin to recognize their own biases, and in turn to recognize how biases affect the development of law. After a couple classes on sentencing, I pass out the following assignment. In half of the papers I name the defendant Sam Johnson and in half I name the defendant Sandra Johnson. I calculate the average sentence imposed on each, first by the whole class and then looking separately at sentences imposed by women and sentences imposed by men. The results prompt substantial discussion.

Sentencing Memorandum

If you were the judge in the following case, what sentence would you impose and why? Write a brief (one-page) memo stating your sentence and explaining your reasons.

United States v. Johnson

Sam Johnson was convicted of possession with intent to distribute 900 grams of cocaine in powder form in Washington, D.C., on January 19, 1995. On that date, officers of the Washington, D.C., task force watched passengers leaving the Amtrak train which had just arrived from New York. Officers noticed Mr. Johnson because he looked nervous, had no luggage other than a large tote bag, and proceeded immediately to a pay phone. A plain-clothes officer stood at the next phone and heard Mr. Johnson describing his own clothing and agreeing to meet someone just outside the station in thirty minutes. The officer identified himself to Mr. Johnson and asked to search his bag. Mr. Johnson began trembling, but handed the officer the bag. The officer opened the bag and found the 900 grams of cocaine.

The officer placed Mr. Johnson under arrest. When asked to cooperate in an ongoing investigation, Mr. Johnson gave the officers two nicknames of persons he had picked the cocaine up from in New York. He said he could provide no other information. Mr. Johnson is twenty years old. He is not married. He has a one-year-old son and a three-year-old daughter. He completed the eleventh grade. From June 1994 until November 1994, Mr. Johnson was employed as a waiter.

After losing a motion to suppress the physical evidence, Mr. Johnson pleaded guilty to one count of possession with intent to distribute 900 grams of cocaine. The statutory mandatory minimum penalty is five years in prison. The maximum penalty is twenty years in prison. A judge can sentence a defendant to less than the statutory minimum only if the court finds that the defendant gave substantial assistance to government authorities to aid a criminal investigation.

Deborah Young
Samford University Cumberland School of Law

#13: Writing Under Pressure

I have recently developed a course designed to prepare students for the shock of the real world by compelling them to write for ninety minutes during twelve classes. They thus write for eighteen hours under pressure.

I develop problems based upon Illinois Civil Procedure. I write up the problems in memo form as if from a partner to a young associate. The students then receive the problem plus a statute plus several cases. Using these materials they are to write letters of opinion, objective memoranda of law, and argumentative memoranda of law.

This technique is especially useful because the twelve writing problems provide a means of repeatedly reviewing the students' work. This increased feedback helps them considerably.

I recently have had quite a continent of students stop in to say their exams in other courses are easier to take, but, most heartening were the visits from those who are clerking and claim to feel much more self-confident about writing under pressure.

Corinne Morrissey
The John Marshall Law School

#14: Fiction Draws Students Into the Culture of Law

While teaching a required course that students did not want to take, I began a little experiment that seems to be working. I required my American Legal History students to read some outside materials they would find entertaining. The students then had to write book reviews of the material. Initially shocked to get an assignment like ones they had learned to dread in high school, they eventually learned the reviews could be a useful part of their law school experience.

Several years ago, the faculty at the School of Law, University of Louisville, decided our students were not being sufficiently exposed to materials outside of the core, rules-oriented courses. The school instituted a requirement that the students take a course from a list of alternatives that included American Legal History. The students were not pleased. None of the law firms that regularly recruited on campus appeared to do very much legal history work. None of the students could recall ever hearing one of our former graduates wax eloquently about a million-dollar legal history case currently in legislation.

I supported the unpopular requirement because I believe law is a reflection of the culture that produces it, and students should have some understanding of that culture. I agreed to teach a section of American Legal History and to let students learn about the culture of law by reading fictional works. To insure they accomplished the reading in a studious manner, I required and graded book reviews.

My first task was selecting the fictional works from which the students could choose. I had several criteria. The works should reflect something about the way in which our culture views law, should present those ideas in a stimulating or thought-provoking manner, and should be exciting to read. In addition, I wanted to find a variety of fictional formats—novels, short stories, and plays. Each student had to select two works, and only one could be a short story.

Naturally, *Billy Budd* by Herman Melville was easy to place at the top of the list. As a short novel that appears in every law and literature discussion, it provided a simple starting place. *To Kill a Mockingbird* by Harper Lee was also an easy choice. Those two items allowed the students to see discussions of right, justice, prejudice, and breakdowns in the judicial process. For the adventurous students, I added *The Trial* by Franz Kafka. Obviously that work does not relate to the American experience, but I felt it was sufficiently universal to be appropriate. That has been a difficult work for students who have tried it.

I selected some shorter works to add a variety of interesting topics. *The Lottery* by Shirley Jackson was a horrifying tale that many students had read when they were younger. When they read it in law school, however, the strict, traditional legal procedure that produced the meaningless execution took on a new meaning. I also added *The Hack Driver* by Sinclair Lewis. It is a delightful short story about the experiences of a new law firm associate. The students enjoyed the work and saw it as a prediction of things to come.

I offered a few plays. Because the course spends a little time on the Salem Witch Trials, *The Crucible* by Arthur Miller was a natural. *Inherit the Wind* and *The Night Thoreau Spent in Jail*, both by Jerome Lawrence and Robert E. Lee, also provided a fictional account of issues that are raised in the course. For the student who wanted a more classical offering, I allowed students to select either *The Taming of the Shrew* or *The Merchant of Venice*. Both of these Shakespeare plays raise issues of the role and rights of women, justice, mercy, and blatant bigotry.

The next problem was to set some limits on the format of the reviews. I wanted the reviews to accomplish a few simple goals. Of course, I had to check to see if the students had actually read the works. And I wanted the students to think and analyze the relationship between law and culture. Finally, in the interest of efficient grading, I wanted the reviews to be short and direct.

The reviews were limited to no more than five pages each. The first page had to contain the name of the work and the author, and it had to answer the question: "Did the student think that other students would benefit from reading the work? Please explain." There were several reasons for this instruction. The first page of every review was removed from the student's work and placed in a ring binder on reserve in the library. This allowed other students to have a quick source as they were selecting the works they would read. I have reused the better ones each year. In addition, the question directs the students to think about why the work may have some relevance to the study of law.

The rest of the review also had specific requirements:

- A brief summary of the work that should extend no more than one paragraph.
- A description of what the student felt was the most interesting part of the work.
- A discussion of what the work revealed about the nature of law or the nature of society.
- An explanation of whether the presentation of the nature of law or society was consistent or inconsistent with the student's own view of that subject.

Using that format, I was able to make some comparisons of the quality of the consideration and analysis that the students had brought to their reading. The summaries of the works and the discussions of the most interesting parts allowed me to determine whether the students had seriously read the material. The discussions of the nature of law or society forced the students to think about the relationship between law and the culture of law.

I continue to teach the course on American Legal History and want to continue the experiment with the book reviews. Both the students and I enjoy this break from the typical law school reading assignment. I have a long reading list of fiction and non-fiction, law-related materials that I have prepared over twenty years of teaching. I intend to select different items from this list as alternatives for the book reviews. In addition, I want to continue to experiment with the format of the reviews.

I also have one additional future experiment in mind. Since today's students are video intensive, and there are a substantial number of excellent law-related movies available, I would like to add movie reviews to the course. I could imagine students writing reviews of the movies *To Kill a Mockingbird, Twelve Angry Men,* or *Inherit the Wind.*

Ronald W. Eades
Louis D. Brandeis School of Law at the University of Louisville

Chapter 10

Classroom Assessment: Feedback to Teachers

Instead of engaging in confrontation, students and I found ourselves co-operating, trying to identify the most troublesome topics and exploring ways to understand and teach that which had not yet been learned or taught. — Walker

[T]he intense nature of the assessments, the increased personal contact, and the overall tone and philosophy of Classroom [Assessment] as a tool to benefit students [have] strengthened and improved the bond between students and myself. — Nakaji

The publication of A NATION AT RISK in 1983 started intense scrutiny of the quality of education in the United States. By the 1990s, higher education reformers were focused on two fundamental questions: "How well are students learning?" and "How effectively are instructors teaching?" Classroom Assessment responds directly to both questions.

A. What Is Classroom Assessment?

Classroom Assessment is a concept that grew out of the movement to improve teaching and learning in higher education. Classroom Assessment encourages teachers to collect frequent feedback from their students about how the students learn and how they respond to particular teaching techniques. Teachers can use that information to modify their instruction to help students learn more effectively.

Classroom Assessment should not be confused with three other types of assessment prevalent in higher education generally and law school in particular. One type of assessment is the evaluation of students by faculty for purposes of assigning grades. In most law school courses, evaluation of students for the purpose of grading occurs through an exam or paper at the end of the course. Classroom Assessment differs from evaluation of students for grades in several respects. First, Classroom Assessment is not used to determine grades. Instead, it is used to provide feedback to teachers about student learning for the purpose of adjusting instruction to help students

261

learn better. Second, Classroom Assessment often involves students evaluating teaching and learning activities rather than teachers evaluating students. Finally, Classroom Assessment occurs regularly throughout the course, rather than at the end.

A second type of assessment in higher education is the evaluation of program quality. Program assessment may be done by faculty, administrators, or outside evaluators. The purposes of program assessment include accreditation, long-range planning, and the restructure of educational institutions. The scope of Classroom Assessment, with its focus on gathering specific information to improve teaching and learning in a specific course, is much more narrow than program evaluation.

A third type of assessment that occurs in most colleges and law schools is the formal student evaluation of teachers and courses. These evaluations usually consist of a standardized list of questions about the course and the teacher. Almost invariably, they are administered once, at the end of the course. Their primary purpose is to provide information for administrators or committees making personnel decisions, such as retention, promotion, and tenure. There are critical differences between Classroom Assessment and student evaluations. Classroom Assessment forms are designed by teachers to gather information from their students on issues relevant to their particular course. As stated above, Classroom Assessment occurs throughout the semester. Moreover, the sole purpose of Classroom Assessment is developmental—to provide teachers with information on the effectiveness of their teaching and their students' learning in order to improve the quality of education in their courses.

B. Classroom Assessment Assumptions

Classroom Assessment is based on the following assumptions about teaching and learning:

- The quality of student learning is directly, although not exclusively, related to the quality of teaching. Therefore, one way to improve learning is to improve teaching.
- To improve teaching effectiveness, teachers first need to make their course goals explicit and then get feedback on the extent to which students are achieving those goals.
- To improve learning, students need to receive focused feedback early and often.
- The type of assessment most likely to improve teaching and learning is conducted by teachers to address issues that apply in their own courses, rather than the assessment conducted by administrators or outside evaluators.

- Classroom Assessment does not require special training; it can be carried out by teachers from all disciplines.
- Classroom Assessment can improve teaching, learning, and personal satisfaction for both teachers and students.

C. Characteristics of Classroom Assessment

Classroom Assessment has six characteristics that make it a powerful tool to improve teaching and learning.

1. *Learner-Centered.* Classroom Assessment places its primary focus of attention on observing and improving learning, rather than observing and improving teaching. As Angelo and Cross put it: "Learning can and often does take place without the benefit of teaching — and sometimes even in spite of it — but there is no such thing as effective teaching without learning. Teaching without learning is just talking."

2. *Teacher-Directed.* Classroom Assessment respects the academic freedom and professional judgment of individual faculty members. The teacher decides what to assess, how to assess, and how to use the information gathered through assessment.

3. *Mutually Beneficial.* Classroom Assessment requires the active participation of both students and teacher. Students improve their self-assessment skills, which are important for lifelong learning. Students' motivation increases when they know that the teacher is invested in the success of their learning. Teachers sharpen their teaching focus and enhance their instructional skills by continually asking themselves three questions: "What are the salient skills and content I am trying to teach?" "How well are my students learning the skills and content?" "How can I help my students learn better?"

4. *Developmental.* Classroom Assessment is not designed to grade or evaluate students. Instead, its purpose is to improve the quality of students' learning in order to help them succeed on subsequent graded assignments, tests, and, most importantly, the world beyond the classroom.

5. *Course-Specific.* Classroom Assessment allows teachers to gather the information they need to meet the needs of the students and the course. Each class is made up of a variety of students with different characteristics that affect their learning processes, such as their attitudes, academic preparation, culture, socioeconomic class, skills, and pre-existing knowledge of the subject. Each class develops its own classroom culture as well. Effective faculty shape their teaching to the context of the class.

6. *Ongoing.* Classroom Assessment is an ongoing process. Teachers use techniques to gather frequent feedback about their students' learning and the effectiveness of teaching methods. Throughout the course, teachers use that information to modify their instructional methods and give feedback to the students about appropriate learning strategies.

D. First Steps with Classroom Assessment

Teachers who are interested in Classroom Assessment but have not used it before should begin by trying one of the most simple Classroom Assessment techniques. The initial foray into Classroom Assessment should take little time and energy. Based on the results of the initial Classroom Assessment experiences, teachers can decide whether Classroom Assessment warrants the further investment of time and effort. Teachers can use a three-step process of planning, implementing, and responding to their first exposure to Classroom Assessment.

Step 1. Planning

Teachers should start by selecting one of their classes in which to try Classroom Assessment. If possible, teachers should choose a course in which they believe the students are reasonably satisfied. Once teachers have more experience with Classroom Assessment, they can use it effectively to deal with problems, but it is best to start with a less threatening situation.

After selecting the course, teachers must choose the first Classroom Assessment Technique (CAT) to use. Two of the CATs described in this chapter, Minute Paper and Three-Sentence Summary, are easily adapted to a variety of courses. Either of these CATs would be appropriate for teachers' initial experience with Classroom Assessment.

Step 2. Implementing

Teachers should inform their students of the CAT they intend to implement and explain why they are doing so. Students will want to know what teachers intend to do with the information. Many students will need reassurance that the purpose of the CAT is to gather information to improve teaching and learning, not to grade students surreptitiously.

When implementing the CAT, teachers should make sure students understand the procedure. Teachers may need to write directions on the board or on an overhead transparency. The students will need to know how much time they have to complete the assessment and whether their responses should be anonymous. (In most cases, the students will be more comfortable and responses will be more useful if they are anonymous.)

Step 3. Responding

Soon after collecting the students' responses to the CAT, teachers should read and analyze the results. The purpose of the analysis is for teachers to understand what their students are learning, what they are not learning, and what teaching methods are effective. A quick read through the responses will often be sufficient for teachers to identify the major themes of the feedback they gathered. Teachers then should decide what, if any, adjustments in teaching and learning methods they should make based on the results of the CAT.

To close the feedback loop, teachers should report to their students the major themes that appeared in the responses. Further, most students will be quite motivated to participate in CATs in the future if teachers tell them how they intend to use the information to hone their teaching and improve student learning.

E. Benefits of Classroom Assessment

Classroom Assessment provides a number of benefits for students and teachers. Students report that CATs result in notable course improvements and a higher-quality education. Student evaluations of the effectiveness of the course and instructor improve significantly.

Faculty using Classroom Assessment report that students participate more actively in class and perform better on exams. In addition, teachers find the CATs motivate students to take more responsibility for their own education. Further, participation in Classroom Assessment increases students' willingness to work cooperatively with their teachers and with one another. Finally, many faculty find that engaging in Classroom Assessment revitalizes their interest in teaching and learning.

F. Classroom Assessment Resource

An excellent resource for teachers using Classroom Assessment is the second edition of CLASSROOM ASSESSMENT TECHNIQUES: A HANDBOOK

FOR COLLEGE TEACHERS. This book, written by Thomas A. Angelo and K. Patricia Cross, is a comprehensive guide to Classroom Assessment. Much of this introduction is based on the Angelo and Cross book. This outstanding monograph contains three parts.

Part One: Getting Started in Classroom Assessment.

Part One begins with a description of the purpose and need for Classroom Assessment, its characteristics, and the assumptions on which it is based. This section also contains an inventory of goals that teachers can use to help them articulate their course and class objectives. Part One then provides a three-step process for teachers to begin using Classroom Assessment. For teachers who want to fully integrate Classroom Assessment in their courses, the book includes a detailed, nine-step guideline. Part One ends with the description of twelve successful Classroom Assessment projects implemented in a variety of courses, from Criminal Justice to Astronomy.

Part Two: Classroom Assessment Techniques.

Part Two is the heart of the book. It describes 50 Classroom Assessment Techniques, including many CATs appropriate for use in law school courses. The CATs can assess students' content knowledge and skills, their attitudes and values, as well as learners' reactions to instruction. Each description contains a summary of the CAT, step-by-step procedures for implementing it, and suggestions for using the data gathered with the CAT. In addition, each description includes examples from various courses of ways to use the CAT and ideas for adapting and extending the CAT to other applications. Finally, Part Two explores the pros and cons of using each CAT.

Part Three: Building on What We Have Learned

Part Three evaluates Classroom Assessment. It summarizes reports from college teachers who have used Classroom Assessment. Those reports address the lessons faculty believed they learned from implementing Classroom Assessment in their courses. The faculty members articulate the costs and benefits of Classroom Assessment.

References

THOMAS A. ANGELO & K. PATRICIA CROSS, CLASSROOM ASSESSMENT TECHNIQUES: A HANDBOOK FOR COLLEGE TEACHERS (2d ed. 1993).

Thomas A. Angelo, *Introduction and Overview: From Classroom Assessment to Classroom Research,* in NEW DIRECTIONS FOR TEACHING AND LEARNING, 7 (Summer, 1991).

K. PATRICIA CROSS & MIMI HARRIS STEADMAN, CLASSROOM RESEARCH: IMPLEMENTING THE SCHOLARSHIP OF TEACHING (1996).

Gerald F. Hess, *Involving Students in Improving Law Teaching and Learning,* forthcoming U.M.K.C. L. REV. (1999).

TEACHING EXCELLENCE CENTER, UNIVERSITY OF WISCONSIN-PLATTVILLE, HANDBOOK FOR STUDENT ADVISORY TEAMS (1991).

Charles J. Walker, *Classroom Research in Psychology: Assessment Techniques to Enhance Teaching and Learning,* in NEW DIRECTIONS FOR TEACHING AND LEARNING, 67 (Summer, 1991).

Specific Classroom Assessment Techniques

#1: Stress Reduction Through Feedback

For many first-year legal writing students, the stress of writing papers and meeting deadlines is nothing compared to the stress of dealing with the constant criticism. "You write the papers," the legal writing professor seems to say, "and then I'll explain in excruciating detail exactly how you screwed up." In an effort to reduce the stress on both the students and me, I have experimented with a variety of techniques designed to reassure the students that I have their best interests at heart and that their opinions and contributions are valuable. As a result, the students seem more relaxed and productive, and I enjoy teaching even more. Some of the techniques I've used are described below.

Student Survey: On the first day of class, I distribute a one-page questionnaire that asks several questions about each student's educational and employment history, prior writing experience, expectations for the course, etc. I explain that the survey information helps me to understand their backgrounds and to tailor my teaching to their needs. Although the survey is optional, nearly every student answers the questions in great detail.

I find that the questionnaires help to reduce stress in several ways. First, the mere fact that I've distributed the questionnaire sends a signal that I view the students as individuals and that I value their contributions to my class. It also reminds me that I am not dealing with some amorphous group of perennially exasperating students, but with individuals who came to law school with high hopes and aspirations and who are entitled to my concern and respect. Second, the questionnaire responses give me a "baseline" sense of the students' communication skills and personalities. With this information in hand, I can tailor my teaching to this particular group of students, thereby avoiding the stress that results from treating students as undifferentiated raw material to be forced into some standard lawyer-mold. Third, few things are more stressful than being compelled to slave over a problem that bores you to tears, and the information on the questionnaires helps me to develop hypotheticals and assignments that are more likely to appeal to my students' particular interests.

One-Minute Response Forms: At the end of each lecture-format class, I ask the students to answer one or two questions on a half-page form. (Typical questions: Please identify any analytical principles that we discussed today and that you didn't understand. What did you like best about your paper? What aspect of your paper satisfied you least? What questions would you like answered about your upcoming oral arguments?) At the beginning of the next class, I try to respond to the students' questions and concerns. This approach reduces stresses because it insures that I address the students' most pressing concerns about the course.

Evaluations and Feedback: In addition to conducting the usual course evaluations for the course and for the tutorial sessions, I frequently invite the students to give me informal feedback. I tell them that I stole some of my best ideas from my students, and I encourage them to talk to me in person or to leave (courteous) anonymous notes in my mailbox if they have any concerns or suggestions about the course. In any given year, approximately 20% of my students will respond to my invitation and give me some sort of written or oral feedback about the course.

Some of the students' comments and suggestions have resulted in major changes to the legal writing curriculum. For example, a number of years ago, several students complained that the first legal-writing assignment of the year (an office memorandum) was especially daunting because they had so little understanding about how to analyze the cases and other legal authorities. The students' comments helped me to see that I was devoting too much time to teaching them how to organize and express their ideas, and not enough time on how to develop those ideas in the first place.

I responded by restructuring the course to include additional reading assignments and in-class exercises on analyzing cases and statutes. The first office memorandum is now an ungraded assignment, and the entire class works together to develop the correct analysis for the client's problem. Only then are the students required to organize these ideas and present them in an office memorandum. Having mastered the basics of legal analysis, they then feel confident about preparing a second (graded) office memorandum on their own. Inviting feedback from the students not only reduced their stress by helping me to make the course more responsive to their needs, but it also made my own job less stressful. The students' analyses are now more cogent and insightful, and consequently, their papers are easier to read and grade.

I didn't immediately recognize the biggest stress-reduction benefit of inviting the students' feedback. I have found, however, that once my students see that I honestly welcome their feedback (both positive and negative), they often become much less defensive about having their own work criticized. By trying to overcome my own defensiveness about criticism, I try to convey to the students that we're in this together, and that thoughtful feedback helps all of us—professors as well as students—to do a better job. I don't know that any of us will ever learn to love criticism, but I'm convinced that inviting candid feedback reduces student stress and hostility and allows them to focus better on the task of learning. What more could any professor ask for?

Kate Lahey
University of Utah College of Law

#2: Minute Papers

Minute papers are a quick and simple way to collect written feedback from students. Periodically, I ask students to respond to some variation of one or both of these questions: "What is the most important thing you learned in class today?" and "What important question remains unanswered?" Students' written responses to these questions provide me with valuable insight into my teaching and my students' learning.

Minute papers are extremely easy to use. Before class, I decide what questions I want to ask. I prepare an overhead with those questions or I write them on the board. I give students two minutes at the end of class to answer the questions briefly in writing. Students hand in their anonymous responses on the way out of class. After class, I review the responses. I can read each paper and jot down notes about the most common responses from a class of 100 students in 15 to 20 minutes.

The responses to the minute papers tell me whether students are getting the main points of a class and what issues I need to address in more detail later. I report the results to the class. Then I make adjustments in future classes or give students suggestions on ways that they can answer their own questions.

Minute papers have several advantages. First, they provide teachers with a reasonable amount of feedback for a modest time investment. The feedback helps teachers assess both the effectiveness of their teaching and the quality of their students' learning. Armed with that information, teachers can make timely mid-course adjustments to maximize their students' learning.

Second, minute papers are quite flexible. Teachers can tailor their questions to their individual course goals. For example, Professor Grayford Gray of the University of Tennessee Law School asks his students to respond to the following questions: "What about the material is the most (1) engaging? (2) alienating? (3) surprising? and (4) confusing?" Teachers can use minute papers to assess student learning from class, reading assignments, simulations, field trips, or virtually any other law school activity. In addition, I have used minute papers at the end of the course to determine which topics should be the focus of a review session.

Third, the use of minute papers sends important messages to students. It shows students that their teachers care about their teaching effectiveness and are willing to make adjustments to be more effective. Further, minute papers demonstrate to students that their teachers are concerned about their students' learning and are willing to help students overcome problem areas. Moreover, the results of the minute papers provide helpful feedback to students about how their learning compares to that of their classmates and their teachers' goals. Finally, minute papers get students actively involved in the assessment of their own learning, an important lifetime skill for everyone.

Gerald F. Hess
Gonzaga University School of Law

#3: Shoe Box Pen Pals

To my large, first-year class each day, I bring a shoe box and 3"x 5" cards. I set it in the back, by the door, when I come in. Students may help themselves to the cards. When they have a question for me which they don't care to ask in front of their mates, they may jot it down on a card, sign it, and return it to the open shoe box lid. In the shoe box itself, cards are divided by alphabetical tabs.

The following class, the inquiring student can check the tab under her last name and retrieve her card with my answer.

Some students hesitate to ask what might be a stupid question. This is my attempt at "back channel" communication. When several students ask the same question, I'm alerted to a potential weakness in my presentation. I'm not adverse to writing "Go look it up!," but only when followed by a place to start.

Addendum: That was what I did before our school-wide network of computers. The shoe box has been retired; its purpose served now by e-mail. These days, an inquiring student e-mails me his question. I reply in the same way, appending my answer below the text of his question. I then take a copy of both question and reply, redact from each the student's name, and post them to an electronic notice board accessible to all in the class, from home, study carrel, or classroom. Volume is up from the shoe box days, and the questions are more sophisticated, probably because the questioner may fiddle with his question more conveniently.

John Paul Jones
University of Richmond School of Law

#4: Feedback to Teachers: Professional Skills Student Consultants

A first-year analysis, research, and writing skills course seeks to provide students with skills that will support them throughout law school and particularly in practice. Evaluating the effectiveness of such a skills course can be difficult. Course evaluations given at the end of the class provide some information. However, because the students have yet to test their legal analysis, problem-solving, research, and other skills in the workplace, their feedback is often based on their grades on their assignments or a comparison of the skills course to doctrinal courses that test their expertise through a single, final exam. Thus, giving evaluations to students at the end of a skills course is like asking someone to assess their driving skills after a Drivers' Education course that consisted of simulations only, with no actual road trips.

Yet using alumni surveys to evaluate skills courses also often proves inadequate. After graduation, alumni often recall favorably the practical nature of the skills introduced in the classes, but few can offer specific, detailed feedback about assignments and content of courses they took years ago.

To gain specific, helpful feedback on our skills courses, we created a program we call Student Consultants. In the spring term, we use data gathered by the Career Services Office to identify six to eight first-year students and six to eight second-year students who have accepted legal employment for the summer. We try to select students who represent a range of practice areas (public interest to intellectual property); a range of workplace settings (judicial clerk; corporate counsel; range of firm sizes); and a geographic range in locations (Dayton, Ohio; East Coast; Chicago). The students are selected and invited to participate in the program.

Student consultants receive a packet of materials, including an overview of the legal skills introduced in the first-year course and forms which ask students to describe the type of work assigned to them during their summer employment. (The packet is reproduced below.)

The detailed responses that come back are excellent, providing better, more precise, more productive student feedback than course evaluations and alumni surveys do. Using this sort of detailed, current response, we have made several adjustments to the skills courses. For example, when students reported increased use of CD ROM research, we added that component to the research portion of the course. When students reported uneven or limited access to CALR, we re-enforced our manual research training with sessions about how to integrate manual and computer-assisted legal research.

In short, the Student Consultants have helped us to shape our skills courses by giving us an accurate picture of how our students use their legal analysis, research, and writing skills when they put them to immediate use during their summer employment.

Packet for Legal Profession Student Consultants (LPSC)

During Legal Profession I-III, students acquire essential lawyering skills. The purpose of the LPSC is to test how well this training holds up in a range of legal workplace settings. This form describes the Legal Profession curriculum and then asks you to describe the tasks, assignments, resources, and skills you used in the workplace this summer.

Legal Profession Lawyering Skills

Research: Manual research using primary and secondary authority

CALR using WESTLAW and LEXIS-NEXIS

Introduction to CD ROM use (workshops held this year)

Integrating different research methods to complete an assignment

Writing: Objective, predictive office memorandum

Persuasive pre-trial brief on pretrial motions such as motion to dismiss or motion for summary judgment

Drafting a complaint and an introduction to formbooks

Procedure & Practice:

Introduction to rules and methods of civil discovery

Introduction to local rules of court

Introduction to depositions

Introduction to negotiations and alternative dispute resolution

Introduction to appellate practice and procedure

Oral Argument:

Oral argument at the pre-trial and appellate court level

For each major task or assignment you undertake in your summer job, please describe: the form of the product, the research resources used, the time frame or turnaround time, the substantive area of the law, and save a copy of the final written product. The product would remain confidential and not be used with client names, copied, or distributed in any way. Use the following form.

Student Consultant _____

Employer _____

Assignment (memo, brief, complaint, document review, deposition preparation, etc.) & **Substantive Area of Law** (tort, criminal, etc.)

_____

Page length of final written product, if any: _____

Turnaround time: _____

Research resources used: _____

Difficulties encountered, or "I wish I had known about…" _____

_____

_____

Successes encountered, or "I could do this because Legal Profession has taught me about…" _____

_____

_____

Law Practice Realities, or "I hate keeping billables" or "Corporate work is more interesting than I thought," or "Partners expect too much…," etc.

_____

_____

_____

Rebecca Cochran
University of Dayton School of Law

#5: Flow Chart Diagnosis

Flow charts have many uses in legal education. Teachers and students can create flow charts to organize, synthesize, and illustrate the connections between related concepts. Flow charts also make effective visual aids in the classroom. Another valuable use of flow charts, and the subject of this piece, is to diagnose students' problems with organization, analysis, and synthesis.

I stumbled upon the diagnostic value of flow charts in my Environmental Law course a couple of years ago. A few days before the final exam, a student called me and asked to meet with me. We set an appointment. Then the student asked, "Can I bring along my charts?" "Sure," I replied, having no idea what the student meant by "charts." The student appeared for our conference with a set of flow charts drawn on huge pieces of butcher paper. The student was a bit sheepish about the charts and we shared a few moments of laughter as the student showed me the text, illustrations, and arrows on the charts. As the student asked questions and referred to the charts, however, the diagnostic value of the flow charts became apparent. I was able to respond easily to the student's questions because the charts served as wonderful visual aids. More importantly, I was able to quickly see not only whether the student grasped individual concepts, but whether the student understood the intricate relationships between various environmental law doctrines.

Since that meeting, I have encouraged students in all of my courses to use flow charts as a method to help them organize and synthesize the material and I encourage students to share their charts with me and to ask me questions about their charts. When I review my students' charts, I get feedback about their understanding of the material and the relationships between concepts we have studied. Then, I am able to give individual students specific feedback to help them better synthesize the material. Further, if I see a consistent problem with the organization of the material in my students' charts, I can spend some time in class clarifying the problem areas.

A dozen or so of the students in my first-year course (Civil Procedure) and my upper-level courses (Environmental Law, Remedies) have accepted my invitation to share their flow charts with me. Every student who has shared charts with me has been enthusiastic about the value of the process. Many students say that they acquired a much deeper level of understanding of the course by preparing the chart and that they were able to quickly correct their organization and synthesis problems after I gave them feedback on their charts.

I am as enthusiastic as my students about the value of flow charts. Reviewing a student's flow chart is the only efficient method I know for me to give students feedback about their organization and synthesis of the material. I can review a two-page flow chart of a complex area of law (personal jurisdiction for example) and spot problems in less than five minutes. As a bonus for me, occasionally students organize or synthesize the material in a creative, accurate way that I had not considered before, so I get new insights into my courses.

I have never required students to prepare flow charts in any of my courses. However, as more students voluntarily prepare and share charts with me, I become more convinced about the value of the process. Consequently, I am considering requiring each student to prepare one flow chart for me during the course so that all my students will participate in the flow chart experience one time; then they can decide for themselves whether to continue to prepare their own flow charts.

Gerald F. Hess
Gonzaga University School of Law

#6: Three-Sentence Summary

For many first-year, first-semester students, what goes on in the classroom is a complete mystery. To help students pierce the mystery, I have introduced the three-sentence summary. I keep it going for about eight weeks (although in some years, students ask that it continue for the whole semester).

From the first day of class, I tell students that in every class I usually have three major points I am trying to convey. (Sometimes they are more concrete than others; sometimes they are an incomplete or undeveloped (as yet) idea.) I tell them that there are a number of minor points as well. After each class, I ask the students to get together with a classmate or two and list the three points they think I was trying to develop from class. I tell students that it is most beneficial if they do this shortly after class ends, while they can still reconstruct the dialogue. Although every year some students never do this exercise, others faithfully sit down after class and list the points.

I begin by doing the exercise myself, putting three sentences on the board explaining on Day Three what I was trying to show on Day Two. (Example: Not all promises are enforceable. Not all statements are promises. Words matter.) A day or two thereafter, students (rather than I) produce the three sentences each day. I begin the next class by asking for student(s) to volunteer to come to the board and list their three major points. (Example: Past consideration is not consideration. Moral obligation is an exception to previous sentence. One needs some sort of ill-defined benefit and detriment to the promisor and the promisee.) For variation, I call on students and write their ideas on the board myself. Usually, this is all done and ready before class actually begins. In some years, it is such a habit that students come up on their own to list the three points.

I then go over the listed points, demonstrating their correctness or indicating their shortcomings. I do this by marking up the sentences on the board, hopefully with colored chalk so students can see corrections and changes more clearly. I focus on big and small issues. I watch carefully for word use and accuracy of explanations. If the volunteer missed a major point, I identify what I was trying to show and how. (No hide-the-ball in the three-sentence summary.) I also indicate how what students thought were major points were actually side issues. All of this serves to summarize the last class and set the stage for the upcoming class. I spend no more than 5–7 minutes each class doing this. I always make it a point to praise the summaries that are good, saying things like, "You got it! Bravo!" Even for those that are less good, I say things like, "On the right track" and "In the ball park."

The three-sentence summary serves several purposes. First, it gets students working together and talking about the material after class. Next, it helps students link one class period to the next and to appreciate that we are building a structure piece by piece. It also helps students feel less lost. Perhaps they didn't get what happened in class on Tuesday but they got all the major points for Thursday's class. It helps them study ahead of time rather than wait for the last minute to piece things together. Even those students who did not prepare the three-sentence summary benefit from hearing the brief discussion. The exercise provides some individual feedback in a relatively non-threatening way. Students who volunteer can see they are on the right path without being called on in class. Even those who do not volunteer can compare their work with that up on the board. Finally, the exercise demystifies the classroom experience and that makes students more willing to listen and participate each day.

Karen Gross
New York Law School

#7: Documented Problem Solutions

Many law teachers, including me, have course goals concerning legal analysis, problem solving, or other thinking skills. Documented problem solving is a way for us to assess how our students analyze issues and solve problems.

To use documented problem solving, teachers first select a problem for students to solve. Teachers then solve the problem themselves, writing down all of the steps they go through in analyzing and solving the problem. Then teachers assign the problem to students. The assignment should make clear that it is not a test, will not be graded, and that the key to the assignment is not whether the students get the "right answer." Instead, for the assignment to work well as an assessment tool, teachers emphasize that the students need to give a detailed, step-by-step, description of how they went about analyzing and solving the problem. For example, it is not enough for students to state what issues the problem raises; students should describe *how* they identified the issues. Likewise, students should not merely state what law applies, but should describe how they decided that law applied and how they concluded other closely related law did not apply. Nor should students simply apply the relevant facts to the applicable law; instead, they should articulate why those facts are important while other facts are not.

Teachers and students can benefit from documented problem solving in several ways. First, teachers can get a sense of the problem-solving skills of the class as a whole. That information can help teachers decide how to teach problem solving in future classes. Second, teachers will be able to diagnose difficulties individual students are having with problem solving and analysis. Responses that contain clear, elegant, or sophisticated analysis can provide helpful examples to students who are having trouble with these skills. Third, as teachers prepare their own documented problem solution, they should become more aware of the process they use to solve problems. That awareness can help teachers be more specific and concrete when they teach problem-solving skills to the class as a whole or they work with students who are having difficulties. Fourth, students will become more aware of their thinking process by articulating their detailed problem-solving procedures and by comparing their analysis to that of their teachers and fellow students. Students should be able to use that awareness to improve their problem-solving process and, therefore, achieve an important goal of many law school courses.

Gerald F. Hess
Gonzaga University School of Law

#8: Teacher-Designed Feedback Forms

Most law schools administer student evaluations of the course and teacher at the end of each course. Often, schools consider student evaluations important sources of information when making salary, promotion, and tenure decisions. Although end-of-the-term student evaluations can provide feedback that teachers can use for development of instructional skills, the developmental aspect of these evaluations is limited for several reasons. First, if the primary purpose of the student evaluations is to provide information for personnel decisions, many faculty are reluctant to give them much weight as developmental tools. Second, since the evaluations are typically administered at the end of the course, the teacher can not use the results to improve the current course. Third, the questions on standardized student evaluation forms are too general to provide the detailed feedback most helpful to improving teaching.

Teachers can administer their own form to students to gather feedback for the purpose of improving teaching and learning. The teacher can tailor the questions to elicit specific information from students. For example, the questions could ask students to rate on a scale particular aspects of the course, the materials, or the teacher's instructional techniques:

> *In preparing your oral argument, please rate the helpfulness of the demonstration in class.*
> *No help　　Little help　　　　Fairly helpful　　Very helpful*
>
> *Please rate the organization of the NEPA unit of the course.*
> *Disorganized　　　　Somewhat disorganized　　Well organized*

Other questions could be more open-ended and intended to gather both feedback and suggestions from students. For example, the form could consist of the following three questions with space for students to write:

> *What teaching/learning activities used in the course to date are most effective for you?*
> *What teaching/learning activities used in the course to date are least effective for you?*
> *What additional teaching/learning activities should we try?*

The procedure for using teacher-designed feedback forms is quite simple. First, design a one-page form with three to five questions you would like students to answer. Before using the forms the first time, explain to the students their purpose—to gather feedback and suggestions in order to make your teaching and their learning more effective. Distribute the forms during the last five or ten minutes of class. Ask the students to respond anonymously. Review the responses, identifying the prevalent themes and suggestions. Within a week of distributing the forms, briefly report back to the class the major feedback they offered and how you intend to use their suggestions. Repeat the process two or three times during the course.

Teachers who design feedback forms and use them with their students can expect several benefits. First, the students' responses to the questions should provide detailed, focused feedback and suggestions that instructors can use to improve their teaching and students' learning. Further, by asking students for feedback and implementing some of their suggestions, teachers demonstrate profound respect for their students and a deep concern for their learning. In response to their teachers' demonstration of respect and concern, most students will work hard to achieve the goals of the course. Finally, by inviting evaluation from students and making appropriate adjustments in their courses, teachers demonstrate, by personal example, the important lifelong skill of welcoming and profiting from constructive feedback.

Gerald F. Hess
Gonzaga University School of Law

#9: Student Advisory Teams

Student Advisory Teams are for legal educators who are seeking new approaches to improve the quality of their teaching and their students' learning. A Student Advisory Team (SAT) is a group of students who meet periodically with the teacher to help the teacher improve the course. The students have two primary roles. First, the students provide feedback to the teacher about the students' learning (what they "get" and what they don't) and the effectiveness of the teacher's instructional methods. Second, the students offer suggestions to improve the course and their learning. The teacher's role is to listen to the students' feedback and to implement reasonable suggestions when appropriate.

The use of student teams to improve teaching and learning grew out of two influential movements in higher education during the last ten years. The first, Classroom Assessment, encourages teachers to gather frequent feedback from their students and to use that information to refocus teaching methods and make learning more effective. The second movement, Total Quality Management, urges teachers to assume the role of facilitator of their students' learning, to allow students significant control over their own education, and to strive for continuous improvement of teaching and learning throughout the course.

Once a teacher decides to use an SAT, the first step is to determine the student members of the team. I solicit student volunteers for the SAT during the second week of the course. I distribute a memo to each student which briefly describes the purpose of an SAT, the SAT format, and the role of the student participants. I also spend a few minutes in class to set out my reasons for using SATs: (1) I view the course as "ours" rather than "mine" and, therefore, believe the students and I share responsibility for its success; (2) I need ongoing feedback about the students' learning and the effectiveness of my teaching so we can make appropriate adjustments throughout the course; (3) I realize that I do not have a monopoly on the world's good ideas and want student suggestions to improve the course; (4) I am forced to think hard about the many teaching and learning issues that SAT members raise during the semester; and (5) I enjoy learning more about my students outside of the classroom. I give students a week or so to volunteer. I have always received at least six volunteers. When I received more than ten, I created two teams.

The first meeting with the SAT is important to provide organization for the group, to help students feel comfortable in their new role, and to begin receiving feedback. To help students prepare for the first meeting, I send each team member a short memo that contains, among other things, the following:

> Attached to this memo is information about SATs. Don't despair! I don't plan on any other required reading for us. Please prepare for our first meeting by reading the material and thinking about the items below. I will not set the agenda for future meetings, but I think that some structure is helpful to make the first meeting productive.
>
> 1. Why did you volunteer to participate in this project?
> 2. Administrative details. The recommended format is for the SAT to meet one week without the teacher and the next week with the teacher. Do you want to follow that format or try a different one? What time and place do you want to meet in the future?
> 3. What has happened so far in this class that is positive and you would like to see continue? What would you like to see happen less often? What else would you like to see happen in this class?

At the first meeting, which typically occurs in the fourth or fifth week of class, we work our way through the agenda. I ask each student to respond to the first item; I respond to it as well, reiterating my reasons for using SATs. The students decide on the format, place, and times for future meetings. I then ask each student to respond to one of the questions in the third item. During this time I listen and take notes, but speak little. By the end of our first meeting, each student has spoken at least twice, they have a good idea of their role, and they have given me valuable feedback.

At subsequent meetings, we follow the students' agenda, discussing their feedback and suggestions. During the meetings, I have several roles. I try to listen carefully to the students' feedback and to ask questions to clarify their comments. I also explore with the students their suggestions for improvement of the course. And, although I generally prefer to have the students decide what issues they should discuss in their meetings, occasionally I will ask the team to address particular topics at their next meeting.

The teacher's response to the students' suggestions is a critical aspect of effective SATs. My SAT members make suggestions relevant to all aspects of the course: (1) administrative matters (a short note on the board each class to remind students of the next assignment), (2) pedagogy (demonstrating case synthesis relevant to a complex issue), (3) content (infusing more ethical issues throughout the course), and (4) educational philosophy (alternatives to a forced-median grading curve that the school mandates in required courses). I begin dealing with student suggestions by asking questions to be sure I understand the issue the students are attempting to address and the nature of their suggestion. Once I understand the issue and we have explored alternatives, I usually implement the students' suggestion or the alternative we worked out in the meeting. For example, as a result of student suggestions I have used more visual aids such as handouts and flow charts, clarified my expectations on written assignments, provided more sample exam questions, helped students tie course material to real life, and given students more feedback on written assignments by putting model and sample responses on reserve in the library. Sometimes I am unable or unwilling to immediately implement a suggestion but attempt to use the suggestion the next time I teach the course. Occasionally, after explaining my reasoning to the students, I decide not to use their suggestion.

The use of Student Advisory Teams to improve teaching and learning in higher education is compatible with the principles of Classroom Assessment and Total Quality Management. Consistent with Classroom Assessment, teachers form the SAT to get feedback from students on their learning and the effectiveness of teaching methods in order to help students learn better. Consonant with the principles of Total Quality Management, students share control over and responsibility for their education by cooperating with the teacher to continuously monitor and improve the course.

Student Advisory Teams have many benefits for students and teachers in law school courses. Most student participants report that SATs improved their attitude toward the course, the teacher, other SAT members, themselves as students, and law school. Further, nearly all participants concluded that SATs improved the course, the teacher's effectiveness, and their learning.

SATs are a valuable tool for teachers who believe that students should share responsibility for the course, that students can give accurate feedback on teaching and learning, and that students can make worthwhile suggestions to improve the course. By listening to student feedback, teachers demonstrate that they care about the quality of teaching and learning in their classrooms. When teachers implement reasonable student suggestions, they show deep respect for their students and a commitment to continuous improvement in their courses.

Gerald F. Hess
Gonzaga University School of Law

#10: More Effective Student Evaluation of the Course and Instructor

Faculty often commiserate on the problems inherent in student evaluations of instructors and courses. When used as tools for assessment of teaching, individual anonymous student evaluations often lack reliability, validity, and fairness. The small-group instructional diagnosis (SGID) system developed for undergraduate schools at the University of Washington effectively addresses these problems and is readily adaptable to the law school classroom.

In the SGID process, students, at the instruction of a trained facilitator, collaborate in small groups to assess the instructor and course. With the help of the facilitator, students then reach a class consensus on strengths and weaknesses which is later reported to the instructor by the facilitator. The beauty of SGID is that, used properly, it can provide a more fair, reliable, and valid assessment of your teaching and course while maintaining student anonymity in the process. Here is how it works:

A facilitator (probably a faculty member from another department on your campus) meets with the class for 30 or 40 minutes. The facilitator begins by explaining the process to the class and assuring them that the process is anonymous, confidential, and voluntary. It is used to help the instructor improve the class and not to help the administration evaluate the instructor. The class breaks into small groups of four or six students who select a reporter for their group. The facilitator writes on the board and asks the groups to answer two questions:

1. What helps you learn in this course?
2. What improvements would you recommend, and how would you suggest they be made?

The students in each group discuss and write answers to the questions in ten minutes. The facilitator elicits from the reporter for each group two or three responses on each question carefully writing the essence of each response on the board to make sure it captures the students' intent. The facilitator questions the class, clarifies, and assists in discussion to reach a consensus and summarize the class responses to the questions. (During this whole-class discussion, it is important that the facilitator focuses on the answers made by the reporters and does not take additional answers from individuals, since such answers have not been peer reviewed in the small groups.) A student records the resulting summary from the board.

After the class, the facilitator meets privately with the instructor and presents the results. The facilitator discusses each of the points with the instructor and answers questions in an attempt to be as accurate as possible in transmitting the students' responses. The facilitator may help the instructor decide improvements that can be readily made so that those changes can be announced in the next class. This reassures students of the responsiveness and effectiveness of the process.

A most important feature of this process is that the comments are peer reviewed and the result of consensus thus avoiding the frustration an instructor feels when a single student makes a stinging criticism that tempts the instructor to change even though no other student may share the opinion. The peer review aspect screens out aberrant personal opinions or remarks that lack foundation, or may be mean-spirited, sexist, or otherwise unprofessional. A faculty member receiving comments from a class through the SGID process may have much greater confidence in the validity and reliability of the student evaluations. Be prepared, however, because valid and fair student observations merit response in the form of change or explanation to the class if change can't be made for some reason. Using the process formatively at mid-term and responding allow the students to see the benefit of their professional evaluation.

The process and changes made result in greater student ownership and responsibility for the class as well as greater participation and satisfaction. For more material on the SGID process and additional references, see Ken White's short paper, *Mid-Course Adjustments: Using Small-Group Instructional Diagnosis to Improve Teaching and Learning* published by the Washington Center for Improving the Quality of Undergraduate Education at the University of Washington. For a broader treatment of such "classroom research," see Thomas A. Angelo and K. Patricia Cross, CLASSROOM ASSESSMENT TECHNIQUES (2d ed. 1993).

Greg Munro
University of Montana School of Law

Chapter 11

The Evaluation of Students

[T]ests are important to students because major decisions are going to be made by, and about, students on the basis of test scores and the grade point average. So out of fairness to students, we must try to improve the tests we give. — Jacobs and Chase

The evaluation of law students is a subject sure to elicit a visceral response from law teachers, who readily recall some memory of the grading process — usually a less-than-pleasant one. Yet the evaluation of law students is extremely important and useful to all of the parties involved. Evaluation serves as a pedagogical tool for teaching and as a means of obtaining future access to law jobs and other educational programs for students.

A. Why Evaluate Students?

The evaluation of students is a time-honored and recurring theme of legal education that may have changed less over the years than any other component of the pedagogical process. Its necessity keeps it from falling into desuetude, because it is clear that many professors — and students — do not recognize the value of evaluation.

1. Ranking and Ordering

The value of evaluation, at a minimum, lies in the ranking and ordering of students for the purpose of assessment by prospective employers, such as private law firms, the government, and judges. The hierarchy established by grades also reflects importantly on a student's chances for admission to other advanced educational programs. Further, the competitive nature of students often seeks affirmation and recognition of their hard work and competency through the evaluation process.

2. Feedback

A benefit of evaluation more closely associated with the pedagogical process is feedback. The feedback function is not merely the objective "mirroring" of a student's performance, but a judgmental appraisal or critique of performance. The critique may assess one or a multiplicity of abilities. In a sense, the high value attached to the feedback function often recreates the evaluation process as an integral part of legal education.

The "mirroring" of mistakes or deficiencies is in itself quite useful. Many students who proclaim their knowledge and understanding of the material are perplexed at why they received low grades. While they may be earnest in their beliefs, they often have no idea how their own habits contribute to mediocre performances. Likewise, students who perform at a superior level may be equally unconscious about their performance, and may, like one famous baseball player, attribute the results to the meal they ate prior to the exam or something similarly irrelevant. For both types of students, the mirroring of performance may help adjust the perception to better fit with the reality.

Feedback also serves the important function of providing a roadmap for improvement. The feedback allows students to recognize performance strengths and weaknesses. Without such recognition, improvement would be haphazard and inefficient. After recognition occurs, and the areas or skills to be improved are identified, specifically directed efforts can be made to improve. Thus, in law school, drafting exercises regularly turn into redrafting exercises, case analysis can be an exercise in creativity, especially in the context of a moot court exercise, and lawyering skills can be improved through repetitive practice.

Significantly, it is not only the students who benefit from feedback, but the professor as well. (See, e.g., Chapter 10.) If it becomes apparent that all or most of the students fail to comprehend a particular area of a course or a particular point made by the professor, this data indicates that the problem may be attributable to the professor. Modification of teaching methods consequently may be in order.

B. The Tools of Evaluation: Instruments and Techniques

Evaluation instruments include: essays, usually consisting of "issue spotters" and sometimes jurisprudential questions; selected response (i.e., objective) questions; oral examinations (although these are much more common in other graduate programs and are limited by ABA rules); reviews of student performance (such as oral argument); and written papers. These assessment instruments can be administered during class, with variable levels of access to materials permitted, or outside of class, usually with plenary access to written materials. The large majority of evaluation occurs in law school at the end of a semester in the form of a final essay examination.

Once a test is administered, the actual evaluation of performance remains. Usually, law schools require only a single letter grade or numerical assessment to be communicated to the student. Some professors go further, providing written comments on the examination or on a separate document. Some teachers meet individually with students or in groups to review the examination, provide students with a copy of the best student paper, offer an answer key or the professor's model answer, or provide feedback in an alternative manner.

While it is commonly accepted in legal education that the professor takes full responsibility for the grading process, there are other sources of evaluation available. Even if these other sources do not participate in the grading process, they can still provide feedback to the students. These sources include teaching assistants, who often get to know the strengths and weaknesses of individual students, and outside attorneys, who may provide feedback about students' lawyering skills, such as interviewing, negotiating, and trial or appellate advocacy.

C. When to Evaluate Students?

Evaluations need not take place at the end of the course, affixed there almost as an appendage; they can be incorporated into the main body of the course as a true part of the learning process. In-class evaluations can occur in the form of quizzes, practice exams, short papers, and even oral exams. These evaluations do not have to count much, if at all, toward the final grade to be viable or to have considerable value to both teachers and students. The feedback they may provide to students and teachers can be invaluable because it is immediate and precedes permanent measurements.

Offering students a one-question, selected response (e.g., multiple-choice) "quiz" during class is illustrative. This technique asks all of the students to participate in actively solving a problem. The students must think independently about an issue and then perform. The subject matter of the question may focus students on a particularly difficult or important doctrinal or conceptual point, serving to highlight and emphasize its importance. The label "quiz," whether it counts or not, likely facilitates student interest and competitive energies. In addition, these questions provide students with instant feedback about their own analytical processes (assuming the proper analysis is communicated to the students in class or at some other time).

The value of assessment during the semester also arises from the fact that there is an implicit educational dimension for the teacher as well as the students. How do teachers know whether the material has been taught successfully? Teachers often have little idea as to how well students are learning during the semester. In fact, professors have been heard to mutter after an examination that they are surprised a class is doing so poorly — or so well. Several minimal evaluation "quizzes" during the semester can provide professors with quick feedback on what students are finding easy, difficult, or complex.

In-semester evaluation instruments need not occupy a considerable amount of the professor's time. The evaluations could be reviewed briefly during class, outside class in optional group sessions, or through a written answer. There is great flexibility associated with such mechanisms, so much so that their "costs" in terms of time and effort are minimal when compared to their benefits.

D. What to Evaluate?

Perhaps the thorniest issue for the professor involves what to evaluate. This delicate question offers a sweeping opportunity to review the goals of the course — in essence, what it is that the students should be learning. Interestingly, thinking about the evaluation process invites a conceptual review of the course on a pedagogical level, sort of the "tail wagging the dog" — the evaluation invites analysis of not just evaluation goals but of methodology and coverage issues as well.

Using this backwards-looking question of what to evaluate, it seems that the traditional essay examination, for example, elevates the skills of legal analysis of doctrine and writing under time pressure above other testable skills. Essay exams often raise questions of coverage — what subjects are important enough to test? — and presentation, namely, how students should adapt their writing to the professor's style. Alternative evaluation forms, such as objective questions, term papers, and skills testing, elevate other skills and present different problems. These alternative tests are sometimes used in traditional classes and often used when the subject matter of the class is skill-oriented, such as legal drafting, negotiation, counseling, and interviewing.

E. How to Evaluate?

1. Methodological Criteria

The two lynchpins of assessment are the concepts of validity and reliability. At a minimum, validity depends on the purpose of the testing instrument—what is it being used to do? That is, what exactly is it testing? The context of the purpose of the instrument, therefore, is important to any discussion of validity. The traditional definition of validity is that the thing being measured is what was intended to be measured. For example, if thinking ability is to be measured, then that is what the test should assess. If knowledge of the rules of law is the target, then that is what ought to be evaluated. If the thing being measured is not what was intended, then the testing instrument is invalid.

This traditional conceptualization of validity glosses over an important point. It is really not the test itself that is valid or invalid, but the validity of the inferences drawn from the test—the indirect evidence of pertinent skills. According to the recent literature, validity is really about the kind of inferences drawn from a test. For example, if a student writes a terrific answer to an issue spotter, does that answer provide indirect evidence of high-level analytical ability or problem-solving skills? If a student writes a poor answer, does that offer evidence of weak analytical ability?

There are three types of validation—content, criterion, and construct. Content validation essentially asks whether the instrument constitutes a fair sampling of the areas covered by the test. Criterion validity compares the testing instrument at issue with other arguably valid test measurements to determine if the measurements are proper. Construct validation simply asks whether the measurement reflects what ought to be measured.

The concepts of reliability and validity are somewhat intertwined. Reliability indicates that the results of the test can be replicated. A reliable test is consistent and will yield the same results on different occasions. A valid test must also be reliable—or it loses its mantle of fairness and ceases to be valid.

2. Effective Evaluation Schemes

Effective evaluation schemes of adult learners have three characteristics: multiple, varied, and fair. Multiple means that students' learning is assessed more than once during the course. Frequent evaluation and feedback allow the students and teacher to monitor progress and to make appropriate adjustments during the course. Research shows that frequent evaluation improves student performance on the final exam. Varied means that the scheme includes more than one type of evaluation tool, such as essay exams, papers, journals, multiple-choice exams, written projects, and performance of practice skills. Different evaluation tools are appropriate to assess student achievement of various objectives. Further, students vary in their preferences for different formats, so using a variety will help students do their best. A fair evaluation scheme reflects several principles: it is designed to assess whether students have achieved the goals of the course; the teacher's expectations and the grading criteria are clear before the evaluation; and the students have an opportunity to practice and get feedback before the evaluation.

3. Some Do's and Don'ts for Law School Examinations

The following suggestions are culled not from the academic literature but from the pitfalls of experience. These suggestions pertain to an end-of-the-course examination.

1. *Do ask more experienced professors* at your school how they approach exams, particularly others who have taught your course (and show them a draft of your exam if you are comfortable in doing so).
2. *Do ascertain whether there is an official or unstated grading curve* at your school.
3. *Do review your examinations* for typos and ambiguities and ask yourself what the point of each question is before submitting the examination to the students.
4. *Do include comprehensive instructions*—provide notice about how the questions will be weighted, what students should do if they encounter a perceived ambiguity, how they should identify themselves on the examination, whether they should skip lines while writing the exam, whether they should write in pen or pencil, and what materials the students may consult during the exam, if any.
5. *Do have students use anonymous grading numbers if appropriate*—contrary to popular opinion, those numbers are for you, not the students (they protect you from bias).
6. *Do adopt some review mechanism* by which students can learn from their examinations. Let students see why they received the grade they did—make an answer key or give students the opportunity to review a "model" or "best" answers. These may include post-examination individual or group reviews, Xe-

roxed answer keys distributed to all students or placed on reserve in the library, or other types of meetings or distribution of information.

7. *Do use a consistent and fair grading method.*

8. *Do minimize the "grade appeals process"* by asking students to look over an answer key or model answer or to attend a review session.

9. *Do take addition seriously.* Watch carefully for math glitches; use a computer program for your curve if you are so inclined.

10. *Do not discuss grades with students* until they are officially released by the Registrar—otherwise there may be appearances of favoritism and you will receive requests for changes before the grades are final.

11. *Do not ruin the section's curve* (see #2 above). If the school does not have a formal curve, find out how other teachers grade and generally follow them.

12. *Do not show how smart you are* by giving an impossible exam, either in length or in subject matter. Students will resent not being able "to show what they know," and ranking and ordering students can be accomplished just as readily with a fair (i.e., easier) exam. Thus, take the exam yourself before administering it to others.

13. *Do not change grades, as a general practice,* unless there is a clerical error—otherwise you may find a line outside your door (see #8 above).

14. *Do not be late* with your grades. Hand them in by the deadline.

References

Lucy Chester Davis & Clinton A. Chose, Developing and Using Tests Effectively (1993).

Philip C. Kissam, *Law School Examinations*, 42 Vand. L. Rev. 433–504 (1989).

Joseph Lowman, Mastering the Techniques of Teaching 251–285 (2d ed. 1995).

A. Neil & M. Wintre, *Multiple-Choice Questions with an Option to Comment: Student Attitudes and Use*, 13 Teaching of Psych. 196 (Dec. 1986).

Norman Redlich & Steve Friedland, *Challenging Tradition: Using Objective Questions in Law School Examinations*, 41 DePaul L. Rev. 143 (1991).

Specific Evaluation Ideas

#1: Practicing What We Preach and Testing What We Teach

Developing my students' analytical skills is one of the most important things I can do, especially in the first-year courses. To develop analytical skills, I think we need to test for them directly. I have started doing this by including case and statutory analysis on exams.

Langdell's Socratic method provided indirect encouragement for learning analytic skills: because his classroom analysis of cases was the only source of the law, students needed to follow the analysis or do poorly on the exam. Today, students have outlines of the law, which means that they no longer need analytic techniques to prepare for finals. It is commonplace to hear students proclaiming how they did well on finals without studying the casebook. Indeed, with Legallines® and other canned briefs, they no longer need to read the material to participate in class.

Neither a supportive nor an abusive learning environment solves the problem. I told students that mistakes in class didn't affect their grade; that no one should be embarrassed by making mistakes, because everyone does; and that the failure to learn to read cases would be a serious handicap in practice. This didn't work, perhaps because students hate to give their peers the impression that they are less than competent, and the case summaries from commercial outlines allow them to seem prepared. Harassing students whose analysis is inadequate simply encourages them to resort to case summaries in Legallines® and the like.

Failing to test for skills creates an inconsistency between our words and our conduct that students tend to resolve in favor of what's easiest for them, which is relying on commercial outlines. If we don't test skills, it's easy for students to conclude that they're not really important. As anyone who has heard, "Will this be on the exam?" can attest, teaching analytic skills by going through cases and statutes in the classroom may not make an impression unless we test for them on an exam.

To address these problems, it has become my practice to include case and statutory analysis on my exams. Generally speaking, I provide a case or statute and require the students to analyze it and use it some way that relates it to other material in the course. In Civil Procedure, I gave them Judge Posner's decision in *In re Rhone-Poulenc Rorer Inc.*, 51 F.3d 1293 (7th Cir. 1995). In Contracts, I gave them the Supreme Court of Illinois's decision in *Academy Chicago Publishers v. Cheever*, 114 Ill. 2d 24, 578 N.E.2d 981 (1991).

In both exams, I had them prepare a summary of the opinion. In *Rhone-Poulenc*, it was in the form of a case brief; in *Academy Chicago Publishers*, it was in the form of a letter to the client explaining the court's reasoning. In *Rhone-Poulenc*, I had them draft a dissent. (I didn't give them Judge Rovner's dissent.) In *Academy Chicago Publishers*, I had them write a petition for rehearing.

In another question in the Contracts exam, I had a drafting exercise that gave them Restatement § 228, which establishes a presumption in favor of an objective standard of satisfaction interpreting contracts that call for satisfaction of one party as a condition of that party's duties. We had not studied that particular section in class, although we had talked briefly about conditions.

In both courses, I gave plenty of advance notice that I was considering doing this. No one complained about the substance of the test.

There are three benefits to this. First, it encourages students to develop their skills by providing a reward for them. I expect the benefit will be even greater in the future, as students learn from past exams that I am serious about doing skills testing. Some teachers try to base exams on the mistakes in commercial outlines; while this responds to the need to get students to try to do analytic thinking, it seems to me preferable to test for skills directly.

Second, it makes our exams measure more of the skills that will be useful in practice. A justice of my acquaintance on a state supreme court requires her prospective clerks, who come from a variety of schools, to complete a performance test to help evaluate them. It's embarrassing that the grades that students accumulate over two years so poorly assess the skills students need in real life that a short performance test is necessary.

Finally, it provides feedback to me as a teacher. Although I'm still developing my teaching methods, it's already clear to me that I need to do more work in class on statutory analysis.

There are some burdens associated with this approach. Finding appropriate cases can take some work, and just scanning U.S. Law Week for recent cases is something I've avoided for fear that the students would catch on. However, it's worth it to me for the benefits it provides.

Greg Sergienko
Southern Illinois University

#2: Using Bloom's Taxonomy to Draft Exams

The last several years have seen a growing inquiry into ways to enhance legal education by drawing on learning theory and cognitive psychology. One potentially powerful tool is Bloom's taxonomy of educational objectives.

Developed to classify the cognitive goals for education, Bloom's taxonomy establishes a set of standard classifications that can provide a framework for discussion and development of many aspects of legal education. This article focuses on using the taxonomy to structure evaluation tools, and provides an example of how I restructured my first-semester Contracts final examination to test specifically for a wide range of student learning.

Bloom's Taxonomy

The taxonomy is a list of six educational objectives. In developing the list, Benjamin Bloom and a group of other educational psychologists sought to develop a classification of objectives consistent with relevant and accepted psychological principles and theories. The classification focuses on student behaviors which are the goals of the educational process. The six categories are:

Knowledge. The student can recall or recognize an idea. Knowledge is remembering what was covered in a way close to the way it was originally encountered in the educational process. This step includes a range of complexity, from remembering simple facts to remembering a complex theory. The progression is from the specific and relatively concrete to the more complex and abstract. An example of a question requiring a student to demonstrate knowledge is: *What are the elements necessary to create a contract?*

Comprehension: The student can grasp the meaning and intent of the material remembered. There are three types of comprehension behavior: translation (being able to put what one knows into other language); interpretation (being able to reconfigure what one knows in a way which makes it more accessible by focusing on the relative importance of the ideas, their interrelationships, and their relevance to generalizations in the original communication); and extrapolation (being able to make inferences with respect to implications, consequences, and effects that flow from the knowledge). An example of requiring a student to demonstrate comprehension would be: *Describe the essence of the objective theory of contract formation.*

Application: The student can select and correctly use the appropriate knowledge to solve a new problem. An example of a question requiring a student to demonstrate ability to apply knowledge would be: *In view of the following facts, was a contract formed?*

Analysis: The student can break down material into its constituent parts and detect relationships among the parts and the way they are organized. Skill in analysis includes five specific abilities: (1) to distinguish fact from hypothesis, (2) to identify conclusions and supporting statements, (3) to distinguish the relevant from the extraneous, (4) to determine how one idea relates to another, and (5) to detect unstated assumptions.

An example of an exercise requiring students to demonstrate analysis is the process of briefing a case.

Synthesis: The student can combine separate elements and parts from multiple sources to create a pattern or structure not clearly there before. Synthesis requires creative behavior. An example of a question requiring a student to demonstrate ability to synthesize would be: *To what extent do the cases of X v. Y, M v. N, and A v. B establish a new rule of contract formation?*

Evaluation: The student can use specified criteria and standards to make judgments about the value of ideas, solutions, methods, or other material presented. It is critical that the student be given clear standards to use in making the evaluation. An example of a question requiring a student to demonstrate the ability to evaluate would be: *To what extent are the cases C v. D and R v. O consistent with the objective theory of contracts?*

Using the Taxonomy to Draft Examinations

Having planned a wide range of learning goals for my Contracts class, I felt obliged to use an evaluation tool that addressed that range of learning. Historically, I used traditional fact patterns to test students' abilities to identify issues raised, articulate legal rules and policies, and apply them to resolve the issues. This type of question evaluates the extent of a student's comprehension and application learning. I supplemented this type of question with multiple-choice questions covering a wide range of substantive law. This type of question tested comprehension and, to a lesser extent, application.

Because I had used Bloom's taxonomy in setting the goals of the course and the design of individual classes, I realized that my traditional questions were insufficient to fully evaluate my students' learning. Therefore, I added three additional types of questions.

To test for analysis and synthesis as well as comprehension and application, I drafted the following question dealing with the doctrines of consideration, reliance, and unjust enrichment as bases for enforcing contracts. (The theories of bargain, reliance, and unjust enrichment were prominent themes throughout the course.)

> *The doctrine of consideration as set forth in Restatement (Second) of Contracts section 71(1) and (2) was once thought to be the central concept in determining whether a promise would be enforced by the courts. As the doctrines of reliance and unjust enrichment gained greater acceptance, promises which would not have been enforceable for lack of consideration became enforceable.*
>
> *Analyze the statement in the preceding paragraph, taking into consideration the following Restatement sections:*
> *A. 71(1) and (2),*
> *B. 73 and 74,*

> C. 86(1) and (2),
> D. 89(a), and
> E. 90(1).
> *Your answer should include:*
> *1. A definition of the concepts of consideration, reliance, and unjust en-richment and an explanation of the policies underlying each concept;*
> *2. An explanation of the elements of each Restatement rule; and*
> *3. A discussion of the relationship between the concepts and the rules in each of the Restatement sections identified, including a brief discussion of a case we read this semester which supports your reasoning.*

The question was particularly effective in determining the degree to which individual students could relate policy to rule and connect apparently different rules that were supported by the same policy.

The second new type of question focused on the students' ability to analyze case law. Because so much of what we do with students early in law school is to work on analyzing cases, I believed it was appropriate to have the students demonstrate the extent to which they had developed the ability to break down a new case into its important component parts. I combined that goal with the presentation of a substantive area of contract law that we had not covered during the semester to test the students' ability to grasp new contract concepts (in this question, third-party beneficiaries). I had told the students before the exam that the exam would include a question that would involve a new area of contracts.

> *The decision in* Sisters of St. Joseph of Peace Health and Hospital Services v. Russell *is attached, along with two sections from the Restatement (Second) of Contracts [defining the kinds of third-party beneficiaries]. The case deals with new subject matter. Analyze the opinion and the Restatement sections. Your analysis should include:*
> *1. A statement of all issues raised by the case;*
> *2. A summary of the court's analysis of the law and facts underlying the resolution of those issues; and*
> *3. An evaluation of the extent to which the case is consistent with the Restatement sections.*

I expected the students to perform very well on parts 1 and 2 because the analytic process required is exactly what they had been doing throughout the semester. I expected excellent results on part 3 even though it called for the most sophisticated aspect of cognitive learning—evaluation—because the standard for the students to use to evaluate the decision was simply the definitions of the two types of third-party beneficiaries recognized under the Restatement.

The responses to the question were highly effective. The aspect of analysis in which the answers varied most was in their discussion of the court's use of facts to support its reasoning.

The last new type of question I used was a drafting problem—pure application. My goal in using the question was to evaluate the students' ability to use their knowledge of the law of conditions to draft some simple contract provisions.

> You have been retained by Kringle Widget Co. to help draft the language for a contract Kringle has negotiated with Hummer Bugg Mfg. Co. Hummer will pay $1 a widget and buy however many widgets it needs for its manufacturing business in 1997. Hummer wanted a quantity discount, and the parties agreed that Kringle would give Hummer a 50% discount on all widgets Hummer buys in 1997 in excess of 10,000. Kringle wanted to have the freedom to end the contract if Hummer does not purchase at least 2,000 widgets within the first six months of 1997. Kringle also wanted to impose a finance charge of 1% per month for late payments (not received within 30 days after the widgets are delivered).
>
> Draft the provisions of the contract to implement the above agreement.

From an application standpoint, the question was only moderately successful. There was only a weak correlation between the students' knowledge of the law of conditions and their ability to draft a series of sentences implementing the agreement. The effectiveness of the draft answers turned as much or more on the students' ability to interpret the agreement and to write precisely, clearly, and succinctly. A question that provided the actual contract and asked the students to identify the conditions would evaluate more effectively the students' ability to apply their knowledge of conditions to new situations.

Bloom's taxonomy can help law teachers to develop clearer evaluation techniques. As more teachers begin using these concepts, we may find that the evaluation process becomes more useful. Using evaluation tools that clearly focus on a range of intellectual skills should allow us not only to evaluate students' performance more accurately but also to help them focus on the skills that need the greatest effort for further development.

Paul S. Ferber
Vermont Law School

#3: Giving Students Potential Exam Questions Before the Exam

Often toward the end of a course I tell students that there may be a policy question on the exam. I then give them a list of six policy questions and tell them that if a policy question appears, it will be one of the six. I also establish exam preparation rules: no outside research and no discussion of the possible questions except with classmates. I give them written guidance about what I look for in their answers.

This pre-exam list of possible policy questions has several positive results. First, especially for first-year students, exam anxiety seems to be reduced by the ability to think through and plan out answers beforehand. Students can walk into the exam with some idea of what to expect and feeling somewhat prepared and a little in control. Second, my exam preparation rules encourage students to prepare cooperatively rather than competitively, a value which I have as a goal in each of my classes. Third, different styles are accommodated to some extent. Students who are not quick on their feet, but who with time to reflect can do well, have a fairer chance to demonstrate their competence than on a traditional timed exam.

Finally, and most importantly to me, the nature of exam preparation (and thus review and internalization of the course) is lifted from memorizing rules to discussing and evaluating them, thus resulting in a higher level of learning. (I often include in my list of possible questions several which I have no intention of asking but on which I want students to focus as they pull the course together.)

Lynn Daggett
Gonzaga University School of Law

#4: The Multiple-Choice Essay

The multiple-choice essay was conceived as an idea to improve the student learning experience, not to reduce costs or optimize resources.

1.   Some weeks before the exercise is due students are given a typical contract law problem. They are told to prepare the answer to the problem in the way they would do if they were going to submit it as a course work but that they will not be allowed to actually submit it. (After all, one of the purposes of this exercise is to reduce the marking burden.) At the same time the nature of the exercise is also explained to them; that is, that they'll be given five different answers to the question. These answers are previous students' actual essay answers (see point 4 below).

2.   Since contract law is taught by a team of teachers at the University of Luton each member of the team marks the five essays (that will be given to the students; see 1 above) in the conventional way, including commenting, in detail, on each essay. The team then meets to discuss the ranking of the essays and a rank order is determined.

[This in itself is a very interesting exercise. Although the staff involved in this exercise did not always agree on the actual mark that each essay should receive there was very little disagreement about the order in which the essays should be ranked. This has interesting implication as to how lecturers mark essays given the research that shows the wide range of mark differences between one lecturer and another.]

3. The team's comments on each of the five essays are collated for future feedback to the students.

4. At the appointed lecture the students are issued with five different answers to the question. These answers are previous students' actual essay answers. The students are told to study each answer carefully and place all five in an order of merit. They are also told to consider where they would place their own prepared answer in the ranking. They have the lecture period, about fifty minutes, to complete the exercise.

5. At the end of the lecture period the students hand in their rank orders. Each student's mark is then calculated by comparing their rank order against the rank order of the contract law team.

6. Within a week the students are given their marked ranking sheets, which shows not only the mark they attained but also the order in which the contract law team ranked the essays. Further, the students are also given the collated comments of the contract law team. Students can then read these comments so as to see why each essay was given the mark it was.

[The actual marking of the exercises takes no more than one hour per 100 students. However, the preparation time takes several hours.]

Max Young
Department of Law, University of Luton, United Kingdom

#5: Practice Exams, Practice Exercises, and Practical Advice

Each fall the blood-sweating behemoth of first-year practice examinations and feedback is courageously undertaken by some of us. Rather than sound and fury signifying nothing, it must be a meaningful experience for our students.

Customarily, I give a two-hour contracts practice exam, designed so I can identify four categories of student performance: the truly lost, the struggling, the proficient, and the distinguished. (For the remainder of the academic year, I work one-on-one with the lost and struggling students with further practice writing exercises which are not discussed in this paper.) Following marking the practice exams, I return them with marginal comments and a "Legal Analysis Handout" (generally 10-15 pages) demonstrating various acceptable and unacceptable "answers." After giving the students an appropriate time to study and compare their exam analysis with the model handout, I hold an extra Q&A session.

I also give my students a two-part handout to help them improve their exam performance. The first part describes common student analysis deficiencies and gives lots of practical advice on writing better exams. The second part details exercises that students can do to improve their skills. An abbreviated version of the second part of the handout follows.

> Notwithstanding the importance of the classroom experience, legal education is essentially self-education (and it takes a lifetime). All of us are continually striving to improve our lawyering skills, especially the skill of effective communication both orally and on paper. The following exercises (outline, practice exam-taking, blue pencil practice, and practice projection) are designed for you to achieve two goals.
> 1. Improve Your Understanding and Comprehension of the Law.
> 2. Improve Your Legal Writing and Communication.
>
> A. *Your Outline*
> Since you are familiar with making outlines, I will limit my comments to ideas that might prove useful to you. To improve comprehension and writing, it is mandatory that you draft (and intermittently revise) your personalized outline for each course. For law-school success, that is a universal truth. Your undergraduate study should provide verification. You cannot improve comprehension and communication by relying solely upon the work and words of others — casebooks, hornbooks, canned outlines, and so forth. You must do the mental push-ups and make these words your own. That takes considerable time and great effort. Yet, it is that time and effort, which you are willing to spend in making (and redrafting) your personalized exam outline, where learning and improving occur. There are no shortcuts.
>
> Just as there is no ideal exam form or content, there is no ideal outline form or content. You must experiment to ascertain what you need in your outline and divine your special outline. For that reason, I cannot peruse your outline and make a judgment for you about its efficacy or substance. That's your judgment call. However, I can make a few observations.
>
> The fundamental notion is that you are taking an entire course, reorganizing and reducing it for clarity, understanding, and recall in the exam context. First, to assure subject matter coverage use the "Table of Contents" of your casebook and class notes (and perhaps a hornbook) for the outline's structure and coverage. Second, the idea is to keep it brief. Your first draft will contain too much information and too many words (prolix). On an ongoing basis, revise and rewrite to make it more brief (concise, precise English). Your goal is to create an outline which effectively allows you to recall the requisite "data" when writing the exam.
>
> Reduce those sentences and words to the least possible number. The result is a few terse but substance-filled sentences. The result is useful on

the exam, especially considering time limitations. For instance, while reading the exam problem, you perceive that bargained-for consideration is an issue. Immediately, from your outline (or mnemonic device) you identify the issue and write the few, terse, substance-filled sentences (from your outline) regarding bargained-for consideration. Now you are reasonably ready to write the most important part of your exam answer by analytically applying those sentences (the "rules") to the unique facts given in the problem.

B. *Practice Taking an Exam Weekly*

In one of your courses, each week practice taking an exam. The only rub is the exam problem. You can find sufficient problems in your casebook. Take the facts of a case in your casebook and assume that is the exam problem. Or take a problem from the notes or questions following a case as the exam question. Give yourself a time limit and write an answer. As you write, you should practice visualization and projection, another exercise explained below. When finished writing, put your "answer" away and let it cool for at least a week. Then read and mark your "answer." By grading and marking your practice answer you will gain new insights and strengths in writing a legal analysis. Finally, when you mark your answer, try the blue pencil exercise.

C. *Blue Pencil Editing Exercise*

Exorcists exist at law and in equity. Unconscionability is an equitable principle (codified in UCC section 2-302) which empowers a court to expunge an unconscionable word, or sentence, or paragraph from a written contract. At law the blue pencil rule permits a court to "blue pencil out" the illegal, objectionable words from an ancillary covenant not to compete in a contract so that the remaining words will be reasonable and enforceable. Printers customarily use a blue pencil to strike words from a manuscript to make it more accurate and readable. This exercise asks you to apply the blue pencil to your "prolix" writing. Beatification of muddle is unacceptable. Plain English is your salvation.

Your legal writings have too many words (and sentences) and similarly need expunging for clarity and precision. The art of writing lies in thrift. Your goal is to write concise, precise, logical English sentences. Your lawyering written products must be readable and comprehendible. Sometime after writing them, take your writings (case briefs, legal research, memos, practice exams) and apply the blue pencil. Strike all superfluous words. Combine words into one word. For example, "In this problem one might argue from the facts that...." becomes "Arguably,...." Combine sentences. Expunge, synthesize, and simplify.

D. *Practice Projection Exercise: The Art of Visualization*

Professionals spend considerable sums learning and applying projection theory (a/k/a visualization). Golfers, tennis players, and many other sports professionals practice projection. Golfers visualize themselves physically striking the golf ball, then see the ball in flight, and watch it land where they want it. Basketball players project the ball into the hoop. Projection sets the mind and body to perform a certain task in a certain way. Scholars have devoted considerable print to this theory in respectable journals. So what is this theory?

In the usual Socratic fashion, let me answer with a question. Who did you project reading your practice exam answer? If you envisioned a reader at all, it was probably the professor which was the worst choice. The professor is so knowledgeable (in your mind) that you will not need to explain your answer logically, clearly, and thoroughly to such a knowledgeable person. Your problem is proper projection.

To practice visualization, you should initially select a person to visualize as your reader. My suggestion is to choose someone in your life that you know well, and who requires a methodical, precise, and careful explanation before comprehending something. Choose a person who will understand and fully comprehend provided you take the time (carefully, deliberately, and thoroughly) to explain. Do you know such a person? If so, that's your reader to visualize throughout your legal career. For me, it's my brother who is a great friend, and good listener. If I'm patient and thoroughgoing, he will comprehend any demanding analysis.

Now practice communicating to your specially chosen person. Hereafter, in drafting, negotiating, litigating, counseling, and so on, continually visualize your chosen person. When you write, imagine that person reading. When in court before a judge, visualize your person before you rather than the judge. When addressing a jury, visualize twelve of that person. I assume by now you understand. My brother would.

Eric Mills Holmes
Dean, Appalachian School of Law

#6: Multiple-Choice Quizzes in Large Classes

In my 55- to 60-student classes in Civil Procedure, I give one-question multiple-choice quizzes in our Monday classes. Students know that they will be quizzed on Mondays based upon material that we have covered in the previous week.

Because the quiz consists of a single multiple-choice question, the quiz takes only about five minutes. Afterwards, we discuss the question and answers.

These quizzes serve several purposes. First, they are an incentive for the students to review each week's material on an on-going basis. Students have told me that the quizzes are very helpful in their review process. Second, the quizzes help me connect one week's material with the material that follows. After our discussion of a quiz, I typically summarize in a few sentences the material that we covered in the prior week and give students a synopsis of how that material relates to what we will cover during the present week. I have found that one of the major problems first-year law students have is making connections between individual cases and segments of material. The discussion that follows Monday morning quizzes gives me a good opportunity to help students make some of those connections.

The discussions that follow the quizzes often are significantly more animated than other class discussions, because students want to know why their answers were wrong or they attempt to convince me that credit should be given for an answer other than the "right" answer for which I was looking. Occasionally I will be convinced to give credit for an answer for which I had not planned to give credit, and I think that seeing me rethink the answers in this fashion may be a good demonstration for the class.

Third, the Monday quizzes give students some low-key feedback on their performance before their final exam. The quiz questions early in the semester are extremely easy. Also, although I give nine two-point questions over the course of the semester, no student can earn more than 14 points. Thus, students can miss one or two questions and still obtain the maximum number of quiz points. Because they can miss two questions without grade penalty, I also don't deal with situations in which students are sick and miss a class for this or other (legitimate or illegitimate) reasons. If I don't get a correct answer from them in a given week, they don't get their two points.

Because most students "max out" on their quiz points and the quizzes typically account for only about 15% of their total grade, the quizzes do not engender the pressures that surround final examinations. The quizzes also make students more comfortable in preparing for and taking final examinations.

I must acknowledge Professor Howard Brill of the University of Arkansas as the source of this idea.

Larry Dessem
Mercer University Law School

#7: Creating Multiple-Choice Questions

Many professors shy away from multiple-choice questions because of the perceived inadequacy of such questions for testing analytical ability and because the apparent difficulty in creating such questions. Effective multiple-choice questions can be created with a modicum of effort, and can be well worth it. Some simple rules govern the construction of such questions, according to the experts. For example, the guidelines governing the creation of multistate bar exam questions include the following:

1. There should be only one clearly correct option;
2. The incorrect options or distractors should be plausible to less knowledgeable examinees but clearly incorrect; and

3. Options should be written so that they do not provide clues for less-knowledgeable but more test-wise examinees.

How to do this? Some other guidelines may be helpful:

1. Create clear question components.
   a. Construct a clear "stem" or call of the question that commands or directs the test-taker to do something.
      1. Avoid using "not" in the stem.
      2. Make the stem relate smoothly with all options to avoid giving clues as to which options are incorrect.
      3. Place words in the stem that otherwise would be repeated in most or all of the options.
      4. Make the stem a complete sentence.
   b. Build an understandable "root" or body of the question.
      1. Be simple and direct.
   c. Design clear options or responses. (Try to reduce the impact of language complexity on item performance.)
      1. Minimize use of multiple or general options that state "none of the above" or "a and b above," etc.
      2. Options should be of similar length and specificity — don't have some options that are much more qualified than others.
      3. All of the options should be somewhat plausible.
      4. Make one option superior to the others.
2. Reduce the odds of guessing.

Sometimes, students learn how to take examinations successfully by becoming skilled in the art of test-taking. These students may discover clues from the structure and nature of the questions, for example. To safeguard against this type of occurrence, several options exist.

   a. Make distractors (incorrect options) viable.
      1. Quality, not quantity of distractors, counts.
         The number of distractors is not as important as the way the question and distractors are framed. A question with two distractors, for example, provides a 50% chance for guessing correctly, a question with three distractors a 33% chance, and a question with four distractors a 25% chance. Thus, adding a fourth distractor reduces the odds from guessing by only 8%. Adding a fifth distractor, moreover, reduces the chance of guessing correctly by only 5%. Consequently, it is more important that distractors be viable than numerous.
      2. Distractors should not provide clues that they are incorrect. Clues may include words such as "always,"

"never," "impossible," and the like. Also, items should correlate grammatically with the stem and not use incompatible wording.

3. One way to correct for guessing is to deduct points for incorrect answers. . . . If a student is permitted to guess without penalty, a poor student will accrue more undeserved points than a good student because a poor student will have more opportunities to guess.

4. Another way to safeguard against guessing is to change the conventional "choose the best/right answer" to "choose the best/right answer and then a secondary or tertiary answer." There is a conflict in the literature as to whether this method enhances the reliability of the test.

5. Viable distractors can include correct but irrelevant statements of law and common errors of law or its application.

b. The number of distractors can vary from question to question. There is no special benefit to having the identical number of distractors for each question, provided of course that guessing is minimized.

3. "Close" counts in horseshoes, hand grenades, slow dancing, and multiple-choice questions.

a. Multiple-choice questions can include stems that ask the students to "choose the best answer," the "most likely" argument, the "least likely" argument, and so on. Professor Josephson calls these "relative judgment" questions, as compared to those that call for absolutes. This type of question promotes comparison and critique by the test-taker, instead of an absolutist search for "right and wrong." These questions may be easier to design as well, since the options can be drawn from more to less incomplete or from more to less accurate.

4. Weed out bad questions—or check for good ones. Evaluate your multiple-choice questions.

Various statistical indices can be used to check your multiple-choice questions.

a. Item Difficulty Index. This determines how difficult your individual questions are. You can compute difficulty by dividing the total number of test-takers getting the question correct with the total number of test-takers overall. If no one gets the question correct, the index will be 0.00. If everyone gets the question correct, the index will be 1.00. The more difficult the item, the lower the index.

   b.   Item Discrimination Index. This correlates the performance on a single question with performance on the exam overall. Here, the performance of the class on the single question is analyzed in terms of how high- and low-ability test-takers performed on the question. The valuation system generally places the correlation on a scale of 1.00 to -1.00. Positive scores indicate that high-scoring test-takers tended to get the question correct more frequently than low-scoring test-takers.

   c.   Some multiple-choice questions may be perceived as "bad" by the students. These questions can be discovered by providing students with the opportunity to explain their answers or to "appeal" or challenge the validity of the question through the use of a special form.

5.   Test for specific objectives.
   a.   One aid to developing good multiple-choice questions is to articulate the objective for a question prior to designing it.
   b.   Specific objectives could include:
      1.   Any of the four learning style questions—Why? What? How to solve? or What if? (See Chapter 2, Idea #6.)
      2.   Any aspect of the trilogy of doctrine-adjudicative facts-environmental facts.
      3.   Critical thinking.

6.   Create questions using all of the different learning styles to reach the broadest number of students.
   a.   "Why?" questions. E.g., Why is the rule constructed in a particular way? Why are some facts more important than others? Why is some precedent more helpful than other precedent?
   b.   "What?" questions. E.g., What is the applicable rule, principle, doctrine, statute, precedent?
   c.   "How to apply?" questions. E.g., Solve a problem after spotting the issue and applying the law to the relevant and significant facts.
   d.   "What if?" questions (ask how a problem or analysis would be affected if one or more facts were changed).

7.   Vary the format.
   a.   One variation is to give students an opportunity to explain their answers. This can be satisfying to students and

professors alike. It may strike a happy balance between the subjectivity of essays and objectivity of selected-response-type questions. One group of researchers studied "answer justification," which is a "technique that allows students to convert multiple-choice items perceived to be 'tricky' into short-answer essay questions."

b. One set of facts can be used for several questions.

c. Create chronology or hierarchy questions. E.g., "Which law/event came first?" "Which is the most important legal rule given the facts?"

e. Explanatory questions. E.g., "Which of the following best explains the judge's conclusion?"

f. Create questions asking students to predict an outcome. E.g., "The most likely outcome of the case or motion presented in this question will be....(a) ; (b) ; etc." This predictive type question requires students to analyze information and draw legal conclusions.

8. Use the "closing argument" method to build questions.

a. Construct the answers first, then the body of the question. Or,

b. Construct the stem of the question first.

9. Use ambiguity. Don't avoid it.

a. Focus on an ambiguity in the law or facts.

b. Create options containing "if, then..." clauses.

10. Practice creating questions during the semester.

a. Use multiple-choice questions as a teaching tool during the semester. Studies show supplementary evaluations during the semester assist in classroom learning.

b. Have the students create multiple-choice questions and hand them in for review and use, either during the semester or on the examination.

c. Use concept mapping to help students create questions, or to determine which areas should be emphasized. (See Chapter 4, Idea #11.)

L. Aiken, *Testing With Multiple-Choice Items*, 20 J. Research and Development in Ed. 44, (1987).

D. Dodd and L. Leal, *Answer Justification: Removing the "Trick" From Multiple-Choice Questions*, 15 Teaching of Psych. 37 (Feb. 1988).

H. Gensler, *Valid Objective Test Construction*, 60 St. Johns L. Rev. 288, (1986).

M. Josephson, Learning and Evaluation In Law School (submitted to the
    Association of American law Schools Annual Meeting, Jan. 1984).
J. Killoran, *In Defense of the Multiple-Choice Question*, 56 SOCIAL
    EDUC. at 106, 107 (1992).
V. Sturtevan & B. Johnson, *Micro-Computer Test-Generation Systems:
    A Software Review*, 16 TEACHING SOCIOLOGY 49 (1988).

Steven Friedland
Nova Southeastern University Shepard Broad Law Center

#8: Evaluation of Oral Lawyering Skills Through a Video Exam

Video exams can be used for a limited but very important purpose. They test a student's ability to analyze another lawyer's performance of a particular interpersonal skill such as counseling or interviewing a client, negotiating with an adversary, or conducting a cross-examination. In part, this ability to prepare a written critique is an indirect reflection of the student's competence in performing the skill itself. It certainly is not a substitute for an evaluation of the student's actual performance of the skill. But a thorough and thoughtful written critique can demonstrate the student's mastery of the concepts integral to a competent performance of the skill. To ensure the realism of the testing experience, a video exam should be accompanied by a factual summary, or, ideally, by a case file that places the video in context. As a complement to other testing methods, video exams can help evaluate students' abilities to perform oral interpersonal lawyering skills.

There are several different learning contexts in which a video exam can be useful. These include: an introductory lawyering skills course, a traditional doctrinal course such as civil procedure, an advanced skills course taught through simulation, and a clinic in which students represent clients on real matters. All that is required is that the teacher have as one of her or his objectives the teaching (and therefore the testing) of interpersonal lawyering skills.

Thus, an important threshold question for a teacher is: can I connect up my answers to how and what I want to evaluate? If teaching applied lawyering skills is part of the what (even a minor part), the challenge is to connect the method of teaching to the method of assessing students' facility in the skills being taught. A video exam can make that connection. It is an evaluative technique that fits nicely with all of the various teaching methods used in skills teaching: direct experiential learning (doing the skill through simulation or on real cases); observational learning (live demonstrations or video depictions); and in all cases, critique of what it is that is done or observed.

When students see the connection between what happens in the classroom or what they are studying or doing during the semester and what they are being tested or graded on, the learning methods are reinforced. Law students often are driven by grades and how and what they are tested on. If a pre-exam focus includes interpersonal skills, it should be appropriately reflected in the method of evaluation used to determine the student's grade.

Consider two examples. First, a first-year lawyering course where one of the objectives is to introduce students to various of the tasks lawyers perform such as interviewing or counseling a client. As part of the teaching the students view various tapes of lawyers performing those skills followed by student critiques of what they observe. If part of the final exam in the course includes a comparable video that students are asked to analyze, the exam appropriately parallels the teaching.

A second example is a simulation skills course such as trial advocacy or a course in interviewing, counseling, and negotiation. Clearly, one way, probably the best and most valid way, to evaluate a student's ability to perform the skill in question is for the teacher to observe the student actually performing the skill. But another, complementary way to test the student's understanding of the skill is to do what presumably had been done throughout the semester in the classroom—namely to ask the students to prepare a critique of a lawyer performance seen on a tape. Combining both evaluative methods seems the optimal way to validate an assessment of a student's skills abilities.

One difficulty or disadvantage in using video exams is that tape production can be time intensive. There are several ways to mitigate this problem. First, working with other teachers of the same subject would enable one video exam to be used by more than one teacher. Second, adapting one of the many professionally produced tapes can save production time. Third, clinicians often produce tapes that might be usable by the non-clinical faculty for exam purposes. Finally, if you have an A/V staff person, I have found that such individuals are willing and often anxious to participate in the creation of original taped productions; they simply have to be asked.

Another hurdle to using video exams is that A/V facilities must be available and easily accessible. If they are not, video exams are not a realistic option.

Occasionally, I hear in response to the suggestion of a video exam the analogy that someone's ability to analyze a championship tennis match does not mean that the analyst can play tennis. That is true. It also is true that a student's ability to complete an effective critique of a negotiation does not a negotiator make. But the analogy misses the point, or several points.

Viewing tapes can assist the student in understanding the multifarious aspects of applied lawyering tasks. Watching a lawyer on tape put all of the pieces together also enables a viewer to apply and test all of the various theories contained in our increasing number of skills texts. As noted above, a video exam validates the importance of the classroom tasks of watching and analyzing lawyering tapes. Finally, a student's ability to critically analyze a lawyer's performance frequently parallels the student's actual performance of the same skill. My own experience in teaching skills is that there is a correlation between the critique skill and the performance skill. The video exam comes as close as possible to actually performing the task. It is a partial, but still very useful answer to evaluating a student's ability to perform interpersonal lawyering skills.

Larry Grosberg
New York Law School

#9: Critiques of Students' Lawyering Skills

Learning lawyering skills, such as negotiations, requires students to participate in exercises that encourage them to consciously develop their skills. Teachers should provide informed and impartial critiques immediately after the exercises.

This quickly becomes a resource problem. Teachers (at least, this teacher) cannot individually critique many (more than two per student per semester) of the student exercises unless the number of exercises or students is unduly restricted. Also, critique by a single instructor can narrow perspectives from which students envision the dynamics of the skill and risk the perception that there is a "right" way (i.e., the instructor's way) to practice the skill.

Part of my solution has been to make extensive use of practitioners and student peer evaluators. There are many collateral benefits to this beyond the availability of evaluators. I train these evaluators in the techniques of the critique method, although time for training is always at a premium. Training is essential because critique is a powerful learning tool. If used inexpertly, it can do more harm than good. I also train students, whose work will be critiqued, about techniques they can use to maximize the learning experience. Again, time restraints are a limitation.

Guide for Evaluators

You will be teaching students basic lawyering skills (client interviewing, oral advocacy, and negotiations) by seeing them perform the skills in simulation exercises and then providing an individualized critique of their performance. We know that "learning by doing" is a very powerful experience. However, its success depends on whether the critique helps the students to understand how they need to improve and encourages them to do so. This learning method demands hard work by faculty and students alike in the form of thorough preparation and diligent application. Here are some guidelines for performing effective critiques:

- *Be prepared to critique.* Read and know the case file. Anticipate what problems may arise. Think about how you would perform the exercise. Take a minute or two to organize your critique before delivering it.
- *Be selective.* Select one or two points on which to critique and fully develop these points.
- *Start with a positive comment.* People tend to be more open to constructive criticism if they hear it after being reassured of their "worth." In every performance, there is something that merits praise.
- *Be specific.* Relate your critique to specific events in the student's performance of the simulation. To do this well, you need to take accurate, detailed notes during the exercise.
- *Be constructive.* If you offer negative feedback, don't just criticize but suggest alternatives of what the person could have done differently. Focus your critique on an area that you think the student will be able to improve.
- *Be succinct.* Get to the point of your critique. Don't ramble on.
- *Be honest.* Your job is not to be popular, but to help the student improve. Tell it like it is, but be supportive. Note what was done well, but only if it was done well.
- *Take responsibility for your critique.* Present the critique in the first person ("I think...", "In my experience...", "I think the better practice is..."). Avoid presenting points of critique as universal principles unless, of course, they are (i.e., "Never address the court as 'Hey, dude!'").
- *Critique the performance, not the person.* Do not be judgmental or sarcastic. Tell the person what you saw or heard and the effect it had on you. Don't just label it as "good" or "bad."

- *Make the student a partner in the critique.* Ask questions. ("What were you trying to achieve?", "What do you think went wrong?", "What alternative approaches might you have tried?")
- *Teach by example.* A critique is a performance unto itself. People learn as much or more from how we say things as from what we say. Incorporate good communications skills into your critique. Use eye contact. Listen intently. Use gestures. Put emphasis in your voice. Be adaptable. Speak in plain English.
- *See the larger picture.* Remember to teach the class as well as the individual student. The students will listen to your critiques of others and compare them to their own. Excessive praise for one may affect how students receive your critiques of others.

Guide for Students

You will be learning basic lawyering skills by practicing these skills in exercises that realistically simulate law practice. You will then receive individualized feedback from experienced practitioners, who have been trained in the techniques of effective critique. To maximize the learning opportunities afforded by this learning method, you need your own "critique skills" — that is, the techniques of how best to receive and implement critique. The following guidelines should be helpful to you:

- *Listen to the critique with care and an open mind.* Try not to take the critique as personal criticism. Don't get defensive or immediately argue with or reject the critique.
- *Be sure you are clear about what has been said.* If you are not clear or don't understand, ask.
- *Focus on specifics.* Try to learn as specifically as possible things you might do to improve your performance in the future.
- *Keep your perspective.* See the critique as offering you new choices, rather than dictating the one right way to do something.
- *Clarify.* If you disagree with the critique, respectfully — but directly — raise the issue and ask for comment (but only after the instructors have completed their critique).
- *Ask questions.* If you want feedback on a specific matter and didn't receive it, ask (time permitting).
- *Don't overly rely on any one person's critique.* Compare it, to the extent possible, with others' (including other students participating in the exercise). Ask others who may know

you and whom you trust about the substance of the critique.

- *Pay careful attention to the critique of other participants in the simulation.* This is an opportunity to learn additional aspects of the skills involved. It also is a more objective perspective from which to observe the dynamics of the critique method.
- *Look for ways to use the information.* At the end of the critique session, ask yourself, "What do I know now (or know better than before)?" Write it down. That is the standard of success of a simulation/critique exercise.
- *Say "thank you."*
- *Look for opportunities to implement what you learned from the critique.*
- *Save your evaluation forms (self and faculty) and any notes of what you learned.* Review them the next time you are about to perform the activity that was the subject of the critique. Learning fundamental skills is an incremental process.

Ralph Cagle
General Practice Skills Program
University of Wisconsin Law School

#10: Extemporaneous Oral Examination

One of the most important skills for students to acquire is the ability to communicate orally. While many institutions, Caldwell College included, are developing and expanding "writing across the curriculum" programs for students, in my observation, there does not appear to be the same emphasis on oral communication. While this oral extemporaneous examination is administered to undergraduate business students, the skills I seek to improve and measure are relevant to law students as well. While I am attempting to prepare my undergraduate students for "real-life" business experiences, such as giving business presentations, indeed, lawyers need to have similar presentation skills in their capacities as litigators, teachers, and business executives.

Rather sadistically, I include this oral extemporaneous examination in my syllabus which is distributed during the first class. From that moment until the date of the examination, at least one student each class asks what it is all about. Of course, part of the effectiveness of the assessment is the element of unpredictability, so I just tell my students that we'll talk about the examination on the date indicated. The closer the date, the more questions. And, the intensity of the questioning increases. I give no explanation until the day of the exam, which is usually towards the end of the semester.

I have found that black letter law, well-settled law, is conducive to this method of examination. Although common law evokes a wonderfully adversarial encounter, because of the time constraints, I purposely avoid controversial areas of law. Although there have been times when a student manages to be quite creative in relating the relevant law, I am primarily seeking to measure the skills required to apply *established* law to a given set of facts. For this reason, I usually test on the Uniform Commercial Code using this method of examination.

First, I introduce the IRAC (Issue, Rule of Law, Analysis, Conclusion) method to my students. I find that this is an easy method for students to grasp and is excellent for organizing thoughts. I usually take part of a class prior to the examination date to go over IRAC.

On the day of the examination, I ask my students to select a number from 1 to 20. I have preselected 20 short Uniform Commercial Code problems and numbered them accordingly. The problems are purposely not complex. In fact, there is only one issue to be addressed. As each student selects a number, I hand the student the corresponding problem, faced down. I continue until each student has a problem. After everyone has a problem, I instruct the students to turn over the paper, read the problem, and use the book and/or class notes to solve the commercial law conflict usually between/among two or more parties. I allow 10 to 15 minutes to prepare an oral presentation on how the conflict would be resolved. Grading is based on technical delivery, correctly identifying the issue, correctly identifying the relevant law, and applying the law to the specific facts. After the initial presentation, if I determine that the student has missed the mark, I Socratically question the student until the student gets on track.

Overwhelmingly, students complete the examination and feel empowered, self-confident, and often surprised that they remembered the law well enough that 10 minutes is sufficient enough time to peruse the code. The underlying learning objective of this exercise: It is not the most important thing to know the law off the top of your head. It is more important to have a sense of the law given the facts and then know where to research to confirm your hunch.

Lori Harris-Ransom
Caldwell College Department of Business

#11: A Call to the Arts

A student submitted a painting for a grade in lieu of the final exam in Antitrust, her last course in law school. This painting was done as research in the study of Antitrust, a regular course and one of the most rigorous law school course offerings.

Because many of my antitrust students have a specialized interest in the field of antitrust or possibly have secured post-law school employment in which they will specialize in antitrust, I invite students with such focus to undertake an independent research project in lieu of the final exam. These students must still attend every class and participate, but they are allowed to tailor their work product for the class to their budding professional interests. In making this option available, I have had in mind that the independent research option in antitrust would produce a work of original jurisprudence, or at a minimum, delve into the problems of applying the law to a specific area.

At the other end of the spectrum from those who are particularly intrigued by antitrust law, lie those students who have a waning interest in law and the entire legal profession. Many such students experience anxiety brought on by pending graduation, which accentuates the perception of dissonance between law school and the real world of the law, the legal profession, and life itself. Such thoughts must be overcome. In a capitalistic society, the value of a person is the value of his or her labor as determined in the market place. This means that each person must choose between doing what he or she most enjoys or what society values most, i.e., those services that society will pay the most to receive. As rational maximizers of utility, we do what society values most because there is greater utility to be had from the money paid for valued services than from indulging personal pleasures. The sacrifice is worthwhile if we earn enough money to command the necessary resources to better our own lot and that of our loved ones. While reason dictates choices, such decisions can be emotionally hardening. Awareness of these growing pains makes the law professor who teaches third-year courses especially mindful of the desirability to be as inclusive as is reasonably possible to attract and retain the intellectual interest of young adults as we shepherd them through the final stages of formal academic development.

The student who submitted the painting is a graduating student for whom the real world was close at hand. As a visiting student with but one pass/fail course left, the classroom window needed widening to become a meaningful learning experience for her. In the fall of 1995, the student was a young artist who was beginning to wonder whether a life in law would be fulfilling and worth the sacrifice. She was looking for ways to apply her legal skills to the arts, her true love. She came to me with an odd request. She wanted to paint a picture depicting an antitrust theme in lieu of a final exam. The difficulty in devising standards to grade art work, the lack of precedent, and the responsibility to ensure that real substantive learning was transpiring were just a few of the problems her proposal presented. However, two thoughts worked in her favor: first was the desire not to discriminate against artistic expression. After all, art history is an especially rich and venerable intellectual tradition. Second, antitrust is sometimes perceived by the uninitiated, mistakenly so, as dealing with complex business crimes explained with mind-deadening economic analysis. A painting would be just the thing to reach new audiences and liven things up. Since I market antitrust, which draws strongly on economic analysis, history, and political developments for explanatory power, as the first truly multi-disciplinary course in law school, it was only fitting that antitrust usher in the integration of a new discipline, namely art. Actually, art is not so new to antitrust. We professors already subject our students to simplistic, two-dimensional graphs of supply and demand curves, which despite our best efforts are too often drawn with an unavoidable sense of comic tragedy. Here was a chance to see real art. Perhaps the most compelling reason for the painting was the sheer gall of the student who proposed it and the insatiable curiosity of the law professor who wanted to see antitrust on canvas.

The Painting. Naked Restraints of Trade is an acrylic painting, which depicts a lesson on antitrust from the case of *United States v. Addyston Pipe & Steel Co.* The artist's abstract reads as follows:

> In this symbolic painting, William Howard Taft, representing both himself and the Federal courts, brandishes a cast-iron pipe against a naked woman, who represents one of several restraints of trade assembled for evaluation by the courts. In *United States v. Addyston Pipe and Steel Co.*, the future Supreme Court Chief Justice's decision developed the rule of ancillary restraints, which meant that the court would strike down all naked restraints of trade, but that restraints clothed in the guise of pro-competitive effects—represented here by athletic apparel and equipment—should be sustained. This rule is the precursor to the rule of reason. As the rule of ancillary restraints is being applied, the Rule of Reason can be discerned, on the verge of materializing, in the background of the painting (which represents the future).

The painting may be criticized in the way that all art is criticized, but the antitrust themes are conveyed in ways which words cannot. The painting captures the origins of the rule of reason lodged in the ancillary restraint test as well as the goal of antitrust law, which is to promote competition in the market place. One notes that the use of athletic figures to symbolize fair competition coincides with the increasing interest in applying antitrust law to major league professional sports. The rule of reason materializes in the background as a rule of interpretation, which strikes down only those restraints of trade whose anti-competitive effects outweigh its pro-competitive effects. The limited role of the judicial branch is reflected by Judge Taft, who represents himself as well as the federal courts, in that Taft acts in conformity with law as indicated by the law book, which he holds in his hand.

The phenomenology of art is exhilarating. Language is often imprecise because words often lose their connectivity to concepts of their origin. For example, the Court initially interpreted Section One of the Sherman Antitrust Act literally as banning all restraints on trade. Later, the Court imposed an interpreted gloss, which limited the ban to restraints which were anti-competitive, while upholding restraints which were clothed in legitimate business reasons and whose pro-competitive effects outweighed their anti-competitive effects, if any. Subsequent decisions have applied this test with varying degrees of understanding and frequently less success. The painting, *Naked Restraints of Trade*, is a constant reminder that the Sherman Antitrust Act is designed to promote free market competition, even if the antitrust players do not always agree on what activity is competitive on balance and how solutions can be structured to ensure a market as free of regulation as is possible. The meaning of the words must change to accommodate a changing society. In visual art, we have a medium where ideas vividly touch reality and expand the contours of its meaning. The canvas at once captures legal relationships in society, but allows for change as society and the sensitivity to problems in society change.

Christo Lassiter
University of Cincinnati College of Law

#12: Student Self-Analysis of Written Assignments

This idea works well with papers (I teach legal writing), but could be adapted for other assignments as well. It is not original with me; I began using something like this when I taught high school English, long ago, and now I can't remember whom to credit.

I ask my students to fill out the sheet below as a form of self-analysis and turn it in with the final version of each assignment. This (hopefully) involves the student in the ongoing writing process, so that the student sees writing as an activity and skill separate from merely putting ideas down on paper. Additionally, it allows the students to identify and recognize their specific, individual pre-writing styles. The students usually assess themselves honestly.

The forms provide me with a great deal of information, including the time a student has put in on a paper, the process (if any) a student uses to organize and write, whether a student is identifying her weaknesses correctly, whether a student has a realistic expectation of a grade, the student's specific concerns (that I might otherwise not detect), and how the student views this product in comparison to earlier papers.

With that information, I know whether a student really worked hard on a paper (and I should therefore be very concerned about writing problems that occur) or blew it off due to time or other pressures (and I therefore should not grade the student any differently, but at least will know the student feels he can do better work than this). I can respond in writing to students' concerns with comments that are more personal than the grading sheet and other correcting suggestions.

Name: _____   Date: _____
Assignment: _____
1. How much time did you spend on this paper? _____
2. Describe the process you went through to create this paper.

a. What prewriting activity did you use to help you explore your subject and get words down on paper? (outlining, mapping, clustering, etc.)

_____
_____
_____
_____

b. What problems did you have with an early draft?

_____
_____
_____
_____

c. What kind of revision strategies did you use to shape and to refine your draft?

_____
_____
_____
_____

3. What are the strengths of your paper? What points still cause you trouble?

_____
_____

_____

_____

4. What do you want me to look for when I evaluate this paper? What questions do you have for me?

_____

_____

_____

5. If you were to grade this paper, what grade would you give it and why?

_____

_____

_____

_____

6. Compared to the last paper you turned in, which one is better? Which one was easier to write? Which one did you spend more time on? Why?

_____

_____

_____

_____

7. Other comments: _____

_____

Kathleen Magone
University of Montana School of Law

#13: Extra Credit

Students in my large Wills and Trusts classes are allowed to earn five points during the semester which can be added to their final exam scores. Points can be earned for a variety of activities including presentations, drills, and research and drafting exercises. The purpose of the extra points is to get the students involved with the material on a different level and to provide some variety during class periods.

Presentations can include original poems and song parodies such as last year's "Get A Will, Bill," reports on pending litigation, or other creative activities approved in advance. (So far no student has taken me up on my offer to give five points for the best original dance depicting "the anguish of a disappointed devisee," although I have had a couple of rap songs.)

Students can earn five points for preparing out-of-class problem sets that help reinforce the material assigned. For example, several students produced crossword puzzles in which the 40-odd "clues" were legal concepts, definitions, and a few facts from cases studied in a particular area of my course, such as intestacy or fiduciary duties. Other students prepared extra problem sets on the Rule Against Perpetuities.

Research activities could include annotated bibliographies of all recent Washington CLE materials on wills located in our library or a short (two-page) analysis on a topic I do not plan to cover in class.

Twice during each semester I offer drafting exercises which qualify for the five-point bonus. These are simple fact patterns with instructions to draft a will or a trust which reflects the client's desires for the distribution of her property.

Students who wish to make presentations, drills, or do research reports must get prior approval and set a definite completion date. Presentations (poems, songs, etc.) are limited to three minutes at the beginning of a class period. Drills and research reports are duplicated and I simply announce that they are available to be picked up at the end of class. Answers to drills and crossword puzzles are put on reserve in the library for students to check their own work. Drafting exercises are announced in advance and must be turned in on a set date. I spend about 15 minutes in class critiquing them when I return the graded papers.

The students seem to like the chance to earn some "extra credit," and perhaps because law students are notorious "grade-grubbers," only five out of 122 students failed to earn the five points last fall.

Kay Lundwall
Gonzaga University School of Law

#14: Debriefing Students

Law school classes often end with students picking up their books and bags and heading for the exit, while a few surround the teacher to ask questions.

In the Academic Support Program at Southwestern, we have formalized the end of class by debriefing students on their classroom performance so they leave class with focus and understanding about the process of the law school classroom.

A student's comfort level with the classroom is essential to her socialization to the study of law and to her academic success. We need to inform students about their performance as class participants.

In our summer program for first-year students, we reserve about 20 minutes each morning to debrief students on their classroom performance. We have also begun using this technique in the Legal Process classes sched-

uled in the first few days of the fall semester. The method is simple. I observe students during class, taking notes about the questions and answers
and the ways students respond. When class is over, I discuss with the students their performance and suggest ways to capitalize on the classroom
experience. Furthermore, I explain why it is important: since law students
receive little if any concrete feedback before they take their first set of
exams, they must take the measure of their intermediate performance by
recognizing and evaluating clues from their classroom performance. These
clues address their grasp of the material as well as their approach to studying that material. By including some discussion about how to study the
material, students move efficiently from novice to expert, and from dependent learners to independent learners. Individual comments might cover
the following areas:

Case Briefs

Two kinds of briefing problems often occur: Briefs are either too long
(the student has not recognized the material from the immaterial), or too
short (the student has leaned toward abstraction and toward knowing only
rules without a clue about their limits and peculiarities). We ask the following kinds of questions:

- How did your notes help or hinder you in class today? When
  students discuss this question, they understand that case briefing is not an end in itself, but a tool for class participation.
  Students soon discover that useful briefs anticipate that day's
  questions, which, in a perfect teaching world, reflect the significance of the assigned material. Often, we can show a student that the answer to a professor's hypothetical was in the
  analysis of a case they have just read.
- When you were unable to respond, was it because of a problem with your brief? If so, what was that problem? Should
  the brief have contained the answer? Should the process of
  creating the brief have suggested the answer? These questions
  help students think critically about their briefs and about the
  specific demands that teachers place on a brief's ability to help
  students in class.
- Why did the teacher ask a particular question? Students begin
  to see the value of anticipating where a line of questions is
  heading.

Teaching Style

We also ask students about the effect of the professor's teaching style that day. Law students seem to concentrate on the differences between teachers, but we try to point out the similarities by cutting through the professor's particular style of teaching.

We ask students about their passive participation. Could they participate vicariously or was there a tendency to tune out when other students were reciting? From these clues, students begin to see the value of preparation and participation, even vicarious participation.

Hypotheticals

Students need to know that a teacher's hypothetical was not merely a convenience but an example of the kind of question they may see on an exam.

Classroom Technology

When teachers write on the board, we tell students to pay special attention: Has the teacher set out the elements of the rule that she expects to see on an exam? Unless alerted, students may not recognize the significance of these doodlings.

Effective Review

Many students come from an undergraduate model that accommodated last-minute review. However, we encourage students to review constantly — before and after each class.

Within two days of the debriefing sessions, the level of student participation increases. More students raise their hands, and the range of responses indicates an increased level of understanding. Furthermore, rather than fighting the process of the law school classroom, students begin to buy into it because they can see where it is going, and they see how they can better prepare to reap its benefits.

Paul Bateman
Southwestern University School of Law

#15: The Speech — "Good Students Who Will Be Good Lawyers and Are Good People Often Get Bad Grades"

At the outset of the second semester when students have not yet received their first grades, I talk about how law school performance requirements differ from those of undergraduate and graduate work in other disciplines. My intention is to prepare students who have always received top-level grades for mediocre-or-worse GPAs, and encourage them to evaluate themselves fairly. Some always accept my invitation to talk with me after grades come out.

The law student's basic task, I suggest, is the scrutiny and memorization of rules and thorough application to the facts, a process that many students find boring and obvious because it differs from good work in other disciplines at this advanced stage of education. As a result, students who naturally think deductively are likely to do well though they may appear to party much and work little. By contrast, many capable, creative students—many of whom thrived in school on inductive thinking—are very disappointed with their grades. Often, this is doubly demoralizing because they have worked harder than ever before in their lives to synthesize the nuances of reasoning presented by the case method. If working harder is impossible in the face of exhaustion, students may ask, why pursue this study?

I want students to realize their hard work pays off in ways beyond grades, an artificial measure at best. First, the ability to do traditional legal reasoning can be learned by work, and probably will be before three years of study. I liken it to a second language. Second, students who accumulate a body of knowledge early build tools for reasoning legally in novel situations in later courses and practice. Third, even these measures of legal scholarship are only part of the requirements for a successful legal career. For traditional practitioners, critical skills for success include in large measure "people skills" (i.e., communication and empathy with clients), particularly in the current mode of improving the public image for the profession. For non-traditional careers, law school learning—reasoning, familiarity with resources, substantive knowledge—generally adds considerable strength. I use the example of the potentially excellent psychiatrist: Often an intuitive and introverted thinker, (s)he is required in medical school to develop skills in objective observation of symptoms and swift response to unfamiliar input from patients and colleagues. This often is a discouraging experience at which performance is mediocre. (The stellar med student is probably headed for surgery...) However, upon achieving the goal of psychiatric practice, all the natural and acquired skills are the tools of excellent, lifelong accomplishment.

Alison Barnes
Marquette University Law School

#16: Recognition of Achievement

At most law schools, the days are long gone since grade point averages were carried out to three decimal points. In fact, in their haste to avoid picayune and unseemly comparisons, some schools have gone to the other extreme, the pass/fail system. But if the former makes too much of little differences, the latter makes too little of big differences — and especially excellence. We should always make much of excellence. In doing so we promote it, and excellence is certainly something to promote.

Each of us, in our own individual courses, can do much to recognize and promote excellence. This includes giving our students appropriate recognition of achievement at the end of the course. This can be done quite simply by sending a letter of congratulations to students who have achieved excellence.

A letter of congratulations can play an especially important role in a course that does not carry a prize for highest achievement. Whether a course carries a prize depends not on the merits of the course or the students, but on the interests of donors. It certainly would be nice if every course had a prize. In the meantime, we would do well to remember that for most prizes, their greatest value lies not in the prize itself but in the recognition it affords. We ourselves can give that recognition, by sending our top student a letter of congratulations for the highest achievement in our course. In fact, even when our course carries a prize, our own congratulations for our student will have high value indeed.

For courses without prizes, our law schools themselves can still give full recognition to the course leaders. They can give them the very same publicity and honors that they give to prize-course winners. If your law school does not already do this, why not suggest it?

Karl J. Dore
University of New Brunswick Faculty of Law

Chapter 12

Teaching and Learning Environment

The classroom is...a communicative and social space where student ambitions and teacher expectations meet.... Your responsibility as the instructor is to take that space—wherever you meet your students—and then turn it into a dynamic site for learning.—Timpson and Bendel-Simso

The teaching and learning environment of a law school class is an invisible but ever-present component of the classroom dynamic. Day in and day out, the students plop their books down at their seats, chat with the person sitting next to them, and ready themselves for class. The teacher walks to the podium, perhaps writes on the board, and the class begins. Yet, the teaching and learning environment that filters into the background of cases, Socratic dialogues, and legal analysis is profoundly important to the quality of the class. Whether noticed or not, the environment of legal education greatly impacts a course.

The teaching and learning environment can be divided into two components: the physical plant and the interpersonal environment. The physical structure of the class includes the books; the seating arrangement; the lighting; the height, size and shape of the classroom; the acoustics; and so on. This physical context is concrete, impermeable, and solid. The interpersonal environment comprises the way the students interact with each other (if at all), the way the teacher interacts with the students during a Socratic dialogue or during discussions about hypotheticals or policy, the way the students interact with the teacher when asking questions in class, the interactions during office hours, during question-and-answer sessions outside class, via e-mail, and so on. The interpersonal environment further includes the way the teacher and students collectively deal with problems, such as noise distractions, a lack of preparation or attendance, or "life" challenges such as family illness or other significant events outside law school. This environment is ethereal, permeable, and penumbral.

A. The Physical Plant

People notice the physical environment of a law school almost immediately. There are urban schools in high-rise buildings and rural schools with sprawling campuses. Within these schools is a mosaic of interiors. Some classrooms have fixed seating in elevated rows; other classrooms are flat, with moveable tables and chairs. Yet, once class begins, the physical environment fades into the background for both teachers and students, and the cases, hypotheticals, and legal reasoning rise to the forefront.

It is only when something goes wrong during a class that the physical plant returns to center stage. Problems and challenges — for both teachers and students — can arise from every aspect of the physical environment. The acoustics, seating arrangement, room design, lighting, size, and proximity to high-traffic areas can pose difficulties.

How a teacher uses the physical space makes a difference in the way students learn in the class, so teachers should devote time and attention to the difficulties posed by the physical plant. For example, if podiums or boards are moveable, then they should be relocated for their best use. If no board is available, the teacher can substitute a flip chart or overhead projector and screen. Teachers should make sure the students in the back of the class can see the board. Seats and tables should be added to over-crowded classes, and students in under-crowded classes should be asked to move up to the front. To overcome acoustical problems, teachers should ask students to repeat their comments with vigor or rearrange seating so students can hear one another.

B. The Interpersonal Environment

The interpersonal environment is less noticeable yet more important than the physical plant. How students relate to each other or the teacher's way of conducting class are seldom-discussed intangibles and often constitute an unconscious backdrop, visible to those outside the experience but not to those who are living it. For example, even without a seating chart, students may regularly take the same seats, may routinely raise their hands (or never do so), or answer in a similar manner to a variety of questions. Teachers may use repetitive speech patterns, ask predictable questions about cases, and have other habits clearly visible to the students, but hidden from the teacher.

With attention and effort, teachers can create an interpersonal environment conducive to learning. The teaching and learning literature emphasizes several means of creating an effective classroom environment. Teachers show respect and concern for students by learning the name of each member of the class. Also, students respond favorably to teachers who demonstrate enthusiasm for teaching the course. Teachers enhance the learning environment by communicating high expectations and clearly informing students of what they can do to succeed in the course.

Large changes in the learning environment may result from modifications in the teacher's class policies, such as how the teacher treats students who are late, unprepared, talking to neighbors in class, answering questions inadequately, etc. These and other policies help to shape the classroom dynamic, and changing the policies can go a long way towards changing student perceptions of the class. One effective technique to improve the classroom environment and to motivate students is to give students a voice in determining classroom policies.

Teachers often create their own class history and traditions. First-year civil procedure teachers may have an "Erie" day, in which students recreate the famous Erie Railroad case, *Erie R.R. Co. v. Tompkins*, 304 U.S. 64 (1938). Torts teachers may do the same with *Palsgraf v. Long Island R.R.* Some teachers become known for playing guitar and singing on the last day of class or a phrase or mannerism that becomes imprinted in students' memories. All of these traditions contribute to an effective class experience.

References

Barbara Gross Davis, Tools for Teaching 193–202 (1993).
William Timpson & Paul Bendel-Simso, Concepts and Choices for Teaching: Meeting the Challenges in Higher Education 3–14 (1996).
Maryellen Weimer, Improving Your Classroom Teaching 18–28 (1993).

Specific Ideas for the Teaching and Learning Environment

#1: Family Day

For many law students, law school becomes an all-consuming enterprise, and it is often difficult for family (broadly and loosely defined as parents, spouses, significant others, children, and close friends) to appreciate fully the law school experience. Indeed, many family members have not spent time at (seen?) the law school and have little idea as to what transpires in the law school classroom. Out of a desire to bridge this gap and ease the tension that often exists between school and family, I developed "Family Day."

Family Day can take place in first-year and/or upper-level courses and works equally well (although differently) in either setting. On Family Day (which is announced well in advance to enable guests to plan), each law student can invite a member of his/her family to attend class. I tell the law students that I will teach a "regular" class so everyone (guests included) will have an assignment and will be called on in class (more on this momentarily). The only requirement in terms of guest selection is that if a child is invited, he/she must be able to read. Over the years, about 70% of the students invite a guest which means class size swells considerably on Family Day! (There are students who do not invite anyone (travel can be a problem for those attending school far from home) or for whom keeping law school separate from family is important.)

Law students and their guests are provided with a duplicated reading assignment two weeks in advance. For example, in Family Day in Contracts II in 1995 (spring semester of a year-long course), we addressed the topic of unconscionability, and everyone was asked to read *Williams v. Walker Thomas Furniture Co.* (the District Court rather than the Circuit Court opinion) and *Vokes v. Arthur Murray, Inc.* Both cases are edited so the reading totaled three typed pages. The cover sheet to the assignment asked everyone to read the cases and familiarize themselves with the facts. Then, the assignment sheet provided: "In thinking about the cases, ask yourselves whether the results seem fair. Are the cases consistent? Is there a single principle that links these cases together? Would you have decided these cases the same way if you had been the judge?" I also give the law students several added cases to read in their text and Section 2-302 of the UCC.

Law students can volunteer a guest to be called on by giving me the name in advance (designating their relationship with this individual if they so choose). I tell students that they can tell the guest they will be called on or I can surprise them. I explicitly tell my students that no guest will be embarrassed or humiliated by the experience—no matter what the guest answers. Before class, I prepare a list of the guests (trying to balance age and relationship) and students I plan to call on for Family Day. I always invite a member of my family (who participates as well).

Family Day has always taken place first thing in the morning. The law school has provided a continental breakfast which is a good ground-breaker and nice for everyone. I arrive in the room early so I can meet family members and guests and chat informally. Then, I go to the front and teach as I usually do.

During class, I call on people—both adults and children; I also take volunteers. The first person I call on is always a family member. That is a tense moment but I usually add some humor about being singled out, and I chat briefly about how hard it is to speak in front of so many people and how no one wants to say something foolish in front of strangers. (In other words, I explain the law school experience and the pros and cons of the Socratic method.) Historically, everyone has been remarkably prepared and willing to participate. Indeed, one unanticipated side benefit of the event is that it has appeared to me that the students and their guests have spoken about the cases (and unconscionability) at some length before class, itself a useful exercise.

I always try to bring in some materials the students and guests have not seen in the readings. In the above Contracts example, I showed the actual cross-collateralization clause from *Williams* on an overhead projector, and we worked on a hypothetical involving several purchases to see how the clause functioned in reality. I also discuss the Circuit Court opinion in *Williams* by Skelly Wright. The discussion of the cases addresses the "tests" for unconscionability and the difficult policy issues of the doctrine (paternalism, certainty, and judicial activism among others).

After class, I answer questions and speak to family members. The reaction of guests and law students over the years has been consistently favorable. And, I think it has helped law students break down the barriers between home and school—which is, above all else, the point of Family Day.

Karen Gross
New York Law School

#2: Personal Statements

> *I can see now that as I read even these words they have a much different tone than those of my personal statement. Words such as compartmentalize, organize, function, and efficient would never have been used to describe my life, yet they seem quite appropriate now...I learned early in my first-year training that emotions or feelings for the people involved in the cases would be only a hindrance and take my focus away from spotting the issue and applying the relevant rule. Thus the people I was reading about took only a two-dimensional nature because they didn't seem real—I had no emotion for them. It is this emotion that I long for, that I need to make me whole.*

Students submit as part of their law school application a personal statement that explores life-changing events, describes the influence of key people, and explains why the applicant wants to become a lawyer. With the admission decision hanging in the balance, applicants craft their words very carefully. Indeed, the essay represents many hours of self-study, revealing priorities and personal goals. Yet for all of its potential value toward sustaining academic discipline and improving legal pedagogy, it is used by the admissions committee principally to verify writing ability and to promote diversity in the entering class. Having served its purpose, it is filed away.

Revisited effectively by the law teacher, a student's personal statement can be an excellent motivational tool and a powerful educational resource. In the former capacity, it keeps the student mindful of original ideals; in the latter role, it prompts the law teacher to turn diverse life backgrounds into a new source of instructional material.

> Reading through my personal statement for the first time [in three years] left me feeling both empty and complete. The emptiness I felt was for the person I was before law school, the idealistic individual who wanted to make a difference.... Looking back my first reflection was that law school robs or strips people of these goals. The whole first year of law school I felt beat down, confused, and lost.

You have probably wondered, as I have, what more we can do to help second- and third-year law students, often appearing jaded and cynical, to reclaim the initial excitement they felt for legal study. Where is a match to reignite "fire in the belly"?

On the first day of class, I ask students what factors contribute to the optimal learning experience. Students are quick to cite natural intelligence as a key factor, but they soon add that discipline and motivation are just as important. Being smart is a big plus, they say, but no more so than the will to excel and good study habits. Pressing on, I ask whether there was a time when they were convinced that becoming lawyers mattered so much that they were prepared to give unrelenting commitment to legal education. As they ponder that question, I tell them the answer is "yes" and that I can prove it *in their own words.*

Puzzled looks turn to surprise and then sheepishness as I inform the class that I have reviewed each of their personal statements and have with me a copy of their essays. I read excerpts, many of which speak eloquently to the denial of justice and the need to press forward in the struggle for equality. I recite from their papers the pervasive theme that the study of law will benefit not only themselves but their "people," their family and friends. I remind them of the zeal they once had to make a positive difference in race and gender relations, to stop the shaming of the poor and outcast, to lend an ear to the unpopular voice.

I then jolt them by announcing that I will distribute to them a copy of their personal statement and that the first paper assignment is to write an updated personal statement. They are to carefully examine the discrepancy between how they imagined law school would deal with their ideals and what in fact law school has done in that regard. As they critically reflect on written promises they made to themselves, would the person they once were recognize the person they have become? Why have they gone back on their word—and at what price?

> [T]he applicant I once was would recognize me because she was hopeful and good. Conversely, I no longer recognize the applicant's positive [outlook], idealism, and hope for change. Perhaps this is merely the result of maturation.... [T]he legal educational process does engender cynicism, disillusionment, the baseness of human nature, and intellectual and emotional exhaustion from constantly conforming to the status quo.

Students report that engaging in this introspective exercise is so unexpected and strange that they do not know how to proceed initially. They tell me that they feel disoriented, as though pulled away from a myopic focus on legal rules to once again behold a broad social vision. Taking this sobering look at where they are in light of where they thought they would be, most students discover that they would apply themselves eagerly to academics were deeply felt convictions at stake instead of mere concepts. They would study harder and take classes more seriously were law school instruction tied to something more important than a final course grade.

> In some ways my personal statement...show[ed] my strong idealistic convictions...I assumed that such aspirations were worthy and valuable to the law school community. "Not so!" said my first year of law school. "The only worthy aspiration for a law student is top-ten grades, law review, and an important and lucrative job with a large firm." I suppose I was and am a little disillusioned with the law school culture.
>
> I have felt a tugging between my intrinsic convictions of wanting to really make a difference and the use of [legal] knowledge to help people, with the more selfish extrinsic conventions of what "success" really is. I don't understand at this point what I want. I don't understand where I fit in and where I will be satisfied with my personal aspirations.... My first year tended to tear me down in many ways.

At this point, revisiting the personal statement becomes a double-edged sword. Once students are challenged to summon and strengthen their heartfelt resolve to become excellent attorneys, the attention shifts to the law teacher. Is the professor prepared to take full educational advantage of students' profound and diverse reasons to excel? Will the instructor do what is necessary to sustain motivation, reforming law school pedagogy to affirm and integrate the beautifully worded aspirations recorded in the personal statements?

This brings us to the second day of class and the use of the personal statements as an educational resource. Students arrive with their newly revised personal statements in hand. The mood swing from the first hour is dramatic. With the instructor looking into their faces, it is as though their first-day expressions—pensive, at best, withdrawn at worst—are now alert and bright, as though a new source of light were shining upon them. Students use other similes, such as it feels like a tightly shut window has been pried open and a fresh breeze has blown in, reinvigorating parts of them that had fallen asleep.

> [O]ne year of law school has actually made me feel less confident... push[ing] my deepest emotions toward discouragement, fear, and intimidation... But when I ponder the many other people (particularly family) who are counting on me... I persist and work harder. My life has become a pattern or example for my younger siblings and other [minority] children in the community.... My personal statement stands as it is and as it was written.

I inform the class that we will engage in an exercise with their updated personal statements that makes plain the limitations of conventional legal study, sheds light on additional problem-solving skills that are otherwise neglected, and sets into motion an instructional pattern that will improve learning relationships among them. In other words, I broaden the purpose of their critical reflection, saying that they revisited their personal statements not only to reinvigorate motivation but moreover to set the stage for our learning adventure together.

I begin the exercise by asking students to list the problem-solving skills that law school training is sharpening. They note such "left-brained" abilities as analytical dissection of facts, spotting of relevant legal issues, selection and application of legal rules, logical argument over the relative merits of a legal position in light of the facts, advocacy of policy considerations, and so on. I then ask whether there has been similar development of other, "right-brained" methods of processing disputes, especially those relying on intuitive, creative, empathic, relational, and spiritual strengths.

> In revisiting my Personal Statement, I am amazed at how optimistic I was about what I could do with my law degree and how I could "make a positive difference".... As for my first year of law school... I was exposed to a "how can I help me and me only" type of world rather than the "how can I learn to help myself and others" type of world that I was expecting. To put it mildly, this stunned me.

I asked students to consider whether the diverse aspirations recorded in their personal statements, especially healing social divisions, could be attained using only logical/intellectual aptitude. Invariably, they realize that to meet the career goals set forth in their personal statements they will need to expand traditional law school problem solving (i.e., theoretical expertise and rights-based advocacy) with far better training in critical reflection, active listening, mediation, goal setting, coalition building, delegation, supervision, accountability, evaluation, and other interactive skills to manage group conflict.

To this end, students in pairs introduce each other to the class as a whole, one asking the other what it felt like to revisit the personal statement. They are expected to convey accurately what was shared, and classmates are motivated to listen, echo sentiments, and offer support. They find themselves pledging to turn law study in a more healthy direction. "Our dreams will no longer be ignored," they say, resolving "to do justice to ourselves and to each other as our first clients. If we were committed to 'doing the right thing' in law practice, let's prepare ourselves now, not just intellectually but interactively."

> [T]hose who are the most respected, and consequently can do the most good, are not separated but connected to everyone else. I need to remember to reach for great heights while at the same time not just visiting those below. I must be with them and take them with me to higher levels.... The simple reading of my Personal Statement has helped return me to my prior course.... I am excited about the chance to continue to do some introspection to make those necessary adjustments in my course to allow me to be an influential lawyer and to become a better person.

As a finishing touch, I challenge students to remain true to their newfound resolve. Specifically, I ask them to consider preparing a videotape at the end of the term that responds to the following questions: Were they chosen to address the entire law school community, what would they say regarding the law school curriculum and educational process? Would they be able to say that they were in danger of losing their connection to their deepest concerns but then recovered, redeeming their ties to ancestry, family, gender, race, economic class, nationality, and other loyalties? Would they look back and take pride in reclaiming aspirations expressed in their revised personal statements?

The personal statement exercise jump-starts a semester-long commitment to integrate student ideals into the learning enterprise. We continue capitalizing on their diverse capabilities by building on the first two days of class, adding such other interactive experiences as interviews, team assignments, videotaped negotiations, teaching on campus and in the community, and other forms of fieldwork.

At the start of this fall semester (1997), I was even more ambitious. I asked students whether they would favor a law school campaign to persuade faculty members and fellow students of the motivational and educational value of the personal statement. In light of our just-completed exercise with their own essays (all excerpts in this article are quoted from students this semester), they could see how our first week turned typical classroom relations into the beginnings of a healthy, integrated community. I asked the 19 students to vote on whether they wanted to be "counted in" the larger campaign, "counted out," or were not sure. Fifteen wanted in; three were not sure; and one was torn between "not sure" and "count me out." Hence, we are now exploring ways to extend the personal statement exercise to those outside our classroom. Dealing honestly and constructively with our diverse, even opposing agendas and perspectives, we hope to model a compelling vision of the optimal law school learning process.

David Dominguez
Brigham Young University Law School

#3: Class Preparation Policy

I borrowed a technique for inducing class preparation and attendance from my colleague Steve Marks (who developed it for his upper-level students). It worked marvelously in my contracts course over the past three years.

For years I have tried every system I have heard of or could imagine to create an incentive for and reward class preparation: from unprepared notes before class (way too demoralizing for me) to a requirement of universal preparation in which grades of unprepared students are subject to being lowered (too intimidating for them and creates an incentive to skip class when unprepared).

Now I do the following: Before each class I come a few minutes early and place on the front desk two clipboards with dated photocopies of the seating chart (one for the left side of the room and one for the right) along with red pens. Students who are prepared for class that day come up and check off their names. (Believe it or not, this takes less than three minutes for a 95- to 105-person class once students get accustomed to finding their names on the sheet.) Students who check their name are subject to being called on that day; those who do not are immune. I am strict about not letting students who forgot to sign their names do so after class. I tell them that though they may have been prepared they did not (however inadvertently) put themselves "at risk" of being called upon and therefore were ineligible for the bonus. This rationale also has been well accepted and students soon stop forgetting.

After class each day, my secretary then compiles the list of prepared students and retains the original sign-up sheets in case a student later questions the calculation. In my one-semester course, every student who signed up prepared for class at least 80% of the time will have their grade raised by one-half (e.g., B to B+; the only exception is that I will not raise an A to an A+) regardless of whether they were ever called on. In my two-semester course, I did the same for those who signed up either 80% in each semester, 85% for the entire year, or 90% in the spring semester only. (This was an attempt to minimize the drop-out rate over the course of a year-long class and it seemed to work.)

I announce to students at the beginning of the term that if they check off their name as prepared and I call on them and find that they are not, I reserve the right to lower their grade by one-half. While this serves to penalize a student for falsely indicating that they are prepared more than a student who simply does not sign up prepared for the requisite number of classes, I think this penalty is more than warranted on a number of grounds I need not elaborate. Fortunately, I have had only one clear-cut case of an unprepared student checking off his or her name and afterwards she could not have been more apologetic, not to mention thoroughly prepared throughout the rest of the course. Although I do not advertise it, I would allow an unprepared student who checked their name to redeem themselves by being called on in subsequent classes and being prepared.

If I discern that a student has really read the material (however well they understood it or are able to discuss it), I exact no penalty. When I am unsure from their responses whether or not the student has really read the material (i.e., he or she is bluffing), I put a question mark on my seating chart and make it a point to call on him or her again soon. This has happened only perhaps two or three times so far (over the course of three contracts courses) and, given that I quietly allow subsequent redemption, I have yet to lower anyone's grade for unpreparedness.

Given the varying numbers of students who check off their names on any given day (and their occasional questions to me about, for example, how far we will get in the material that day) I have found that the students police themselves quite honorably. Indeed, the only drawback I have noticed is that some students hold themselves to a higher standard of preparation before they sign up than I do. For example, I recently inadvertently called on a student who had not checked her name off as prepared. (I apologize to the class in advance for ever doing this and tell students that they definitely should bring my error to my attention should it occur.) She did quite well in response and after class asked if she could check her name off since she had been called on. I told her she certainly could, expressed my regrets for calling on her, but also commented that in my view she was entirely prepared and I was surprised to learn that she had not checked her name. She told me that she had not been feeling well that day and just didn't think she was up to being called on. Clearly, she was a normally prepared student who was using one of her permitted "unprepared" days to take the pressure off a particular class.

Given our mandatory grading curve and the fact that perhaps upwards of 90% of the students qualify for the bonus, this policy has the obvious effect of penalizing those who are unprepared but, though they realize this as well as I, it has nonetheless been received very positively by the students. Indeed, far more positively than any other system I have tried. A "reward" for which nearly everyone can qualify is simply much more favorably perceived than is an explicit "penalty" (a lesson for law-and-econ folks). And before each class I am presented with a gratifying line of prepared students (and a sheet full of red checks) rather than a depressing pile of notes from the unprepared.

Moreover, this policy amounts to a de facto attendance bonus as well, since only those in attendance for the requisite days are eligible for the bonus and it has eliminated the need for any independent attendance requirement which in the past I have found necessary to counter legal writing and moot court assignments. This policy also encourages students to come to class on time rather than have to go to the front of the room to sign the sheets after class had begun. (I do permit this, though others may not wish to.)

Most importantly, of course, preparation (and attendance) levels have been uniformly excellent (even during legal writing and moot court seasons) without the need for any hectoring by me. Students can come to class without fear on days when they are unprepared; those few who are simply too fearful of being called upon can opt out and accept the de facto penalty, while experiencing the class without "terror."

Randy E. Barnett
Boston University School of Law

#4: No Notes

Here's a teaching tip that may improve your classroom performance and impress your students: Use no notes (not even the assigned course book) in class sessions *for the entire semester*.

This simple idea offers several advantages for the professor who walks into class empty-handed for some forty-plus hours of classes in a semester:

- *It gives you freedom.* You're not anchored to the podium or table where your lecture notes or coursebook would be located. You can move about and use the blackboard more freely. You can speak more extemporaneously as you are forced away from both exact words and established organization fixed by your notes or coursebook. You can have more eye contact.
- *You'll impress students.* Students observe virtually every other law professor carry substantial materials (notes or coursebook) into their classes and follow those materials religiously, and they will notice that you're not saddled with those mate-

rials. They are impressed that you have such a mastery of the material that you can teach an entire course without notes, or they appreciate that you prepare so diligently that you can do so.

- *You'll put students at ease.* The idea here is that if the professor can teach the course without notes or a casebook, then students should certainly be able to comprehend it with the help of the coursebook, classroom lectures, and study aids. Students are more likely to view your relationship with them as non-adversarial if they see that the subject is manageable. This approach does not mean the course will be less rigorous, because the professor still must demand thorough preparation and full understanding from the students.

- *You'll be forced to go out among the students.* One of the big advantages of this teaching trick is that it gets me away from the podium and out into the classroom, because there are regular occasions when I need to use the exact words of a statute, a case, or whatever. When this happens, I just go out into the class and read from the coursebook with one of the students over his or her shoulder. Often, I stay there and continue a dialogue with the class from that location. Reducing the distance between the prof and the students seems to be effective. Students tend to warm up to you, and they seem less intimidated.

- *You'll enhance your classroom preparation.* Although we all prepare diligently for all of our classes, I think you must be even better prepared to guide the class without coursebook or notes at your side. Incidentally, if I have a case or statutory citation, or any other item of detail, that does not appear in the assigned reading and that I want to share with the students, I simply scribble it on a scrap of paper, put it in my pocket before class, and retrieve it at the appropriate moment in the lecture. Again, students are impressed; they see that I have prepared for that particular class.

Michael L. Closen
John Marshall Law School

#5: Teaching Statutory Analysis

For some years I have taught a section of Civil Procedure in the first-year and upper-level electives in environmental law. All my courses are "statutory" (the Federal Rules of Civil Procedure are, for teaching purposes, the functional equivalent of statutes). The federal environmental statutes are lengthy, complex, and (as one court has stated regarding a particular statute) "mind numbing." A colleague and I have developed a new first-year course, Sources of Law in the American Legal System; one of the objectives of the course is to develop some skill, and comfort, in analyzing statutes.

Before offering some thoughts on teaching statutory analysis, I wish to offer some background observations that affect how I view the task. First, I believe that almost all new law students have a strong aversion to reading statutes. (I remember that I was one of those students.) Many new students may enjoy reading cases because of their story value and because, in discussing common law decisions, they can talk about principles of justice and fairness. Second, I think that, with a significant number of students, the aversion to statutes develops into a phobia. These students will avoid statutory courses or, if they are unable to do so (because of curriculum requirements), they will never confront the statutes themselves but will look instead for summaries or explanations of the statutes (from the instructor or from study aids). Many of these students develop the belief that "I'm not good with statutes"—a statement that is reminiscent of the undergraduate's statement that "I'm not good at math (science)." Third, I think that some students may believe that it is beneath their dignity to undertake a close reading of a statute. These students believe that they came to law school to study theory and principles of justice, not to engage in unintellectual verbal nitpicking. Finally, I believe that, in the present legal world (a world, to borrow Calabresi's term, of "statutorification"), all lawyers must be able to attack and dissect complex statutes and regulations; ideally, they should enjoy the task.

Here are some ideas for teaching statutory analysis.

(1)   My primary objective is to get the students to read the statute carefully. I do not move to discussions of legislative history, intent, purpose, etc., until there has been a careful (some might say nitpicking) dissection of the statutory language.

(2)   I have come to believe that, in a classroom (especially when there is a large number of students), students will not confront the precise language of a statute unless the relevant statutory language is visually presented on a screen. Even if students have a statutory supplement before them, they resist looking down at the statutory language. If the language is presented on a screen (with an overhead projector or a computer projector), the students, I believe, are more likely to look carefully at the language. Also, the projection of the language on the screen makes the task of statutory analysis more of a com-

munity effort. (For example, I often stand at the back of the room and ask students to go up to the projector and underline the statutory language that they consider important.)

(3) I try to give the students a few basic tips that make it easier to analyze lengthy and complex statutory provisions:

   (a) Put brackets around the dependent clauses and then ignore them until you have analyzed the main clause. Students are sometimes overwhelmed by numerous "except" and "when" clauses and focus upon these clauses before they understand the main clause.

   (b) There is an exception to tip (a) — "dependent" clauses that begin with "if" or its functional equivalent. These are "triggering" clauses and, though "dependent" in the grammatical sense, must be examined first because they "trigger" the application of the main clause.

(4) Finally, I reward (verbally) the student who identifies an ambiguous word or phrase—especially if the student can explain why the word or phrase is ambiguous and how the word or phrase could be changed to eliminate ambiguity. I absolutely gush over the student who suggests that I have misread some word or phrase.

John Hyson
Villanova Law School

#6: Teaching Law, Learning French

I've been teaching law for twelve years. In struggling to keep myself and my students interested, I have read, reflected, and experimented, diagnosed, and evaluated.

I've talked with students, practitioners, other professors, and, on occasion, myself. All of these activities have been useful. Quite fortuitously, however, the best thing I've done was to audit a course in introductory French.

For the teacher like myself whose own law school memories have begun to dim, who (finally) has gotten to the point where she feels she has mastered her subject matter and technique, and for whom the classroom has become a comfortable place that holds no terror, I recommend a temporary exchange of roles.

Put aside the persona of the confident professor, with years of teaching and practice experience, and become, for three hours a week, the student. And not the dean's list student, either. Study something that has always interested you, but at which you don't excel. For me, speaking French was a long-time dream. When I began to study it, I realized that a thick tongue and a tin ear were not exactly assets.

Traveling between my professor and student roles gave me a much greater insight into the feelings and behavior of my students. I thought I understood, even sympathized, with students who sit in the back row, avoid eye contact, want to say the answer but aren't sure they understand the question.

In my French student role, I, the formerly "A" student from kindergarten on, found myself dismayed when the chairs in the room were arranged in a semi-circle so as to eliminate the back row. I rehearsed my answers in my head before I raised my hand and, when I didn't know the answer, was relieved when the professor's eyes looked to the other side of the room. Most of all, despite the fact that I have come to think of myself as an adult person who does not require approval to sustain her well-being, I was ecstatic when the professor smiled, nodded, or, wonder of wonders, said "Good!" after I uttered "C'est moi."

Back in my own classroom, my sympathy turned into empathy. Feeling ridiculously like Bill Clinton, I wanted to say "I feel your pain" to the students who tried hard to look elsewhere when I asked a question. I, too, knew what it was like to be called on, have someone speak in a foreign language, and want an answer. While I had never seen myself as being stingy with positive reinforcement, I had gained a heightened awareness of how powerful a simple nod of the head can be. Moreover, I had experienced that awful, difficult-to-admit-to comparison of myself to others, who, it seemed to me, probably dreamed in French and had the conditional and imperfect tenses for breakfast.

A couple of things saved me. One was that nothing important rode on the quality of my performance. I was, thank God, already happily employed. I was there in the most voluntary of senses, purely for the fun of it.

But I wondered: What if I had been, like most of my classmates, 18 or even 21 years old? What if I felt as if my fate were inextricably bound to achieving in a course in which my answers were more often wrong than right?

For those who would like to skip the pain and, upon reading this, might say to themselves that they can imagine all of these feelings without signing on for the rigors of becoming an actual student, I say I once thought so, too. Imagining the feelings and experiencing them are two entirely different things, however. Drawing from my insights from clinical teaching, it's the difference between imagining how a lawyer might feel conducting her first deposition and actually doing it. My advice is that you don't cheat yourself out of the authentic experience.

Susan B. Apel
Vermont Law School

#7: Storytelling

Do you tell stories in the classroom? I do. My suspicion is that most of us do in one form or another.

In order to establish what I am about, it is necessary to digress a bit and talk about several of my experiences with storytelling. (By the way, the digression is one of the main elements of a type of storytelling that I find quite compelling. It has been raised to a high level by a colleague who tells stories about law, and everything else, in the western campfire tradition, with baroque twists and turns that after perhaps hours of digression turn back on themselves to somehow support the main story line.)

My first experience with storytelling goes back to my law school days. My Contracts professor spent (I swear!) the whole year talking about the facts in *Hawkins v. McGee*, 146 A. 641 (N.H. 1929). You remember that case: the infamous hairy hand, where the doctor was held to his "promise" to make the hand 100% when the result was a hairy palm. Now, this case can be abstracted to stand for an important proposition about the objective theory of contract formation. *See* John D. Calamari and Joseph M. Perillo, *Contracts* § 2-6, at 33 n. 51 (3d ed. 1987). But it obviously served a much more important purpose in that class, becoming instead a vehicle for discussion of the whole nature of the contracting process. To me, what is important is that I still remember the story of the hairy hand 25 years later, and with but a small effort can reconstruct a good deal of the law of contracts. It only occurred to me a few years ago that my recall of contract law was dependent on the power of the story.

Another experience I had with storytelling (and still continue to have, with variations) is that of listening to students champion adjunct teachers (always practicing lawyers) because they tell such good "war stories" — teaching their subjects by reference to "real events." In my younger days, I rolled my eyes at such encomiums because they seemed to be nothing more than praise for a pedagogy that avoided the hard stuff of "teaching the law." I do not roll my eyes anymore. (At least as much.)

My last experience is again more personal. I teach Administrative Law. For a good part of the time that I have taught, *INS v. Chadha*, 462 U.S. 919 (1983) has been a part of all the casebooks. It is important doctrinally in the separation of powers context, but I have found myself over the years using the compelling facts in *Chadha* first to tell Chadha's story and then to retell it at many points during the course. Chadha's story serves, in my thinking, as an important reminder of basic human dimensions in administrative law. (If you are interested in the story, *see* Barbara Hinkson-Craig, *Chadha: The Story of an Epic Constitutional Struggle* (1988).)

So, what is my point? It is that storytelling, with "thick" elucidation of the facts, may be an important teaching technique that has not been very seriously explored in the setting of the "ordinary classroom" (the phrase is borrowed from Roger Crampton for a purpose). I am aware of the explosion of interest in the use of storytelling (coming out of developing feminist theory) for consciousness-raising and as a way to counter traditional (and arguably masked) ideologically based and illegitimate theory. I find that movement illuminating. (I also recognize that I may entirely misunderstand those storytellers' points of view. I intend to educate myself on that point more thoroughly, but, as the saying goes, that is another story.)

James M. Vaché
Gonzaga University School of Law

#8: Students' Need to Translate Ideas

A student says, "Excuse me, professor. I did not understand that." The professor then repeats the statement in a louder voice, enunciating all the words more clearly.

Sometimes a louder repetition is exactly what students need. More often, students' questions indicate that they have not been able to connect the concept to something significant for them. If so, they need different words to make the professor's communication meaningful. They need words that touch their knowledge base and experience.

Recently, a student made this point by telling me that one of her professors routinely explained every concept in two different ways. The professor's first explanation was often like a foreign language to the student, but the second explanation, usually more experientially based, was more comprehendible. The student made it a practice to write down both explanations and to put an equal sign between them so she could work on learning the terminology and meaning of the first explanation from her understanding of the second. She described her experience as "translating."

Why "Translate"?

One reason for the need to "translate" is the inherent difference in starting points between an expert and a novice. For an expert who has already put together a framework or mental map of an area of law, concepts have context and fit within a larger picture or pattern of relationships. This "seamless web" is a reflection of the integrated knowledge of the legal expert.

Students, however, start as novices, bringing only their interest in learning and whatever experiences and knowledge their lives and academic backgrounds provide. Instead of the multidimensional, intricate pattern of the expert, law students must sort through a variety of mental maps developed for other academic disciplines or created to help them function in life situations. They scan their information base for similarity of content or pattern to connect this new concept their teacher is presenting with their own past knowledge and experiences. Only on identifying a match or partial match between what they know and what the teacher seems to be saying can they begin constructing simple frameworks for new concepts.

The difference between a teacher and another expert is the teacher's willingness to stop and make "seams" or entry points that help the novice. The expert may try to reach back to recall early experiences with legal concepts, but while important, this will still be limited because the expert cannot easily erase current insights or complex connections and the expert may have discarded as inaccurate or incomplete the original construct that allowed the expert to move from a novice state to an expert status. For example, in modernizing an old building one might use extra supports while connecting the new to the old, but when the building is finished these connectors are either unnecessary and discarded or incorporated into the design and not distinguishable as separate from the new structure. Additionally, there are many learning factors that impact the ways a person moves from being a novice to being an expert.

Variety of Learning Styles

The teacher's particular experience is but one of many possible processes for learning the same material. For the teacher, this explanation may be the clearest, easiest way to understand: It worked for her or him! However, many students will require different methods and metaphors. The need for other ways to cognize material is prescribed by past experience and learning style, not intelligence. Even when the student develops a complex, integrated pattern of understanding, it will not exactly match the professor's. However, if learning is accurate, the pattern will have the same basic elements, similar relationships, and corresponding application outcomes.

In any class, there probably are more students who learn in ways different from the professor than students who learn similarly to that professor. How do teachers bridge the gap? How do students cross the bridge? In fact, most students do make that leap, sometimes because of the teacher, sometimes in spite of the teacher.

I believe good teachers invite students to participate in a joint project as equal partners with different resources and responsibilities. To ascertain what students need, we should look to them to give us clues about how to build the bridge. What are they doing to translate, understand, integrate, and apply the material? How can we use this information to improve our communication with students?

Translation Aids

Students who use commercial or "grapevine" study aids may provide one clue. Many students use these materials to help them identify basic vocabulary and simple relationship patterns, or to help them sort major concepts. The teacher who believes students who use study aids are lazy overlooks the reality that many students need resources to consult that reinforce or clarify their understanding from a different perspective and in different words.

In my experience, students may benefit from using study aids as a tertiary source, to confirm or illuminate their understanding of the material or the process of analysis that they encounter in reading for class and in class discussion. It often helps to see something simplified so that the primary elements are identified more easily when they are applied to another context or in another problem. An outline, flow chart, or diagram provides insight by helping separate the main points and analytic relationships from the minor points and examples. Going over the terminology and concepts in a somewhat different form also provides a review. A discrepancy between their professor's presentation and these other materials motivates students to learn more in order to clarify or resolve the contradiction.

The Process of "Translating"

However, for some students who need to translate, study aids are not effective. I recall one student who tried a number of study aids at the urging of his study group, but he succeeded only when he started analytically flow-charting his courses. Another student came to see me because she was having difficulty outlining. She needed to have a visual image of analyses. She loved to flow-chart. In fact, it was so much fun for her to use that process that she assumed it was wrong. Everyone she knew was working on outlines, and all the organizational models she had seen were in outline form, so she thought she needed to work harder to make outlines. When she could visualize the material through creating a flow chart, her grades shot up.

In the classroom, visually oriented students need to take the professor's oral message and translate. For these students, charts or visual schematics showing the relationship of the different elements of a concept can be helpful. Encouraging students to work through the development of a flow chart or decision tree in class can reinforce concepts. Asking them to apply their visual structures to hypotheticals will help them to refine their conceptual framework.

Other students learn better auditorially. A useful translation aid for these students is to let them tape-record classes. For this type of learner, taking notes interferes with the learning process, but without a record of what happened in class, they cannot do the next important step of learning: reviewing. Handing out an outline of important class points at the beginning of class also can free students to use their auditory learning by listening with their full attention. Having space on the outline for students to add notes allows them to insert their own insights, making the outline a richer tool.

A realistic problem method makes the material more useful and concrete for many students. They learn by using and applying the material. These learners usually want to be able to see how something works. They want to know when and how it is used. They like to draw from their experiences, so increasing their bank of relevant experiences increases their learning. Problems, role-plays, and small-group tasks help these students to translate.

Other Ways to Facilitate "Translating"

Some students need a framework or overview to have a context within which to put details. Their process of translating involves relating cases to the big picture. Without the big picture for reference, they are often confused and have a difficult time sorting through all the information. Giving an overview and assigning materials that provide a brief synopsis of the material to be covered and its relationship within the course are beneficial for these students.

Other students find overviews so shallow as to be meaningless without the factual situations that give the general principles depth. Providing a summary when finishing a section helps them bring the material together to develop their own big picture. Without the encouragement to look for the larger themes and patterns, these students may collect much information about individual cases and miss the ways these data illustrate strategies and tests for new or different factual situations.

"Translating" for Exams

I have found that students who need to translate what a professor has said in order to make it meaningful within their context need to be careful about accuracy when translating back on exams. Not surprisingly, those students with the greatest need to "translate" often find themselves hard-pressed to get this process accomplished within the time limits imposed by most exams. Also, their class preparation often includes translating into their understanding, which takes more time than just reading the next day's assignment.

The more congruent the student's learning style is with the professor's, and the more the student and professor have in common, the more likely it is that the student will share and understand the professor's constructs and examples. The challenge in a diverse classroom is finding ways to communicate with students who have dissimilar experiences, interests, and learning styles. Bridging that gap requires teachers to learn and discover new ways of perceiving and translating their knowledge. The satisfaction of accomplishing this successfully is a significant reward of teaching. What teachers can learn from students through this process of translating is the fertile soil for new insights and increased expertise.

Martha M. Peters
University of Florida College of Law

#9: Cultural Legends

The Republic of Palau, a small island nation in the Western Pacific Ocean, has a population of 15,122 persons. The country has been independent since October 1, 1994. From 1994 to 1995, I worked as Court Counsel to the Palau Supreme Court. I also volunteered to help Palauan students who were learning English at the Palau High School. Using one of the legends of Palau, I created mock trials for the high school students. The legend was the sacrifice of Surech and Tulei.

Surech was a beautiful woman from a village in Ngiwal on the large island of Babeldaob. Tulei, her handsome boyfriend, was from Ngkeklau village in Ngaraard. Tulei was also the nephew of the great chief Mad ra Ngebuked. Hearing Tulei speak of Surech's beauty, the chief said, "Bring me her face so I can see it." Tulei was horrified by his uncle's request. For Tulei, these words had three possible interpretations. First, the chief could have wanted simply to meet the beautiful Surech. This, however, seemed too easy. Second, the chief might have wanted to see Surech in case he wanted her for himself. The chief had the right to have the most beautiful woman; if he demanded, Tulei would have to give her up. Third, the chief might have wanted Tulei to cut off Surech's head so that he could see only "her face." Tulei knew that the chief kept a collection of the heads of his enemies.

Tulei took Surech to a remote island, where he remained silent for several days. Surech asked Tulei to explain his strange silence. He told Surech of his dilemma: The chief either wanted her head or wanted to steal her from him. Surech asked sorrowfully, "How long have you been keeping this to yourself?" Surech sadly began to weave a basket. When Surech finished, she bent over the basket, and Tulei used his machete to cut off her head.

Tulei took the basket to the chief, who then banished Tulei from the village.

We used a courtroom at the Palau Supreme Court to put Tulei on trial for the murder of Surech. The Palauan students assumed the roles of prosecutors, defense attorneys, witnesses, judges, and court clerks. The classes discussed whether Tulei was acting on the chief's orders (the Nuremberg defense), whether by weaving the basket Surech consented to be killed (and whether a person can "consent" to be killed), whether the possibility that the chief would steal Surech would justify her murder, and whether Tulei had any factual defenses to the crime. In presenting their cases, the students were especially proud of their use of scientific evidence and lawyering techniques they learned from broadcasts of the O.J. Simpson trial on the Palauan television.

The exercise was important for these students. Because judicial proceedings in Palau are conducted in English rather than Palauan, the students gained familiarity with the procedures, language, and translation process used in their own courts. They transcended the language barrier that bars access to the courts. (The situation is similar to that in Haiti, where the courts use French rather than Haitian Creole.) If enough Palauan students become interested in law, the need for American lawyers may someday subside as Palauan lawyers and judges bring the Palauan language into the Palauan courts. The alternative would be to lose the rich Palauan language.

Also, the students gained familiarity with the court proceedings and with career opportunities they may not have considered previously in this country which has no law school. And the students learned a Palauan legend that, sadly, few of them knew. The tradition of teaching legends to children may fail when there are distractions such as broadcasts of foreign murder trials on television.

Teaching a Palauan legend to Palauan students made me realize that here in the United States there must be hundreds of local legends of which I am unaware, and which might provide useful classroom hypotheticals while preserving the important tradition of oral history.

Mark Wojcik
The John Marshall Law School

#10: Kinetic Classroom

One student, the driver, is riding piggy-backed on another, who is a motorcycle. Careening around the classroom, they unfortunately collide with another motorcycle. Both drivers fall to the floor, while a fifth student, a police officer, gestures animatedly at the scene.

One motorcycle continues to roll and eventually crashes to a stop in a corner. Several other students, bystanders all, shake their heads. One moves to drape an arm around a driver, while the others compete to tell the police officer who is at fault and why.

John Rassias, professor of French at Dartmouth College, leaps from his seat in the front row, and assuming the role of Fellini in this fantastical sequence, shouts, "Cut!" It is early in the morning, and it is a typical beginning of French class.

I became intimately familiar with the Rassias method when I enrolled in his French course. His teaching techniques are unique, and have been captured on film by television shows like *Good Morning America* (which filmed the above scenario) and *60 Minutes*.

As I experienced the Rassias method, I became particularly intrigued with the use of physical movement in the classroom. Like Professor Rassias, I noticed how I, too, move around, gesture, use my hands while I speak to my students. The difference in our classrooms was that in his, students moved as well. The picture of my own classroom started to appear out of balance. Why was I in almost constant motion, while the students sat, and continued to sit, and sit some more for over an hour, their physical movements limited to a raised hand and moving lips?

Sitting, I have come to believe, and more importantly, *having the expectation that one will not be called upon to do anything else*, made it possible for students to disengage more easily. There is a quietness, a security of physical attachment to a desk that allows one's eyes to wander to the window. Most obvious is that a sitting student can sleep, physically or at least mentally; a moving student, or *a potentially moving student*, cannot.

I do not recommend that one's class be turned into an aerobics course. Too much, and non-purposeful, movement might cause its own set of problems. But now I try to structure interaction in the classroom that moves beyond the verbal. Previously, I have made use of buzz groups, breaking larger classes into smaller groups to discuss a particular point. Now I include an activity. For example, the last time I used buzz groups, I asked them to present their conclusions on a flip chart, which required them to physically gather around the paper and write.

Other examples are perhaps more novel. In past years, I have always begun my Family Law class by having students reflect, through a class discussion, on the meaning of family. Last year, I divided students into small groups, and asked each group to come to a consensus on one feature of the definition or function of family. Instead of orally reporting their discussion, they put together a short skit (one minute or less) exhibiting the characteristic upon which they had decided. As an example, one group of students stood up and demonstrated that they shared the same address. Another group explained pooled resources as a feature of family life by tossing their money into a pile and then withdrawing certain sums for various group expenses. Another showed the concept of nepotism by inventing a skit in which one individual was pressured by other family members to hire a relative. My favorite was a group of two whose presentation involved one standing up and nagging the other.

I've illustrated the need for the Uniform Child Custody Jurisdiction Act by having students physically grab and abduct baby dolls or stuffed animals from one another, running to various corners of the room that represented different jurisdictions. In another exercise, ten students role-played various pieces of marital property. They stood in the front of the room while other students physically moved them into varying configurations to demonstrate equal and equitable distributions.

Some of this is, of course, flash, a break from the ordinary that keeps students interested. But I think it is more than that. Watching movement itself is stimulating; moving oneself is even more so. However, even if only one or two students are moving in the room, it presents the possibility of movement to the remainder. Simply put, if one feels that one may be called upon momentarily to get up and do something, one's mental faculties cannot afford to slump. Additionally, movement seems to have created better memory. When I try to weave things together by referring to past classes, some students remember what one or the other said about whether it is equitable to split the shares of stock 50/50 or award them all to one party. More students remember the specter of a student, role-playing the stock, standing in front of the room while two of the students, one on each side in the roles as lawyers, make the "stock" the object in a physical tug-of-war.

For the unconvinced, a simple and low-risk experiment can begin by monitoring one's own movement in the classroom and then purposefully doing something else. Generally, I pace back and forth across the front of the room. Should I decide to move differently—for example, stroll down the center aisle—the student reaction is subtle but definitely detectable. Heads move in a different direction; depending on where they sit, students perceive me moving closer or farther away from them than is usual. Their postures change. Something unexpected has happened, which means that something *else* unexpected could happen, for which they don't want to be caught unaware.

A variation of this experiment is one that most teachers have already used. If your students normally sit while they speak in class, ask one to stand up, or to move and stand in the front of the room while speaking. Eyes turn to catch the movement and ears and minds open.

My teaching has been a torrent of words, sometimes written on handouts or on the blackboard, more often simply auditory, my own voice speaking to students as they listen and speak back to me, and sometimes to each other. I've experimented with many different forms of verbal communication, from free-flowing discussions to buzz groups to pairs and circles, all of which have contributed to my classrooms. Movement, as its own form of communication, or as an adjunct to words, or as a momentary respite from the speaking/listening barrage, offers unexplored but promising possibilities.

Susan B. Apel
Vermont Law School

#11: Voices

> The reason we're here is because someone important once listened to us. Not because someone once told us something.
>
> Janet Emig, English professor, to a group of
teachers; quoted in Peter Elbow, What is English

That's what teaching *should* be about but isn't: discerning the gift. Too often the central activity of our discipline is judging. The major thing we have learned to do in life is to assign grades.

Mary Rose O'Reilley, The Peaceable Classroom

The first goal of education—if we think it has anything to do with values— is to bring students to a knowledge of the world within: its geography and anthropology, depths and heights, myths and primary texts....Our second goal should be to help the student bring his subjective vision into community....The classroom, then, must be a meeting place for both silent meditation and verbal witness, of interplay between interiority and community.

The Peaceable Classroom

Human beings, no matter what their background, need to feel that they are safe in order to open themselves to transformation. They need to feel a connection between a given subject matter and who they are in order for knowledge to take root. That security and that connectedness are seldom present in a classroom that recognizes the students' cognitive capacities alone. People often assume that attention to the emotional lives of students, to their spiritual yearnings and their imaginative energies, will somehow inhibit the intellect's free play, drown it in a wash of sentiment, or deflect it into realms of fantasy and escape, that the critical and analytical faculties will be muffled, reined in, or blunted as a result. I believe the reverse is true.

Jane Tompkins, A Life in School:
What the Teacher Learned

Stories are the most basic way we have of organizing our experience and claiming meaning for it.

James Boyd White, Heracles' Bow

The plural of anecdote is data.

Deborah Rhode, *Gender and*
Professional Roles, FORDHAM L. REV.

Conventional classroom hierarchies encourage extremes of both unre-
flective passivity and aggressive competition. The structure of professional
control over the content and evaluation of the learning process discourages
independent thought and encourages participation more designed to impress than to inform.

Gender and Professional Roles

A class doesn't get to know itself until it has been let go. People's personalities won't be visible, their feelings and opinions won't surface, unless
the teacher gets out of the way on a regular basis. You have to be willing
to give up your authority, and the sense of identity and prestige that come
with it, for the students to be able feel their authority. To get out of the students' way, the teacher has to learn to get out of her own way. To not let
her ego call the shots all the time. This is incredibly difficult. But I think
it is a true path for a teacher.

A Life in School

Argument can be...a form of violence. We pile up evidence as the kids in
my neighborhood used to pile up snowballs, each with a rock in the middle, on the rims of their winter forts. If the other side has more rocks, we
concede.

The Peaceable Classroom

War begins in banality, the suppression of the personal and idiosyncratic.
By contrast, "[a] language that takes our emotions seriously and gives
them real weight in our lives encourages us to think and be and act differently.... [A]t Harvard...the first thing they learn is not to say 'I.' That
is forbidden.... In learning the language of domination these students
learn to give up their subjectivity, their emotionality, their range of experience, their partisanship." Such education feeds the purposes of author-
itarian structures, governmental and religious...fostering "a compulsive
need for order, a fear of confusion or chaos, a desire for clarity and control...a culture of obedience."

Dorothy Soelle, Theologian,
quoted in *The Peaceable Classroom*

Our capacity to resist has nothing to do with our intelligence but with the
degree of access to our true self.

Alice Miller, *For Your Own Good: Hidden*
Cruelty in Child-rearing and the Roots of Violence

What we are taught is not as important as the *method* by which we are taught. We may forget algebra and second year Latin, but we remember how to obey orders, suppress our own experience, and think like everyone else.
Jerry Farber, The Student as Nigger,
in The Peaceable Classroom

When I look back at my schooling today, I see...a person who was taught not to feel.... When I look at my undergraduate students, I see how their schooling is forcing them into the same patterns I have struggled to overcome: a divided state of consciousness, a hypertrophy of the intellect and will, an undernourished heart. I see how compartmentalized the university is, with the philosophy department at one end of the campus, the gymnasium at the other. I see how conditioned the students are—though not terminally so—to keep their own experience out of the learning process.
A Life in School

Still, I may as well confess that the most startling debasements of character I have ever observed...have taken place during the three years of law school.
Wayne Booth, The Vocation of a
Teacher: Rhetorical Occasions

I would like to meet the concern about turning the classroom into "some kind of therapy group"...by observing that good teaching *is*, in the classical sense, therapy: good teaching involves reweaving the spirit. (Bad teaching, by contrast, is soul murder.)
The Peaceable Classroom

There are an infinite number of approaches to every concept. One can only wonder at the risks involved in grabbing a single way of looking at a topic and presenting it as a lesson.
Vivian Paley, The Boy Who
Would Be a Helicopter

What we usually call "historical consensus" all too often reflects the judgment calls of people in power, usually men; critical canons are formulated by winners; what is and what is not an important question is determined by those with the most clout. The women in my classes, by contrast, tend to raise issues of people on the edges: issues of racism, sexism, homophobia, violence, problems that the powerful have not felt in their bodies and hence dismiss as "unimportant."
The Peaceable Classroom

The powerful man worries about what he doesn't know, about the information that could hurt him, never realizing that his success has already hurt him. I thought of the powerful people I knew: my mother, now dead; magazine editors, a corporation president, an investment banker, any number of movie directors; some famous critics and university professors—yes, especially them, the professors. At a panel discussion they would complain of the exclusion of minorities and women from the culture of the past in a thick-textured jargon, whose precise function was to exclude anyone whose mind worked differently from theirs. They were great at seeing everyone's power needs but their own. I had rarely met a powerful person who knew himself. Or herself. Women were no different in this regard. How could they see everything and remain what they were? You cannot have complete self-recognition and continue to be a public man or woman, an authority, a lawgiver, a benefactor. Blindness was *necessary* to the powerful, who fight an upheld mirror as if it were the devil himself; they know that self-recognition can destroy them.

David Denby, Great Books

How a community treats its outsiders is the mirror of its moral landscape.
The Boy Who Would Be a Helicopter

If research universities... are going to become places where people like to come to work in the morning, where the employees have a stake and feel they belong, then they will have to model something besides an ideal of individual excellence. By the way they conduct their own internal business, they'll need to model our dependence on one another, our need for mutual respect and support, acceptance and encouragement. If the places that young people go to be educated don't embody the ideals of community, cooperation, and harmony, then what young people will learn will be the behavior those institutions do exemplify: competitiveness, hierarchy, busyness, and isolation."

A Life in School

[E]very effective teacher owes to students to teach them the arts of reflecting on the personal and social meaning of what they are being taught.
The Vocation of a Teacher

Teachers teach what they are as much as what they know.
Peter Elbow, What is English

The longest journey a person can take is the twelve inches from the head to the heart. Who is helping our students to make this journey?
A Life in School

Mark Weisberg
Queen's University Faculty of Law, Kingston, Canada

#12: Tributes

In an effort to change the pace in my classes (which generally proceed through cases, statutory analysis, questions, hypotheticals), I have introduced *tributes*. Generally speaking, the tributes are an opportunity for me to speak about someone related to the course (more on this momentarily). The idea of tributes was inspired by Professor George Priest who gave such a tribute in a commercial law course when he taught at the University of Chicago Law School. I try to give a tribute in at least one course a semester.

The tributes are usually unannounced and, to the extent possible, I relate them to current events. Several examples are useful. When Justice Thurgood Marshall died, I delivered a tribute to him in my Bankruptcy class based on his bankruptcy jurisprudence. (Before I did the tribute, I did not even know if Justice Marshall had a bankruptcy jurisprudence.) In the year Mary Joe Frug died, I gave a tribute to her in my Contracts class. I have given a tribute to Karl Llewellyn (on the anniversary of his birthday). Once, I gave a tribute to the author of my Contracts casebook (it must have been a slow year). When we read *Wood v. Lady Lucy* in Contracts, I give a tribute to Lady Lucy.

These tributes have several functions. First and foremost, they provide a different kind of intellectual exercise. They break the flow and allow a class to think about material in a different way. Indeed, I tell students to put away their pens, papers, and books for the day and just to listen and reflect. Second, they expand the nature of the legal enterprise. In a tribute, I commonly refer to material outside the course itself and use non-legal sources. This moves us away, at least for a day, from purely legal and doctrinal issues. Third, the tributes are humanizing. They always contain important personal stories of the individuals involved. They provide a context for the legal issues we address. In other words, tributes are a form of storytelling, and they frequently touch students, particularly if I am moved or inspired by the subject of the tribute.

There are several upsides and downsides to tributes. (Not surprisingly, they are related at some level.) Not all students like or appreciate the tributes. They sometimes remark that they are irrelevant. Some students respond as follows: Why spend time on material that will not be tested? Why waste the time, they say, when we are already so pressed for time in class to cover the material in the text? I have several responses to this. I accept the reality that tributes will not be appreciated by all. Although some students may come to appreciate them in the future, others never will.

However, tributes are an opportunity for exposure to context (namely people and the lives they lead). And, the arbitrariness of law school categories and studying material in isolation is worth noting because law practice is, after all, about intersecting categories. But, perhaps most important for me, tributes have been a way to capture the interest of students who otherwise may have been turned off partially or completely to the law school approach. In a tribute, these students suddenly see and feel something that they had not experienced before. If a single class can do this for some people, then the class is worthwhile. The latter point has been brought home to me because every year some second-year students ask if they can come back to Contracts I and hear the tribute to Lady Lucy. This has made tributes something of a tradition in my classes. The idea of tributes has taken hold at a deeper level.

There is also one other feature of tributes worth observing. They take a good deal of preparation time and, for those tributes that cannot be repeated, this is troubling. I have to say that, despite the work, the tributes have provided me with other benefits. I transformed the Thurgood Marshall tribute into a speech and, shortly thereafter, an article. In other semesters, with less "noteworthy" tributes, I have found it useful just to think about and read other materials for class. Putting away the text, statutes, and class notes has freed up my mind as well. So, the tributes provide a breath of fresh air for students and teacher that hopefully lasts beyond the day that they are delivered.

Karen Gross
New York Law School

#13: Students Adopt a State

Trust and Estates classes at Loyola University Chicago are upper-level, elective, large classes, with an emphasis on rules, lots of old rules, and virtually all of them are about dead people—not exactly a winning combination from a student's perspective. About four years ago, as I began switching my own thoughts from teaching to learning, I tried something new. Each student in my three-hour Estates class has the casebook as well as a copy of the Illinois statutes on intestacy and wills. In addition each student must choose, by a posted sign-up sheet, another jurisdiction and thereby becomes the class expert in that jurisdiction's probate code. I require that all jurisdictions must be chosen once (except for Louisiana) before duplicates can be chosen.

The students are to copy their relevant statutory materials and have them in class at all times. As we discuss cases in intestacy and wills, students include insights from what the other jurisdictions' statutes provide. Discussion may be prompted by an individual student volunteering or by my taking a poll, e.g., "How many of your jurisdictions limit the pretermitted child/heir statute to after-borns?"

Our discussions move easily among three venues: (i) the relevant law of the particular case which we all have in common, (ii) Illinois law which we all have in common, and (iii) each student's law which is not common to all. Thus we get practice in analyzing a particular court's interpretation of relevant laws, moving the fact pattern to the Illinois statute and discussing this transition in common, and finally the student's individual assessment of his or her jurisdiction's statute to the fact pattern.

This approach is limited, I think, to the intestate and will provisions (the first half of course) because the materials thereafter on trust, powers, and future interests are based less on statute. The involvement, however, does not die at spring break. About that time, I hand out to the class the first question of the final exam (20% of grade). That question requires the students to choose a section of the Illinois statutes (or their particular jurisdiction) and compare/contrast it with the relevant statute, if any, from their jurisdiction (or Illinois). The paper cannot exceed two typewritten pages. They may do research or choose not to do it. They may do the question in advance or choose not to do it in advance. Papers are handed in with the final exam. Grades are based on the choice of topic (5 points), writing style (5 points), and legal analysis (10 points). There is no reason why students cannot do well on this question. In fact, the majority of students do fairly well, some not so well — very few fall in between.

Overall these are the benefits I have seen with this technique:

1. Each student has ownership of unique material — therefore is a stakeholder for class discussion. This is especially useful in a large-class situation where passivity could be an issue.
2. Very easy to generate discussion — even from reticent students who are "just" reporting.
3. An easy way to stay on top of new statutes and to get a sense of majority/minority positions.
4. Shows that these "rules" are not divine immutable truths, but manmade, and could be reformed.
5. Likewise, shows amazing similarity and common origin of these rules.
6. Great exercise in statutory reading, interpretation, and drafting, especially when we try to rewrite an Illinois statute.
7. Gives a modest research/writing/library exercise.
8. A great way to show differences in outlooks and philosophies (although Louisiana can overwhelm students).
9. Built-in exam question.

Anne-Marie Rhodes
Loyola University Chicago School of Law

#14: Hollywood Squares

I taught Torts last year. As part of a review we played the game "Hollywood Squares." As you may recall, this T.V. game show was quite popular at one time. In my version of the game nine students, selected at random, are called down to be part of the "expert panel." They are seated in three rows, with three in a row. Two players are selected to start the game. A tic-tac-toe grid is drawn on the blackboard.

I have prepared questions; each player selects a question and then calls upon one of the "experts" to answer the question. The expert gives a response. The response may be correct or false. As is true of the original version of "Hollywood Squares," if the expert does not know the answer to the question she may make up an answer in hopes of tricking the player. The player must indicate whether she believes the response given by the expert is true or false. Although I know the correct answer, I have the rest of the class determine whether the choice made by the player is right or wrong.

How does the class designate the right choice? The students remaining in their seats clap and cheer with great enthusiasm if the player made the right choice. The right choice earns the player an "X" or "O" on the board. The player then places the "X" or "O" strategically on the board, in hopes of winning the game. (I'm the game show host so I'm the one who actually writes on the blackboard.)

If the class believes the answer given is wrong, they are to exhibit a definite "lack" of enthusiasm. No mark is earned for a wrong answer.

Play continues until one of the players gets "tic-tac-toe."

Two new players are selected for each round. If time permits you could also replace the nine experts.

The day after the game, we discuss the questions and the correct answers. The correct answers could be typed up and distributed to students.

Pamela McKinney
Albany Law School

#15: Considering Audience: Using A Writing Concept to Enhance Legal Learning

An exciting aspect of teaching law is to discover how many ideas from other areas of teaching can enrich the law school classroom. Relating law school classes, by either substance or pedagogy, to students' previous learning experiences helps them to begin to see the relationships that bind law to so many facets of life. I offer here one example developed from my experience teaching composition and business/technical writing.

A basic concept in teaching writing is to encourage student writers to consider the audience that might be reading a particular type of writing. A personal narrative about a high school escapade would look quite different when written for a teenage audience, a parents' group, and a close friend. A complaint letter to a business should seem reasonable from the perspective of the business owner, not the righteously indignant customer. These considerations of audience extend naturally and logically to teaching law, whether in the doctrinal, legal writing, or clinical classroom.

1. The doctrinal classroom.

Using the several audiences that are present in any case (plaintiff, defendant, judge/court, practitioners, society), teachers can encourage students to explore the many views present in cases. For instance, student 1 could be asked to articulate the arguments of the plaintiff in a case, student 2, the defendant. Student 3 could represent the judge hearing (or the court deciding) the case. The professor could ask the following questions of the students:

For students 1 and 2:

- As the attorney trying this case, what is the first best argument that you could anticipate the other side making?
- How would you shape your arguments in anticipation of the other side's arguments?
- What arguments will the (pick one party) find hardest to counter? Easiest?
- What arguments have no corollary argument? Are those strong or weak arguments?
- How were any of your arguments treated by the court in its opinion? What does that tell you about the expectations of that audience?
- What types of argument are most effective?
- What (pick one party) arguments are the easiest for you to counter?
- What societal goals or interests could be affected by the outcome of the case?
- How would you structure an argument to support the interests of (pick a special-interest group affected by this legal issue)?

For student 3:

- Which party's arguments were more persuasive? What kind of arguments were they?
- What are the characteristics of a legally sound argument?
- To what extent does a court consider precedent?
- To what extent did the court consider policy?

- What level court decided the case? Relate that court to the type of argument that it considered favorably in deciding the case.
- How would another court (higher, lower, in a different time frame or jurisdiction or whatever) have considered this same issue? Would its concerns have been the same or different? Would it have found the same arguments persuasive?
- (If reading included opinions at more than one level) How did the courts' approaches differ? Why?
- What are the implications of this opinion on the practicing bar?
- What special-interest groups will be affected by the court's opinion?

Using the multiple-audience approach is especially useful for students who can only see one side of an issue or who have difficulty understanding what arguments judges find to be persuasive or to have legal merit.

2. The legal writing classroom.

Because legal writing is simply a specialized form of writing, the concepts that apply in other writing situations apply in the legal writing classroom also. Whether the students are working on a client letter, an objective memorandum, an appellate brief, documents, or discovery materials, putting themselves in the position of their audience is imperative for clear and effective writing. Here are some sample questions:

- Who would be reading this document? Who else? Who else?
- How much time will those readers have to study this document?
- What are the interests of those readers? Are they seeking information? Providing input? Making a decision based upon the document? Responding to the document?
- What is the attitude of the reader to the document? Friendly? Skeptical? Critical?
- What specific ways have you drafted/revised this document to fit those interests and attitudes?
- What information have you glossed over/left out because you as the writer think that it's obvious? Re-examine that information. Do your assumptions about its obviousness apply to every foreseeable audience?
- Have you explained the relationships between ideas clearly based upon the knowledge level of the audience(s) who will be reading it?

Discussing these questions helps students to shape their writing for the reader, rather than producing written work that can be understood only by its drafter.

3. The clinical classroom.

In clinical work, students are often so concerned about dealing with their first clients that they approach the experience in a self-centered fashion. These questions can help them to broaden their approach.

- What do you know about your client outside of the legal issue that brought you together? Consider education, living arrangements, ethnicity, socioeconomic status, etc.
- What words will you use to speak with your client? Can you explain the law without using jargon? Would you have understood your explanation of the legal problem before you started law school? Before you started college? Before you started high school?
- What processes have you mentioned to your client (e.g., petitioning the court, filing a motion)? Did you explain how each step worked? What knowledge did you assume that your client "must be aware of"?
- Have you considered how your client can be presented effectively in contact with any other audiences in the case—opposing party, judge, social services representatives, etc.?
- How do you think your client will perceive you? How are you presenting yourself—attitude towards client, attire, confidence level?
- What does your client think of the legal system? Is it a sure thing, a crapshoot, corrupt, inefficient?

Because students tend to be so immersed in the learning process themselves, they often need a little help to see the world through someone else's eyes.

In conclusion, this introduction to using the concept of audience demonstrates how helping students to see the law, their writing, and their clients from perspectives other than theirs can enhance learning, communicating, and practicing law.

Nancy Soonpaa
Albany Law School

#16: Thoughts for the Day

I often send pieces of paper out to students, such as revisions of the syllabus, reflections on the last class or block of materials, study questions for the next class or series of classes, and so on. When I do I often accompany them with what I call my "thought for the day." In the best of situations, I try to remember or find a quote from some luminary that relates to what I have written or will be saying. I use these thoughts to provoke, amuse, or (I hope) encourage deeper thinking by the students. I have a variety of sources and collect "thoughts" as others might collect stamps. I use sources such as the collected writings of various people, including Martin Luther King, Holmes, Learned Hand, Shakespeare, Plato, Bertrand Russell, and so on. I also clip quotes from various sources. One of the richest veins to mine is THE CHRONICLE OF HIGHER EDUCATION. Letters to the editor and the end page essays are good sources. In addition, various editions of *Bartlett's* and *The Oxford Dictionary of Modern Quotations* are good sources. Finally, some of my favorite books, such as *Zen and the Art of Motorcycle Maintenance* and the *Tao*, provide inspiration.

Here are some examples of what I might do in several teaching situations.

In discussing the relationship between ethics and professional responsibility, and dealing with the inevitable observation that abstract moral theory has little place in the world of making a living, I might offer Brecht's thought in *Threepenny Opera*: "Food comes first, then morals." Or I might use that one, and then add Socrates's (Plato's) observation in the *Apology* that "the life which is unexamined is not worth living."

One of the themes that also emerges from many of my professional responsibility students is that the rules cannot make lawyers act morally. This is a specific reflection on the generally held view that one cannot legislate morality. I might respond in a "thought for the day" with Martin Luther King's observation, made to the National Press Club in 1962 (and elsewhere as well): "It may be true that morality cannot be legislated, but behavior can be regulated. The law may not change the heart, but it can restrain the heartless." (Source: *A Testament of Hope: The Essential Writings of Martin Luther King, Jr.*, James M. Washington, editor.)

Teaching administrative law allows one countless opportunities to bring the observations of good writers to bear. A couple of examples:

In discussing the role that government should play, as a prelude to close examination of the bureaucratic state:

> John Maynard Keyes: "The important thing for Government is not to do things which individuals are doing already, and to do them a little better or a little worse, but to do those things which at present are not done at all." Source: *The Oxford Dictionary of Modern Quotations*.

In discussions of entitlement, I might ask the students to think about the role of government in dealing with poverty, in part because I don't think one can understand the entitlement cases without thinking about the transformation in expectations brought about by social changes in the last 60 years. Long ago, I found a comment from William Penn on this matter:

> "It is a reproach to religion and government to suffer so much poverty and excess."

I also from time to time reflect with the students on some of my ideas about learning and teaching. Two favorites:

> From the *Tao Te Ching,* translated by Stephen Mitchell: "The more you know, the less you understand.
> From Pirsig's *Zen and the Art of Motorcycle Maintenance* (This one takes a little background information. Phaedrus is talking to a friend about the friend's frustration in trying to put a bar-b-que together by following the instructions that come with the kit).
>
>> "What's really angering about instructions of this sort is that they imply there's only one way to put this rotisserie together — *their* way. And that presumption wipes out all the creativity. Actually there are hundreds of ways to put the rotisserie together and when they make you follow just one way without showing you the overall problem the instructions become hard to follow in such a way as not to make mistakes."

Now, two final comments. One risk in doing this is that students will find your quotes to be a reflection of a particular mind set, ideology, etc. I plead guilty to this charge, but do try to balance my temptation to be one-sided by finding counter positions. I also invite the students to submit their own, or comments to mine, and then distribute those to the class as well. A second risk is that you will seem pedantic or patronizing by referring to literature or other sources with which the readers might be unfamiliar. I respond to this in two ways. I try to indicate that I am not always familiar with the work from which the quote is taken, most often by citing to the compilation where I found it. I also prick myself with a little irony:

Again from the *Tao:* "True words aren't eloquent; eloquent words aren't true."

James Vaché
Gonzaga University School of Law

#17: Student Conferences

When I was in law school, I seldom met with my professors outside class. When I did, these conferences were not always helpful. As someone who has always had a "problem" with authority figures (I respect and revere them too much), I was often too intimidated to effectively concentrate while conferring with a professor.

During a conference, I would nod my head profusely as the professor responded to one of my prepared questions. I would ask very few follow-up questions for a number of reasons: I did not always fully understand what my professor was saying, I did not want my professor to realize I did not fully understand what he was saying, I wanted to show the professor I respected his elevated status and his brilliant intellect, and I did not want to take up too much of my professor's time.

As a law teacher, I try to avoid having my students feel that sense of inferiority I often felt when conferring with a professor. I try to create an environment where my students and I are on equal footing. In this article, I will suggest a few ways to level the "balance of power" to make student conferences as effective as possible.

I teach legal research, writing and oral advocacy courses ("legal skills" courses). My suggestions, however, can be applied to courses in all areas.

Know Something Significant About the Student

To avoid any student feeling unrecognized and insignificant, I make sure I know a student's name and background *before* that student walks through my office door. During the first class of the semester, I have students complete an information sheet that requests such facts as prior education, professional work experience, prior writing experience, and interests outside law school. Additionally, to help attach names to faces, a photo of each student is put on my seating chart. (At Cal Western, a photo is taken of each student at registration for fall classes.)

I spend a significant amount of time at the beginning of the semester reviewing the names, photos, and backgrounds of my students. Also, if a student has signed up in advance for a conference (which I encourage but do not require), I review that student's information again before the conference.

I try to make the most of relevant background information. Although I never hesitate to talk with a student who brings up an interesting aspect of her background, I also try to relate a student's background to matters being addressed in our conference. For example, I might mention to a student who was a journalist for a few years, and who is frustrated by her performance on a legal skills assignment, that we will need to work together to help her make the transition from writing as a journalist to writing as a lawyer.

Make the Student Feel at Home

Before we even begin to confer, I try to relax a student and level any imbalance of power. To the surprise of some students, I greet them by their first name as they come into my office. I offer the student one of the two chairs in front of my desk. I then get up from behind my desk and sit next to the student. More than a few students have commented that sitting next to me, rather than across from me, is much less intimidating.

I often do something else that surprises students: I ask if they would like a cup of coffee. I make numerous trips to the coffee pot in the faculty lounge, and it is never a problem to bring back another cup for a student. Even if a student does not want a cup, this simple gesture can be a very powerful tool for putting a student at ease and putting us on more equal footing.

Make the Conference Your Top Priority

I always try to remember that students pay my salary and are my biggest and most important client. They are entitled to the same significant, undivided attention that I would give to a client meeting with me for legal advice.

Prior to a conference, I move all my work to the side of my desk so I can give the student my undivided attention. During our conference, I try not to let anything divert my attention. As I would do with any law client, if the phone rings during our meeting, I do not pick it up. If my computer beeps to tell me I have an e-mail message, I disengage the beep without looking at the message.

I also try to listen carefully and patiently to what a student is saying. Like law clients, students come to my office because they need to get questions answered and problems solved. Important work must be done during the conference. Minimizing a student's concerns or rushing a student out before fully and comprehensibly answering her questions is an abuse of power (would you treat your faculty colleagues in such a manner?). In a balanced relationship, the student's understanding of the subject matter should be as urgent and important to you as it is to your student.

Leveling the balance of power also means allowing a student to complain and vent during a conference. One of the "joys" of teaching legal skills courses is returning graded assignments to students *during* the semester. I have had my share of students (especially first-semester students who have not received any other grades) challenge their grade and my teaching ability.

For some students, the sheer cathartic effect of speaking their mind to a professor is enough to make them feel better (at least temporarily). I have seen, however, other students' angry reactions turn into sobbing. As a friend who is a psychiatrist once told me, these students were able to cry because they felt relatively safe and unthreatened during our conference.

Let Students Know They Are Not Alone

I tell students that although writing is an individual struggle I am their coach and colleague and will work with them as a partner to develop their writing. As their partner, I significantly increase my office hours and conference times during the busiest parts of the semester: before writing assignments are due and after assignments are returned.

During these busy periods, I sometimes do student conferences on a Saturday or a Sunday. Additionally, I usually extend my office hours if there are people outside my office waiting to see me after my last conference. Finally, I encourage people to call my voice-mail and leave a message; I check and return messages over the weekend if an assignment is due early the following week.

Although not all students need to see or talk with me over a weekend, students greatly appreciate my availability. My availability and concern over their assignments help to convince students that we are partners on projects they are completing and that I am willing to make some sacrifices to be an effective partner.

Conclusion

Obviously, law teachers have many different styles and approaches to conferring with individual students. I do not know whether my approaches will work for you. Nonetheless, if a simple gesture helps a student get more out of your conference (and your course), it may be worth considering.

Mark Broida
California Western School of Law

Index

—